V

STALINISM

Books by Robert C. Tucker

Philosophy and Myth in Karl Marx

The Soviet Political Mind

The Great Purge Trial (Co-Editor)

The Marxian Revolutionary Idea

The Marx-Engels Reader (Editor)

Stalin as Revolutionary, 1879–1929:
  A Study in History and Personality

The Lenin Anthology (Editor)

STALINISM

Essays in Historical Interpretation

Edited by Robert C. Tucker, Princeton University

with contributions by

WŁODZIMIERZ BRUS
KATERINA CLARK
STEPHEN F. COHEN
ALEXANDER ERLICH
LESZEK KOLAKOWSKI
MOSHE LEWIN
ROBERT H. MCNEAL
MIHAILO MARKOVIĆ
ROY A. MEDVEDEV
T. H. RIGBY
ROBERT SHARLET
H. GORDON SKILLING
ROBERT C. TUCKER

W · W · NORTON & COMPANY · INC ·
NEW YORK

First Edition

Stalinism.
  Based on papers presented at a conference on "Stalinism and Communist political culture"
held at Bellagio, Italy, July 25–31, 1975, and sponsored by the Planning Group on Comparative
Communist Studies of the American Council of Learned Societies.
  Includes bibliographical references.
  1. Communism Russia—History—Congresses. I. Tucker, Robert C. II. Brus, Włodzimierz.
III. American Council of Learned Societies Devoted to Humanistic Studies. Planning Group on
Comparative Communist Studies.
HX313.S683 1977   335.43′0947   76–56110
ISBN 0-393-05608-2

2 3 4 5 6 7 8 9 0

Contents

Preface

This book grew out of an international research conference on "Stalinism and Communist Political Culture." The conference was held at the Rockefeller Foundation's conference center, Villa Serbelloni, at Bellagio, Italy, July 25–31, 1975. Its sponsor was the former Planning Group on Comparative Communist Studies, created by the American Council of Learned Societies in 1967 with a grant from the Carnegie Corporation.

The Planning Group's mission was to promote comparativism in Communist studies. In seeking to do so, it sponsored a series of workshops and research conferences to explore various approaches to comparative analytic understanding of twentieth-century Communism as the diverse phenomenon which in our time it has more and more shown itself to be. The approach embodied in the Bellagio conference on Stalinism was historical. In the historical context, some efforts were made to view the Communist system as a form of culture—or "political culture."

No attempt was made, however, to prescribe to the conference a unified point of view worked out in advance. The participants were chosen from different disciplines, ranging from history and politics through economics and sociology to philosophy and literary scholarship; from among authorities on Eastern Europe and China as well as Russian specialists; and were encouraged to prepare essays on one or another aspect of Stalinism according to their own lights.

The one request made of the authors of the papers was that they contribute *interpretive* essays on the aspect of Stalinism of interest to them. Historical episodes and historical material were naturally not to be excluded from consideration, but were to be used for illustrative or evidentiary purposes rather than treated as the subjects of the papers. The aim was to produce a collection of scholarly papers which would seek in their different ways to be interpretive and explanatory in nature. This collective effort to illuminate the Stalinist phenomenon, and to reexamine past such efforts critically, was based on the view that even now, nearly twenty-five years after Stalin's death, the nature and causes of the "ism" that his reign embodied remain in many ways a mystery.

The outcome, as the reader will see, is a symposium that reflects a diversity of viewpoints as well as of disciplinary orientations. This diversity became clear, often dramatically so, when the participants met in Bellagio in the summer of 1975 for what proved to be an absorbingly intense week-long discussion of papers prepared and circulated in advance of the meeting. Although the writers of the papers in this volume later had the opportunity to take the Bellagio discussions into account in revising their papers for publication, the original diversity of viewpoints has not been effaced. On one central philosophical issue—was the Stalinist phenomenon in Communism's history the logical and inevitable outcome of the original Marxist world-view?—the volume shows not simply diversity but a direct clash of views presented by two eminent philosophical minds from Eastern Europe: Leszek Kolakowski and Mihailo Marković. Given the present, still developing state of scholarship on Stalinism, such diversity and outright opposition of interpretive positions seems healthy and best calculated to advance our understanding of the very complex set of problems involved.

The following scholars took part in the Bellagio conference as paper-givers and discussants: Zygmunt Bauman of the University of Leeds; Włodzimierz Brus of St. Antony's College, Oxford; Hélène Carrère d'Encausse of the Institute of Political Studies, Paris; Katerina Clark of the University of Texas; Stephen F. Cohen of Princeton University; Alexander Dallin of Stanford University; Alexander Erlich of Columbia University; Sheila Fitzpatrick of Columbia University; John Gardner of the University of Manchester; Leszek Kolakowski of All Souls College, Oxford; Moshe Lewin of the University of Birmingham; Mihailo Marković of the Serbian Academy of Sciences and Arts; Robert H. McNeal of the University of Massachusetts; Roger Pethybridge of the University College of Swansea; T. H. Rigby of the Australian National University; Robert Sharlet of Union College; H. Gordon Skilling of the University of Toronto; Robert M. Slusser of Michigan State University; Robert C. Tucker of Princeton University; and Lynn T. White III of Princeton University. In addition, Professor White served as rapporteur, and Professor Dallin, a past chairman of the Planning Group on Comparative Communist Studies, was the official observer on behalf of the Planning Group.

Although he did not take part in the Bellagio conference, Roy A. Medvedev of Moscow has since contributed, by invitation, an essay to the symposium. Mr. Medvedev is well known internationally as the author of the single most important study of Stalinism to come from Soviet Russia: *Let History Judge: The Origins and Consequences of Stalinism* (New York, 1971). Alone of the essays in this volume, his is not primarily interpretive in character but rather, as he explains in his introductory note, a set of new material on the political biography of Stalin and, as such, an addendum to *Let History Judge*. Although the conference and resulting symposium have focused on the "ism" rather than on the man Stalin, the addition of this essentially biographical essay seems appropriate in the light of the conferees' generally accepted view that Stalinism, along with all the other dimensions discussed in the various essays, had a personal dimension—to which a further contribution by Mr. Medvedev to the political biography of Stalin cannot fail to be pertinent.

In conclusion, on behalf of all the participants in the Bellagio conference and contributors to the symposium, I wish to thank all those who have contributed material resources, advice, and other forms of help in this venture: the Carnegie

Corporation for the original grant to promote comparativism in Communist studies; the American Council of Learned Societies for administering the funds and providing the facilities for the work of the Planning Group; Dr. Gordon B. Turner of the ACLS for his participation in the Planning Group's work from beginning to end and for his valuable advice on various problems that arose for me as the organizer of the conference and editor of the resulting volume; Princeton University for administering the Planning Group's grant for this project; my fellow members of the Planning Group for their encouragement and sponsorship of the conference on Stalinism and their advice to me in this connection; the Rockefeller Foundation for making available its superb conference center in Bellagio as the meeting-site; Dr. Ralph W. Richardson, Jr., Dr. Jane Allen, and Dr. William C. Olson of the Rockefeller Foundation for their many-sided assistance; all the personnel of Villa Serbelloni for making the conference week a pleasant experience as well as an illuminating one; and Mrs. Lorna Giese for her able help with the conference correspondence and related matters. I also owe a special debt of gratitude to my colleagues and fellow conference participants, Professors Cohen and Lewin, for their thoughtful advice and assistance on many matters involved in the preparation of this book.

Finally, I wish to thank James L. Mairs, senior editor at W. W. Norton, and Emily Garlin, editor, for the interest which they have taken in this work, and for their editorial assistance.

R.C.T.

Stalinism and Comparative Communism

Robert C. Tucker

The present volume is not the first to discuss the nature and causes of Stalinism. But I believe that it is the first such concerted, systematic, group inquiry into the Stalinist phenomenon, primarily in its Soviet Russian manifestation.

Two questions arise here: Why did it take so long for Stalinism to become the subject of such concerted study? And, why should the quest for comparativism in Communist studies—a field that at present covers fourteen different Communist party–ruled countries and dozens of non-ruling Communist movements in other countries—focus upon the Stalinist phenomenon, given the latter's historical nature, the fact that it arose in Soviet Russia at the end of the 1920's and in the 1930's, when Russia was the only Communist-ruled country (save for its Outer Mongolian dependency), and inevitably reflected the particular forces operative in the Soviet situation of that time?

Apropos the first question, perhaps it would be helpful to recall Hegel's dictum that the owl of Minerva spreads its wings when dusk is falling. He meant that wisdom—the philosophical mind—is never really able to comprehend in depth such a complex reality as a form of civilization until the latter has run its historical course and can be seen as a whole. It must be said that Stalinism is not yet dead, either in its birthplace, Russia, or in the numerous other countries and political movements which have undergone Stalinization in their histories. In the one Communist-ruled country where a reform movement was struggling to create, finally, a socialism with a radically non-Stalinist face—Czechoslovakia—the Russian army intervened in 1968 to restore a Stalinist kind of order. But while Stalinism is not dead in the Communist-ruled parts of the world, it survives as a pervasive or not-so-pervasive remnant, as the dead hand of the Stalinist past on the post-Stalin present rather than as the dynamically pulsating Stalinism of Stalin's era. Consequently, we can now begin to see the phenomenon framed in historical time. We may not be Minerva's owl, but we have a better view.

One reason why it took so long for our scholarship to address itself directly and explicitly to the problem of Stalinism is that in its time of emergence, development, and domination, Stalinism was never officially called by its own name. Nikita Khrushchev, who became a member of Stalin's Politburo in 1938, recalls in his memoirs that Lazar Kaganovich, the most sycophantic of Stalin's courtiers, would occasionally propose to Stalin the introduction of "Stalinism" into official Communist usage, but that Stalin, flattered as he was by the idea, never adopted it.[1] Although the Soviet press would refer in Stalin's time to the "teaching of Marx-Engels-Lenin-Stalin," the Communist ideology retained the designation "Marxism-Leninism." And all the ideological, political, social, economic, and cultural phenomena which gave their special stamp to the Stalin period, including the hypertrophy of the state and its secret police, the terror system, the strident Great Russian nationalism, the hierarchical society, the revival of elements of tsarism and so on, were officially treated—insofar as their existence was acknowledged—as aspects of Soviet society in its "socialist" stage of development, or Marxism-Leninism in action.

Even at that time the concept of Stalinism was being elaborated along one line by those dissident Bolshevik-Leninists, as they called themselves, who accepted Stalin's rival in exile, Lev Trotsky, as their leader and mentor; and we find in Trotsky's book *The Revolution Betrayed* (1937), for example, an extended discussion of Stalinism as a system of deviations from the developmental guidelines of original Leninism or Bolshevism. A critical reexamination of Trotskyist interpretations of Stalinism appears below in the essay by Robert McNeal.

With the Western scholars who began in the later 1940's to elaborate what was called "Soviet studies" as an academic field, it was a different matter. The great majority were ready to see the phenomena that we are calling "Stalinism" as the logical unfolding of what had been implicit in the Bolshevik (Russian Communist) movement from the beginning. True, they were well aware of such features of the fully developed Soviet system as the terror, the omnipresence of the secret police, the existence of a vast network of forced-labor camps, the hyper-authoritarian character of Soviet political life, the censorship, the party-controlled cultural system, and the class structure of what was supposedly a society en route to classlessness. The reader has only to turn to a classic product of the sovietological scholarship of that period, Merle Fainsod's *How Russia Is Ruled* (1953), to verify this statement.

These phenomena, however, were neither called "Stalinism" nor conceptualized as such. Symptomatically, there was no entry under "Stalinism" in the index to Fainsod's weighty volume. The term employed as an overall designation of the Communist sociopolitical system as it existed in the time of Stalin was "totalitarianism." The official (Stalinist) claim that the developed Communist system was Marxism-Leninism in action was not disputed. But this outcome was conceptualized as a system of totalitarian single-party dictatorship of which Stalin, by virtue of his abilities and various historical circumstances, had become the supreme leader in succession to Lenin.

The concept of totalitarianism had been elaborated in the 1930's and 1940's by a series of able German émigré thinkers who in many cases had been forced to flee from Hitler's Germany. They saw the totalitarian system as a novel twentieth-century form of ideologically motivated, thoroughly bureaucratized, terroristic total tyranny which was everywhere identical in substance though it

---

1. *Khrushchev Remembers* (Boston, 1970), pp. 46–47.

varied somewhat in externals, and which found classic manifestation in two countries: Nazi Germany under Hitler and Communist Russia under Stalin. Since the notion of "totalitarianism" seemed to fit the reality of Soviet Communism, Western Soviet studies tended to treat Communism simply as a variety of totalitarianism and not to bother overmuch, if indeed they bothered at all, with the phenomenon of Stalinism. These studies didn't regard the latter as problematic.

In the notion of totalitarianism there was a lacuna which history in Soviet Russia and some other Communist-ruled states exposed after Stalin's death, when the terror subsided and Soviet Communism under Khrushchev embarked upon a period of de-Stalinizing reforms which were accompanied by official criticism of Stalin's so-called mistakes. The lacuna consisted in the fact that the theory of the totalitarian regime made no provision for the possibility of such a regime embarking on a course of de-totalitarianizing change by, for example, curbing the terror which was taken to be the fundamental hallmark of totalitarianism. The theory had treated the novel form of party-dictatorial total rule as possessing an inner dynamic that would go on producing totalitarianism's characteristic manifestations permanently unless the system was overthrown, as Hitler's was, by force. Fainsod nicely expressed this position in the closing sentences of the above-cited work: "The governing formula of Soviet totalitarianism rests on a moving equilibrium of alternating phases of repression and relaxation, but its essential contours remain unchanged. The totalitarian regime does not shed its police-state characteristics; it dies when power is wrenched from its hands." [2]

For this reason, among others, the totalitarianism paradigm came under increasingly widespread criticism by scholars in Soviet studies in the later 1950's and after.[3] One result was that the field was left without a generally accepted theoretical organizing idea, although some minds clung to the familiar paradigm at the time when others were ready to relinquish it. For those who were prepared to rethink our analysis of Soviet Communism, and of Communism in general, a number of possibilities were open. One was to build up the analysis historically. Starting with the Soviet system as it existed in its first decade (1917–27), the scholar would re-examine its nature and historical circumstances, identify the different currents that existed in it, and then seek to show how and why the Stalinist current became ascendant at the end of the 1920's and what this meant for Soviet Communism and for other Communist movements as well. For Moscow's control of the Third International made all the affiliated parties and movements subject to the influence of Soviet developments in the 1930's and after. Soviet studies would, in short, become a kind of a "comparative politics" of the Soviet system over time. The reader will readily see that such an approach propels the problem of Stalinism into the foreground of scholarly inquiry. The nature, causes, and dynamics of Stalinism, and its mode of transmission to Communist

---

2. Merle Fainsod, *How Russia Is Ruled* (Cambridge, Mass., 1953), p. 500. For the same point of view, see Zbigniew Brzezinski, *The Permanent Purge* (Cambridge, Mass., 1956). The quoted sentences did not appear at the end of *How Russia Is Ruled* when its second edition was published in 1963.

3. For an example of such criticism, see Stephen Cohen's essay, below.

movements outside of Soviet Russia, are opened up anew as subjects for research and analysis. The problem, of course, had been there all along. But the scholarly mind moves tortuously to its goals, as well as at a snail-like pace.

This brings us to the second question posed at the outset. If Soviet studies are to take on the character of a comparative politics over time, why should not Communist studies in the larger sense become a comparative politics (and economics, society, ideology, etc.) over space? Here again, new developments in the social reality being studied were a spur to a comparative approach. As Stalinism partially subsided in Khrushchev's Russia, the compulsory uniformity that Stalinism had tried to impose upon Communism everywhere gave way to a visible diversity of tendency. Khrushchev's denunciation of Stalin in a closed session of the Twentieth Soviet Party Congress in February 1956, a speech which has not yet been published in Russia, became known through much of the world when a version of it appeared in *The New York Times* in June of that year. This intensified the ferment already developing in various Eastern European countries under Communist party rule. Polish Communism underwent a temporary liberalization under a new leadership which sought successfully to contain the demand for more far-reaching change; Hungary exploded in a popular insurrection which it took a Russian army to suppress; and Mao's China began to back away from what it would one day openly denounce as "Khrushchev revisionism."

Through a whole series of subsequent events (among them the overthrow of Khrushchev in 1964 and the invasion of Czechoslovakia in 1968), a basically conservative Soviet political leadership, consisting of men who came to political maturity under Stalin, has since managed to restore some semblance of stability at the cost of the democratizing reforms which Russia and various other Communist-ruled countries urgently need but which this leadership obviously sees as threatening to its own position and to the authoritarian, bureaucratic, single-party system over which it presides. Even so, what used to be called the "Communist world" is rife with inner division nowadays. The shaky hegemony of Russia's Communism is challenged by China's. The continued validity of some of Marxism-Leninism's most time-honored tenets, such as the necessity of a "dictatorship of the proletariat" in the revolutionary transition period, is openly questioned by some West European parties that are not in political power but hope to be. The presence of Soviet armed forces not only in East Germany but in Poland, Hungary, and Czechoslovakia is very likely a precondition of the predominance of the Soviet model of Communism in Eastern Europe over the long range. Meanwhile, Yugoslavia continues to go its own way, Hungary proceeds with surreptitious reform, Poland has thrown off the incubus of Gomulka's brand of Communist conservatism, Rumania seeks to assert its national independence as a Communist single-party state, and Albania is an anti-Soviet friend of Communist China. At present, it almost seems that the only solid increment to Russia's position in Eastern Europe as a result of the Second World War is that she acquired a dependable ally in Bulgaria.

If international Communism's enforced emulation of the Soviet Russian model is gone for good, comparative Communist studies are here to stay. Depending on one's approach and interests, such studies may mean different things. One possibility is the search for analytical comparison between Communist and non-Communist sociopolitical systems within the genus of that widespread twentieth-century phenomenon, the revolutionary mass-movement regime under single-party auspices, or "movement-regime." [4] Further, various theories of "convergence" or "the post-industrial society" pose as a problem the analytic comparison of, say, Communism in the highly industrialized Soviet Russia of our time with such non-Communist—and non–movement-regime—systems as those existing in contemporary Western Europe and the United States. But comparative Communist studies have so far sought primarily to comprehend the Communist systems themselves, with reference both to what they have in common and to their significant differences.

Those of us who have been involved in it can testify that the quest for a comparative Communism in this sense of the term has been more difficult than we realized when we started, and that positive results have been slower to materialize than we expected. We face, to begin with, the fundamental methodological question: how is one to proceed in the effort to build a comparative analysis of, say, the existing fourteen Communist-ruled states? One answer, which may appeal to some scholarly minds trained in the contemporary social sciences in America, is that we should mentally juxtapose the objects of comparison and then measure the degrees of likeness and/or difference under this or that "variable" on which the requisite information is available; and, having achieved empirical comparative results by this method, we could then form hypotheses, hopefully testable, as to what it is that the likenesses and/or differences under one or another variable are a "function" of. Possibly such a procedure may be worth pursuing for certain purposes, but I doubt that the attainable results would be other than superficial. To comprehend the fissiparous tendency in modern Communism, a different approach and theoretical foundation seem called for.

One possibility, which has appealed to the author of these lines, is an historical approach based on the idea that Russian Bolshevism and the Communist revolutionary movements that later emerged under its tutelage have been would-be culture-transforming movements, and that the sociopolitical system which they create upon coming to power is a new form of culture, or "political culture." The concept "culture-transforming movement" is derived from that of a "revitalization movement," advanced by the anthropologist Anthony F. C. Wallace and defined by him as "a deliberate organized conscious effort by members of a society to construct a more satisfying culture" and, alternatively, as the "attempted and sometimes successful innovation of whole cultural systems, or at least substantial portions of such systems." [5]

---

4. In "Towards a Comparative Politics of Movement-Regimes," *The American Political Science Review* (June 1961), reprinted in *The Soviet Political Mind,* Rev. ed. (New York, 1971), Chap. 1, I suggested that the movement-regime is encountered in three different though comparable varieties: the Communist, the fascist, and the nationalist.

5. See Wallace's article "Revitalization Movements," *American Anthropologist,* Vol. LVIII (1956), pp. 264–65, where he classifies Russian Communism as one form of twentieth-century revitalization movement, and his elaboration of the revitalization-movement idea in his book *Culture and Personality,* 2nd ed. (New York, 1970). For the argument that the Communist revolutionary movement is

The cultural approach to Communism has a prehistory, going back to such early studies as René Fülop-Miller's *The Mind and Face of Bolshevism* (1928). This approach was eclipsed, however, when the totalitarian theory came into ascendancy later on. Characteristic of the latter was the view of Communism, whether in Russia or elsewhere, as in essence a system of power—or total power. Accordingly, Communist revolutionary movements were understood as power-seeking in their fundamental nature. Given this orientation, the analyst's attention inevitably focused upon such phenomena of Communist systems as their power structures, control devices, and organizational weapons. One of the resulting difficulties, from the standpoint of the needs of comparative Communist studies, is that structurally and organizationally the different Communist socio-political systems show a great deal of sameness. Simply as a system of power—which of course it is, among other things—Communism in one country is normally not so different from Communism in another. Even such Communisms in collision as those of Russia and China, or Russia and Yugoslavia, have more in common structurally, as party dictatorships with a host of formally non-party mass organizations subject to party control, than their leaders may like to admit. This helps to explain why the rise of comparativism in Communist studies had to await upon the decline of the totalitarian theory's hold upon the scholarly mind. Incidentally, it may also help to explain why numerous persons, political practitioners as well as scholarly researchers, were belated in recognizing the serious significance of rifts in the "Communist world" when these made their often subtly nuanced early appearance, as in the post-1956 prenatal period of the Sino-Soviet conflict. If Communism was in essence a system of total power owing allegiance to Marxism-Leninism as its ideology, how could mere differences of formula and emphasis be important?

From the standpoint of a cultural approach that takes Communism to be a form of political culture or sociocultural system, there is no difficulty in recognizing the patent fact that these movements are also power-seeking ones and that, once they achieve political dominance in a country, they are also—indeed, as a vital part of their political culture—systems of power.[6] But at the same time, the cultural approach sensitizes the observer to the enormous significance of symbolism and hence to the potential meaning of differences that the adherents of the system-of-power position are apt to dismiss as atmospheric or "merely symbolic."

---

best understood as a culture-transforming one, and Communism itself as a new form of political culture, see the present writer's article "Culture, Political Culture, and Communist Society," *Political Science Quarterly*, Vol. 88, No. 2 (June 1973), and its further elaboration in "Communist Revolutions, National Cultures, and the Divided Nations," *Studies in Comparative Communism*, Vol. VII, No. 3 (Autumn 1974). The former was prepared for a conference on political culture and Communist studies held in November, 1971, under the auspices of the Planning Group on Comparative Communist Studies.

6. A cultural approach has no need to slight the importance of the organizational or power aspect of Communism, since the form of organization is properly viewed as an integral part of Communist political culture. For an interpretation of Stalinism in basically organizational and institutional terms, see T. H. Rigby's essay, below.

To the culturalist student of Communism, it is a matter of genuine importance when, to take a hypothetical example, one Communist party lays special stress on one theme in Lenin (say, the proletarian dictatorship as canonized in *The State and Revolution*) while another strongly emphasizes a different theme (say, the danger of Left sectarianism as argued by Lenin in *"Left-Wing" Communism: An Infantile Disorder*); for this may represent a Communist way of disagreeing over what is the desirable political line for Communist movement to take in the present period.

Why the cultural approach to Communism goes along with the historical one is easily stated: cultures, especially in the modern world, change over time; and culture-transforming movements, even when securely in power, confront serious obstacles to rapid sociocultural change in that the revolutionaries are always a minority among the people and the cultural ways of the past are bound to live on in the minds and lives of the popular majority. Furthermore, the very idea of innovating a sociocultural system as different from the existing one as movements like Communism envisage is utopian. The outcome of the political revolution by which the revolutionaries gain power, followed by their efforts—through legislation, education, propaganda, agitation, coercion, and whatnot—to change the cultural ways of the people, is never anything more than *partial* sociocultural change. What emerges is some sort of amalgam of the pre-revolutionary culture with the sociocultural innovations that the revolutionary regime has succeeded in implementing. Thus, as has often been pointed out, the administrative centralization characteristic of French monarchical political culture reappeared in different trappings in the republic that grew out of the French Revolution.

It follows from this argument that if we wish to understand the sociocultural development of a country which has undergone the kind of political revolution that brings a culture-transforming movement to power, we must investigate the amalgamating process which is invariably, although not necessarily avowedly, a part of it. To put the matter in more concrete terms, the revolutionary new sociocultural system will incorporate into itself elements of the national cultural past, as Soviet Communism did, for example, when in 1924, on Lenin's death, it established an official Lenin cult, replete with the mummy in the mausoleum on Red Square, which struck some protesting Communist revolutionaries at that time as a revival of the Russian Orthodox Church's old custom of preserving the bones of saints for display to the faithful. There will take place, in short, a certain nationalization of the revolutionary new way of life. Perhaps we may even formulate it as a rule—though not as an iron law—that Communism in power tends to become national Communism; and add that Bolshevism, the first case in point, became under Stalin and Stalinism a form of Russian national Communism which did not, however, shed its international expansionistic impulses.

The nationalizing of Communism will be the tendency, given the impossibility of total innovation of cultural systems, the popular impediments to cultural change, the fact that the revolutionaries themselves were acculturated under the old regime and hence bear elements of the old culture within their own personalities, and, finally, the further fact that *some* of the revolutionaries—for example, a Stalin—are more inclined than others are to become imbued with nationalist feeling and to find things in the national cultural past, Russia's in this case, which seem worth preserving or reviving. It is at this point, among others, that the cultural approach must take into account the potential influence of leader-personality as a factor in historical development.

The thesis to which this reasoning leads, which I offer only as one of the propositions in this book and not as an agreed position of the authors as a group, is that Stalinism represented, among other things, a far-reaching Russification of the already somewhat Russified earlier (Leninist) Soviet political culture. How and in what ways the further Russification occurred under Stalin's leadership in the Soviet revolution from above of the 1930's is a main subject of one of the essays that follow and is shown to one or another extent in some of the others as well. To sum it up briefly, the original Bolshevik culture-transforming movement developed during its early years in power a Soviet culture in which elements of the Russian and general human past were blended with the movement's manifold innovations in economics, society, politics, art, and everyday life; and in the ensuing time of Stalin the further transformations that took place under the ideological banner of "building socialism" both reflected patterns out of the Russian past—including the pattern of revolutions from above—and yielded such revivals of tsarism as the absolute autocracy which Stalin recreated through the Great Purge of the later 1930's.

The relevance of the cultural-and-historical approach in general, and of an inquiry into Stalinism in particular, to comparative Communist studies, should now be clear. Against the background of the Marxist Social Democratic movements of the later nineteenth century, Communism arose in Russia under the name of Bolshevism in the early twentieth; and having under Lenin during the First World War taken a hostile stance toward Social Democracy because of the tendency of its various member parties to adopt a national "defensist" position regarding the war, i.e., to support their respective governments in what Lenin saw as an imperialist war unworthy of any socialist's support, the Bolsheviks soon after taking power developed under their aegis a third or Communist International (Comintern) which deliberately set about the encouragement of amenable radical groups in various countries to form revolutionary parties on the Bolshevik model. That central element of the Bolshevik political culture, the self-styled vanguard party committed to revolutionary action aimed at the establishment of a party-led "dictatorship of the proletariat," a party functioning under Moscow's influence as a "section" of what was in theory one world-wide Communist revolutionary movement, became thereby the kernel of "international Communism." In effect, the Communist parties of other countries became agents of the diffusion of Russian Communist political culture in the revolutionary movements of those countries. And having undergone through the purges of the foreign Communist leaderships in the Stalinist 1930's a further process of combined sovietization and Russification, indeed of *Stalinization,* those Communist parties that acquired power in the aftermath of the Second World War, in most cases under conditions of Red Army occupation of their countries, presided over internal revolutionary processes which involved the forcible transplantation of Soviet Communism in its highly Russified Stalinist form.

The countries that came under Communist rule by one or another means—the imposed revolution under Russian occupation or revolution by guerrilla warfare, as in China, Yugoslavia, Albania, and Vietnam—varied significantly both from one another and from Russia in their national politico-cultural heritages. Hence a tendency toward diversity was bound to be latent in "international Communism," even in the later Stalin years. For just as Russian Communism had innovated a sociocultural system in which elements of old Russian culture were present, so every other Communist movement in power would incline toward some degree of nationalization of Communism. If only to make the movement more acceptable and effective in the country that it controlled, the leaders would seek to blend various elements of the national cultural heritage (and not simply their own language, which even Stalinism tolerated) into the amalgam that was Communist culture in its Chinese or Yugoslav or Polish or Czechoslovak or other form. I do not claim that this is the sole source of diversity in Communist development, but only that it is one of the powerful sources and that it will predictably manifest itself wherever a successful Communist political revolution occurs. So long as Stalin's terroristic despotism existed, i.e., so long as he lived, the polycentric tendency was largely suppressed in the countries where Communism took over during and after the Second World War. But the situation changed considerably after Stalin died and the terroristic despotism was dismantled. However, his successors have tried and are still trying by various means, not excluding military intervention, to hold Communist diversity in check.

In scholarship, as in war, it is often useful to follow what has been called the strategy of the "indirect approach." [7] The cultural-and-historical approach is an indirect strategy in comparative Communist studies. Instead of moving straight to the comparing of Communisms, the distinguishing of observable similarities and differences between them, it delves into the developmental history of Communism, starting with Russian Communism. It does this in search of understanding not simply of the ways in which different Communisms are alike or differ, but of the underlying sources and dynamics of differentiation or non-differentiation within the Communist sociocultural universe.

Adopting the strategy of the indirect approach in comparative Communism, the central importance of addressing ourselves to the problem of the Stalinist phenomenon is beyond question. Even though, as in this volume, we examine the nature and causes of Stalinism primarily in its original Russian setting and only to a small degree in its extension to other countries, whatever progress we make may possibly redound to the benefit of Communist studies in their comparative dimension. For what we try here to illuminate is the developmental dynamics of Russian Communism, which impinged in countless ways upon every other

---

7. In *Strategy: The Indirect Approach* (New York, 1954), p. 18, B. H. Liddell Hart writes: "The history of strategy is fundamentally a record of the application and evolution of the indirect approach."

Communist movement in the world and which *most* heavily impinged upon the others precisely in Stalin's time. No matter whether Stalinism's imprint upon a given Communist movement or party-state was indelibly deep, or whether it was an incubus which one or another movement in a particular non-Russian national cultural setting had the power and inclination to throw off, comparative Communist studies must take account of this influence; and to take account, it must comprehend Stalinism itself much more adequately than we have done so far.

I believe that I speak for all the contributors to the symposium in saying that we are conscious of its incompleteness even as a group of interpretive studies of Stalinism in its Soviet Russian setting. Since an examination of Stalinism anew is drawn unavoidably to its formative period, these essays are concerned much more with the rising Stalinism of the 1930's than with that of the period of the Second World War and after. Our collection does not do justice to all important aspects of Stalinism. Thus, the problem of Stalinism as a system of terror, although dealt with in several of the essays and touched upon in others, has not been singled out as the exclusive subject of an entire essay. Nor does the book contain, as it might well have, a full essay on the problem of whether Stalinism signified the eclipse of the Communist party-state by an *oprichnina*-state under the Soviet secret police.

Cognizant of the collection's incompleteness, we nevertheless hope that the reader will take it for what it is meant to be: a new beginning toward the solution of an old problem, a partial inquiry into the meaning of Stalinism as an historical phenomenon, and an indirect contribution to the eventual rebuilding of Communist studies on a comparative basis.

Part One

OLD AND
NEW APPROACHES

Bolshevism and Stalinism

Stephen F. Cohen

Every great revolution puts forth, for debate by future scholars and partisans alike, a quintessential historical and interpretative question. Of all the historical questions raised by the Bolshevik revolution and its outcome, none is larger, more complex, or more important than that of the relationship between Bolshevism and Stalinism.

It is, most essentially and generally, the question of whether the original Bolshevik movement that predominated politically for a decade after 1917, and the subsequent events and social-political order that emerged under Stalin in the 1930's, are to be interpreted in terms of fundamental continuity or discontinuity. It is also a question that necessarily impinges upon, and shapes the historian's perspective on, a host of smaller but critical issues between 1917 and 1939. With only slight exaggeration, one can say to the historian of these years: Tell me your interpretation of the relationship between Bolshevism and Stalinism, and I will tell you how you interpret almost all of significance that came between. Finally, it is—or it has been—a political question. Generally, apart from Western devotees of the official historiography in Moscow, the less empathy a historian has felt for the revolution and Bolshevism, the less he has seen meaningful distinctions between Bolshevism and Stalinism.

A reader unfamiliar with Western scholarly literature on Soviet history would therefore reasonably expect to find it full of rival schools and intense debate on this central issue. Not only is the question large and complex, but similar ones about other revolutions—the relationship of Bonapartism to 1789 being an obvious example—have provoked enduring controversies. Still more, the evidence seems contradictory, even bewildering. If nothing else, there is the problem of interpreting Stalin's revolution from above of the 1930's, an extraordinary decade which begins with the abrupt reversal of official policy and the brutal collectivization of 125 million peasants, witnesses far-reaching revisions of official tenets and sentiments, and ends with the official destruction of the original Bolsheviks, including the founding fathers, and their historical reputations.

All the more astonishing, then, is the fact that the question has produced very little dispute in our scholarship. Indeed, during the great expansion of academic Soviet studies (I speak here mainly of the Anglo-American school) between the late 1940's and 1960's, a remarkable consensus of interpretation formed on the

3

subject of Bolshevism and Stalinism. Surviving various methodologies and approaches, the consensus posited an uncomplicated conclusion: no meaningful difference or discontinuity was seen between Bolshevism and Stalinism, which were viewed as being fundamentally the same, politically and ideologically. Inasmuch as the two were distinguished (which was neither frequent nor systematic since the terms Bolshevik, Leninist, Stalinist were used interchangeably), it was said to be only a matter of degree resulting from changing circumstances and necessary adaptation. Stalinism, according to the consensus, was the logical, rightful, triumphant, and even inevitable continuation, or outcome, of Bolshevism. For twenty years this historical interpretation was axiomatic in virtually all of our major scholarly works.[1] It prevails even today.

The purpose of this essay is to reexamine this scholarly axiom, to suggest that it rests upon a series of dubious formulations, concepts, and interpretations, and to argue that, whatever its insights, it obscures more than it illuminates. Such a critique is long overdue for several reasons.

First, the view of an unbroken continuity between Bolshevism and Stalinism has shaped scholarly thinking about all the main periods, events, causal factors, actors, and alternatives during the formative decades of Soviet history. It is the linchpin of a broader consensus, also in need of critical re-examination, about what happened, and why, between 1917 and 1939.[2] Second, the continuity thesis has largely obscured the need for study of Stalinism as a distinct phenomenon with its own history, political dynamics, and social consequences.[3] Finally, it has strongly influenced our understanding of contemporary Soviet affairs. Viewing the Bolshevik and Stalinist past as a single undifferentiated tradition, many scholars have minimized the system's capacity for reform in the post-Stalin years. Most of them apparently share the view that Soviet reformers who call upon a non-Stalinist tradition in earlier Soviet political history will find there only "a cancerous social and political organism gnawed by spreading malignancy."[4]

---

1. I base this judgment on a survey of the literature published from the late 1940's onward. Other writers have commented, approvingly or disapprovingly, on this consensus. See Hannah Arendt, "Understanding Bolshevism," *Dissent*, January–February 1953, pp. 580–83; Isaac Deutscher, *Russia in Transition* (New York, 1960), p. 217; and H. T. Willets, "Death and Damnation of a Hero," *Survey*, April 1963, p. 9. A major exception over the years has been Robert C. Tucker, who sees major discontinuities, even a "gulf," between Bolshevism and Stalinism. See the essays collected in his *The Soviet Political Mind*, rev. ed. (New York, 1971). Barrington Moore's *Soviet Politics—The Dilemma of Power*, rev. ed. (New York, 1965) differs from the consensus interpretation in important respects but generally falls into the continuity school.

2. This essay grows out of a larger study which includes a more general critique of Western literature on Soviet history and politics.

3. For a similar point, see Robert M. Slusser, "A Soviet Historian Evaluates Stalin's Role in History," *American Historical Review*, Vol. 77, No. 5 (December 1972), p. 1393. Until recently there were few academic studies of Soviet Stalinism as a specific phenomenon. For an early and interesting attempt to define and analyze Stalinism as a political movement in Western Communist parties, see Irving Howe and Lewis Coser, *The American Communist Party: A Critical History* (Boston, 1957), Chap. 11.

4. Abraham Rothberg, *The Heirs of Stalin: Dissidence and the Soviet Regime* (Ithaca, N.Y., 1972), pp. 377–78. For a similar critical point, see Tucker, *Soviet Political Mind*, p. 19.

Two disclaimers are in order. A single essay cannot explore fully all the dimensions and aspects of this long-standing interpretation. I can do so here only elliptically, with the purpose of raising critical questions rather than providing adequate answers. Nor do I wish to devalue the many important scholarly works which adhere to the continuity thesis. Indeed, it is testimony to their enduring value that many contain rich materials to refute it.

I

The history and substance of the continuity thesis warrant closer examination. Controversy over the origns and nature of Stalin's spectacular policies actually began in the West early in the 1930's.[5] For many years, however, it remained a concern largely of the political Left, especially anti-Stalinist Communists, and most notably Trotsky. In the mid-1930's, after an initial period of inconclusive and contradictory statements, the exiled oppositionist developed his celebrated argument that Stalinism was not the fulfillment of Bolshevism, as was officially proclaimed, but its "Thermidorian negation" and "betrayal." By 1937, Trotsky could add: "The present purge draws between Bolshevism and Stalinism . . . a whole river of blood." [6]

Unequivocal, though somewhat ambiguous in its reasoning, Trotsky's charge that Stalinism represented a counter-revolutionary bureaucratic regime "diametrically opposed" to Bolshevism became the focus of an intense debate among Western radicals, and among Trotskyists (and lapsed Trotskyists) themselves. The discussion, which continues even today, suffered from an excess of idiomatic Marxist labeling and ersatz analysis—Was the Stalinist bureaucracy a new class? Was Stalin's Russia capitalist, state capitalist, Thermidorian, Fructidorian, Bonapartist, still socialist?—and from some understandable reluctance, even on the part of anti-Stalinists, to tarnish the Soviet Union's legitimacy in the confrontation with Hitlerism.[7] Nonetheless, the debate was interesting, and it has been unduly ignored by scholars; it anticipated several arguments, favoring both dis-

---

5. Perhaps the first writer to argue that Stalin's policies should be termed "Stalinism" and "not Marxism or even Leninism" was Walter Duranty. See his series of dispatches to the *New York Times* in June 1931, collected in *Duranty Reports Russia* (New York, 1934), pp. 186–219. They were answered, and the term "Stalinism" rejected, by the leader of the Communist opposition in the United States. Jay Lovestone, "The Soviet Union and Its Bourgeois Critics," *Revolutionary Age*, August 8 and 22, and September 15, 1931.

6. Leon Trotsky, *Stalinism and Bolshevism* (New York, 1972), pp. 15, 17; and his *The Revolution Betrayed* (New York, 1945). See also "Does the Soviet Government Still Follow the Principles Adopted Twenty Years Ago?" *Writings of Leon Trotsky, 1937–38* (New York, 1970), pp. 169–72; and *Their Morals and Ours* (New York, 1937).

7. Many Soviet and non-Soviet Communists later said that their critical attitude toward Stalinism was diminished in the 1930's by their perceived choice between Soviet Russia and Hitler's Germany. This explanation is often dismissed unfairly. Such an outlook also influenced the thinking of non-Communists, including some anti-Communist Russian émigrés. See, for example, Nicholas Berdyaev, *The Origin of Russian Communism* (Ann Arbor, Mich., 1960), p. 147.

continuity and continuity, that later appear in academic literature on Bolshevism and Stalinism.[8]

Academic commentary on the subject began in earnest only after the Second World War, with the expansion of professional Soviet studies. The timing is significant, coinciding with the high tide of Stalinism as a developed system in the Soviet Union and Eastern Europe, and with the onset (or resumption) of the Cold War. This may help explain two aspects of the continuity thesis which are not easily documented but which seen inescapable. One is the dubious logic, noted by an early polemicist in the dispute, that "Russian communism *had* to turn out as it has because it now can be seen to have, in fact, turned out as it has." [9] The other is that early academic works were, as a founder of Russian studies once complained, "too often written in the atmosphere of an intense hatred of the present Russian regime." [10] These perspectives undoubtedly contributed to the scholarly view that the evils of contemporary Stalinist Russia were predetermined by the uninterrupted "spreading malignancy" of Soviet political history since 1917.

The theory of a "straight line" between Bolshevism (or Leninism, as it is regularly mislabeled) and major Stalinist policies has been recently popularized anew by Aleksandr Solzhenitsyn.[11] But it has been a pivotal interpretation in academic Soviet studies for many years, as illustrated by a few representative statements.

Michael Karpovich: "Great as the changes have been from 1917 to the present, in its fundamentals Stalin's policy is a further development of Leninism." Waldemar Gurian: "All basic elements of his policies were taken over by Stalin from Lenin." John S. Reshetar: "Lenin provided the basic assumptions which—applied by Stalin and developed to their logical conclusion—culminated in the great purges." Robert V. Daniels: "Stalin's victory . . . was not a personal one, but the triumph of a symbol, of the individual who embodied both the precepts of Leninism and the techniques of their enforcement." Zbigniew Brzezinski: "Perhaps the most enduring achievement of Leninism was the dogmatization of the party, thereby in effect both preparing and causing the next stage, that of Stalinism." Robert H. McNeal: "Stalin preserved the Bolshevik tradition . . ." and approached the "completion of the work that Lenin had started." Adam B. Ulam:

---

8. The main sources for the debate include Trotsky's *Biulleten' oppozitsii,* 4 vols. (New York, 1973), and Trotskyist and radical journals published in Europe and the United States. Several interesting books grew out of the debate. Some are cited below.

9. Dwight MacDonald, in *Partisan Review,* Winter 1945, p. 186. He was criticizing an article in the same issue by James Burnham, "Lenin's Heir," which argued that "under Stalin, the communist revolution has been, not betrayed, but fulfilled" (p. 70). For a similar methodological point, see Tucker, *Soviet Political Mind,* p. 6.

10. Michael Karpovich, "The Russian Revolution of 1917," *Journal of Modern History,* Vol. II, No. 2 (June 1930), p. 253.

11. *The Gulag Archipelago,* Vol. I–II (New York, 1974), p. 137, and his "Understanding Communism," *The New Leader,* August 4, 1975, p. 8.

Bolshevik Marxism "determined the character of postrevolutionary Leninism as well as the main traits of what we call Stalinism." Elsewhere Ulam says of Lenin: "His own psychology made inevitable the future and brutal development under Stalin." Arthur P. Mendel: "With few exceptions, these attributes of Stalinist Russia ultimately derive from the Leninist heritage. . . . " Jeremy R. Azrael: "The 'second revolution' was, as Stalin claimed, a legitimate extension of the first." The recitation could continue; but finally H. T. Willets, who confirms that non-Soviet scholars regard Stalinism "as a logical and probably inevitable stage in the organic development of the Communist Party." [12]

What is being explained and argued in this thesis of "a fundamental continuity from Lenin to Stalin" should be clear.[13] It is not merely secondary features, but the most historic and murderous acts of Stalinism between 1929 and 1939, from forcible wholesale collectivization to the execution and brutal incarceration of tens of millions of people. All this, it is argued, derived from the political—that is, the ideological, programmatic, and organizational—nature of original Bolshevism.[14] The deterministic quality of this argument is striking, as is its emphasis on a single causal factor. It is generally characteristic of our scholarship on Soviet history to explain social and political development after 1917 almost exclusively by the nature of the party regime and its aggression upon a passive, victimized society. Authentic interaction between party-state and society is ignored. Not surprisingly, the literature of academic Soviet studies contains little social history or real social studies; it is mostly regime studies.

None of this is wholly explicable apart from the "paradigm" that dominated Soviet studies for so many years. Much has been written in recent years critical of the "totalitarianism" approach in terms of political science. But its unfortunate impact on our historiography has gone relatively unnoticed. In addition to obscuring the subject by using "totalitarianism" as a synonym for Stalinism, the approach contributed to the continuity thesis in two important ways.

---

12. See, respectively, Karpovich in *Partisan Review,* July 1949, pp. 759–60; *The Soviet Union: Background, Ideology, Reality,* ed. Waldemar Gurian (Notre Dame, Ind., 1951), p.7; Reshetar, *Concise History of the Communist Party* (New York, 1960), pp. 218–19; Daniels, *The Conscience of the Revolution: Communist Opposition in Soviet Russia* (Cambridge, Mass., 1960), p. 403; Brzezinski in *The Development of the USSR: An Exchange of Views,* ed. by Donald W. Treadgold (Seattle, Wash., 1964), p. 6; McNeal, *The Bolshevik Tradition: Lenin-Stalin-Khrushchev* (Englewood Cliffs, N.J., 1963), pp. 136–37; Ulam, *The Unfinished Revolution* (New York, 1960), p. 198, and *The Bolsheviks* (New York, 1965), p. 477; *Essential Works of Marxism,* ed. Arthur P. Mendel (New York, 1965), p. 199; Jeremy R. Azrael in *Authoritarian Politics in Modern Society,* ed. Samuel P. Huntington and Clement H. Moore (New York, 1970), pp. 266–67; H. T. Willets in *Survey,* April 1963, p. 9. See also Alfred G. Meyer, *Leninism* (New York, 1962), pp. 282–83.
13. Waldemar Gurian, *Bolshevism: An Introduction to Soviet Communism* (Notre Dame, Ind., 1952), p. 3.
14. This has been the customary explanation of collectivization and the purges. Many examples could be cited, but see two standard works: Zbigniew K. Brzezinski, *The Permanent Purge: Politics in Soviet Totalitarianism* (Cambridge, Mass., 1956), p. 50 and passim; and Naum Jasny, *The Socialized Agriculture of the USSR* (Stanford, Calif., 1949), p. 18.

While most Western theorists of Soviet "totalitarianism" saw Stalin's upheaval of 1929–33 as a turning point, they interpreted it not as discontinuity but as a continuation, culmination, or "breakthrough" in an already ongoing process of creeping "totalitarianism." Thus Merle Fainsod's classic summary: "Out of the totalitarian embryo would come totalitarianism full-blown." [15] As a result, there was a tendency to treat the whole of Bolshevik and Soviet history and policies before 1929 as merely the antechamber of Stalinism, as half-blown "totalitarianism." The other contribution of the approach, with its deterministic language of "inner totalitarian logic," was to make the process seem not just continuous, but inevitable. To quote one of many examples, Ulam writes: "After its October victory, the Communist Party began to grope its way toward totalitarianism." He adds: "The only problem was what character and philosophy this totalitarianism was to take." [16]

The continuity thesis was not the work of university scholars alone. A significant role was played by the plethora of intellectual ex-Communists (Solzhenitsyn being among the more recent) whose intellectual odyssey carried them first away from Stalinism, then Bolshevism-Leninism, and finally Marxism. As their autobiographical thinking developed, once-important distinctions between the first two, and sometimes all three, faded. Armed with the authority of personal experience (though often far from Russia) and conversion, lapsed Communists testified to the "straight line" in assorted ways. Some became scholarly historians of "totalitarianism." [17] Others, including James Burnham and Milovan Djilas, produced popular theories presenting Soviet Communism in a different light—as a new class or bureaucratic order. But they, too, interpreted the Stalinist 1930's—the victorious period of the new class (or bureaucracy)—as the "continuation" and "lawful . . . offspring of Lenin and the revolution." [18] Historiographically, their conception differed chiefly in terminology: an unbroken continuity from half-blown to full-blown new class or ruling bureaucracy. Finally, there was the unique contribution of Arthur Koestler, whose novel *Darkness at Noon* presented Stalin's annihilation of the original Bolsheviks as the logical

---

15. *How Russia Is Ruled,* rev. ed. (Cambridge, Mass., 1963), p. 59. One of the best books in Soviet studies, it is marred chiefly by an interpretative perspective of an inexorable process toward a "full-blown totalitarian regime" (pp. 12, 31, 37, 91, 95, 102, 109, 116, 128). For similar allusions see Tucker, *Soviet Political Mind,* p. 178; Robert V. Daniels, *The Nature of Communism* (New York, 1962), p. 111; Gurian, *Bolshevism,* p. 72; Brzezinski in *Development of the USSR,* p. 6; McNeal, *Bolshevik Tradition,* p. 70; Ulam, *The Bolsheviks,* p. 541; John A. Armstrong, *The Politics of Totalitarianism* (New York, 1961), p. x.

16. Adam B. Ulam, *The New Face of Soviet Totalitarianism* (New York, 1965), pp. 48, 49. Similarly, "The steady advance of the Soviet system to the absolutism, or totalitarianism, of full Stalinism makes the process seem inevitable." Robert G. Wesson, *The Soviet Russian State* (New York, 1972), p. 96.

17. See, for example, Bertram D. Wolfe, *An Ideology in Power: Reflections on the Russian Revolution* (New York, 1969).

18. Milovan Djilas, *The New Class: An Analysis of the Communist System* (New York, 1957), pp. 51, 53, 56, 57, 167–68; and his "Beyond Dogma," *Survey,* Winter 1971, pp. 181–88. For Burnham, see his *The Managerial Revolution* (New York, 1941), pp. 220–21; and above, note 9.

triumph of Bolshevism itself.[19] The continuity thesis was fulsome, the consensus complete.

Just how complete is indicated by the two major historians whose work otherwise fell well outside the academic mainstream—E. H. Carr and Isaac Deutscher. Neither shared the mainstream antipathy to Bolshevism; Deutscher was a partisan of the revolution, and Carr viewed it with considerable empathy. Both presented very different perspectives on many aspects of Soviet history.[20] And yet both, for other and more complex reasons, saw a fundamental continuity between Bolshevism and Stalinism. Carr's great *History of Soviet Russia* concludes before the Stalin years. But his extended treatment of 1917–29, and the alternatives to Stalinism, is consistent with his early judgment that without Stalin's revolution from above, "Lenin's revolution would have run out in the sand. In this sense Stalin continued and fulfilled Leninism. . . . "[21]

Deutscher's views on the subject were more complicated and interesting, partly because he, almost alone, made it a central concern in his historical essays and biographies of Stalin and Trotsky. He carefully distinguished between original Bolshevism and Stalinism. He described major discontinuities, even a "chasm between the Leninist and Stalinist phases of the Soviet regime," and he was an implacable critic of scholars who imagined a "straight continuation" between the two. On balance, however, because the nationalized foundations of socialism were preserved, because Stalin's regime had carried out the revolutionary goal of modernizing Russia, and because the Bolshevik alternative (Trotskyism, for Deutscher) seemed hopeless in the existing circumstances of the 1920s, Deutscher believed that Stalinism "continued in the Leninist tradition. . . . " Despite Stalinism's repudiation of cardinal Bolshevik ideas (chiefly internationalism and proletarian democracy, according to Deutscher) and grotesque bureaucratic abuse of the Bolshevik legacy, the "Bolshevik idea and tradition remained, through all successive pragmatic and ecclesiastical re-formulations, the ruling idea and the dominant tradition of the Soviet Union."[22]

In short, for all their other disagreements, an "implicit consensus" on an "unbroken continuity of Soviet Russian history from October 1917 until Stalin's

---

19. Many other ex-Communists contributed to the continuity thesis. On this, see Isaac Deutscher's intemperate but interesting essay "The Ex-Communist's Conscience," *Russia in Transition,* pp. 223–36. A notable exception is Wolfgang Leonhard, who insists that "Stalinism does not by any means represent the logical or consistent continuation of Leninism." *The Three Faces of Marxism* (New York, 1974), p. 358. See also his solitary position in a survey on the question in *The Review: A Quarterly of Pluralist Socialism* (Brussels), No. 2–3 (1962), pp. 45–68.

20. For a discussion of Carr and Deutscher, see Walter Laqueur, *The Fate of the Revolution: Interpretations of Soviet History* (New York, 1967), pp. 96–108, 111–33.

21. E. H. Carr, *Studies in Revolution* (New York, 1964), p. 214.

22. "Russia in Transition," *Dissent,* Winter, 1955, p. 24; *Russia in Transition,* pp. 216–18; *Russia after Stalin* (London, 1969), pp. 21–22, 28–29, 33–34, and Chap. 2 passim; and *The Prophet Unarmed: Trotsky, 1921–1929* (London, 1966), p. 463. Deutscher regarded the "balance between change and continuity" as the "most difficult and complex problem by which the student of the Soviet Union is confronted." He disclaimed having "struck any faultless balance" on the question. *Ironies of History* (London, 1966), p. 234; *Russia in Transition,* p. 217.

death" joined the mainstream scholarship and the counter-tradition represented by Carr and Deutscher.[23] On this issue at least, the only dispute seemed to be whether the inexorable march of Stalinism should be dated from 1902 and the writing of Lenin's *What Is to Be Done?*, October 1917 and the subsequent abolition of the Constituent Assembly, 1921 and the ban on party factions, or 1923 and Trotsky's first defeat.

Scholarly consensus, even in Soviet studies, is unnatural and impermanent. The first sustained revision of the historiography of the reigning "totalitarianism" school came in the early 1960's from mainstream scholars who looked at Stalinism in the broader perspective of underdeveloped societies and modernization. Their achievements are not to be minimized. They began to see Stalinism in terms of Russian history and social change, and as being historically limited. But rather than challenge the continuity thesis, they embraced, or reformulated, it. Stalin's social policies of the 1930's—sometimes including even the purges—were interpreted as *the* Bolshevik (or Communist) program of modernization, functional in the context of Russia's backwardness and the party's modernizing role, and thus the "logical conclusion" of 1917.[24] In a kind of amended version of the "totalitarianism" view, Stalinism was portrayed as full-blown Bolshevism in its modernizing stage.

---

23. I am quoting Hannah Arendt. Speaking of participants at a conference in 1967, she continued: "Those who were more or less on the side of Lenin's revolution also justified Stalin, whereas those who were denouncing Stalin's rule were sure that Lenin was not only responsible for Stalin's totalitarianism but actually belongs in the same category, so that Stalin was a necessary consequence of Lenin." *Revolutionary Russia,* ed. Richard Pipes (Cambridge, Mass. 1968), p. 345.

One other scholarly tradition should be mentioned. Some writers interpreted the Stalin years in the context of Russian historical and cultural traditions. This emphasis on the resurgent Russianness of Stalinism might have led them to conceptualize discontinuities between Bolshevism and Stalinism. Instead, they blurred dissimilarities by treating both as "Communism" and continuous, or by tracing resurgent traditions back to early Soviet history. See, for example, Nicholas S. Timasheff, *The Great Retreat: The Growth and Decline of Communism in Russia* (New York, 1946); Berdyaev, *Origins of Russian Communism;* Dinko Tomasic, *The Impact of Russian Culture on Soviet Communism* (Glencoe, Ill., 1953); and Edward Crankshaw, *Cracks in the Kremlin Wall* (New York, 1951). More recently, Zbigniew Brzezinski has treated Soviet political history in terms of a dominant autocratic "Russian political culture." He interprets Bolshevism-Leninism as a "continuation of the dominant tradition," and thus Stalinism as "an extention—rather than an aberration—of what immediately preceded." "Soviet Politics: From the Future to the Past?" (This article will appear in a volume of essays in honor of Merle Fainsod to be published by Harvard University Press. I am grateful to Professor Brzezinski for allowing me to read and cite it in advance.)

24. Maximilien Rubel in *Revolutionary Russia,* p. 316. Similarly, see Cyril E. Black, "The Modernization of Russia," in *The Transformation of Russian Society: Aspects of Social Change since 1861,* ed. Cyril E. Black (Cambridge, Mass., 1967), p. 678; Theodore H. Von Laue, *Why Lenin? Why Stalin?* (Philadelphia, 1964), pp. 202, 205; Alec Nove, "Was Stalin Really Necessary?" *Encounter,* April 1962, pp. 86–92. One advocate of the development approach says that the "most salient fact about the Soviet Revolution . . . is its remarkable history of continuity. . . . " Alex Inkeles, *Social Change in Soviet Russia* (New York, 1971), p. 41. Another problem with the modernization approach to the Soviet 1930's is that it obscures other important developments in economic, social, and political life which were not "modern" but traditional and even retrogressive.

A direct challenge to many aspects of the continuity thesis has finally developed in the last few years. Benefiting from the availability of new Soviet materials, the scholars involved are less dependent on a single approach than on a critical re-examination of Soviet history and politics from 1917 onward. But although these few revisionist books have been reviewed respectfully,[25] their impact on scholarly thinking evidently remains limited. The academic consensus on Bolshevism and Stalinism is no longer intact. But the great majority of scholars, including the new generation, still believe that "Stalin epitomized the Communist mind . . . ," that his acts were "pure, unadulterated Leninism," that "Lenin was the mentor and Stalin the pupil who carried his master's legacy to its logical conclusion." [26]

II

The voluminous scholarship devoted to the continuity thesis has certain tenacious conventions. They are, loosely defined, of two sorts: a set of formulations, historical approaches, and conceptual explanations of how and why there was a political "straight line" between Bolshevism and Stalinism; and a series of interlocking historical interpretations said to demonstrate Bolshevik programmatic continuity between 1917 and Stalin's upheaval of 1929–33. Both need to be re-examined fully, though I can do so here only very briefly and, again, elliptically. I leave the question of programmatic continuity to the next section and begin with conceptual matters.

The problem begins with the formulation of the continuity thesis. Among its most familiar assertions is that Bolshevism contained the "seeds," "roots," or "germs" of Stalinism. To this proposition even the most ardent proponent of

25. Among them are Moshe Lewin's *Lenin's Last Struggle* (New York, 1968), *Russian Peasants and Soviet Power: A Study of Collectivization* (Evanston, Ill., 1968), and *Political Undercurrents in Soviet Economic Debates: From Bukharin to the Modern Reformers* (Princeton, N.J., 1974); Robert C. Tucker's *Stalin as Revolutionary, 1879–1929: A Study in History and Personality* (New York, 1973); and my *Bukharin and the Bolshevik Revolution: A Political Biography, 1888–1938* (New York, 1973). An early work that challenged the thesis indirectly was Alexander Erlich, *The Soviet Industrialization Debate, 1924–1928* (Cambridge, Mass., 1960).

26. The first comment is from Adam B. Ulam, *Stalin: The Man and His Era* (New York, 1973), p. 362; see also pp. 282, 294, 362. The other two are from Richard Gregor's introduction to *Resolutions and Decisions of the Communist Party of the Soviet Union*, Vol. 2, ed. Richard Gregor (Toronto, 1974), p. 38. I base this statement on a survey of recent historical writings by scholars of both generations, and of scholarly reviews of five recent books that treat the relationship between Bolshevism and Stalinism: Roy Medvedev, *Let History Judge: The Origins and Consequences of Stalinism* (New York, 1971); Solzhenitsyn, *The Gulag Archipelago;* Ulam, *Stalin;* Tucker, *Stalin as Revolutionary;* Cohen, *Bukharin and the Bolshevik Revolution.* It should be noted here that, unlike an earlier generation of historically minded political scientists, recent political scientists specializing on the Soviet Union, because of their methodological and contemporary interests, have rarely concerned themselves with these questions of Soviet historical development. One exception is Frederick C. Barghoorn. See, for example, his interesting and problematic treatment in "The Post-Khrushchev Campaign to Suppress Dissent," in *Dissent in the USSR*, ed. Rudolf L. Tökes (Baltimore, 1975), pp. 38–42.

discontinuity must say—yes, of course.[27] Unfortunately, this is to say very little, indeed only the obvious. Every historical period—each political phenomenon—has antecedents, "seeds," in the preceding one: 1917 in tsarist history, the Third Reich in Weimar, and so forth. In itself, however, this demonstrates nothing about continuity, much less causality or inevitability.

The Bolshevism of 1917–28 did contain important "seeds" of Stalinism; they are too fully related in our literature to be reiterated here. Less noted, and the real point, is that Bolshevism also contained other important, non-Stalinist, "seeds"; and, equally, that the "seeds" of Stalinism are also to be found elsewhere —in Russian historical and cultural tradition, in social events such as the Civil War, in the international setting, etc. The question is, however, not "seeds," or even less significant continuities, but fundamental continuities or discontinuities. Moreover, to change metaphors and quote Victor Serge on this point, "To judge a living man by the death germs which the autopsy reveals in a corpse—and which he may have carried in him since birth—is that very sensible?" [28]

Even less helpful are the three definitional components of the continuity thesis: Bolshevism, Stalinism, continuiy. In customary usage, these terms obscure more than they define. The self-professed *raison d'être* of the "totalitarianism" school was to distinguish and analyze a wholly new kind of authoritarianism. Yet precisely this critical distinction is often missing, as illustrated by the familiar explanation of Stalinism: "authoritarianism in prerevolutionary Leninism naturally and perhaps inevitably gave birth to Soviet authoritarianism." [29] Variants of this proposition explain that Stalinism continued the illiberal, non-democratic, repressive traditions of Bolshevism.

This argument misses the essential comparative point. (It also assumes, mistakenly, I think, that some kind of democratic order—liberal or proletarian—was a Russian possibility in 1917 or after.) Bolshevism was in important respects—depending on the period—a strongly authoritarian movement. But failure to distinguish between Soviet authoritarianism before and after 1929 means obscuring the very nature of Stalinism. Stalinism was not simply nationalism, bureaucratization, absence of democracy, censorship, police repression, and the rest in any precedented sense. These phenomena have appeared in many societies and are rather easily explained.

Instead, Stalinism was excess, extraordinary extremism, in each. It was not, for example, merely coercive peasant policies, but a virtual civil war against the peasantry; not merely police repression, or even civil war–style terror, but a holocaust by terror that victimized tens of millions of people for twenty-five years; not merely a Thermidorian revival of nationalist tradition, but an almost fascist-like chauvinism; not merely a leader cult, but deification of a despot. During the Khrushchev years, Western scholars frequently spoke of a "Stalinism without

---

27. As does, for example, Medvedev, in *Let History Judge.*

28. *The New International,* February 1939, pp. 53–55. On the question of "roots" see also Trotsky, *Stalinism and Bolshevism,* p. 23.

29. Thomas T. Hammond, "Leninist Authoritarianism before the Revolution," in *Continuity and Change in Russian and Social Thought,* ed. Ernest J. Simmons (Cambridge, Mass., 1955), p. 156.

the excesses," or "Stalinism without the arrests." This makes no sense. Excesses were the essence of historical Stalinism, and they are what really require explanation.[30]

Similar problems arise from the customary treatment of original Bolshevism, which is to define it in such a selectively narrow fashion as to construe it as Stalinism, or "embryonic" Stalinism. I have tried to show elsewhere that Bolshevism was a far more diverse political movement—ideologically, programmatically, generationally, etc.—than is usually acknowledged in our scholarship.[31] Another related convention of the continuity thesis should also be protested: the equating of Bolshevism and Leninism. Lenin was plainly the singular Bolshevik; his leadership, ideas, and personality shaped the movement in fundamental ways. But Bolshevism was larger, and more diverse, than Lenin and Leninism. Its ideology, policies, and politics were shaped also by other forceful leaders, lesser members and committees, non-party constituents, and great social events, including the First World War, the Revolution, and the Civil War.[32] I am not suggesting that Leninism, rather than Bolshevism, was nascently Stalinist. Those who do so rely similarly upon an exclusionary selection of references, emphasizing, for example, the Lenin of *What Is to Be Done?* and 1919, while minimizing the Lenin of *The State and Revolution* and 1922–23.

What, then, of formulating continuities and discontinuities? It is among the most difficult problems of historical analysis. Most historians would agree that it requires careful empirical study of historical similarities and dissimilarities, and that the question of degree, of whether quantitative changes become qualitative, is critical. Not surprisingly, perhaps, this venerable approach plays a central role in our thinking about differences between tsarist and Soviet political history, and almost none in our thinking about Bolshevism and Stalinism. Thus a major proponent of the continuity thesis warns against equating the tsarist and Soviet regimes: "it is important to stress that there is a deep gulf dividing authoritarianism and totalitarianism, and if we treat the two as identical political formations, we end by revealing our inability to distinguish between continuity and

---

30. The issue of whether Stalinism can be defined apart from its excesses figures prominently in recent Soviet discussions. Soviet revisionist historians have argued, for example, that the collectivization drive of 1929–33 is incomprehensible apart from its excesses *(peregib)*. A Soviet leader then complained that for these historians "collectivization was a whole chain of mistakes, violations, crimes, etc." "Rech' tov D. G. Sturua," *Zaria vostoka*, March 10, 1966, p. 2. Answering a *samizdat* writer, Roy Medvedev makes the same point: "The *essence* of Stalinism was those very 'imbecile savage extremes' that Mikhailov regards as a minor detail." *On Socialist Democracy* (New York, 1975), pp. 398–99. For a Western concept of Stalinism without "excessive excesses," see Nove, "Was Stalin Really Necessary?"

31. *Bukharin and the Bolshevik Revolution*, pp. 2–5 and passim.

32. For example, Bukharin's writings considerably influenced Leninist and Bolshevik ideology on imperialism and the state. Ibid., pp. 25–43. In a new book, *The Bolsheviks Come to Power: The 1917 Revolution in Petrograd* (New York, 1976), Alexander Rabinowitch shows us a Bolshevik party in 1917 dramatically unlike the stereotype of a conspiratorial, disciplined vanguard, a party responding to, and gaining from, grass-roots politics. The enormous impact of the Civil War remains to be studied.

change." [33] But if we were to apply this sensible admonition to Soviet history itself, it would be difficult not to conclude, at the very least, that here, too, 'differences in degree grew into differences of kind. . . . What had existed under Lenin was carried by Stalin to such extremes that its very nature changed." [34]

As our scholarship stands, however, it appears that special approaches are reserved for interpreting Soviet history. One is the extraordinary determinism and mono-causal explanations on which the continuity thesis so often depends. The vocabulary used to posit a direct causal relationship between the "political dynamics" of Bolshevism and Stalinism, especially collectivization and the Great Terror, may be unique in modern-day political and historical studies. It abounds in the language of teleological determinism: "inner logic," "inexorably totalitarian features," "inevitable process," "inescapable consequences," "logical completion," "inevitable stage," and more. Or, to give a fuller illustration, a standard work explains that Stalin's collectivization campaign of 1929–33 "was the inevitable consequence of the triumph of the Bolshevik Party on November 7, 1917. . . ." [35]

Serious questions about historical approach are involved here. For one thing, our language betrays a rigid determinism not unlike that which once prevailed in official Stalinist historiography, and which was properly derided by Western scholars. [36] For another, while claiming to explain so much, this sort of teleological interpretation actually explains very little. It is, as Hannah Arendt observed many years ago, more on the order of "axiomatic value-judgment" than authentic historical analysis. [37] And it is vulnerable logically. Replying to similar arguments circulating in the Soviet Union, Roy Medvedev has pointed out that if Stalinism was predetermined by Bolshevism, if there were no alternatives after 1917, then 1917 and Bolshevism, must have been predetermined by previous Russian history. In that case, "to explain Stalinism we have to return to earlier and earlier epochs . . . very likely to the Tartar yoke." He adds, on a political note, "That would be wrong . . . a historical justification of Stalinism, not a condemnation." [38]

Implicit in all this is, I think, a sovietological version of what Herbert Butterfield called the Whig interpretation of history. The past is evaluated in terms of the present, antecedents in terms of outcome. Or as one interpreter of continuity in Soviet political history has argued, "Sometimes the past is better understood by examining the present and then defining the relationship of the present to the past." [39]

---

33. Fainsod in *Continuity and Change in Russian and Soviet Thought,* p. 179.

34. Boris Souvarine, "Stalinism," in *Marxism in the Modern World,* ed. Milorad M. Drachkovitch (Stanford, Calif., 1965), p. 102.

35. Jasny, *Socialized Agriculture of the USSR,* p. 18.

36. As has been pointed out before: Isaac Deutscher, "The Future of Russian Society," *Dissent,* Summer 1954, pp. 227–29; Robert D. Warth, *Lenin* (New York, 1973), p. 171.

37. *Dissent,* January–February 1953, pp. 581–82.

38. *Let History Judge,* p. 359.

39. Brzezinski in *Development of the USSR,* p. 40. Brzezinski was replying to Robert C. Tucker in an exchange on Soviet political history. Arguing against Brzezinski's continuity thesis, Tucker had suggested that study of Soviet history must start at the beginning, proceeding "layer by layer."

The approach is modified here by "sometimes," but it is clear and widespread. It is not wholly indefensible. The historian, as Carr reminds us, is unavoidably influenced by the present and by established outcomes.[40] In addition, careful application of contemporary insights may illuminate the past. But the Whig tradition in Soviet studies has given rise to unsatisfactory conventions on the subject of Bolshevism and Stalinism. Accompanying the teleological determinism, there is a tendency, projecting outcome backward upon the past, to Stalinize early Soviet history and politics; to ignore, for the "straight line" to 1917, the actual period, 1929–33, when historical Stalinism first appeared; and, throughout, to interpret the party ahistorically, as though it acted above society and outside history itself.

Two familiar, and equally questionable, lines of analysis are among the corollaries of our Whig historiography. One argues that the inner "political dynamics" (or "nature") of the Bolshevik party predetermined Stalinism. The other insists that changes in the Soviet political system under Bolshevism and Stalinism were superficial or secondary to continuities which were fundamental and observable. Whatever the partial truths of the first argument, it suffers from the implicit ahistorical conception of a basically unchanging party after 1917, an assumption easily refuted by evidence already in our literature. What is meant by "the party" as historical determinant when, for example, its membership, composition, organizational structure, internal political life, and outlook underwent far-reaching alterations between 1917 and 1921 alone?[41]

The causal "dynamic" cited most often is, of course, the party's ideology.[42] Several obvious objections can be raised against this explanation of social and political development. It is even more one-dimensional. It ignores the fact that a given ideology may influence events in different ways, Christianity having contributed to both compassion and inquisition, socialism to both social justice and tyranny. And it relies upon a self-serving definition of Bolshevik ideology as being concerned mainly with the "concentration of total social power."[43]

More important, the nature of Bolshevik ideology was far less cohesive and fixed than the standard interpretation allows. If ideology influenced events, it was also shaped, and changed, by them. The Russian Civil War, to take an early instance, had a major impact on Bolshevik outlook, reviving the self-conscious theory of an embattled vanguard, which had been inoperative or inconsequential for at least a decade, and implanting in the once civilian-minded party what a

---

40. *What Is History?* (London, 1964), p. 42.

41. I have learned much from discussions on this point with Moshe Lewin.

42. Solzhenitsyn's theory that the ideology "bears the entire responsibility for all the bloodshed" is only a recent, though somewhat extreme, version. A. Solzhenitsyn, *Pis'mo vozhdiam Sovetskogo Soiuza* (Paris, 1974), p. 41. For academic versions, see, for example, Ulam, *Unfinished Revolution,* p. 198; Donald W. Treadgold, *Twentieth-Century Russia* (Chicago, 1959), p. 263; and Zbigniew K. Brzezinski, *Ideology and Power in Soviet Politics,* rev. ed. (New York, 1967), p. 42.

43. The interpreter can then define "Stalinism . . . as mature Leninism." Philip Selznick, *The Organizational Weapon: A Study of Bolshevik Strategy and Tactics* (New York, 1952), pp. 5, 39, 42, 216, and the index entry at p. 348. The movement's "original sin," according to Ulam, was "lust for power." *Stalin,* pp. 261, 265.

leading Bolshevik called a "military soviet culture." [44] Above all, official ideology changed radically under Stalin. Several of these changes have been noted by Western and Soviet scholars: the revival of nationalism, statism, anti-Semitism, and conservative, or reactionary, cultural and behavioral norms; the repeal of ideas and legislation favoring workers, women, schoolchildren, minority cultures, and egalitarianism, as well as a host of revolutionary and Bolshevik symbols; and a switch in emphasis from ordinary people to leaders and official bosses as the creators of history.[45] These were not simply amendments but a new ideology which was "changed in its *essence*" and which did "not represent the same movement as that which took power in 1917." [46]

Similar criticisms must be leveled against the other causal "dynamic" usually cited, the party's "organizational principles"—the implied theory that Stalinism originated with *What Is to Be Done?*[47] It, too, is one-dimensional and ahistorical. Bolshevism's organizational character evolved over the years, often in response to external events, from the unruly, loosely organized party participating successfully in democratic politics in 1917, to the centralized bureaucratic party of the 1920's, to the terrorized party of the 1930's, many of whose executive committees and bureaus no longer existed.[48]

Moreover, the argument is, in effect, an adaptation of Michels' "iron law of oligarchy," which was intended to be a generalization about all large political organizations and their tendency toward oligarchical rather than democratic politics. This may suggest a good deal about the evolution of the Bolshevik leadership's relations with the party-at-large between 1917 and 1929, as it does about modern parties generally. But it tells us nothing directly about Stalinism,

---

44. N. Osinsky in *Deviatyi s'ezd RKP(b). Mart–aprel 1920 goda: protokoly* (Moscow, 1960), p. 115.

45. See Timasheff, *The Great Retreat;* Frederick C. Barghoorn, *Soviet Russian Nationalism* (New York, 1956); Robert V. Daniels, "Soviet Thought in the Nineteen-Thirties: An Interpretative Sketch," *Indiana Slavic Studies,* Vol. I, ed. Michael Ginsburg and Joseph T. Shaw (Bloomington, Ind., 1956), pp. 97–135; and Paul Willen, "Soviet Architecture: Progress and Reaction," *Problems of Communism,* No. 6 (1953), pp. 24–34. Soviet scholars have commented on the change in focus from masses to leaders. See M. V. Nechkina in *Istoriia i sotsiologiia* (Moscow, 1964), p. 238. For a vivid illustration, compare the films made to commemorate the tenth and twentieth anniversaries of the 1917 revolution: *October,* or *Ten Days That Shook the World* (1927), and *Lenin in October* (1937).

46. Daniels, "Soviet Thought in the Nineteen-Thirties," p. 130. In 1932 Ol'minsky complained that ideological changes in party historiography were leading to a "castrated Leninism." Quoted in L. A. Slepov, *Istoriia KPSS—vazhneishaia obshchestvennaia nauka* (Moscow, 1964), p. 11.

47. See, for example, Selznick, *The Organizational Weapon;* and S. V. Utechin's introduction to V. I. Lenin, *What Is to Be Done?* (Oxford, 1963), p. 15. For a polemical but effective critique of this theory, see Max Shachtman, *The Bureaucratic Revolution: The Rise of the Stalinist State* (New York, 1962), pp. 202–23. As Shachtman points out, few Western scholars have missed the chance to quote approvingly Trotsky's 1904 prediction: "The organization of the party will take the place of the party; the Central Committee will take the place of the organization; and finally the dictator will take the place of the Central Committee."

48. See *Ocherki istorii kommunisticheskoi partii Turkmenistana,* 2nd ed. (Ashkhabad, 1965), p. 495; *Ocherki istorii kommunisticheskoi partii Kazakhstana* (Alma-Ata, 1963), p. 377. And see the evidence in Robert Conquest, *The Great Terror: Stalin's Purge of the Thirties* (New York, 1968), Chaps. VIII, XIII; and Medvedev, *Let History Judge,* Chap. 6.

which was not oligarchical but autocratic politics,[49] unless we conclude that the "iron law of oligarchy" is actually an iron law of autocracy.

The party's growing centralization, bureaucratization, and administrative intolerance after 1917 certainly promoted authoritarianism in the one-party system and abetted Stalin's rise. To argue that these developments predetermined Stalinism is another matter. Even in the 1920's, after the bureaucratization and militarization fostered by the Civil War, the high party was not (nor had it ever been) the disciplined vanguard fantasized in *What Is to Be Done?* It remained oligarchical, in the words of one of its leaders, *"a negotiated federation between groups, groupings, factions, and 'tendencies.'"*[50] In short, the party's "organizational principles" did not produce Stalinism before 1929, nor have they since 1953.

There remains, then, the argument that discontinuities were secondary to continuities in the working of the Soviet political system under Bolshevism and Stalinism.[51] Though ideally an empirical question, here, too, there would seem to be a critical methodological lapse. The importance of distinguishing between the official, or theatrical, façade and the inner (sometimes disguised) reality of politics has been evident at least since Bagehot demolished the prevailing theory of English politics in 1867 by dissecting the system in terms of its "dignified" and "efficient" parts. The case made by Western scholars for fundamental continuities in the Soviet political system has rested largely on what Bagehot called "dignified," merely apparent, or fictitious parts.

Looking at the "efficient," or inner, reality, Robert C. Tucker came to a very different conclusion several years ago: "What we carelessly call 'the Soviet political system' is best seen and analyzed as an historical succession of political systems within a broadly continuous institutional framework." The Bolshevik system had been one of party dictatorship characterized by oligarchical leadership politics in the ruling party. After 1936 and Stalin's Great Purge, despite an outward "continuity of organizational forms and official nomenclature," the "one-party system had given way to a one-person system, the ruling party to a ruling personage." This was a ramifying change from an oligarchical party regime to an autocratic "Führerist" regime, and was "reflected in a whole system of changes in the political process, the ideological pattern, the organization of supreme power, and official patterns of behavior."[52] The apparent continuities regularly itemized—leader, the party, terror, class war, censorship, Marxism-

---

49. Tucker, *Soviet Political Mind,* Chap. 1 and p. 212.

50. Nikolai Bukharin, *K voprosu o trotskizme* (Moscow and Leningrad, 1925), p. 11. To put this point differently, the infamous 1921 ban of factionalism in the party was not, as most scholars suggest, the culmination of the Bolshevik-Leninist tradition, but a quixotic attempt by a panicky leadership to constrain, or legislate away, its own tradition. As official historians have complained over the years, party history has been a history of "factional struggle." M. Gaisinskii, *Bor'ba s uklonami ot general'-noi linii partii: istoricheskii ocherk vnutripartiinoi bor'by posleoktiabr'skogo perioda,* 2nd ed. (Moscow and Leningrad, 1931), p. 4; Slepov, *Istoriia KPSS,* p. 22.

51. See, for example, Inkeles, *Social Change in Soviet Russia,* p. 41; and Bertram D. Wolfe in *The USSR after Fifty Years,* ed. Samuel Hendel and Randolph L. Braham (New York, 1967), p. 153.

52. Tucker in *Development of the USSR,* p. 33; *Soviet Political Mind,* pp. 18, 179.

Leninism, purge, etc.—were synthetic and illusory. The terms may still have been applicable, but their meaning was different.[53]

Tucker's conclusion that Stalin's terror "broke the back of the party, eliminated it as a . . . ruling class," has been amply confirmed by more recent evidence.[54] After the purges swept away at least one million of its members between 1935 and 1939, the primacy of the party—the "essence" of Bolshevism-Leninism, in most scholarly definitions—was no more. Its elite (massacred virtually as a whole), general membership (in 1939 70 percent had joined since 1929 or after), ethos, and role were no longer those of the old party, or even the party of 1934. Even in its new Stalinist form, the party's political importance fell well below that of the police, and its official esteem below that of the state. Its deliberative bodies—the party congress, the Central Committee, and eventually even the Politburo—rarely convened.[55] Accordingly, the previous and different history of the party could no longer be written about, even to distort: between 1938 and 1953, only one Soviet doctoral dissertation was written on this once hallowed subject.[56]

It is sometimes pointed out, as a final defense of the continuity thesis, that "Stalinism" was never acknowledged officially during Stalin's reign, only "Marxism-Leninism." With Bagehot's method, of course, this tells us nothing.[57] Moreover, it is not entirely accurate. As the cult of the infallible leader (which, it should be said, was very different from the earlier Bolshevik cult of a historically necessary, but not infallible, party) grew into literal deification after 1938, the adjective "Stalinist" was attached increasingly to people, institutions, orthodox ideas, events, and even history. This was a departure from even the early 1930s, when they were normally called Leninist, Bolshevik, or Soviet. It reflected, among other things, the sharp decline in Lenin's official standing.[58] Catchphrases such as "the

---

53. On "purge" and "class war," for example, see Robert M. Slusser's review of Brzezinski's *The Permanent Purge,* in *American Slavic and East European Review,* Vol. XV, No. 4 (December 1956), pp. 543–46; and Tucker, *Soviet Political Mind,* pp. 55–56.

54. *Soviet Political Mind,* p. 135. See Conquest, *The Great Terror,* Chaps. 8, 13; and Medvedev, *Let History Judge,* Chap. 6. Conquest calls the crushing of the party "a revolution as complete as, though more disguised than, any previous changes in Russia" (p. 251).

55. Between 1918 and 1933, there were ten party congresses, ten party conferences, and 122 Central Committee plenums. Between 1934 and 1953, there were three party congresses (only one after 1939), one party conference, and twenty-three Central Committee plenums (none in 1941–43, 1945–46, 1948, or 1950–51). *Sovetskaia istoricheskaia entsiklopediia,* Vol. 8 (Moscow, 1965), p. 275. According to Medvedev, the expression "soldier of the party" was replaced by "soldier of Stalin." *Let History Judge,* p. 419. For an example of the cult of the state, see K. V. Ostrovityanov, *The Role of the State in the Socialist Transformation of the Economy of the USSR* (Moscow, 1950).

56. *Vsesoiuznoe soveshchanie o merakh uluchsheniia podgotovki nauchno-pedagogicheskikh kadrov po istoricheskim naukam, 18–21 dekabria 1962 g.* (Moscow, 1964), p. 242.

57. As Boris Souvarine has argued in "Stalinism," in *Marxism in the Modern World,* pp. 90–107. Since Stalin's death, the official euphemism for Stalinism has been, of course, "cult of the personality."

58. Compare, for example, references to the party leadership, the Central Committee, political ideas, etc., at the following gatherings: *XVII konferentsiia vsesoiuznoi kommunisticheskoi partii (b): stenograficheskii otchet* (Moscow, 1932); *XVII s"ezd vsesoiuznoi kommunisticheskoi partii (b). 26 ianvaria–10 fevralia 1934 g.: stenograficheskii otchet* (Moscow, 1934); and *XVIII s"ezd vsesoiuznoi*

teachings of Lenin and Stalin" remained. But less ecumenical ones arose to characterize the building of Soviet socialism as "the great Stalinist cause," Stalin alone as "the genius-architect of Communism," and Soviet history as the "epoch of Stalin." [59] The term "Stalinism" was prohibited from official usage; but the concept was ingrained, tacitly and officially.[60]

If symbols can tell us anything about political reality, we do best to heed Leonid Petrovsky's commentary on the statue of Dolgoruky, which Stalin built on the spot where Lenin had once unveiled a monument to the first Soviet Constitution. "The monument to the bloody feudal prince has become a kind of personification of the grim epoch of the personality cult. The horse of the feudal prince has its back turned to the Central Party Archives, where the immortal works of Marx, Engels, and Lenin are preserved and where a beautiful statue of Lenin stands." [61]

III

Underlying the other arguments of the continuity thesis is, finally, that of a programmatic "straight line" from 1917. It is the view, widespread in Soviet studies literature, that Stalin's wholesale collectivization and heavy industrialization drive of 1929–33, the paroxysmic upheaval he later properly called "a revolution from above," represented the continuation and fulfillment of Bolshevik thinking about modernizing, or building socialism in, Russia. In other words, even if it is conceded that the events of 1936–39 were discontinuous, what about those of 1929–33?

The argument for programmatic continuity rests upon interlocking interpretations of the two previous periods in Bolshevik policy: War Communism—the extreme nationalization, grain requisitioning, and monopolistic state intervention effected during the Civil War of 1918–20; and NEP—the moderate agricultural and industrial policies and mixed public-private economy of 1921–28. In its essentials, the argument runs as follows: War Communism was mainly a product of the party's original ideological-programmatic ideas (sometimes called "blueprints"), an eager crash program of socialism.[62] These frenzied policies collapsed

kommunisticheskoi partii(b), 10–21 marta 1939 g.: stenograficheskii otchet (Moscow, 1939). As time passed, there was a partial ban on literature about Lenin. *Spravochnik partiinogo rabotnika* (Moscow, 1957), p. 364. The diminishing of Lenin began earlier. On the anniversary of the Revolution in November 1933, an American correspondent counted in the shop windows on Gorky Street 103 busts and portraits of Stalin, fifty-eight of Lenin, and five of Marx. Eugene Lyons, *Moscow Carrousel* (New York, 1935), pp. 140–41.

59. *XVIII s"ezd*, p. 68; V. K. Oltarzhevskii, *Stroitel'stvo vysotnykh zdanii v Moskve* (Moscow, 1953), pp. 4, 214.

60. The term "Stalinism" appears to have been used privately, by high leaders as well as others. See *Khrushchev Remembers: The Last Testament* (Boston, 1974), p. 193; Medvedev, *Let History Judge*, pp. 506–7. It has been used widely in *samizdat* literature.

61. "Open Letter to the Central Committee," *Washington Post*, April 27, 1969.

62. See, for example, Treadgold, *Twentieth-Century Russia*, p. 165; Ulam, *The Bolsheviks*, pp. 467–68; Paul Craig Roberts, " 'War Communism': A Re-examination," *Slavic Review*, June 1970, pp. 238–61. Craig is arguing against the view that War Communism was primarily expediency, which he calls the "prevalent interpretation." This is not my impression.

in 1921 because of the population's opposition, and the party was forced to retreat
to the new economic policy of concessions to private enterprise in the countryside
and cities. Accordingly, official Bolshevik policy during the eight years of NEP—
and NEP itself as a social-political order—are interpreted in the literature as
being "merely a breathing spell," "a holding operation," or "a strategic retreat,
during which the forces of socialism in Russia would retrench, recuperate, and
then resume their march." [63]

How these two interpretations converge into a single thesis of programmatic
continuity between Bolshevism and Stalin's revolution from above is illustrated
by one of our best general histories. War Communism is presented as "an attempt,
which proved premature, to realize the Party's stated ideological goals," and
NEP, in Bolshevik thinking, as "a tactical maneuver to be pursued only until
the inevitable change of conditions which would make victory possible. . . ." The
author can then marvel over Stalin's policies of 1929–33: "It is difficult to find
a parallel for a regime or a party which held power for ten years, biding its time
until it felt strong enough to fulfill its original program." [64] The problem with
this interpretation is that it conflicts with much of the historical evidence. Having
discussed these questions at some length elsewhere,[65] I shall be concise.

There are three essential points to be made against locating the origins of War
Communism in an original Bolshevik program. First, odd as it may seem for a
party so often described as "doctrinaire," the Bolsheviks had no well-defined
economic policies upon coming to office in October 1917. There were generally
held Bolshevik goals and tenets—socialism, workers' control, nationalization,
large-scale farming, planning, and the like—but these were vague and subject
to the most varying interpretations inside the party. Bolsheviks had done little
thinking about practical economic policies before October, and, as it turned out,
there were few upon which they could agree.[66]

Second, the initial program of the Bolshevik government, in the sense of
officially defined policy, was not War Communism but what Lenin called in
April–May 1918 "state capitalism," a mixture of socialist measures and concessions to the existing capitalist structure and control of the economy.[67] If this first
Bolshevik program resembled anything that followed, it was NEP. And, third,
the actual policies of War Communism did not begin until June 1918, in response
to the threat of prolonged civil war and diminishing supplies, a situation that
immediately outdated Lenin's conciliatory "state capitalism." [68]

---

63. The concluding quotation is from Adam B. Ulam, *The Russian Political System* (New York,
1974), p. 37. The first two are from Arthur E. Adams, *Stalin and His Times* (New York, 1972), p.
7; and John A. Armstrong, *Ideology, Politics and Government in the Soviet Union,* 3rd ed. (New York,
1974), p. 22. Similarly, see Fainsod, *How Russia Is Ruled,* pp. 528–29; Gurian, *Bolshevism,* p. 76;
and Solzhenitzyn, *The Gulag Archipelago,* p. 392, where it is said that the "entire NEP was merely
a cynical deceit."

64. Treadgold, *Twentieth-Century Russia,* pp. 165, 199, 258.

65. *Bukharin and the Bolshevik Revolution,* Chaps. 3, 5–9.

66. For a fuller discussion, see *Bukharin and the Bolshevik Revolution,* pp. 53–57.

67. V. I. Lenin, *Sochineniia,* Vol XXII (Moscow and Leningrad, 1931), pp. 435–68.

68. E. H. Carr, *The Bolshevik Revolution,* Vol. II (New York, 1952), pp. 51, 53, 98–99.

None of this is to say that War Communism had no ideological component. As the Civil War deepened into a great social conflict, official measures grew more extreme, and the meaning and the "defense of the revolution" became inseparable, Bolsheviks naturally infused these improvised policies with high theoretical and programmatic significance beyond military victory. They became ideological.[69] The evolution of War Communism, and its legacy in connection with Stalinism, require careful study (though the similarities should not be exaggerated). But the origins will not be found in a Bolshevik program of October.

The question of NEP is even more important. Not only were the official economic policies of 1921–28 distinctly unlike Stalin's in 1929–33, but the social-political order of NEP, with its officially tolerated social pluralism in economic, cultural-intellectual, and even (in local soviets and high state agencies) political life, represents a historical model of Soviet Communist rule radically unlike Stalinism.[70] In addition, the standard treatment of Bolshevik thinking about NEP is more complicated because all scholars are aware of the intense policy debates of the 1920's, a circumstance not easily reconciled with a simplistic interpretation of NEP as merely a programmatic bivouac, or the antechamber of Stalinism.

Tensions inherent in the interpretation are related to secondary but significant conventions in our literature on NEP. The programmatic debates of the 1920's are treated largely as an extension of, and in terms of, the Trotsky-Stalin rivalry (or, perpetuating the factional misnomers of the period, "permanent revolution" and "socialism in one country"). Trotsky and the Left opposition are said to have been anti-NEP and embryonically Stalinist, the progenitors of "almost every major item in the political program that Stalin later carried out." Stalin is then said to have stolen, or adapted, Trotsky's economic policies in 1929. Having portrayed a "basic affinity between Trotsky's plans and Stalin's actions," these secondary interpretations suggest at least a significant continuity between Stalinism and Bolshevik thinking in the 1920's, and underlie the general interpretation of NEP.[71] They are, however, factually incorrect.

The traditional treatment of the economic debates (we are not concerned here with the controversy over Comintern policy or the party bureaucracy) in terms of Trotsky and Stalin bears no relationship to the actual discussions of 1923–27. If the rival policies can be dichotomized and personified, they were Trotskyist and Bukharinist. Stalin's public policies on industry, agriculture, and planning

69. A classic example is Nikolai Bukharin's *Ekonomika perkhodnogo perioda* (Moscow, 1920). For an interesting Soviet study of this question, see E. G. Gimpel'son, *"Voennyi kommunizm": politika, praktika, ideologiia* (Moscow, 1973).

70. For a discussion of NEP in these terms, see my *Bukharin and the Bolshevik Revolution*, pp. 270–76; and Lewin, *Political Undercurrents*, Chaps. 4, 5, 12.

71. Alfred G. Meyer, "Lev Davidovich Trotsky," *Problems of Communism*, November–December 1967, pp. 31, 37, and *passim*. Meyer's is a rather pristine example of the interpretation, but variations run through our literature. See, for example, Leonard Schapiro, "Out of the Dustbin of History," *ibid*, p. 86; Reshetar, *Concise History of the Communist Party*, pp. 230–31; Basil Dmytryshyn, *USSR: A Concise History*, 2nd ed. (New York, 1971), p. 121; Ulam, *Stalin*, p. 292, note 3; and Isaac Deutscher, *Stalin: A Political Biography*, 2nd ed. (New York, 1967), p. 295, which seems to be contradicted on p. 318.

were Bukharin's, that is, pro-NEP, moderate, evolutionary. This was the cement of the Stalin-Bukharin duumvirate that made official policy and led the party majority against the Left oppositions until early 1928. During these years, there were no "Stalinist" ideas, apart from "socialism in one country" which was also Bukharin's.[72] If "ism" is to be affixed, there was no Stalinism, only Bukharinism and Trotskyism. This was understood at the time. As the opposition of 1925 complained, "Comrade Stalin has become the total prisoner of this political line, the creator and genuine representative of which is Comrade Bukharin." Stalin was no prisoner, but a willing adherent. He replied, "We stand, and we shall stand, for Bukharin." [73]

Bukharin's economic proposals for modernizing and building socialism in Soviet Russia in the 1920's are clear enough. Developing the themes of Lenin's last writings, which constituted both a defense and further elaboration of NEP as a road to socialism, and adding some of his own, Bukharin became the party's main theorist of NEP. Though his policies evolved between 1924 and 1928 toward great emphasis on planning, heavy industrial investment, and efforts to promote a partial and voluntary collective farm sector, he remained committed to the NEP economic framework of a state, or "socialist," sector (mainly large-scale industry, transportation, and banking) and a private sector (peasant farms and small manufacturing, trade, and service enterprises) interacting through market relations. Even during the crisis of 1928–29, NEP was for the Bukharinists a viable developmental (not static) model, predicated on civil peace, that could reconcile Bolshevik aspirations and Russian social reality.[74]

But what about Trotsky and the Left? Though his political rhetoric was often that of revolutionary heroism, Trotsky's actual economic proposals in the 1920s were also based on NEP and its continuation. He urged greater attention to heavy industry and planning earlier than did Bukharin, and he worried more about the village "kulak"; but his remedies were moderate, market-oriented, or, as the expression went, "nepist." Like Bukharin, he was a "reformist" in economic policy, looking to the evolution of NEP Russia toward industrialism and socialism.[75]

Even Preobrazhensky, the avatar of "super-industrialization" whose fearful arguments about the necessity of "primitive socialist accumulation" based on

---

72. Cohen, *Bukharin and the Bolshevik Revolution,* pp. 147–48, 186–88. For a different view of Stalin in the 1920's, see Tucker, *Stalin as Revolutionary,* pp. 395–404. Tucker argues that much of Bukharin's programmatic thinking was antithetical to Stalin psychologically, and that Stalin's later policies were already adumbrated in differences of emphasis between the two. Even so, the fact remains that there was no meaningful difference on the level of public policy and factional politics between 1924 and 1927.

73. *XIV s"ezd vsesoiuznoi kommunisticheskoi partii (b). 18–31 dekabria 1925 g.: stenograficheskii otchet* (Moscow and Leningrad, 1926), pp. 254, 494.

74. Cohen, *Bukharin and the Bolshevik Revolution,* Chaps. 6, 8, 9.

75. The economic ideas of Trotsky and the Left are treated elliptically and somewhat inconsistently by Isaac Deutscher, though he does call Trotsky a "reformist" in economic policy. *The Prophet Outcast: Trotsky, 1929–1940* (London, 1963), p. 110. For a fuller study, see Richard B. Day, *Leon Trotsky and the Politics of Economic Isolation* (Cambridge, England, 1973); and Lewin, *Political Undercurrents,* Chaps. 1–3.

"exploiting" the peasant sector are often cited as Stalin's inspiration, accepted the hallmark of NEP economics. He wanted to "exploit" peasant agriculture through market relations by artifically fixing state industrial prices higher than agricultural prices.[76] Both he and Trotsky, and the Bolshevik Left generally, thought in terms of peasant farming for the foreseeable future. However inconsistent their ideas may have been, neither ever advocated imposed collectivization, much less wholesale collectivization as a system of requisitioning or a solution to industrial backwardness.[77]

The debates between Bukharinists and Trotskyists in the 1920s represented the spectrum of high Bolshevik programmatic thinking, Right to Left. The two sides disagreed on important economic issues, from price policy and rural taxation to the prospects for comprehensive planning. But unlike the international and political issues which most embittered the factional struggle, these disagreements were limited, within the parameters of "nepism," which both sides accepted, though with different levels of enthusiasm.

In fact, the revised Bukharinist program adopted as the first Five-Year Plan at the Fifteenth Party Congress in December 1927, and calling for more ambitious industrial investment as well as partial voluntary collectivization, represented a kind of amalgam of Bukharinist-Trotskyist thinking as it had evolved in the debates of the 1920's.[78] When Stalin abandoned this program a year and a half later, he abandoned mainstream Bolshevik thinking about economic and social change. After 1929 and the end of NEP, the Bolshevik programmatic alternative to Stalinism, in fact and as perceived inside the party, remained basically Bukharinist. From afar, the exiled Trotsky leveled his own accusations against Stalin's regime, but his economic proposals in the early 1930's were, as they had been in the 1920's, far closer to, and now "entirely indistinguishable from," Bukharin's.[79]

NEP had originated as an ignoble retreat in 1921, and resentment at NEP economics, politics, and culture continued throughout the 1920's. It was perpetuated in the heroic Bolshevik tradition of October and the Civil War, and probably strongest among cadres formed by the warfare experience of 1918–20, and the younger party generation. Stalin would tap these real sentiments for his Civil War re-enactment of 1929–33. But, for reasons beyond our concern here, by 1924 NEP had acquired a general legitimacy among Bolshevik leaders. Not even Stalin dared challenge that legitimacy in his final contest with the Bukharinists in 1928–29. He campaigned and won not as the abolitionist of NEP, or the proponent of "revolution from above," but as a "calm and sober" leader who could make it work.[80] Even after defeating the Bukharin group in April 1929, as NEP crumbled under Stalin's radical policies, his editorials continued to insist

---

76. E. Preobrazhensky, *The New Economics* (London, 1965), pp. 110–11; Erlich, *Soviet Industrialization Debate,* pp. 32–59.

77. As Preobrazhensky later pointed out, in *XVII s"ezd,* p. 238.

78. See Lewin, *Political Undercurrents,* Chaps. 2 and 3.

79. Ibid., pp. 68–72; Cohen, *Bukharin and the Bolshevik Revolution,* pp. 347–48.

80. Cohen, *Bukharin and the Bolshevik Revolution,* pp. 328–29. This question is treated in terms of Stalin's leadership role in Tucker, *Stalin as Revolutionary,* Chaps. 12–14.

that "NEP is the only correct policy of socialist construction," a fiction still officially maintained in 1931.[81]

The point here is not to explain the fateful events of 1928–29, but to illustrate that Stalin's new policies of 1929–33, the "great change," were a radical departure from Bolshevik programmatic thinking. No Bolshevik leader or faction had ever advocated anything akin to imposed collectivization, the "liquidation" of the kulaks, breakneck heavy industrialization, and a "plan" that was, of course, no plan at all.[82] These years of "revolution from above" were, historically and programmatically, the birth-period of Stalinism. From this first great discontinuity others would follow.

IV

In treating Stalinism as "full-blown" Bolshevism, and the Soviet 1930's as a function and extension of 1917, the main scholarly disservice of the continuity thesis has been to discourage close examination of Stalinism as a specific system with its own history. I am persuaded by Tucker's argument that essential, even definitive, aspects of Stalinism, including critical turning points in its history and the "excesses," cannot be understood apart from Stalin as a political personality.[83] Nonetheless, the agenda of what remains to be studied by way of broader political, social, and historical context and factors is very large. The present would seem to be a good time to begin this kind of innovative research. In addition to the availability of new materials and longer perspectives, the same questions are now being discussed in the Soviet Union, though for the moment largely by *samizdat* writers.

It is important, first of all, to shed the ahistorical habit of thinking of the Stalinist system as an unchanging phenomenon. The historical development of Stalinism must be traced and analyzed through its several stages, from the truly revolutionary events of the early 1930's to the rigidly conservative sociopolitical order of 1946–53.[84] The 1930's themselves must be divided into periods, including at least the social upheaval of 1929–33; the interregnum of 1934–35, when future policy was being contested in the high leadership; and 1936–39, which witnessed the final triumph of Stalinism over the Bolshevik tradition and the political completion of revolution from above.

---

81. *Pravda*, April 28, 1929, p. 1; *Pravda*, March 21, 1931, p. 1.

82. It is true that the Bolshevik economist Iurii Larin was accused of having proposed a "third revolution" against kulak farms in 1925. But Larin was a secondary figure unaffiliated with the leadership factions, whose suggestion was derided by all. Medvedev is mistaken, I think, in suggesting that he was a Trotskyist. *Let History Judge*, p. 97. See also Deutscher, *Stalin*, pp. 318–19.

83. See Tucker's *Stalin as Revolutionary* and *Soviet Political Mind*.

84. I refer here to the internal Soviet order of 1946–53, and not to the transformations effected in Eastern Europe. The ahistorical "totalitarianism" approach saw the Stalinist regime of 1946–53 as still being revolutionary and dynamic. For a different approach and conclusion, see Tucker, *Soviet Political Mind*, pp. 174, 186–90. The conservatism of late Stalinism is noted even in official Soviet accounts. See, for example, N. Saushkin, *O kul'te lichnosti i avtoritete.* (Moscow, 1962), pp. 26, 32.

The years 1929–33, obscured in both Western and official Soviet theories of Stalinism,[85] are especially important. They were the formative period of Stalinism as a system; they presaged and gave rise to much that followed. For example, several characteristic *idées fixe* of full Stalinism, including the murderous notion of an inevitable "intensification of the class struggle," first appeared in Stalin's campaign to discredit all Bukharinist and NEP ideas in 1928–30. Stalin's personal role in unleashing imposed collectivization and escalating industrial targets in 1929, when he bypassed councils of party decision-making, augured his full autocracy of later years.[86] More generally, as Moshe Lewin has shown in a social history of 1929–33, many administrative, legislative, class, and ideological features of the mature Stalinist state took shape as makeshift solutions to the social chaos, the "quicksand society," generated by the destruction of NEP institutions and processes during the initial wave of revolution from above. In Lewin's view from below, the first in our literature and rich testimony to the need for social history, the Stalinist system was less a product of Bolshevik programs or planning than of desperate attempts to cope with the social pandemonium and crises created by the Stalinist leadership itself in 1929–33.[87]

As for subsequent events, it would be a mistake to interpret Stalin's terrorist assault on Soviet officialdom in 1936–39 as a "necessary" or "functional" by-product of the imposed social revolution of 1929–33. A very different course was advocated by many party leaders, probably a majority, in 1934–35. More telling, there is plain evidence that the purges were not, as some scholars have imagined, somehow rational in terms of modernization, a terrorist Geritol that accelerated the process, weeding out obsolete functionaries, etc. The terror wrecked or retarded many of the real achievements of 1929–36.[88]

Nevertheless, there were important linkages between these two great upheavals, and they require careful study. The enormous expansion of police repression, security forces, and the archipelago of forced-labor camps in 1929–33 were clearly part of the background and mechanism of 1936–39. There were also less obvious, but perhaps equally important, consequences. Even though forcible wholesale collectivization had not originated as a party, or even collective leadership, policy, the entire party elite, and probably the whole party, was implicated in the criminal and economic calamities of Stalin's measures, which culminated in the terrible

---

85. The Khrushchevian theory dated Stalinism's rise from 1934, a fiction preserved even in more detailed accounts. Saushkin, *O kul'te lichnosti i avtoritete.*

86. For a fuller discussion of these two points, see my *Bukharin and the Bolshevik Revolution,* pp. 314–15, 332–33; and Medvedev, *Let History Judge,* pp. 85–86, 89–90, 101, 103. Medvedev points out that many of Stalin's orders came "in *oral* form."

87. Moshe Lewin, "Class, State and Ideology in the *Piatiletka*" (unpublished paper delivered to the conference on "Cultural Revolution in Russia, 1928–1933," Columbia University, November 22–23, 1974). See also Lewin, *Political Undercurrents,* Chap. 5, and his "Taking Grain," in *Essays in Honour of E. H. Carr,* ed. C. Abramsky (Cambridge, England, 1974), pp. 281–323.

88. See, for example, Medvedev, *Let History Judge,* pp. 314–15; A. F. Khavin, *Kratkii ocherk istorii industrializatsii SSSR* (Moscow, 1962), pp. 305–6; and A. Nekrich, *22 iunia 1941* (Moscow, 1965), Part II.

famine of 1932–33. Every semi-informed official must have known that collectivization was a disaster, wrecking agricultural production, savaging livestock herds,
and killing millions of people.[89]

In official ideology, however, it became obligatory to eulogize collectivization
as a great accomplishment of Stalinist leadership. This bizarre discrepancy between official claims and social reality, uncharacteristic of original Bolshevism,
was a major step in the progressive fictionalization of Soviet ideology under
Stalin. It must have had a profoundly demoralizing effect on party officials,
contributing to their apparently meager resistance to Stalin's terror in 1936–39.
If nothing more, it implicated them in the cult of Stalin's infallibility, which grew
greater as disasters grew worse, and which became an integral part of the Stalinist
system.[90]

The few authentic attempts to analyze Stalinism as a social-political system
over the years have been mostly by Marxists who offer "new class" or "ruling
bureaucracy" theories of the subject. This literature is fairly diverse and features
wide-ranging disputes over whether the Stalinist bureaucracy can be viewed as
a class or only as a stratum, and of what kind. It also contains valuable material
on the sociology of Stalinism, a topic habitually ignored in academic studies, and
reminds us that the new administrative strata created in the 1930's strongly
influenced the nature of mature Stalinism, particularly its anti-egalitarianism,
rigid stratification, and cultural and social conservatism.[91]

As a theory of Stalinism, however, this approach is deeply flawed. The argument that a ruling bureaucracy-class was the animating force behind the events
of 1929–39 makes no sense, logically or empirically. Quite apart from the demon-
strable role of Stalin, who is reduced in these theories to a replicable chief
bureaucrat, it remains to be explained how a bureaucracy, which is defined as

---

89. Anecdotes about the disaster were rife. The following one circulated in Moscow in the early
1930's: The party leadership was attacked by body lice. Doctors were unable to get rid of the lice.
One wit (allegedly Radek, as always) proposed: "Collectize them, then half of them will die and the
other half will run away." Lyons, *Moscow Carrousel*, p. 334.

90. A survivor tells us that Stalinism "not only destroyed honest people, it corrupted the living."
Vsesoiuznoe soveshchanie, p. 270. Medvedev also links the growth of the cult to the disasters of the
early 1930's. *Let History Judge*, p. 149. The birth of the notion of Stalin's infallibility probably should
be dated from his famous article "Dizzy with Success" in March 1930. Despite the objections of some
high party leaders, he managed to place full blame for the "excesses" of collectivization on local
officials. The fictional, or mythical, character of Stalinist ideology remains to be studied in historical
and sociological terms. For a study of its ideological aspects, which unfortunately confuses Bolshevism and Stalinism, see Roman Redlikh, *Stalinshchina kak dukhovnyi fenomen: ocherki bol'sheviz-
movedeniia*, Book I (Frankfurt, 1971).

91. See, for example, Trotsky, *The Revolution Betrayed;* Shachtman, *The Bureaucratic Revolution;*
M. Yvon, *What Has Become of the Russian Revolution?* (New York, 1937); Peter Meyer, "The Soviet
Union: A New Class Society," *Politics*, March and April 1944, pp. 48–55, 81–85; Adam Kaufman,
"Who Are the Rulers in Russia?" *Dissent*, Spring 1954, pp. 144–56; Djilas, *The New Class;* and Tony
Cliff, *State Capitalism in Russia* (London, 1974). Class-bureaucracy theories of Stalinism are also
proposed by some *samizdat* writers. See, for example, S. Zorin and N. Alekseev, "Vremia ne zhdet"
(Leningrad, 1969); and *Seiatel'*, No. 1 (September, 1971), in *Novoe russkoe slovo*, December 11, 1972.

being deeply conservative, would have decided and carried out policies so radical and dangerous as forcible collectivization. And, indeed, Stalin's repeated campaigns to radicalize and spur on officialdom in 1929–30, and after, suggest a fearful, recalcitrant party-state bureaucracy, not an event-making one. Nor is it clear how this theory explains the slaughter of Soviet officialdom in 1936–39, unless we conclude that the "ruling" bureaucracy-class committed suicide.

We are confronted here, as elsewhere, with the difficulty inherent in applying Western concepts, whether of the Marxist or modernization variety, to a Soviet political and social reality shaped by Russian historical and cultural tradition. One reason Western-inspired theories apply poorly to the Stalinist administrative elites created in the 1930's is that the latter were more akin to the traditional tsarist *soslovie,* an official privileged class that served the state—in this case a resurgent Russian state [92]—more than it ruled the state. Arguably, there is today a Soviet ruling class or bureaucracy which has emancipated itself; but during its formation and agony in the Stalin years, for all its high position and great power over those below, it did not ultimately rule.

Approaches that take into account historical-cultural tradition are therefore essential, though they, too, sometimes have been abused in Western scholarship. Early studies of Stalinism in historical-cultural terms tended to become monocausal interpretations of a revolution (or Communism) inevitably undone or fatally transformed by history. Instead of viewing tradition as contextual, they treated it as virtually autonomous and deterministic.[93] As Carr has said, however, "Every successful revolution has its *thermidor.* "[94] But the outcome is not predetermined; it is a problematic admixture of new and old patterns and values, and the nature of this outcome depends upon contemporary social and political circumstances as well. In 1932–33, for example, the Stalinist regime reinstated the internal passport system, once thought to typify tsarism and despised by all Russian revolutionaries. Here was an instance of revived tradition, but also of contemporary policy and crisis, since the retrogression came about in direct response to the social chaos, particularly wandering peasant masses in search of food, of 1929–33.

Cultural approaches can contribute to an understanding of many things, from Stalin's personal outlook and political autocracy, as Tucker has shown, to the social basis of Stalinism as a system. There is, in particular, the important question of Stalinism's popular support in Soviet society, a problem largely ignored and inconsistent with the imagery of a "totalitarian" regime dominating a hapless, "atomized" population through power techniques alone. Though the coercive aspects of the Stalinist system can scarcely be exaggerated, this seems no more adequate as a full explanation than would a similar interpretation of Hitler's Germany.

---

92. Tucker, *Soviet Political Mind,* pp. 133–34.
93. See, for example, Timasheff, *The Great Retreat;* and above, note 23.
94. E. H. Carr, "Stalin," *Soviet Studies,* July 1953, p. 3.

While its nature and extent certainly varied over time, it seems evident that there was substantial popular support for Stalinism, inside and outside officialdom, from the beginning and through the very worst. Some of this sentiment probably demands no special explanation, though it must be taken into account. Revolution from above was an imposed upheaval, but it required and obtained enthusiastic agents below, even if only a small minority, from the cultural to the industrial and rural fronts.[95] In addition, revolutions from above (a little-studied category) are by definition a great expansion of the state and its social functions, which means a great proliferation of official jobs and privileges. While many were victimized, many people also profited from Stalinism, and identified with it. Not just the "whole system of smaller dictators" throughout Soviet administrative life, but the millions of petty officials who gained opportunity and elevation of status.[96] Even the purges, Medvedev suggests, elicited the support of workers, who saw in the downfall of bosses and bureaucrats "the underdog's dream of retribution with the aid of a higher justice. . . . Impotence seeks the protection of supreme avenging power." [97] And there can be little question that the war-time patriotism of 1941–45 translated itself into considerable new support for the increasingly nationalistic, and victorious, Stalinist system.

Other aspects of Stalinism usually regarded as only imposed from above and without social roots also need to be reconsidered in this light and in longer perspective. The main carriers of cultural tradition are, of course, social groups and classes. In the 1930's, as Lewin has shown, the "petty bourgeois" majority of Russia swarmed into the cities to become large segments of the new working class and officialdom, the Drozdovs of tomorrow. In this context, is it sufficient to view Stalinist popular and political culture as merely artifices of censorship? Did not the literature, or the state nationalism, of 1936–53, for example, also have authentic social roots in this newly risen and still insecure officialdom, whose values, self-perceptions, and cultural Babittry it so often seemed to reflect? [98]

Finally, a dramatic example of cultural tradition and popular support was the Stalin cult, in some ways the major institution of the autocracy. Stalin promoted it from above, but it found fertile soil, becoming (as many Soviet sources tell us) an authentic social phenomenon. It grew from an internal party celebration of the new leader on 1929 into a mass religion, a "peculiar Soviet form of wor-

---

95. See, for example, Sheila Fitzpatrick, "Cultural Revolution as Class War" (unpublished paper delivered to the conference on "Cultural Revolution in Russia, 1928–1933," Columbia University, November 22–23, 1974).

96. Medvedev, *Let History Judge,* pp. 415–16, 536. David Schoenbaum's concept of a "revolution of status" in Hitler's Germany may apply here. See his *Hitler's Social Revolution* (Garden City, N.Y., 1967), Chaps. 8, 9. Stalin's personal popularity is acknowledged in official critiques of Stalinism. See, for example, *Kratkaia istoriia SSSR,* Part II (Moscow and Leningrad, 1964), p. 271.

97. Medvedev, *On Socialist Democracy,* p. 346. For similar testimony on this point, see *The Times* (London), May 25, 1937. Medvedev called this popular sentiment "an implicit criticism of bureaucracy." It may, however, have been implicit anti-Communist sentiment.

98. For similar points, see I. Zuzanek quoted in Medvedev, *Let History Judge,* p. 529; Hugh Seton-Watson, "The Soviet Ruling Class," *Problems of Communism,* May–June 1956, p. 12; and Barghoorn, *Soviet Russian Nationalism,* p. 182.

ship." [99] Neither Bolshevik tradition, the once modest Lenin cult, nor Stalin's personal gratification can explain the popular dimensions it acquired. For this we doubtless must return to older values and customs, to "unwritten mandates borne by the wind." [100] Not surprisingly, these popular sentiments have outlived Stalin himself.

---

99. Medvedev, *On Socialist Democracy,* p. 346. Elsewhere Medvedev objects to the theory that the Stalin cult was rooted primarily in traditional village religiosity, arguing that it originated in the city and was strongest among workers, officials, and the intelligentsia. This leaves open, however, the question of the social origins of these city groups. *Let History Judge,* pp. 429–30. There are many other firsthand testimonies to the religious and authentic nature of the cult. See, for example, *In Quest of Justice: Protest and Dissent in the Soviet Union Today,* ed. Abraham Brumberg (New York, 1970), pp. 320, 329. Soviet scholarly studies of religion often read like implicit analysis of Stalinism. See Iu. A. Levada, *Sotsial'naia priroda religii* (Moscow, 1965).

100. The expression is G. Pomerantz's, in *In Quest of Justice,* p. 327.

Trotskyist Interpretations
of Stalinism

Robert H. McNeal

"Stalinism is the syphilis of the workers' movement." [1] Thus did Trotsky, near the end of his life, sum up the phenomenon that had defeated not only his political aspirations but also his attempts to comprehend it. There is no point in asking with whom the working-class movement had been consorting, nor otherwise subjecting the metaphor to literary criticism. It is simply a cry of anguish from a man who deeply believed in human progress, most particularly in the progressive meaning of his life as a revolutionary, and could not come to terms with the cruel irony that confronted him in Stalin's Russia and Comintern. Although he once denied any "subjectivity and sentimentalism" in facing the possibility of rejecting his own October Revolution, even maintaining that "old Freud" would agree with him on this, Trotsky would have been more than human if he had not felt anguish, rage, and frustration concerning Stalinism. [2]

The problem can be compared to theodicy. Marxism, like mainstream Christianity, assumes a fundamental, long-term benignity of the universe toward human beings. Also like Christianity, it faces the problem of squaring this assumption with the woeful state of man in the present and most of the past. Unlike Christian theology, Marxism finds the answer to this problem in the dialectic, the idea that contradiction not only is in the nature of things but is the dynamic that eventually lifts man to ever higher levels and eventual fulfillment. It is both psychologically understandable and philosophically sound that Trotsky in his last months engaged in a passionate defense of the dialectic as the key to any revolutionary thought. [3] Without it the critic of the existing order is doomed to pessimism. If the dialectic could explain how capitalism at its worst is the prologue to the first truly human stage of civilization, then surely it could handle the problem of Stalinism. But how? Trotsky did not face the question in any *summa*, starting with the most fundamental philosophical questions, partly because he had never been much given to this kind of work, partly because of his continual

---

1. All writings referred to in this paper are by Trotsky, unless otherwise noted. *Writings of Leon Trotsky (1937–1938)* (New York, 1970), p. 78. The title of this series is hereafter abbreviated *WLT,* followed by the years.

2. *In Defense of Marxism* (New York, 1973), p. 24.

3. Ibid., pp. 43–56, 49–52, 72–85.

hope that Stalinism was ephemeral and would soon disappear, and partly because he was dealing with a living historical problem that evolved as it was observed.

What we have from Trotsky, then, is a lot of writing about Stalinism over many years, displaying some fundamental continuity but also alternative formulations, shifts of opinion, and even self-contradictions. Since Trotsky was more a brilliant theoretical journalist than a philosopher, it would not be fair to the man and his mind to present Trotsky's concept of Stalinism as if it were a fixed, integrated whole. What follows is an attempt to describe the evolution of Trotsky's thinking about Stalinism in two main periods, granting that there are some elements that cut across these divisions and others that are not quite stable within them.

The first of these periods runs from the intra-party struggle in the mid-1920's, when Trotsky first began to speak of Stalinism, to 1935. The period is characterized by Trotsky's frequent and consistent use of the word "centrism" to describe Stalinism. As explained by Trotsky, this term characterizes "all those trends within the proletariat and on its periphery which are distributed between reformism and Marxism, and which most often represent various stages of evolution from reformism to Marxism—and vice versa." [4] Nevertheless, it is rooted in the proletariat. Centrism occurs in times of relative prosperity or of the ebbing of revolution when "different layers of the proletariat shift from politically left to right, clashing with other layers who are just beginning to evolve to the left." Centrism "in general" serves as "a left cover for reformism." [5] Such a highly pejorative interpretation of Stalinism occurs in Trotsky's writings in the later twenties, in which he drew an analogy between Stalinism, on one hand, and Menshevism and the German Social Democrats, on the other. The latter parallel was particularly attractive to Trotsky because the "national socialist" betrayal by the German Social Democrats in 1914 could be compared with Stalin's "national messianism" and "social patriotism" in exchanging internationalism for "socialism in one country." [6] But Trotsky was not consistent in equating Stalinism and Menshevism. In the early thirties he explicitly gave Stalin credit for standing on the left side of centrism, apart from the Mensheviks. "There exist only two firm and serious lines: the line of the imperialist bourgeoisie and the line of the revolutionary proletariat. Menshevism is the democratic mask of the first line. Stalinism is the centrist deformation of the second." [7] Deformed but in good company. On another occasion Trotsky explained that Rosa Luxemberg's disagreements with Lenin were also centrist and in this sense resembled Stalin, even though "he did not come up to her knees," "politically, theoretically or morally." [8]

This placement of Stalinism within the framework of proletarian rather than

---

4. *The Struggle Against Fascism in Germany* (New York, 1971), pp. 211–12.

5. Ibid., p. 211.

6. *The Third International After Lenin* (New York, 1970), pp. 70–71, 133. *Permanent Revolution* (New York, 1969), pp. 134, 139, 149, 160.

7. *WLT (1930–1931)* (New York, 1973), p. 20ᶯ

8. *The Struggle Against Fascism in Germany,* ₁   ₁lso *WLT (1932)* (New York, 1973), p. 245, which refers to Stalin's "Bolshevism."

bourgeois politics was in keeping with Trotsky's attitude toward the party in this period. Steadfastly rejecting the validity of his expulsion from the party and Comintern, Trotsky thought of his own faction, before and after expulsion, as the "Left Opposition" *within* the movement. Whatever the Stalinists might say, Trotsky considered himself their party comrade, whose criticism was partly responsible for the "left turn" associated with the First Five-Year Plan and collectivization. Trotsky even seemed eager to associate himself with policies that most historians consider Stalinist, in particular the destruction of the kulaks (which Trotsky considered insufficiently thorough) and the first major political trials (Shakhty and Mensheviks). In 1930 Trotsky was quite willing to contemplate political coalition with Stalin, hardly out of any personal attachment, but because he considered himself and Stalin to be members of the same proletarian party, sharing to some degree the cause of resistance to truly bourgeois, right-wing trends.[9]

Trotsky's conception of the Right was not the same as Stalin's. The latter attached this label to Bukharin and his associates. Both before and after Stalin's split with Bukharin, Trotsky accepted Bukharin as part of centrism, albeit a much less important part after his fall from the Politburo. In fact, Bukharin and Rykov were among those with whom Trotsky seemed willing to join forces *against* the Right in 1930.[10] The right wing as Trotsky conceived it in this period was headed by persons whose power bases were not really in the party at all—military figures such as Voroshilov and Tukhachevsky, or Chekists such as Yagoda and Deribas.[11] Typically Trotsky did not speak of leadership in this connection, but simply referred to "Ustrialovists" (anonymous Soviet adherents of the émigré publicist who maintained that capitalism would be restored by the Soviet regime), or "the Bessedovskys and Agabekovs" (diplomats who defected to the capitalists). Such out-and-out traitors represented the Right in Trotsky's thinking. In his somewhat fantastic perception of the USSR in the late twenties and early thirties, Trotsky's main concern was less Stalinism itself than the danger that Stalinism would be replaced by the Right. Trotsky perceived "the formation of a bourgeois party at the right wing of the CPSU." [12] It was this "party" that Trotsky usually had in mind when he spoke of Thermidor and Bonapartism up to 1935. True, he had spoken of Thermidor or the pressing danger of Thermidor in the debates of 1926–27, but he soon repented this, and he even denied in 1932 that he had ever called the regime Thermidorean.[13] His point was that the *threat* of Thermidorean or Bonapartist takeover was serious, but he did not identify the existing Soviet regime (Stalinism) with this right-wing menace. By 1933 Trotsky would grant that the division between Thermidorean and non-Thermidorean elements passed *through* the apparatus and not *between* the apparatus and the other military-

---

9. *WLT (1930–1931)*, pp. 54–55, 64, 299, 300, 308.
10. *The Stalin School of Falsification* (New York, 1972), p. 172; *The Struggle Against Fascism in Germany*, p. 103.
11. *WLT (1930–1931)*, p. 53.
12. *The Third International After Lenin*, p. 286. See also *WLT (1930–1931)*, pp. 52, 200.
13. *The Stalin School of Falsification*, pp. 143 ff. See also *WLT (1932)*, p. 47.

bureaucratic-kulak interests, but the man thrust of his argument in 1923–1933 separated Stalinism and Thermidor or Bonapartism. The transition from the workers' state to Thermidor/Bonapartism, Trotsky argued in 1931, must involve a violent overthrow, civil war.[14] Since these had not been seen in the USSR, one could deduce that there was as yet neither Thermidor nor Bonapartism. When the Left Communist Hugo Urbahns proposed in 1933 that the Soviet Union was Bonapartist, Trotsky rebuffed him with the verity that all Bonapartism is based on bourgeois property, and this had not been restored in the USSR.[15] Granted, the Stalinist regime was "plebisicitary," in Trotsky's repeated expression, and in March 1932 he predicted that the Red Army would support Stalin against the party—"This is a new stage in the systematic, planned, persistent preparation of Bonapartism." [16] But all this was potential rather than actual, and there was always the hope that the Soviet working class would defeat this bourgeois counter-revolution.

In Trotsky's perception, "bureaucratism" was common to both Stalinist centrism and the Thermidorean-Bonapartist Right. Trotsky's discussion of this category is either very subtle or not very consistent. At times bureaucratism is treated as a major foundation of the right-wing danger, linked directly to the resurgence of the "proprietors," the neo-bourgeoisie.[17] In this context the bureaucracy was largely *anti*-Stalin, because his left turn had betrayed their rightist expectations.[18] At other times, Stalinist centrism is considered to be intrinsically bureaucratic, rising as a third force above the proletarian and the Thermidorean-Bonapartist wings of the party.[19] There probably is a contradiction here, but, given the promiscuous use of the word "bureaucratism" in Communist (and other) literature, one should not be too hard on Trotsky on this account.

Finally, Trotsky's perception of Stalinism in the late twenties and early thirties acknowledged that the regime was building socialism. For all Trotsky's continued fulminations against "socialism in one country," there was little difference between him and Stalin on this issue, a debate into which Trotsky was foolish to have been drawn. The narrowness of the gap between him and Stalin on the possibility of building socialism in one country is revealed by Trotsky's remarkably favorable statements about the development of socialism even under "bureaucratic centrist" leadership. "Successful socialist construction is proceeding in the USSR," Trotsky wrote in 1930. "Academically, it is understood, one can construct within the boundaries of the USSR an enclosed and internally balanced socialist economy." [20] His point in this relatively pro-Stalinism phase was not that socialism was not being built in the USSR, but that it was vulnerable to a

14. *WLT (1930–1931)*, pp. 221–22.

15. *WLT (1933–1934)*, p. 107.

16. *WLT (1932)*, p. 68.

17. *The Third International After Lenin*, p. 294; *WLT (1930–1931)*, p. 217; *WLT (1932–1933)*, p. 48–49.

18. *WLT (1930–1931)*, p. 63.

19. *WLT (1932–1933)*, p. 309.

20. *WLT (1930–1931)*, pp. 73, 208; *The Third International After Lenin*, p. 54. To be sure, Trotsky repeatedly denied that the Soviet Union had actually built socialism.

counter-revolutionary overthrow because of capitalist encirclement and domestic hostile elements. The road to socialism would be blocked if "those in charge of industry on one hand and the top strata of workers on the other break loose from party discipline." [21] The whole outlook resembles very closely what is usually regarded as the Stalinism of this period: successful socialist construction, the danger of capitalist encirclement, the need for party discipline and vigilance against domestic class enemies.

Trotsky fundamentally changed his mind about Stalinism by the beginning of 1935. The central point of Trotsky's new conception of Stalinism was that it should be classified as "Bonapartism" or "Thermidor." He acknowledged that this was a direct contradiction of his previous interpretation of the analogy with the French Revolution, while attempting to deny that he had really changed his mind very much. "It is not a question of *changing* our principled position . . . but only a question of rendering it more precise." [22] The category of "centrism," which he had used in the previous period, was now quietly dropped with reference to Stalin. The last such usage that occurs in his published works appears to be in October 1933.[23] Since there is no specific and generally accepted system of cross-reference between the framework of the politics of the French Revolutionary era and the politics of twentieth-century socialism, it does not appear that Trotsky was logically *obliged* to drop the label "centrism" when adopting the label "Bonapartism" or "Thermidor." That Trotsky chose to replace "centrism" with "Bonapartism" or "Thermidor" as his standard characterization of Stalinism seems to be the result of his generally darkening appraisal of the situation in Soviet and world Communism. Shortly after the establishment of Nazi power in Germany (January 1933), Trotsky argued that the docile acceptance of Hitler by the Comintern signaled its demise.[24] The Soviet Communist party, too, had in effect ceased to exist.[25] Stalin's policies were in general taking a right turn, and police repression was increased.[26] The idea that Stalinism was part of the proletarian and Marxist camp was no longer something Trotsky could stomach. In a private letter of October 10, 1937, he explained that "Stalinism is no longer centrism but the crudest form of opportunism and social patriotism.[27]

The change from a conceptual framework directly associated with Social Democratic policies to one based on the French revolution posed various problems for Trotsky. For one thing, he never delved deeply into the history of the French Revolution or Karl Marx's writings on Bonapartism (more Louis than Napoleon), so that "Bonapartism" or "Thermidor" as a model remained quite sketchy. Trotsky variously stated that there was "young" and "old" Bonapartism,

21. *WLT (1930–1931)*, p. 74.
22. *WLT (1934–1935)*, pp. 183, 173.
23. *WLT (1933–1934)*, p. 18.
24. *WLT (1932–1933)*, p. 305.
25. Ibid., pp. 238, 309; *WLT (1934–1935)*, p. 131; *The Struggle Against Fascism in Germany*, p. 424.
26. *WLT (1934–1935)*, p. 157.
27. *WLT (1933–1934)*, p. 340.

that Stalin represented the Bonapartism of the rising bourgeoisie, that Stalinism resembled the Bonapartism of the First Consulate, that it was closer to the Empire than the consulate, that "the scientific sociological definition of Bonapartism" is that a "saviour" (leader) preserves the "new property forms by usurping the political functions of the ruling class." [28] The application of the concept, vague as it was, to the Soviet Union involved some problems of social observation, too. His main effort in this work, *The Revolution Betrayed* (1936), written in the difficult conditions of near-isolation in Norway, is a pioneer work in describing the emergence of a new elite in Stalin's Russia, but it has serious shortcomings. Trotsky was intent upon proving that the social roots of the new privileged elements were in the old bourgeoisie, which simply was not the case with respect to most of the new elite. This being so, Trotsky was obliged to over-emphasize the Soviet diplomatic corps as a sample of the new elite. The corps did include ex-bourgeois persons in the thirties, just as it had in Lenin's time, but it surely was an unrepresentative group within the new managerial-military-political elite. On a humbler level, Trotsky imagined that there was an influential class of well-to-do collective farmers in Stalin's Russia, the immediate heirs to the kulaks. As for the party itself, Trotsky had very little to say, because he either lacked data or was embarrassed by the degree to which its members really were proletarian and peasant in origin, and even, to a considerable extent, in occupation. Generally speaking, Trotsky had little to say about the party as an institution, apart from broad generalizations about the morally edifying role that a *real* proletarian party should play.

The impression that Trotsky's concept of Soviet Bonapartism or Thermidor is more polemical than analytic is enhanced by the difficulties that he had with the sequential aspects of the two terms as applied to the Soviet Union. In 1935, when he first asserted that Stalinism was a form of Bonapartism, Trotsky openly asked how this could be possible if, in keeping with his previous conceptions, the country had never entered the stage of Thermidor. [29] At this time he proposed a model that was internally inconsistent: Thermidor had come to Russia in 1924, and "the hypertrophy of bureaucratic centrism" had gradually led to the establishment of Bonapartism. [30] This formulation not only broke with his previous denials that the revolutionary decline had reached the Thermidorean stage, it also abandoned his thesis of the early thirties that the transition from a workers' state to Thermidor must involve a revolutionary overthrow of the revolutionary regime. [31] But Trotsky found himself unable to stick to this analysis. Although he had characterized Stalinism as Bonapartism in 1935, *The Revolution Betrayed*, completed in August 1936, contained a substantial chapter on "The Soviet Thermidor," which Trotsky treated as a rising phenomenon from around the death

28. *WLT (1934–1935)*, pp. 182, 208.
29. Ibid., p. 173.
30. Ibid., pp. 173–80.
31. See above, p. 33. Even in 1935 Trotsky had explicitly rejected the assertion of the Democratic Centralists in 1926 that the workers' state was dead. *WLT (1934–1935)*, p. 170.

of Lenin right up to 1936. Later in the same book he characterized Stalinism as "Bonapartism," again with the implication that this category covered both the present and a number of years past. This overlapping of Thermidor and Bonapartism did not seem to disturb Trotsky in the next few years, although it is fair to say that he relied mainly on "Bonapartism." [32]

The sense that either label was more a handy epithet than a seriously thought-out theory is enhanced by Trotsky's tendency in 1939–1940 to add "totalitarian" to his anti-Stalinist vocabulary. This neologism, drawn from bourgeois political science, might have been thoughtfully related to "Bonapartism," but Trotsky never took up this possibility. To be sure, it is natural enough that Trotsky was attracted by the idea of consigning Hitler and Stalin to the same camp.[33] But Stalinism did not *simply* equal Fascism in Trotsky's perception. "The USSR minus the social structure of the October Revolution would be a Fascist regime," he wrote at the end of 1939; but the point of the statement was that this socialist foundation had not yet been subtracted.[34] This question of the economic base of the USSR was Trotsky's most serious problem with the idea that Stalinism was (as you prefer) Bonapartism, Thermidor, or totalitarianism. As long as he had maintained that Stalinism was basically within the proletarian camp, it was not so difficult to defend the idea that the Soviet state, the product of the October Revolution, remained basically a workers' or socialist state. Trotsky did in fact maintain this, but in these earlier years the issue did not seem very pressing in his writings. How different the problem was after he had characterized Stalinism as something far worse than centrism, something clearly outside the proletarian camp. How could one characterize the USSR as a workers' state if the political regime was "Bonapartist" or worse? But if it was not a workers' state, what could one say of the historic role of the October Revolution and its principal hero?

This dilemma was highly divisive in Trotsky's relations with his disciples and fellow travelers in the anti-Stalinist left. While many of these people attempted to grasp one horn of the dilemma and acknowledge that Stalin's Russia was not socialist, Trotsky sought to slide between the horns, maintaining that it was a "degenerated" workers' state but that its nationalized economic base survived as a defense against the restoration of capitalism or the formation of some new form of exploitation. In the debate that Trotsky carried on with such (non-Russian) Marxists as Urbahns, Laurant, Craipeau, Carter, Rizzi, Shachtman, and Burnham it appears that the latter were more imaginative than Trotsky in attempting to apply Marxian analysis. Trotsky rejected their ideas with towering contempt but also with a literal-minded, mechanical Marxism about which even he seems to have harbored doubts. His basic argument was simply that the

---

32. *The Revolution Betrayed* (New York, 1972), passim; *WLT (1937–1938)*, pp. 88, 93; *The Transitional Program for the Socialist Revolution* (New York, 1973), pp. 102 ff. *WLT (1939–1940)* (New York, 1969), pp. 51–97; *In Defense of Marxism,* p. 9.

33. *WLT (1939–1940),* p. 164; *The Struggle Against Fascism in Germany,* p. 53; *In Defense of Marxism,* pp. 9, 13, 31.

34. *In Defense of Marxism,* p. 53.

economic base in the USSR, a planned economy and nationalized means of production, *must* mean that the country was a workers' state.[35] Trotsky was willing to grant that the Stalinist bureaucracy was "parasitic" and consumed a large share of the country's production, but this he considered merely akin to embezzlement rather than the expropriation of surplus product.[36] Another equally semantic solution to the problem was his insistence that the new elite be labeled a "caste" rather than a "class." Even if the bureaucracy established the "right of parasitism," according to Trotsky, it would require the "virtual liquidation of the planned economy" and nationalized ownership to constitute a "new social base." [37] When Burnham and Shachtman expressed doubts on the helpfulness of the dialectic, Trotsky responded by attempting to reassert his position in dialectical terms. The process of degeneration in the Soviet Union, he argued, had not gone so far that quantity had changed into quality.[38]

Although his writings against these particular heretics in 1939–40 did not offer any particular demonstration of his proposition, one might look back to several of his previous writings for a deductive argument on behalf of the point. The transition of any new class basis for a society, Trotsky had stated in 1936–38, required a violent revolution.[39] Since the Soviet Union had not yet experienced an anti-Stalinist revolution, it followed that its working-class basis still survived. This seems internally consistent and possibly persuasive within a Marxist frame of reference, but Trotsky exacerbated his quarrel with the "ultra-left" (as he called it) by rather gratuitously defending the Stalinist regime in various aspects that many socialist observers did not find very attractive. The bureaucracy, he wrote in 1934, "protects the workers' state with its own peculiar methods." [40] It seems that the purge was one of these methods, for in 1937 he asserted that the very fact that it could "throw thousands upon thousands of the families of the bureaucrats into the greatest poverty" demonstrated that real bourgeois property rights did not exist in the USSR.[41] (To be sure, this was not all that Trotsky had to say about the purges, but most of his voluminous writing on this topic was in self-defense or on current Kremlinology. It did not relate very closely to the general theory of Stalinism.) [42]

Trotsky was willing to give Stalin credit for contributing to the "defense" of nationalized property "from the all too impatient and avaricious layers of this very bureaucracy." [43] Not only the Stalinist purge but even the personal dictator-

35. *WLT (1935–1936)*, pp. 121–22; *The Revolution Betrayed; WLT (1937–1938)*, pp. 86 ff., 90 ff.

36. *WLT (1933–1934)*, p. 111; *WLT (1934–1935)*, p. 118; *WLT (1937–1938)*, p. 88.

37. *WLT (1937–1938)*, p. 122.

38. *In Defense of Marxism*, pp. 43, 84, 121.

39. *The Revolution Betrayed*, p. 253; *WLT (1937–1938)*, pp. 87, 91.

40. *WLT (1934–1935)*, p. 124.

41. *WLT (1937–1938)*, p. 88.

42. For an exhaustive study of Trotsky's writings on the purges, see Thomas R. Poole, *"Counter Trial,"* in "Leon Trotsky on the Soviet Purge Trials" (dissertation, University of Massachusetts at Amherst, 1974).

43. *WLT (1937–1938)*, p. 92; *WLT (1938–1939)*, p. 324.

ship of one leader seemed to Trotsky to have its positive side. In a polemic against Burnham he noted that the rule of the proletariat could express itself, among other possibilities, "through a factual concentration of power in the hands of a single person." While this is a danger to the rule of the proletariat, "at the same time, under certain conditions," it could be "the only means to save that regime" (i.e., the rule of the proletariat).[44]

Much as Trotsky struggled to reject the idea that Stalinism and the workers' state were mutually exclusive, he understood the force of this argument all too well and most particularly understood its depressing implications for Marxist optimism about the long-term prospects for mankind. He acknowledged that Stalinism *might* lead to the restoration of a system of class exploitation. There was even a clear danger that this would happen if the workers in Russia remained "isolated" from other revolutions, and particularly if Fascism triumphed in Western Europe.[45] His opponents were merely a little premature in their timing. Or was it Trotsky who was belated, as he had been in recognizing the establishment of Thermidor in the late twenties and early thirties? When he lashed out at Stalinism as "Fascism" (a well-known variant on bourgeois rule), as "Bonapartist gangsterism," when he stated that the bureaucracy "contains within itself to a tenfold degree all the vices of a possessing class," one senses that Trotsky was nearly ready to agree with his adversaries on the "left." [46]

That he did not do so seems partly attributable to his awareness of the pessimistic conclusions to which such thinking led. If Stalinism really did represent a transition to a new ruling class, while the proletarian revolution in other countries failed to materialize, "we should doubtless have to pose the question of revising our conception of the present epoch and its driving forces. . . . Have we entered the epoch of social revolution and socialist society or, on the contrary, the epoch of the declining society of totalitarian bureaucracy?" [47] If the latter, Trotsky admitted that this meant "the foundering of all hopes for a socialist revolution." [48] Here he drew back. "Marxists do not have the slightest right (if disillusionment and fatigue are not considered "rights") to draw the conclusion that the proletariat has forfeited its revolutionary possibilities and must renounce all aspirations to hegemony in the era immediately ahead." [49]

Trotsky's refusal to succumb to such pessimism is expressed ideologically in his determination to demonstrate that Stalinism, the degeneration of the workers' state, is a short-term phenomenon, while the proletarian revolutionary movement is bound to revive in the USSR in the long run. The fundamental problem here was to connect the degeneration of the revolution with the heritage of economic backwardness in Russia *without* accepting the Menshevik argument that the

---

44. WLT *(1937–1938)*, p. 90.
45. *WLT (1934–1935)*, p. 162; *WLT (1937–1938)*, pp. 86, 170.
46. *WLT (1938–1939)*, p. 325.
47. *In Defense of Marxism*, pp. 14–15, also 8–9.
48. Ibid., p. 15.
49. Ibid., p. 15.

proletarian revolution had come prematurely to Russia. Trotsky's solution was to place the blame on the German Social Democrats. If they had made a revolution on time, it would have rescued the Soviet Union from its bureaucratic, Stalinist distortions, the evil result of attempting to build socialism in one country. Instead, "the Social Democrats rescued the bourgeoisie." The triumph of the proletarian revolution in Germany "was prevented solely and exclusively by the Social Democrats." [50] Salvation in this situation could come through the revival of revolution in the West, with the help of the Fourth International, and the dialectical development of the Soviet economy. It would only take one serious success on the part of the European Left to inspire the Soviet workers to remove the Stalinist bureaucracy. "Can we doubt for an instant that, if the Spanish workers had been victorious and if the French workers had been able to develop their May–June offensive of 1936 to its conclusion, the Russian proletariat would have recovered its courage and overthrown the Thermidoreans with a minimum of effort?" [51] Within the Soviet Union, Stalinism was preparing its own demise. The more it developed the economy (and Trotsky gave it credit for achieving quite a lot), the more the needs of economic development stood in contradiction with the bureaucratic system, leading to a "crisis," a "second revolution." [52] Trotsky did not ask himself about the possible pessimistic implications of this application of the classical Marxian analysis of capitalism to Stalinism. If the revolution had been so surprisingly belated in the capitalist countries, for all the economic contradictions, what should one expect of the Soviet system? Trotsky expected its fall. As late as 1939 he implied that its fall was likely in "a few years or even months," a theme that he had maintained steadily through the thirties, despite some shifting from an expectation of imminent crisis to a recognition that some stabilization might occur in Stalinism. [53] This was Trotsky's least prophetic insight but a very natural, human response to the dismal situation that he faced in his last years.

Trotsky died in 1940, but his movement proved to be remarkably durable, despite the absence of any imposing leader or solid institutional basis. Indeed, the vitality of organized Trotskyism seems to lie not in unity but in an amoeboid capacity to reproduce by dividing. The factional history of Trotskyism has yet to be

---

50. *The Revolution Betrayed,* pp. 59, 23.

51. *WLT (1937–1938),* p. 88.

52. *The Revolution Betrayed,* p. 289. See also *The Struggle Against Fascism in Germany,* p. 221; *WLT (1933–1934),* p. 115; *WLT (1934–1935),* p. 120; *In Defense of Marxism.* However, for a different interpretation of the consequences of Soviet economic growth, see *The Revolution Betrayed,* pp. 235–36: "The very dynamic of economic progress involves an awakening of petty bourgeois appetites, not only among the peasants and representatives of 'intellectual' labor, but also among the upper levels of the proletariat." Perhaps one can square this with the main line of Trotsky's argument by supposing that up to a point economic growth stimulates appetites, then proves unable to advance fast enough to satisfy them.

53. *In Defense of Marxism,* pp. 9, 14. For other references on this subject, see my essay "Stalin's Interpretation of Stalin," *Canadian Slavonic Papers,* Vol. V (1961), pp. 87–97.

written, but it is clear enough that there has never been a time when the diverse Trotskyist groups in the world all have been on good terms with one another. It would require many years and a polyglot team of researchers to track down the recorded statements of all Trotskyist organizations since 1940. This is beyond the reach of the present paper, which rests on a sampling of the pertinent materials, mainly in English and heavily weighted toward the Socialist Workers' party. This limitation does not, however, appear to be terribly serious with respect to the theme of the paper: the concept of Stalinism. Within the mainstream of post-1940 Trotskyism this problem has not been subject to any serious further exploration. Indeed, the very definition of orthodox Trotskyism rests on the acceptance of Trotsky's interpretation of Stalinism.[54] The numerous disagreements among the orthodox have turned on many issues,[55] but the conception of classical Stalinism, the origins and nature of this degeneration of the workers' state in Russia, has not been one of the divisive points. The main theses have been reiterated frequently, but with scant amplification or reconsideration. The most authoritative and consensual statements of the Trotskyist idea of classical Stalinism were resolutions adopted by the Fourth and Fifth World Congresses of the Fourth International, (1954 and 1957, respectively), entitled "The Rise and Decline of Stalinism" and "The Decline and Fall of Stalinism." As the latter title suggests, the optimism that Trotsky displayed concerning the early end of Stalinism remains an article of faith. In the first years after 1953 the real signs of stress in the USSR and in other Communist parties and states encouraged the Trotskyists to think that the end of the era of degeneration and deformation was actually at hand. That this crucial turn should have been precipitated by the death of an individual whose importance Trotsky and his followers had always belittled raised a somewhat awkward point. The resolution of 1954 somewhat gingerly and abstractly tried to deal with this problem by suggesting that Stalin was the link between the socialist base and the bureaucratic superstructure in the USSR, that he at once represented a guarantee to the bureaucracy of their privileges and to the proletariat that the socialization of the means of production would remain. This theme, however, was not elaborated. But Stalinism, as understood by Trotskyists, did not perish in the aftermath of its namesake's death, which is more compatible with the traditional Trotskyist disassociation of the personality and the "ism."

But if the basic concept of Stalinism is a settled matter among orthodox Trotskyists, its application to Communist states outside the Soviet Union has confronted them with problems of interpretation that cannot be answered by reference to the words of a man who died in 1940. In this area opinions have varied among Trotskyists, drastically at times, and this material is of some interest to the comparative discussion of Communist systems.

---

54. *Quatrième internationale,* no. 11–12 (1957), pp. 59–103. This includes both the 1954 and 1957 resolutions cited, because the former was re-adopted, and re-published along with the additional resolution of 1957.

55. Ibid., p. 67.

The initial reaction of Trotskyists to the expansion of Soviet control over Eastern Europe at the end of World War II was not very favorable. In 1939–40 Trotsky, to the indignation of some of his former admirers, supported Stalin's annexations on the grounds that the statization of the annexed economies was a step toward socialization.[56] But this was not the way that Trotskyists perceived the early post-war scene in Soviet-occupied, but unannexed, Europe. For several years it was maintained in the journal *Fourth International,* which seems to have reflected the views of a large portion of West European and American Trotskyism at this time, that Stalin had made a typically anti-revolutionary deal with the imperialist powers and was supporting the national bourgeoisies in such countries as Poland and Bulgaria, just as he was suppressing revolution in France and Italy. These governments, it was observed, were mixed Communist and non-Communist affairs, and their economies were not fully statized. Even Yugoslavia was not exempt from this interpretation before 1948. The states of the buffer zone, as the area was often called by Trotskyists, were the fruits of Stalinist conciliationism with capitalism, but were not themselves Stalinist states.[57]

This interpretation was revised as the reality of Communist power in East Europe became unmistakable. No error was admitted in the previous interpretation, but it was maintained that the pressure of the masses had compelled Stalin to move to the left, statizing more of the economy. Stalinism, it seems, could not be a dynamic revolutionary force, but it could be obliged to carry out a revolution against its will, especially in countries in which bourgeois power was too weak to be propped up.[58] I have not encountered any substantial attempt by orthodox Trotskyists to explain just how this was supposed to have worked, probably because it is not easy to find evidence that the workers of, say, Bulgaria were compelling Stalin to bend to their will. In any case, it was admitted by the end of the forties that the Communist states of the buffer zone, excepting Yugoslavia after 1948, were deformed workers' states on the Stalinist Soviet model. ("Deformed" rather than "degenerated" because, unlike the USSR, the East European Communist states had never experienced the pre-Stalinist workers' state).

The Communist states that did not owe their birth to the Stalinists posed different problems for Trotskyists. The possibility of Communist parties that were not Stalinist came naturally to the Trotskyists, who had always considered themselves in this category and had predicted that the future belongs to such organizations. When Tito's break with Stalin surfaced in 1948, the Socialist Workers' party was quick to send an open letter to the Yugoslav Communists, proposing that the two parties enter into discussions with one another and share advice.[59] For the next few years Trotskyists displayed an avid interest in the Yugoslavs,

---

56. *In Defense of Marxism,* pp. 18–19, 56–59, 87–90, 130–37.

57. *Fourth International* (hereafter abbreviated *FI*), March 1945, pp. 67–69; May 1945, pp. 136, 170.

58. *FI,* June 1948, p. 118; a long polemic against Deutscher, who considered that Stalin had imposed the revolution from above in East Europe, appears in *FI,* July–August 1950: George Clark, "Leon Trotsky—A New Vindication."

59. *FI,* August 1948, pp. 176–81.

but were disappointed. The 1951 Congress of the Fourth International adopted a resolution on the Yugoslav question which summed up the ambivalence of this model of de-Stalinization.[60] On one hand, it was formally recognized that the Yugoslavs had broken with Stalin in 1941 (the Fourth International reproached itself for having failed to notice this until 1948) and was now only "semi-Stalinist." The Yugoslav attempt to deal with "bureaucratism" was appreciated as an attempt to deal with Stalinism. "Yugoslav conquests against Soviet bureaucratism" should be defended by the Fourth International, which would support Yugoslavia in case of a war with the Soviet Union and would attempt to form a united front with the Yugoslav Communists for specific actions. On the other hand, Yugoslav Communism, having partially de-Stalinized, had become "centrist," "opportunist." The official Yugoslav critique of Soviet Stalinism erred in calling the Stalinist system state capitalist. (This was before Djilas' independent publication of *The New Class,* which even more directly opposed orthodox Trotskyism on this point.) The failure of the Titoists to revise their Stalinist attitude toward Trotskyism also rankled. This issue, said the resolution, is a test of whether a given Communist party had "definitely and decisively" surmounted Stalinism. In the next decade many Trotskyists found fault with the program of workers' councils in Yugoslavia, which were deemed too decentralized for a socialist economy.[61] In 1960 Murray Weiss, who was more or less the chief authority on Russia and East Europe in the Socialist Workers' Party, even maintained that the Yugoslav Communists "had never ceased to be Stalinist." [62] All in all, the case of Tito's Yugoslavia seems to have added nothing but confusion to the Trotskyist concept of Stalinism and what it takes to de-Stalinize a workers' state.

China presented similar problems. At the time of the establishment of the People's Republic the few surviving Chinese Trotskyists who had escaped regarded Mao as a Stalinist and his state a result of Stalinist compromise with capitalism.[63] Although this interpretation was printed in Western Trotskyist organs, it was not long before the latter began to detect major stresses between Moscow and Peking. In fairness, it must be acknowledged that at least some Trotskyists saw the coming of the Sino-Soviet antagonism far ahead of the non-Marxist observers in the West. At the opening of 1951 Ernest Mandel (writing as "Ernest Germain") called attention to these tensions, while rightly forecasting that an open split in the near future would be surprising.[64] Later that year, the World Congress of the Fourth International noted this problem and, with explicit

---

60. *FI,* November–December 1951, pp. 202–7.

61. This emerges in many short allusions in *ISR* (e.g., Winter 1960, p. 21). It appears that the decline of interest in Yugoslavia is related to the decline of Michel Pablo's influence in the Fourth International after 1952. Pablo, the general secretary of the organization, had shown special interest in Yugoslavia at the Second World Congress in 1948. In 1966 *ISR* accused him of pro-Titoism (Summer, p. 99).

62. *ISR,* Spring 1960, p. 109.

63. *FI,* January–February 1950, p. 3; January–February 1951, pp. 10–12.

64. *FI,* January–February 1951, p. 21.

reference to Yugoslavia, Korea, and China, stated: "It is not excluded that certain communist parties with the bulk of their forces can be pushed out of the orbit of the Soviet bureaucracy and can project a revolutionary orientation. From that point they would cease to be strictly Stalinist parties." [65] The evolution of Maoism and its independence from Moscow received mixed reviews from Trotskyists. Predictably, Chinese anti-Americanism and anti-Sovietism drew praise, while the cults of two individuals, Stalin and Mao, did not. In recent years one can find Trotskyist writers who conclude that Mao's China is or is not Stalinist.[66] A resolution of the 1965 World Congress of the Fourth International, which represented only some of the major Trotskyist factions of that date, leaned toward Mao.[67] The Chinese Communist Party was not "Stalinist in the strict sense of the term." Mao had not committed great crimes against revolutionaries, and his regime does more than the Soviets to set egalitarianism against bureaucratism. "The material forces that give rise to such a hardened and fully crystallized bureaucracy as appeared in the Soviet Union no longer exist anywhere else in the world." Trotsky had been right in regarding Stalinism as the result of "a completely special combination of forces and circumstances," so there is no inevitable period of Stalinism following workers' revolutions in China or elsewhere. On the other hand, bureaucratism was a problem in China, which explained why the Maoists respected the person of Stalin, "the very incarnation of bureaucratism." The Great Leap Forward had been a disastrous attempt at socialism in one country, a policy that, it was hoped, had been replaced by "uninterrupted revolution." As for the Sino-Soviet dispute, most Trotskyists have favored "critical support" for the Chinese, some factions being more critical and others more supportive.[68] In any case, the Sino-Soviet schism, like the earlier Yugoslav case, frequently is hailed as a sign of the break-up of Stalinism.

Cuba posed still different problems. With the exception of the Healyist group, which has simply regarded Fidelism as capitalism (not Stalinism), most American and European Trotskyists have shown remarkable tenacity in attempting to interpret Castro's state as non-Stalinist. Their enthusiasm for it at first is understandable. The July 26 Movement had not grown out of a Stalinist Communist party, it was socially radical and—wonder of wonders—it initially permitted a small Trotskyist organization to function openly. This pleasing situation did not last long. Castro suppressed the Cuban Trotskyists in 1961–63, merged his July 26 Movement with the Communists, grew increasingly dependent on Moscow, and in a major speech of 1966 denounced Trotskyism as "this discredited thing, this anti-historical thing, this fraudulent thing which emanates from elements so

---

65. *FI,* November–December 1951, p. 186.

66. It is Stalinist, according to Tony Thomas, *Marxism versus Maoism* (New York, 1974), p. 13; *ISR,* Fall 1960, p. 109. Among those arguing the contrary is Nahuel Moreno in Ernest Mandel, ed., *Fifty Years of World Revolution,* p. 157.

67. *ISR,* Spring 1966, pp. 78–80.

68. The position of the Socialist Workers' party is summarized by Joseph Hansen, in a polemical article that suggests that only the Pabloists fail to give "critical support" to the Chinese in the Sino-Soviet dispute (*ISR,* Spring 1965, pp. 8–19).

clearly at the service of Yankee imperialism." [69] This has led some Trotskyists to acknowledge the danger of a drift toward Stalinism, but the main thrust has been remarkably pro-Castro, even while admitting that his attack on Trotskyism was "reminiscent of the frame-up charges in the famous Moscow trials of the thirties." [70] As late as 1972, George Novack, a stalwart of the Socialist Workers' party, paid the supreme compliment by referring to "a Lenin, a Trotsky, a Castro." [71] The explanation of this puzzling incongruity might be sought in doctrine: Castro's anti-imperialism and the alleged mildness of bureaucratism in Cuba. However, I am inclined to see it mainly as a pragmatic response to the politics of the 1960's. The rise of the New Left in Europe and America offered the Trotskyists unprecedented opportunities for recruitment and united front activities, for many of the new radicals shared the Trotskyist belief in revolutionary militancy and the rejection of Stalinism. Almost all new leftists were passionately enthusiastic about the Cuban revolution, and especially its (non-Cuban) hero, Ché Guevara. For the Trotskyists to have offended this conviction would have been politically suicidal. The New Left was pleased to overlook the aspects of Castroism that might have been considered Stalinist, so it behooved the Trotskyists to do no less. This represented the least sacrifice with respect to Guevara, who entered the Trotskyist pantheon. He had no substantial record of the anti-Trotskyist statements and died a martyr's death before becoming involved in Cuban tendencies toward bureaucratism or Soviet dependency.[72] All in all, the case of Cuba, which might have defined Stalinism by its opposite (an undegenerated workers' state), contributed its share of ambiguity to the Trotskyist conception of Stalinism.

If orthodox Trotskyism after 1940 contributed little to the conceptualization of Stalinism, what of the unorthodox? I refer here not to those writers who left the Trotskyist movement or merely were influenced by Trotsky's ideas, but only to those who openly differed with the founder, while still considering themselves disciples in some measure. Such a writer was Max Shachtman, who had been a major figure in American Trotskyism in the 1930's but broke with Trotsky in 1940 and founded his own group. Although he was on the bitterest terms with the orthodox heirs of Trotsky ("epigones," in Shachtman's pointed allusion to Trotsky's label for Lenin's successors), Shachtman continued to express his admiration for Trotsky and for *most* of his analysis of the degeneration of the workers'

---

69. Robert J. Alexander, *Trotskyism in Latin America* (Stanford, Calif., 1973), p. 229. A survey of Trotskyism and Cuba appears on pp. 215–35. This is the only scholarly work that I know of that provides a survey of the factional history of Trotskyism in a large area from its inception to the present, with the partial exception of Yves Craipeau, *L'Origine de Trotskysme en France* (Paris, 1971). On the world movement, the nearest thing to a satisfactory introduction is Pierre Frank, *La Quatrième Internationale* (Paris, 1969).

70. *ISR,* Summer 1966, pp. 96–106.

71. George Novack, *Understanding History* (New York, 1972), p. 81.

72. It appears that Guevara was not uncritical of Trotskyism, but this is not widely known, nor publicized by Trotskyists. Robert J. Alexander, *Trotskyism in Latin America,* p. 231.

state and the rise of Stalinism. Trotsky, he thought, simply had failed to carry his analysis to its logical conclusion: recognition that Stalin's Russia was not a workers' state but a new form of society which Shachtman called "bureaucratic collectivism" or "bureaucratic state socialism." [73] He even suggested that Trotsky was not far from seeing the light near the end of his life. Did not "The USSR in War" admit the *possibility* that a new exploiting class would emerge under Stalin? [74] But his desire to emphasize the similarity of his own ideas and Trotsky's did not keep Shachtman from offering a sharp critique of the master's reasoning. The state owned the means of production and exchange in Russia, but this did not demonstrate that it was a workers' state, contrary to what the orthodox Trotskyists (and their founder) seemed to think. Rather persuasively, Shachtman argued that much of Trotsky's analysis of Stalinism showed precisely that the workers in Russia had lost control of the state.

This argument was elaborated in various ways. At one point, Shachtman advanced the thesis that a proletarian state is unlike capitalism in that the latter separates social and political power, while in a proletarian state, in the absence of private property, the social power of the workers is inseparable from their political power. Lose political power, as Trotsky admitted they had in Russia, and the workers lose control of the means of production. No more workers' state.[75]

A related logic could be seen in post-war Eastern Europe. Surely the bourgeoisie was not in power in the Communist countries, but they had never experienced a proletarian revolution, so the proletariat could not be in power. Therefore, the bureaucracy must be in command in its own right.[76]

For a number of years Shachtman denied that the theory of bureaucratic collectivism need be discouraging to socialists. He did not regard this system as the wave of the future in capitalist countries and the Soviet Union alike (as did Rizzi and Burnham in their somewhat similar but non-Trotskyist books), but remained a Trotskyist in regarding the Stalinist degeneration as an exceptional phenomenon. It was the "barbarism" that Marx and Engels had predicted as the successor to capitalism, should the workers not build socialism soon enough.[77] It was doomed to collapse once *true* socialism had appeared in other countries, as Shachtman hoped it would. But this optimism seemed little justified by his appraisal of Stalinism at the opening of the sixties. He considered the Soviet collectivist bureaucracy to be "robust, ambitious, predatory, self-conscious, socially trained and a politically well represented class reality." It would not withdraw readily and was not to be undermined by its own economic progress, which simply contributed to the "maintenance of the machinery of repression." [78]

---

73. Shachtman's writings on Stalinism are conveniently collected in his book *The Bureaucratic Revolution: The Rise of the Stalinist State* (New York, 1962).

74. Ibid., pp. 39–40.

75. Ibid., pp. 43–45, 62, 92, 95.

76. Ibid., pp. 82–83.

77. Ibid., p. 32.

78. Ibid., p. 16.

Shachtman may have scored in his argument with the orthodox concerning the logic of Stalinism and the workers' state, but his victory faced him with that dismal reappraisal of proletarian revolution which neither he nor Trotsky could accept.

Another factional leader who regards himself as a disciple of Trotsky, while openly acknowledging theoretical differences with him, is Tony Cliff (Ygael Gluckstern). His group, which is based in Britain, calls itself the International Socialists, but it is generally referred to by orthodox Trotskyists as the "state capitalists," because the principle revision introduced by Cliff is the conception of Stalinism as "state capitalism."

More than any orthodox Trotskyist of the post-war period, Cliff has devoted serious research to the Soviet Union and Eastern Europe, utilizing a wide variety of Soviet sources in his books, *Russia: A Marxist Analysis* and *Stalin's Satellites in Europe.*[79] Pursuing many of the themes that Trotsky opened in *The Revolution Betrayed,* Cliff sees them leading to the conclusion that the Stalinist bureaucracy is a class in the classical Marxist sense and that the society is capitalist, but not in the normal sense, owing to the absence of private ownership of the means of production.[80] Like Shachtman, whose writing he snubs, Cliff maintains that the loss of worker control over the economic system in a planned, statized economy implies loss of political power.[81] Therefore, a social and not only a political revolution (contrary to Trotsky) is needed to overthrow the state capitalist order.

Also like Shachtman, Cliff calls attention to the signs that Trotsky himself was uncomfortable with his defense of the Soviet Union as a "workers' state" near the end of his life. Cliff emphasizes that Trotsky's last and unfinished book, the biography of Stalin, refers to class struggle in the Soviet Union.[82] Nevertheless, Cliff recognizes that Trotsky did not adopt the "state capitalist" interpretation, and he concludes that this was the result of Trotsky's "conservative attachment to formalism," that this was non-Marxist, failing to take into account the "law of combined development," to which Trotsky, himself, had contributed much. According to Cliff, this should have led him to understand that reaction need not mean a restoration of traditional capitalism, but might be a "spiral decline" to a form combining old and new elements.[83]

Cliff finds the foundations of the theory of state capitalism more in the works of Marx, Engels, Lenin, and (interestingly, for few Trotskyists have shown much regard for him) Bukharin than in the works of Trotsky. Cliff sees state capitalism as a transitional form which is practically impossible before the proletarian revolution but quite possible after the proletarian revolution has statized owner-

---

79. The former book was published in London in 1955 and again around 1964, with the addition of a section on "Russia after Stalin." The latter book was published in London in 1952 under the name Ygael Gluckstern, which I take to be the author's natal name.

80. Tony Cliff, *Russia: A Marxist Analysis* (London, 1964), pp. 106, 117–18, 142.

81. Ibid., p. 126.

82. Ibid., p. 139.

83. Ibid., p. 145.

ship.[84] Its mission is to complete the task of capital accumulation, after which it will fall victim to "a new, glorious edition of the proletarian revolution on a much stronger base than in 1917." [85] Cliff offers a hypothesis concerning the reasons for the unexpectedly long delay in this upheaval. He acknowledges that during the early stage of Stalinist industrialization many of the ablest workers took advantage of the opportunities for upward mobility and left the working class, while raw recruits flooded in. With the diminution of such expansion one can look forward to a more militant working class.[86] This characteristic Trotskyist optimism regarding the future of Soviet society would be more persuasive if Cliff's substantive writing about the USSR had identified signs of a growing disaffection of the industrial workers. In fact, he has merely shown that opportunities for upward mobility have diminished and that even official Soviet sources reveal some degree of worker dissatisfaction with assembly-line labor and managerial practices. Cliff acknowledges that real income has increased but maintains that this simply increases expectations. In the main, his discussion of the problems of Soviet Russia follow the lines on non-Marxist sovietologists, dealing with such issues as agricultural productivity and the disaffection of the minority nationalities. This seems sound enough, but it is hard to see why much of it should be called a "Marxist analysis."

Nor has Cliff illuminated the long-term historical issues connected with a Marxist analysis of Stalinism. From a few, brief references one would gather that he is willing to accept the Menshevik argument that Russia after 1917 had to experience a period of capitalism in order to complete the task of accumulation. On the other hand, he refers to "the workers' state of Lenin and Trotsky (1917–23)," without explaining whether this was an alternative path to state capitalism or simply a utopian effort of leaders who failed to understand the imperatives of history.[87] Still more confusing, he refers in passing to the great purge of the thirties as a "civil war" between the bureaucracy and the workers, in which the former won and thus restored capitalism, albeit in the new, statized form.[88] This not only suggests that the workers' state lasted well beyond 1923, but also contradicts all the evidence about the relative roles of the workers and bureaucrats in the purge. Surely it was the latter who bore the brunt, while the former showed no signs of revolutionary resistance of the sort that would characterize any recognizable form of civil war.

In a sense, then, the "state capitalist" interpretation of Stalinism is more optimistic than Trotsky's concept of the "degenerated workers' state." At least Marxism provides a general theory that forecasts the overthrow of capitalism in general, which presumably includes state capitalism, while it is hard to know

---

84. Ibid., pp. 108–9.
85. Ibid., pp. 33–39, 340.
86. Ibid., p. 342.
87. Ibid., p. 126.
88. Ibid., pp. 127–28.

what hope Marxism offers concerning the process of socialist restoration in a degenerated workers' state, or, for that matter, in Shachtman's "bureaucratic collectivist" regime. On the other hand, Cliff's study of Stalinist society, which he considers to have survived its founder, reveals scant sign of impending revolution. One may deduce proletarian revolution from his general theory, but this seems little supported by his inductive labors.

Isaac Deutscher seems to have departed from any form of organized Trotskyism shortly after appearing in 1938 at the Founding Congress of the Fourth International, which he regarded as a fiasco. Nevertheless, he remained a great admirer of Trotsky and became in effect his authorized biographer, for Natalya Sedova granted Deutscher the sole exception to the ban on using a large part of the Trotsky archives before 1980. In his address at her graveside in 1962, Deutscher acknowledged that he was "unorthodox," but his eulogy confirmed his commitment to his own kind of Trotskyism.

One of Duetscher's great assets, his fluent, allusive, and metaphorical style (in a language that he learned as a mature man), is an obstacle to the analysis of his ideological position. For example, his use of Dostoyevsky's Grand Inquisitor to explain Stalin's purge is an eminently readable and psychologically suggestive device, but it is difficult to compare ideas presented in this way with the more literal theoretical writing of the Marxist tradition. Although the word "Deutscherism" appeared in Trotskyist publications, his work is really too little structured to become an "ism," and the following sketch to some extent imposes on Deutscher a doctrinal clarity that is absent from most of his writings. He accepted the fundamental Trotskyist conviction that Stalinism was a regrettable detour on the road from the proletarian revolution of October 1917 to the achievement of socialism. Like Trotsky, he found the terminology of the French Revolution helpful in understanding this phenomenon. Stalinism is a mixture of Thermidor and Bonapartism. Deutscher (unlike Trotsky) would add Jacobinism.[89] Like Trotsky, Deutscher was ever ready to forecast the downfall of Stalinism and the regeneration of the revolution.[90] Like Trotsky, Deutscher attributed the origins of the Stalinist detour to the post-revolutionary state of weariness and the insubstantial working class in an immature industrial economy.[91] Like Trotsky, he maintained that the resulting rule of the bureaucracy did not constitute a new

---

89. Deutscher, *Russia in Transition* (New York, 1957), p. 144. *In the Prophet Outcast* (New York, 1963) Deutscher takes a somewhat different tack, suggesting that "such an analogy [Thermidor] did indeed serve more to obfuscate than to enlighten . . ." (pp. 313–18).

90. The most eloquent and perhaps most widely renowned of Duetscher's many statements in this spirit concludes his book *Russia After Stalin* (New York, 1968; published in 1953 as *Russia, What Next?*): "For many decades freedom was banned from Russia because it was, or was supposed to be, the enemy of socialism. If Russia had been free to choose her own road she would hardly have marched in the direction in which Bolshevism had led her. But freedom may once again become the ally and friend of socialism; and then the forty years of wandering in the desert may be over for the Russian revolution."

91. Deutscher, *Stalin* (New York, 1949), p. 289; *The Prophet Unarmed* (New York, 1959), Chap. I; *Ironies of History* (New York, 1966), pp. 21, 31.

class regime in the Marxist sense because the system was still basically a workers' state with socialized means of production.[92] The degree to which the bureaucracy contradicts the further development of the productive forces of the country increases the likelihood of its reform or replacement.[93] The objectively impressive growth of the Soviet economy, combined with the innate democratic striving of the proletariat, offers increasing grounds to hope for such a change.[94] All of this constitutes the solid foundation of Trotskyism in Deutscher's perception of Stalinism. But he modified and extended these ideas.

One issue on which he revised a major orthodox Trotskyist position is socialism in one country. Seeing more clearly than Trotsky the ambiguities in Trotsky's argument on this matter, Deutscher dismisses it as a non-problem or a quibble.[95] This leads to qualified approval of Stalinism, including the cult of personality, as "an amalgamation of Marxism with the semi-barbarous and quite barbarous traditions and primitive magic of an essentially pre-industrial, i.e., not merely pre-socialist but pre-bourgeois, society." [96] Odious, it seems, but necessary in view of the backwardness of Russia in 1917. This stress on the historical necessity of Stalin as modernizer, especially an industrializer, seems to be Deutscher's main difference with Trotsky, who was loath to admit that *he* could not have carried out this task.

Thus Stalinism is a transitional state, in which the *muzhik* is forced toward an advanced level of industry and culture.[97] Here one has the impression that Deutscher's conception of Stalinism is analagous to the Menshevik idea of capitalism. Both are conceptions of a stage of modernization that cannot be avoided, however distasteful politically. Both Deutscher's interpretation and Menshevism argue for a period of political quietism on the part of true socialists, who must wait for the Stalinist or capitalist stage, respectively, to outlive itself. Trotsky could never stomach such an attitude toward Stalinism (or capitalism) and continually called for revolutionary forces to prepare for action, but Deutscher was sure that everything would turn out well through the action of the Dialectic. Deutscher, to be sure, explicitly rejected Menshevism.[98] Evidently he considered it preferable (or inevitable) that Russia should undergo the unpleasant transition to advanced industrialization under the auspices of Stalin rather than the likes of Miliukov or Kerensky.

This optimistic confidence in the regenerative powers of socialism, without the help of any Fourth International, led Deutscher into further revisions of Trotskyism after the death of Stalin. Convinced that "Stalinism has exhausted its historical function," Deutscher was remarkably ready to see fundamental socialist

---

92. Deutscher, *The Unfinished Revolution* (New York, 1967), pp. 53–58.

93. *Russia After Stalin*, pp. 64, 165; *The Great Contest* (New York, 1960), pp. 20–21; *The Unfinished Revolution*, pp. 38, 104–7.

94. Deutscher, *Russia After Stalin*, pp. 55, 101; *Ironies of History*, pp. 30–31.

95. Deutscher, *Stalin*, pp. 285–87.

96. Deutscher, *Ironies of History*, p. 21; *Stalin*, p. 344; *Russia After Stalin*, pp. 53–55.

97. Deutscher, *Russia in Transition*, p. 88.

98. Deutscher, *Ironies of History*, pp. 207–25.

regeneration under Malenkov and then Khrushchev.[99] Contrary to orthodox Trotskyism, Deutscher considered that the bureaucracy itself was capable, under the pressure of historically developed social forces, of beginning the necessary reforms. In 1953 he even asserted, "What Malenkov's government is carrying out now is precisely the 'limited revolution' envisaged by Trotsky." [100] The revelation of Khrushchev's secret speech gave further sustenance to this optimism, but at the same time drew Deutscher's attention to the ambiguities of official Soviet anti-Stalinism. Writing in the fall of 1956, he maintained that "circumstances have forced Malenkov and Khrushchev to act *up to a point* as the executors of Trotsky's political testament."[101] On one hand, de-Stalinization had become a social necessity (owing to the economic and cultural modernization under Stalin), and "the resistance [to de-Stalinization] of all these groups [bureaucracy, labor aristocracy] has proved to be weaker, far weaker, than might have been expected." On the other hand, Deutscher recognized that "the job which it should have been the historic right and privilege of authentic anti-Stalinists [Trotskyist or *other* old Bolshevik oppositions] to tackle has thus fallen to the Stalinists themselves who cannot tackle it otherwise than halfheartedly and hypocritically." [102] On balance, he seems to have had difficulty restraining the optimistic interpretation of de-Stalinization. While admitting that one might have to wait quite a long time for the replacement of the reforming Stalinists, Deutscher suggested that either a rapid transition to a non-Stalinized generation or a violent upheaval might accelerate the process.[103]

But events did not sustain the hopeful mood of 1953–1956. In 1959 the " 'political revolution' which Trotsky once advocated" was neither "precisely" the policy of the Soviet leadership nor its policy "up to a point," according to Deutscher. It was at some indeterminate stage in the future, apparently after the time "in another few years" when "there will hardly be a trace left of the Russia of the muzhiks." [104] Was this an admission that Deutscher had over-rated the degree of economic modernization attained by 1953? Like Trotsky before him, Deutscher had learned to his sorrow that Stalinism was not such a short episode. In his last years, like Trotsky, Deutscher clung to the hope that the dialectic would make everything right in the end, but his analysis of the downfall of Stalinism grew quite vague. In 1965 "the opening, the unequivocal opening, of a truly new phase of the Russian—and not only the Russian—revolution is long overdue." [105] Because of these difficulties, Deutscher's admirer Marcel Liebman, in introducing a re-issue of one of Deutscher's works in 1968, felt obliged to improve on the prophetic powers of the writer whose foresight he had just praised. Noting that Deutscher had in 1953 considered that the USSR might

---

99. Deutscher, *Russia After Stalin,* p. 96.
100. Ibid., p. 164.
101. Deutscher, *Ironies of History,* p. 23 (emphasis in the original).
102. Ibid., p. 23.
103. Ibid., p. 25.
104. Deutscher, *The Great Contest,* pp. 20–21.
105. Deutscher, *Ironies of History,* p. 17.

revert to Stalinism, become a military dictatorship, or evolve toward democratic socialism, Liebman added that there seemed to be a fourth choice for "the short, and even average, run. . . . Soviet Russia may get bogged down in a regime which, like bourgeois societies, will aim, under the 'enlightened' control of its administrators, at increased consumption in an atmosphere of contentment and collective apathy." [106] This may have a good deal to recommend it as an analysis of the Soviet Union, but it leads toward the intellectual option that Trotsky resisted so desparately in his last years, and which Deutscher, too, resisted: that the October Revolution had in time led to the establishment of a new form of exploitation by a ruling class.

What has Trotskyism contributed to the understanding of Stalinism? One should at least pay tribute to Trotsky's role as a pioneer in the study of Soviet politics and society, in the company of other Marxist émigrés, such as Nicolaevsky and Dallin. But this does not speak to the broader problem of conceptualization with which this anthology is primarily concerned. Here one might hope that Trotsky-ism represented a challenging application of Marxist thought to the question of Stalinism.

In a sense Trotsky struggled to *avoid* making a Marxist analysis of Stalinism. There is something to this with respect to both the question of the origins of Stalinism and the question of its destiny. Trotsky's analysis of the origin of Stalinism could not be pressed to its conclusion without embracing the kind of classical Menshevism that he had consigned to the trash can of history in October 1917. The important factor in the rise of Stalinism, he argued, was Russia's backwardness and isolation. (In this context the factor of proletarian weariness merely follows from the struggle with backwardness and isolation.) If examined thoughtfully, this seems to mean that Stalinism, the degeneration of the workers' state, came about because Trotsky (among others) failed to heed the warning of the Mensheviks, who considered that the proletarian revolution in Russia should await the fulfillment of capitalism in Russia, by which time the expected socializa-tion of the West should have been achieved. But this was much too unpalatable a conclusion for Trotsky and his school. In the literature of Trotskyism this question is mainly bypassed, or simply blamed on the Social Democrats in casual allusions to their failure to lead the revolution in approximately 1918.

As for the destiny of Stalinism, the Trotskyist tradition has been unable to confront the possibility that it could be a solidly founded or long-term phenome-non. The relationship of Stalinism to the Communist party as an institution has never been subjected to sustained examination by any Trotskyist. The problem here is that Trotsky accepted the Leninist idea of the elite, omnicompetent party and regarded it as a model for the Fourth International. Because of this commit-ment, no Trotskyist, not even the "revisionist" Deutscher, has thus far been willing to apply Marxian analysis to the instititional basis of the political and social system of Soviet-style Communism. This shortcoming is related to the

---

106. Deutscher, *Russia After Stalin,* p. xx.

Trotskyist avoidance of the problem of Stalinism outside the USSR. For understandable polemical reasons the Trotskyists have regarded many non-Russian Communist parties and states as Stalinist, but the supposedly exceptional conditions of backwardness and isolation which affected Russia in the 1920's do not explain why such bodies exist, and in such profusion. As Trotskyists have acknowledged, isolation ceased to be a factor after approximately 1950, and backwardness characterizes neither Communist states like the German Democratic Republic nor countries such as France, in which masses of workers follow a Stalinist party not in power. It was this unwillingness of Trotskyism to analyze the institutional foundations of Stalinism that led the founder and his successors to predict the approaching downfall of Stalinism for almost half a century. Sometimes this millenium is just at hand (e.g., during the turbulence of the early thirties, the approach of the Second World War, the aftermath of Stalin's death, the Sino-Soviet dispute), at other times a less impatient forecast appears. But Trotskyism, even in the heretical forms discussed above, has always been characterized by the conviction that Stalinism is an accidental and short-lived anomaly in history. It was Trotsky, however, who first popularized the expression "Stalinism," and he and his followers have stressed that they did not conceive of this as merely the personal regime of one mortal. Having called attention to the conception of Stalinism as something more deeply rooted in the society and the political institutions of this century, the Trotskyists could not, however, follow up this insight as uninhibited Marxists without threatening their eschatological faith, which was more fundamental than their commitment to a science of society.

Stalinism and the Mono-Organizational Society

T. H. Rigby

The policies and methods pursued by Stalin played a vital part in establishing the Soviet social and political system as we know it today. And yet these policies and methods were also means to or attributes of a form of personal rule that disappeared with its founder. Is there a paradox here? What *was* the role of Stalinism in the genesis of modern Soviet society?

The Soviet Sociopolitical System

The Soviet Union may be termed a mono-organizational society, since nearly all social activities are run by hierarchies of appointed officials under the direction of a single overall command.[1] Organizations are also, it is true, the most characteristic social structures in modern Western society, but here traditional and especially market structures not only retain a significant role in various societal sub-systems, but are crucial to overall coordination of the society, which is achieved largely through processes of competition and mutual accommodation within the framework of established rules and conventions. In the Soviet Union, by contrast, overall coordination of the multifarious discrete organizations operating in the various societal sub-systems is itself achieved *organizationally,* i.e., through superordinated structures of command, much as in war-time the Supreme Command directs and orchestrates the numerous formations, branches, and services operating in a particular theater of war.

The problems of coordination are obviously stupendous in an organizational complex that seeks to embrace nearly all the socially relevant activities of scores of millions of people, and in its efforts to cope with these problems the system has evolved a number of distinctive devices and processes. Structurally most of these are focused on the Communist party, which has been largely redeployed from its earlier purposes to serve the needs of societal coordination. Most obvious here is the hierarchy of full-time party officials staffing the so-called party committees at the various territorial-administrative levels, who are primarily engaged in steering, monitoring, and reconciling the operations of the numerous special-

---

1. A fuller characterization of the Soviet social and political system in the terms presented here will be found in T. H. Rigby, "Politics in the Mono-Organizational Society," in *Authoritarian Politics in Communist Europe: Uniformity and Diversity in One-Party States* (Berkeley, Calif., 1976).

ized organizations in their area. The activities and responsibilities attaching to ordinary party membership have also been reoriented to serve the purposes of societal coordination. The party sees to it that some scores of thousands of responsible and other sensitive posts are restricted to its members, that substantial membership levels are maintained in all influential occupations, and that every work group has its leavening of Communists. Intra-party indoctrination and information programs, discipline and accountability procedures are employed to orient members, both "cadres" and rank-and-file, and through them, their non-party colleagues, towards overall party goals and current priority tasks as defined by the leadership, rather than the special values and interests of the group concerned.

The running of practically all sectors of social activity by organizations which are themselves integrated organizationally into a single vast structure has given rise to one of the most influential ways of looking at Soviet society. This is sometimes referred to as the "bureaucratic model," [2] although it requires a good deal more than a perception of the fundamentally bureaucratic character (or organizational, administrative, or managerial character—at a certain level of generalization the terms may be used interchangeably) before one has a "model"; for there are many varieties of "bureaucracy," and we cannot yet claim to have a satisfying specification of the essential structures and processes of Soviet society as a bureaucratic entity and of the systemic inter-relationships of these structures and processes.

The nature of this problem may be better appreciated if we recall the "classical" accounts of bureaucratic or managerial systems. These envisage a hierarchical pyramid with a more or less elaborate division of labor, the activities of each participant being governed by rules and instructions handed down by his superior. Goals, formulated at the apex of the pyramid, are broken down at successive levels to ever simpler sets of tasks, and organizational success depends on each participant precisely performing his tasks as prescribed, without his needing to understand the system as a whole or even support its goals (in fact, if participants substitute for the instructions of their superiors their own view of what will best serve the organization's goals, the system will tend to be disrupted). Conversely, the information required for the formulation of goals and the assignment of tasks is progressively assembled as it is funneled upwards, and the full picture is visible only at the apex. In a large system, top management will usually have

---

2. The ordinary Soviet citizen did not, of course, require a scholarly "model" to convince himself of the salience of bureaucracy in the USSR, and, indeed both Trotsky in *The Revolution Betrayed* and his subsequent writing and James Burnham in *The Managerial Revolution* long ago focused their respective characterizations of Soviet society on the dominance of the bureaucrats or managers. However, it has taken a later generation of scholars familiar with the work of Max Weber and modern organization theory and prompted by post-Stalin developments to challenge the prevailing concept of "totalitarianism," to look seriously at the structural characteristics of the USSR viewed as a bureaucratic system. A pioneering role was played here by Alfred G. Meyer in his article "U.S.S.R. Incorporated," *Slavic Review,* Vol XX (1961), pp. 369–76, and his book *The Soviet Political System: An Interpretation* (New York, 1965).

at its disposal, in addition to the pyramid of reporting and command (the "line" officers), groups of specialists ("staff" officers) to vet performance with respect to personnel and technical standards, to provide related services, and to assist with the organization's external relations.

All of this will look familiar enough to connoisseurs of Soviet society. Whatever activity you engage in in the USSR, will you not find yourself at some point in a hierarchical chain of command where the main expectation will be that you fulfil the *zadaniia* assigned to you from above, under the watchful eye of various control agencies? Do not all lines converge on the Politburo, where alone, allegedly, the full picture is available for orienting decisions on all fields of activity? Could not all Soviet institutions be seen as the various line and staff divisions of a single hierarchical pyramidal structure?

This is all very well as far as it goes, but deeper probing reveals other aspects of the Soviet system that do not fit at all well into this "classical" bureaucratic model. I will briefly refer to three of them.

First, the parallel party and governmental hierarchies, with their overlapping jurisdiction and blurred division of labor. Party bodies are supposed to "guide and check" the work of governmental and para-governmental agencies and their field units without "supplanting" their officials. Party officials should not become involved in the routine administrative work of bodies subject to their supervision, but must be prepared to closely direct operations in situations of crisis or where matters defined as urgent or important are at stake. In seeking to satisfy these ambiguous requirements, the party official will get some help from rules, instructions, and objective criteria, but must rely largely on his political judgment.

Second, the totality of demands that Soviet officials receive from their direct superiors and other bodies authorized to instruct them is frequently such that some demands cannot be met without sacrificing others, either because of inadequate resources or because in the given conditions the different demands conflict operationally. This phenomenon, first noted in the study of Soviet industrial management,[3] can be detected in various forms and degrees in most fields of activity. Seemingly both a product and a source of inefficiency and confusion, it can also have important advantages. Operatives down the line, obliged constantly to make decisions about which demands to meet and what to sacrifice in meeting them, become more responsive to the current priorities of the most important relevant authorities. This introduces greater flexibility into the organization, decentralizes effective decision-making, and in Weberian terms generally fosters substantive rationality at the expense of formal rationality.[4]

A third major departure of the Soviet system from the "classic" bureaucratic model is the salience of mobilizational methods. In Soviet parlance "mobilization" may simply mean a campaign, usually involving a mixture of exhortation

---

3. See Joseph Berliner, *Factory and Manager in the U.S.S.R.* (Cambridge, Mass., 1957).

4. The positive aspects of this phenomenon are ably discussed by Andrew Gunder Frank in his article "Goal Ambiguity and Conflicting Standards: An Approach to the Study of Organization," *Human Organization,* Vol. 17 (1958–59), pp. 8–13.

and coercion, for achieving some collective objective in the normal sphere of responsibilities of those concerned, e.g., fulfilling their production plan. But it may also involve, e.g., in getting in the harvest, the redeployment of persons from their normal tasks, the suspension of normal rules, and the substitution of an *ad hoc* role allocation and authority structure in place of those normally applying.

To emphasize such "anomalies" is not to deny the bureaucratic character of Soviet society but to point up the question of *what kind* of bureaucracy it is. And we are now in a position to provide a partial answer to this question by reference to the distinction which some contemporary organization theorists have drawn between "mechanistic" and "organic" systems of management and administration. The mechanistic system, appropriate to stable conditions and routine programs, corresponds by and large with the "classic" model of bureaucracy outlined above. By contrast, "the *organic* system is appropriate to changing conditions, which give rise constantly to fresh problems and unforseen requirements for action which cannot be broken down or distributed automatically arising [sic] from the functional roles defined within a hierarchic structure." [5] In these circumstances participants are constantly faced with problems that oblige them to redefine their tasks and make *ad hoc* decisions in collaboration with others directly involved (whatever their place in the formal organization), and such decisions must be informed by an appreciation of the overall goals of the organization and its immediate priority objectives. These two forms must be seen as "ideal-types," the poles of a continuum, and actual organizations will usually evolve some mixture of mechanistic and organic elements in their actual mode of operation.

I would suggest that the "anomalous" features of the USSR as a bureaucratic system are largely explicable as vehicles for a partially organic mode of operation, which represents a response to the frequently unstable and volatile conditions generated by social and technical innovation, organizational growth and change, and the disruptions attendant on complexity. Thus, while the state apparatus can be largely left to itself so long as mechanistic processes suffice, the party can come to the fore where circumstances necessitate operating more organically. Mobilizational methods and the action-patterns evoked by mutually conflicting demands are textbook organic devices. The shared "culture" and orientation towards the organization's goals, values, and programs which are necessary for it to function effectively as an organic system are facilitated by the permeation of all groups with party members, whose special indoctrination, information, and accountability sensitize them to the general thrust and changing priorities of the system.[6]

Soviet society, then, can be seen as a single vast and immensely complex

---

5. Tom Burns and G. M. Stalker, *The Management of Innovation,* (London, 1966), p. 121. In this book, originally published in 1961, Burns and Stalker provided the pioneering, and still the most elaborate and satisfying, characterization and explanation of this distinction. The basic concepts have since gained wide acceptance, but some have seen the term "organic" as misleading, and in a recent edition of their book Burns and Stalker have substituted "organismic."

6. The view proposed in this paragraph is argued at much greater length in my article "Politics in the Mono-Organizational Society."

organization, displaying a distinctive blend of mechanistic and organic characteristics. This picture, however, will remain misleadingly incomplete unless we take account of certain further features which derive precisely from the fact that this is a *society-wide* organization, which not only runs the production and distribution of nearly all goods and services, but seeks to monopolize the socialization and moral guidance of its members and has full responsibility for such basic functions of "the state" as military defence and internal order. What we must note here is not merely the global range of functions but the effects of combining them in a single organization. There is no space here to explore all the ramifications of this but certain aspects require our attention.

First the salience and distinctive characteristics of ideology and repression in the Soviet mono-organizational system. As anyone soon becomes aware on joining a large organization—be it an industrial firm, military formation, or government department—it will always have its own peculiar "ideology" or "culture," and this, for the reasons we have noted, can become crucial to successful performance where the system is operating "organically." At the same time any state must possess its legitimating beliefs and symbols, enjoying a wide degree of acceptance in the population. Furthermore, people growing up in any society must not only acquire the technical skills necessary for their future work roles but also the values, attitudes, and behavior-patterns enabling the society to cohere and operate effectively as a system. What is peculiar to the mono-organizational society is that all three of these phenomena—the organizational culture, the political legitimation and the socialization of individuals—come together in a single purportedly comprehensive ideology. For this is what "Marxism-Leninism" has evolved into in the USSR. Further, while we now understand that the "goal-system" governing the behavior of members in any large organization cannot be reduced to a single all-embracing goal (e.g., making soap, winning the war, saving souls), such a "basic" goal will always be there as the *raison d'être* of the organization and the ultimate (even if rarely invoked) touchstone of action. In the ideology of the Soviet mono-organizational system the "construction of communism" performs this role.

The combination and consequent interpenetration of functions in this system has other important consequences for the ideology. This may be illustrated from the example of the arts. Since the "production" and "distribution" of artistic values is directed by the same organizational system that is responsible for, *inter alia,* material production, the civic training of youth, and national defense, the system's managers will naturally be concerned that the impact of their artists on, say, work motivation, acceptance of existing authority-patterns, or attitudes to military service should be entirely positive.

It follows from what has been said that the ideology of the mono-organizational system will be not only global in scope but also monopolistic in its claims. Cultural pluralism and tolerance for heterodox ideas may be not merely acceptable but actually functional in a "market" society, with its largely autonomous sub-systems and coordination through processes of competition and mutual accommodation. In a mono-organizational society, by contrast, while they might be functional to the sub-systems, they will be *dys*functional to the system as a whole. The very comprehensiveness and internal coherence of the ideology mean that a challenge to any part of it threatens the whole. It is an intangible seamless web which, if torn, will reveal the emperor naked. Hence it is no mere perversity when Soviet leaders apprehend heresy amongst historians or poets as ultimately threatening their overthrow. And, along with the legitimacy of the rulers, the whole pattern of shared attitudes, symbols, and concepts in terms of which (largely through the mediation of the party) societal coordination is achieved both within and between its constituent sub-systems is similarly vulnerable to the voicing of discordant facts or ideas.

All human societies set limits to deviant expression and behavior and to opposition to established authorities and institutions, beyond which they will be prepared to employ coercive controls. In the Soviet mono-organizational system one tends to run up against such limits far more quickly than in modern Western societies, and coercive controls are correspondingly more salient. There are three main reasons for this. First, the monopolistic position of the official ideology in all its ramifications needs to be policed and enforced: not just its social and philosophical doctrines, but its democratic symbols and forms—so manifestly at variance with the bureaucratic structure of power—and its claims about the character of Soviet life—so often inconsistent with the personal experience of citizens. Second, the Soviet political system lacks legitimate channels of opposition to existing leaders and their policies—like other large-scale formal organizations, and also like *most* historically known political systems, but unlike those of the modern West, where such arrangements can be seen as functional to the processes of competition and mutual accommodation through which societal coordination is achieved. And finally, since the effective functioning of the mono-organizational system depends on the faithful transmission of messages (bearing commands, reports, etc.) through its immensely complex communication channels, special controls and sanctions are required to ensure that such messages are not intentionally or unintentionally distorted.

It is clear, then, that the salience of coercive social controls has an objective basis in the functional needs of the system and does not merely flow from the repressive attitudes of its leaders. These functional needs also explain the relative prominence of the political security and auditing-inquisitorial components in the pattern of coercive controls rather than the protection of persons and private property component which predominates in the West.

The effort to embrace practically all social activities within a single organizational system also has important consequences for the character of politics in the USSR. This has much in common with the politics one finds in any large organization or bureaucracy, i.e., it is for the most part "crypto-politics," not overt and channeled through specialized "political" institutions, but covert, masquerading as the faithful performance of assigned organizational roles. It involves competition between constituent organizations and their formal sub-divisions, biased reporting of information relevant to the formation or vetting of policy, informal networks or cliques, the use of personnel powers to reward friends and punish enemies, and bias in the execution of policy so as to facilitate or prejudice its success or to favor certain affected interests rather than others.

The crypto-politics of this organizational system, however, also displays some distinctive features deriving from its societal scope. On the one hand the full coercive and informational resources of the society are involved, both as instruments and prizes, in Soviet bureaucratic politics. On the other hand, all social cleavages and special interests, be they local, professional, ethnic, generational, or what have you, must feed into and be played out in the bureaucratic political arena if they are to be reflected in policy outcomes.

Essentially Soviet crypto-politics may be regarded as an aspect—but only one aspect—of the "informal organization" of the system. In all large organizations informal arrangements evolve to supplement and often modify or even supplant their formally prescribed structures and rules, serving to adapt the operation of the system to the interests, convenience, and limitations of the participants. They inject contractual and customary elements into what usually purports to be a "pure" command hierarchy. The informal organization may assume such importance in the operation of a system that "working to rule" would lead to its speedy breakdown, and this is notably the case in many parts of the Soviet system. The informal arrangements in and between Soviet organizations arise, in part, from their quasi-organic mode of operation, and to this extent enjoy a qualified legitimacy. These, however, shade through numerous grades of strictly improper but usually tolerated plan-fulfilling devices into the labyrinthine underworld of *blat.*

Despite the vast scope of the mono-organizational system there are important areas of human action in the USSR which the system seeks only to regulate without, however, directly managing them. On the one hand, a considerable autonomy of choice is vested in an acknowledged personal-family-domestic sphere, to which the system concedes a major influence over such societally important matters as quantitative and qualitative changes in the population, child-rearing, personal consumption and leisure-time activities. On the other hand, the substantial (though varying) element of self-selection in job-allocation and the private plot sector in farm production represent significant market enclaves in the centrally managed economy. Further, the retention of pre-existing ethnic entities with their languages and much of their elite and folk cultures— however pruned and channeled to serve the interests of the system—entails considerable traditional influence on the behavior, beliefs, and loyalties of the population. A special and uniquely anomalous case here is the tolerance— however limited, grudging, and combined with repression—of religion: for this involves permitting *organized* activity aimed at perpetuating behavior and beliefs deemed to conflict fundamentally with the basic goal of the system.

Stalinism

This, then is how I would characterize Soviet society. It is a society in which, despite significant traditional and market "survivals," most activities are directly managed by innumerable organizations or bureaucracies, all of which are linked up in a single organizational system. In its operation this system displays a distinctive blend of mechanistic and organic aspects, and the party, which combines a bureaucracy superordinated over all other bodies with a membership permeating all segments of the system, plays a crucial role in its coordination. The range and combination of functions performed by this mono-organizational system have engendered an ideology comprehensive in scope and monopolistic in its claims, a highly salient system of coercive social controls dominated by its political security and vetting-inquisitorial aspects, and a lively crypto-politics within and between its bureaucratic structures, on whose outcome the conflicting ambitions and interests of individuals and groups primarily depend.

While this account of the USSR as a mono-organizational society has been presented in the present tense, it would be applicable, as I hope any reader who has followed the discussion so far would concur, at any time from the 1930's on. As I shall argue later, however, only with crippling qualifications could it be applied to the Soviet Union of the 1920s. The fully fledged mono-organizational society, in fact, crystallized simultaneously with the establishment of Stalin's dictatorship. The question logically suggests itself, therefore, whether what I have been presenting is actually an analysis of *Stalinism:* suggests itself, but only to be answered, surely, with a resounding negative. For who would be satisfied with a characterization of Stalinism that left out the police terror and the personal power and cult of the dictator? It follows, then, that the history of the Soviet mono-organizational society can be divided into two stages: a first, "Stalinist," phase, during which the characterization I have given above is applicable but inadequate, and a second, "post-Stalinist," phase, during which it is both applicable and adequate. "Stalinism," in other words, was the mono-organizational system in combination with something else, and we must now look more closely at what this "something else" was.

Let us begin by bringing to mind some of its main ingredients. First and most obvious was one-man rule, contrasting with the oligarchical pattern of power before and afterwards. This does not mean, of course, that Stalin personally decided everything, which would have been physically impossible, but that he personally decided anything he wanted to, unconstrained by the power of any individual, group, institution, or law.[7] Even the most powerful of his officials knew better than to query his commands.[8] This untrammeled power extended to the liberty and indeed existence of any individual or group in the population. He could have members even of his immediate entourage incarcerated or killed without his needing to inform, let alone consult, the others. For such purposes he had at his disposal a political police enjoying arbitrary powers of arrest and punishment and maintaining a spy network permeating the whole of society. This enabled him not only to destroy opposition but to forestall it, by removing

---

7. Khrushchev makes and illustrates this point repeatedly in his memoirs. See *Khrushchev Remembers: The Last Testament,* tr. and ed. Strobe Talbot (Boston, 1974), pp. 11, 20, 45, 158, 177, 238, 241, 357.

8. See, e.g., ibid., p. 93.

"over-mighty subjects," by striking at suspect segments of the population, by inhibiting discussion, and by the "atomizing" effects on human relationships of the prevalent mutual distrust.

Stalin's fiat not only ran in all fields of practical policy, he was also the final arbiter in matters of faith, truth, and public taste and morals. His spoken and written utterances were accorded the reverence of received truth, and ritually repeated in season and out. They formed the core of a body of official doctrine which drew also on the writings of Marx, Engels, and Lenin, and which, like the dictator himself, was not subject to critical discussion but only affirmation. Truth was what conformed to this doctrine rather than what conformed to observed facts. This was of course deadly to true art and scholarship, and artists and scholars of independent mind were arrested or otherwise silenced, leaving the field to sycophants and time-servers.

It goes without saying that overt association to further particular interests or policies was out of the question in these circumstances, and crypto-political life, though persisting very actively, came to center mainly round the rivalries of personal followings and cliques. The public arena, emptied of spontaneous political life, was, however, noisy with contrived activity as the citizens were kept busy acclaiming the leader and his regime and policies in meetings, processions, and other manifestations, and engaging in "voluntary" services at the behest of the soviets, Komsomol, trade unions, and a host of other official organizations. Moreover, "building communism" meant under Stalin the sacrifice of mass living standards to grandiose industrialization projects, imposing an exhausting and enervating burden on the ordinary citizen in merely coping with conditions of day-to-day life. Thus, between his "heroic labors" and all these extra demands, the latter was left with little time, heart, or energy to engage in self-motivated activities.

Many features of Stalin's regime may be subsumed under the principle *divide et impera*. Resentments engendered by the dictator's policies were redirected against target groups in the population: against "bourgeois specialists," "kulaks," "enemies of the people," "homeless cosmopolitans," and so on. Younger, technically better-trained officials were set against the generation of their superiors, who had won their positions through political loyalty (and thus knew not only too little, but also too much). The dictator's lieutenants and the bureaucracies they commanded were given overlapping jurisdictions, and thus brought into conflict.

The term "cult" is appropriate to the presentation of Stalin in the media, at meetings, in schools and kindergartens, and in the arts. But the pseudo-religious character suggested by this term permeated the whole ideology, which partook of the quality of holy scripture, subject to constant public affirmation in ritualistic and sometimes even incantational terms.

Now, all this is familiar enough—indeed all too familiar. But that is precisely the point. For, whereas those features of Soviet mono-organizational society common to both its Stalinist and its post-Stalinist phases constitute a system qualitatively new in human experience, that "something extra" that we must add to the first phase to get an acceptable account of Stalinism consists of ingredients that have recurred with singular unoriginality throughout the history of complex societies. It is indeed the sort of thing you are *likely* to get when one man attains absolute power, and "tyranny" will serve as well as anything else as our name for it.

"What kind of Sovereign is this that cannot take away any life that she pleases!" exclaimed the chamberlain of Emir Nasrullah of Bokhara, when informed of the constitutional position of Queen Victoria.[9] Periander of Corinth, the Emperor Tiberius, the Emperor Ch'in Shih-Huang, or Cesare Borgia might have reacted with the same incredulous scorn. Tyrants everywhere are apt to be deified, to impose their standards of truth and beauty on all, to crush all signs of independence, and to carry out prophylactic purges.[10] For a brief, systematic characterization, we still cannot do better than Aristotle's summary of what he called the "traditional method" of maintaining tyranny:

> Here belong all the old hints for the preservation (save the mark!) of tyranny, such as 'Cut off the tops and get rid of men of independent views', and 'Don't allow getting together in clubs for social and cultural activities or anything of that kind; for these are the breeding grounds of independence and self-confidence, two things which a tyrant must guard against', and 'Do not allow schools or other institutions where men pursue learning together, and generally ensure that people do not get to know each other well, for that establishes mutual confidence'. Another piece of traditional advice to a tyrant tells him to keep the dwellers in the city always within his view and require them to spend much time at his palace gates; their activities then will not be kept secret and by constantly performing servile obligations they will be used to having no minds of their own. . . .
>
> Similarly a tyrant should endeavour to keep himself aware of everything that is said or done among his subjects; he should have spies like the Tittle-tattle women, as they were called at Syracuse, or the Eavesdroppers whom Hiero used to send to any place where there was a meeting or gathering of people. It is true that men speak less freely for fear of such men, but if they do open their mouths, they are more likely to be overheard.
>
> Another traditional way is to stir up strife amongst all possible opponents of the tyranny, by slander setting friends against friends, class against class, and one monied set against another. It is also in the interests of a tyrant to keep his subjects poor, so that they may not be able to afford the cost of protecting themselves by arms and be so occupied with their daily tasks that they have no time for rebellion. As examples of works instituted in order to keep subjects perpetually at work we may mention the pyramids of Egypt. . . . Friends are a source of protection to a king but not to a tyrant; it is part of his policy to mistrust them as being potentially more dangerous to him than the rest. . . .

---

9. Fitzroy Maclean, *A Person from England and Other Travellers* (London, 1958), p. 87.

10. Han Fei Tzu, whose prescriptions were well regarded by the first Ch'in emperor, recommended that "the ruler of men must prune his trees from time to time and not let them grow too thick for, if they do, they will block his gate. . . . If the trees are pruned from time to time, cliques and parties will be broken up. Dig them up from the roots, and then the trees cannot spread. . . . Search out the hearts of men, seize their power from them. The ruler himself should possess the power, wielding it like lightning or like thunder." Han Fei Tzu, *Basic Writings,* tr. Burton Watson (New York, 1964), pp. 41–42.

The typical tyrant dislikes serious and liberal-minded people. He regards himself as the only authority; if anyone sets himself up in rivalry and claims the right to speak his mind he is felt to be detracting from the supremacy and absolute mastery of the tyrant. Thus his dislike of intellectual pretensions is based on fear; such people are potential destroyers of his rule.[11]

Does not this, allowing for incidental features deriving from the conditions of the Greek city-state, read like a paraphrase of large parts of our characterization of the rule of Stalin? Aristotle does not set out to list all the "traditional" devices of tyranny, but argues that they can be summed up under three headings: namely that the tyrant's subjects should '(a) have no minds of their own, (b) have no trust in each other, and (c) have no means of carrying out anything.' [12] He goes on, however, to point out that while it is along these lines that the tyrant usually seeks to maintain his rule, he has an alternative method, namely to cultivate the image of a "king," that is a *good* absolute ruler who seeks the public benefit rather than his own. To this end he will avoid squandering the people's money on personal ostentation and gifts to favorites; he will represent his demands for services as necessary to the economic well-being of the people; he will take advantage of war to establish a reputation for military leadership and to pose as the savior of the nation; he will link himself personally with the bestowal of honors but not, if he can help it, with the infliction of repression, and so on.[13]

Aristotle's two patterns of tyranny should, perhaps, properly be regarded as "ideal types," since actual tyrannies have frequently combined elements of both. Even the most obnoxious of tyrants, including Adolf Hitler, have sometimes displayed attributes of "kingly" rule alongside the traditional devices of tyranny. And this, it should be plain, was true of Stalin as well.[14]

Now, the argument here is not one of *plus ça change . . .*—quite the contrary. Tyrannies vary, and not only because tyrants vary, but also because of the particular circumstances of their assuming and exercising power, and the character of the societies they rule. It is this last factor that interests us here. In the past, tyrannies have been limited for technical reasons either in geographical scale or the depth and generality of their penetration. It was possible for a tyrant acting within the confines of an ancient Greek or renaissance Italian city-state to exercise a profound and continuing influence over the lives of all his subjects, though even here the traditional and market relationships which governed routine daily activities tended to cushion his impact. In the great despotic empires the ruler's hand was directly, continually, and profoundly felt only by limited (mainly elite) segments of the population and in specific fields of activity. The more humble the subject, the more remote from the capital and major administrative centers, the more indirectly, superficially, and intermittently would he feel that hand

---

11. Aristotle, *The Politics*, tr. T. A. Sinclair (Harmondsworth, 1961), pp. 225–27.

12. Ibid., p. 227.

13. Ibid., pp. 228–31.

14. For a comparative analysis of tyrannical regimes, including that of Stalinist Russia, resting heavily on Aristotle's approach, see Maurice Latey, *Tyranny: A Study in the Abuse of Power* (London, 1969).

(though if it chanced to fall, say, to summon him to military or labor service or to inflict exemplary punishment, his life might never be the same). Hence Russian folk wisdom enjoined: "Do not keep your household near the prince's household, or your settlement near the prince's settlement" *(Ne derzhi dvora bliz kniazha dvora, ne derzhi sela bliz kniazha sela)*, for "Near the Tsar, near to death" *(Bliz tsaria—bliz smerti)*, even if "Near the Tsar, near to honor" *(Bliz tsaria—bliz chesti)*. In such empires the tyrant, in effect, ceded vast segments of the life of society to the virtually autonomous operation of traditional and market forces.

Stalin's tyranny, by contrast, disposed of the technical resources, most crucially in the fields of communication and transport, that enabled it to achieve on an imperial scale the deep and generalized penetration of society previously possible only on a mini-state scale. More than this, however, the drastic curtailment of the role of autonomous traditional and market forces in the regulation of social activity, and the substitution of hierarchical organizations, culminating in the person of the tyrant, for managing most areas of life, opened up a series of channels for transmitting the tyrant's will *directly* to *every* subject: one to order his work; one to demand his manifold manifestations of submission and acclaim; one to guide his thinking; one to spy on him and punish his actual, suspected, or potential misdemeanors; and so on. And now we are ready for definitions. Stalinism was not just the mono-organizational society, nor was it just tyranny. It was tyranny exercised under the conditions of a mono-organizational society, or, as I would prefer it, the mono-organizational society as run by a tyrant.

Here, however, a further question immediately arises: if Stalinism was a combination of these two components, was this combination purely fortuitous, or was some necessary relationship involved? Since the Soviet mono-organizational society has now functioned for nearly a quarter-century without the ingredient of personal tyranny, the latter is evidently not an essential feature or condition of such a society. Yet, as mentioned earlier, the establishment of Stalin's tyranny and of the mono-organizational society did coincide closely in time. Was the one therefore necessary to the *establishment* of the other? And if so, what was the historical connection between the two phenomena? It is to these questions that we must now turn.

The Making of Stalinism

It is easy to detect factors in pre-Stalinist Russia making for both personal tyranny and a mono-organizational society. These factors are reasonably familiar, and it will suffice to recall them briefly. Russia entered the twentieth century as an autocratic monarchy in both theory and practice, and the attendant attitudes were deeply embedded in both the "elite" and "mass" political culture: "Truth is God's, but freedom [to decide] is the tsar's" *(Pravda bozh'ia, a volia tsarskaia);* "No one judges the tsar's judgment" *(Tsarskoe osuzhdenie bessudno)*. It is true that conventions of restraint and elements of a *Rechtstaat* had been painfully evolving for some generations, and that the political reforms following the 1905 revolution, despite the reaction that soon set in, represented significant steps towards a constitutional monarchy which ultimately *might* have led to some genuine form of elected parliamentary government. However, liberal and anti-authoritarian politics had little chance to take root before being swept away, along with the middle classes, where such support as they enjoyed mainly lay.

The traditions of the Russian revolutionary intelligentsia, out of which the Bolshevik movement emerged, were predominantly and often scornfully anti-liberal and had no patience for procedural democracy or compromise with opponents. Although—despite all that has been written about Russian "messianism"—these traditions did not focus on individual leaders or saviors, they invested the revolutionary organization (as such) with an unqualified claim to rule which flowed from its "correct" doctrine; and in the inevitable struggles to establish what *was* correct doctrine, dominant personalities were bound to emerge and establish followings, so that in practice the thrust of these traditions was towards dictatorship, a fact that was clearly recognized by such of Lenin's fellow-Marxists Leon Trotsky and Rosa Luxemburg when he set about grafting these organizational traditions (in the form of "democratic centralism") on a section of the infant Russian Social Democratic Workers' Party.

Lenin, admittedly, although always prepared to fight tooth and nail for the policies he believed right, was not despotic by personality, and could tolerate being contradicted, criticized, and overruled on nonessential issues. This partly explains why the potential for personal dictatorship embodied in his organizational methods was not realized in Lenin's lifetime. In practice what emerged was an oligarchy of party leaders, resting on a state machine from which they had extirpated all opposition, and a party machine run by officials formally elective but in practice chosen from the center. The panic reaction of this oligarchy, in the form of its ban on "factions," to the surfacing of intra-party opposition groups in 1920–1921, ensured that henceforth no effective alternative to their collective dictatorship could develop—so long as they hung together.

Aristotle's perception of the inherent instability of oligarchy, of the tendency of such collective dictatorships to soon break down, failing special efforts and particularly favorable conditions, has been abundantly borne out over the intervening two millenia—and in the Soviet case neither the efforts nor the favorable conditions were forthcoming. Without assuming that a personal dictatorship was "inevitable," we must recognize it as now a likely outcome.

Turning to those elements in pre-Stalinist Russia making for the crystallization of a mono-organizational society, one may again detect relevant antecedents well back in the tsarist past. First there was the great preponderance of the state over society, marking tsarist Russia, as some would have it, as an oriental despotism.[15] Because social forces were too constrained to allow much scope for spontaneous evolution, change, when it occurred, mainly took the form of "social engineering" from above, most dramatically in the reforms of Peter the Great and Alexander II. Related to this was the notion of society as consisting of "estates," each of which was defined in terms of its distinctive obligations to the state, which were

15. See especially Karl A. Wittfogel, *Oriental Despotism: A Comparative Study of Total Power* (New Haven, 1957).

enforced by a centralized bureaucracy. The realization of this notion in actual practice was always somewhat untidy and became progressively more so, but its influence remained important. A further point was the major involvement of the state in a variety of social activities, from the promotion of industrial development to science and higher education.

We must beware of exaggerating these features of pre-revolutionary Russia. For one thing, capitalist market relations made considerable headway in the generation or so before the Revolution. The dominance of tradition in the villages, where four-fifths of the population still lived, modified the picture even more drastically. Yet these qualifications should themselves be qualified. Russian industrial capitalism remained heavily dependent on the state. As for the peasantry, the commune—the main vehicle of tradition—operated as a kind of "primitive totalitarianism" which left little scope for autonomous individual choice and on top of this was also caught up in administering important programs of the state, for instance the poll tax and army recruitment before the 1861 reforms, and subsequently implementing the terms of the emancipation.

Nonetheless, caution is called for in drawing comparisons with the "West." In the salience of features which seem partly to prefigure those of the mono-organizational society, tsarist Russia stood out in sharp contrast, say, to England, but less so to both pre- and post-revolutionary France, and even less to Prussia-Germany. There is no justification for assuming that, even without the Bolsheviks' coming to power, Russia would necessarily have been the country to pioneer the mono-organizational society.

Once the Bolsheviks were in the saddle, however, the probability of such an outcome was enhanced enormously. For the two main components of their movement, namely their Marxism and their Russian revolutionary traditions, conspired mightily to this effect. From their Marxism they received the concept of a society totally remade from the basic economic structure up, their confidence in the feasibility and indeed inevitability of this, and their resort to the state as the main instrument of this transformation. From the Russian revolutionary tradition, as we have noted, they received, and perfected, the centralized "military" pattern of organization and their belief in the absolute claims of the revolutionary will, which should brook no opposition or resort to avoidable compromise. Pestel' as early as the 1820's looked to a "temporary" dictatorship of revolutionary leaders to bring about *his* good society. The two components came together in the concept of the "dictatorship of the proletariat," an *obiter dictum* of Marx's unearthed by Lenin and borne aloft like the Holy Grail. This dictatorship, defined as "power unlimited by any laws," was to be exercised, as Lenin acknowledged, "essentially" by the "revolutionary vanguard."

The measures collectively known as War Communism went a long way towards transforming Soviet Russia into a centrally managed society during the very first years of the regime, although how far this was due to the drive to remake society and how far to improvisations provoked by the demands of the Civil War it is not easy to say. Much of industry was nationalized and run by centralized government agencies, and the rest of the economy was placed under close supervision and direction. The market in goods and services for both production and consumption was almost entirely replaced by centralized allocation. Official agencies moved in busily to take charge of non-economic activities such as the arts, media, science, education, and health care. Opportunities for expressing views at variance with Bolshevism were progressively curtailed, while massive campaigns to transform people's beliefs and attitudes were mounted. Moreover, the party was already asserting a major coordinating role in keeping the specialized bureaucracies entrusted with various aspects of national life running in harness.

Despite this mammoth surge towards the centralized bureaucratic management of society, Soviet Russia even in the full tide of War Communism fell considerably short of the mature mono-organizational society as we have described it above, and the substantial abatement of centralized economic and, in some degree, other controls during the NEP further widened this gap. Nonetheless the USSR in the mid-1920's was much closer to the mono-organizational pattern than any other society that had yet existed, and especially any society in peacetime.

Thus the ground was now well prepared for both the constituent elements of Stalinism. It would be a mistake to infer, however, that Russia was already teetering on the brink, that one sharp push was all that was needed to plunge it into the Stalinist abyss. There remained a number of restraining factors, and these must be examined before we can grasp the dynamic relationship between the two components of Stalinism.

First, there was still much that was not centrally managed. In the economy agriculture formed one vast exception, and after 1921 most small-scale industry and distribution was also in private hands, while market relationships again came into their own as the major coordinating mechanism in the economy. In non-economic activities, although access to resources was for the most part determined by official agencies, there was a considerable degree of autonomy at operative levels. This leads to a second point: there was still substantial scope for independence of thought during the 1920's. Of course, "counter-revolutionary" views could not be publicly expressed, but in most fields this left a wide range within which conflicting opinions and attitudes could compete. This was most conspicuously so in the case of science but was also marked in the arts, the aspirations of Proletkul't notwithstanding. On matters with more direct political implications, such as legal or economic policy, the forums within which open debate could occur tended to be more restricted, but sharply differing views were nevertheless vigorously pressed throughout the 1920s. In general, differences of opinion enjoyed a degree of legitimacy, and there was no assumption that there must be a "correct" line authoritatively dispensed on all issues.

Finally, significant obstacles to one-man rule were built into the Russian communist movement itself. I said earlier that Lenin bequeathed an oligarchical power-structure institutionalized in the Politburo, which seemed likely to degenerate into a personal dictatorship unless the oligarchs could, rather improbably, hang together. This picture now needs to be qualified. To start with, the oligarchy was not wholly restricted to the seven or eight members of the Politburo. On the one hand, the party Central Committee, numbering three to four dozen at this period, was not yet a mere rubber stamp for "its" Political Bureau. On the other hand, both the Council of People's Commissars and the party executive machinery (run by the Orgburo and the Secretariat) remained important, if subordinate, decison-making centers. Further, the authority of the major oligarchs lent a degree of autonomy to the official bodies directed by them (the industrial administration (VSNKh), the political police (GPU), the Army and Navy Commissariat while Trotsky was in charge, the trade unions, the Leningrad party organization while dominated by Zinoviev, the Moscow party organization while dominated by Kamenev, and so on), and so injected a considerable element of bureaucratic pluralism into the operation of the system.

There was also a more general and pervasive inhibition on dictatorship, deriving from democratic elements in the party's traditions and structures. Largely under the influence of German Social Democracy, Marxism as a political movement came to Russia heavily imbued with democratic values. The tradition of democracy, moreover, was one that rejected populism of either a Rousseauesque or charismatic variety, and stressed such procedural aspects as free and open discussion of policy, collective decision-making by majority vote, election of executive bodies and officials, etc. It is this, of course, that explains the widespread disquiet within the infant Russian Social Democratic Workers' Party at Lenin's quasi-military, centralist concepts of organization, and it explains why he had to present these as "democratic" centralism. At the same time the Bolshevik affirmation of procedural democracy was not pure sham, despite their readiness to make a virtue of the necessity of operating *un*democratically in the conditions of the conspiratorial underground. While accepting the authority of directives and "cadres" sent from the center, local party organizations did elect committees, did discuss policy issues, did take votes. In the language of genetics, the organizational patterns and concomitant attitudes that established themselves in the prerevolutionary period may be characterized as centralism dominant and democracy recessive.

These patterns were further reinforced during the Civil War, as the necessity of curbing democracy in the interests of strict discipline and the centralized deployment of personnel was accepted. It was only as peace and victory were in sight that the centralist and democratic strands of the party tradition came sharply into conflict. The resolution of this conflict in favor of the former, through the leadership's success in rallying the Tenth Congress to support its suppression of intra-party opposition and factions, can be regarded as a reconfirmation and entrenchment of the established centralism dominant–democracy recessive patterns. The leadership was now armed with the disciplinary and personnel powers to break up centers of opposition, to install compliant secretaries and committees, and to keep criticism and discussion on a low key. Nevertheless the democratic forms were observed so far as consistent with these purposes, as was the right of party members to debate "unresolved" issues, a right that was exercised with marked vigor at the annual conferences and congresses.

The Soviet political system as bequeathed by Lenin may be described as an oligarchy focused in the Politburo but overflowing to a second level of several dozen other officials, an oligarchy marked by a considerable degree of bureaucratic pluralism, and operating in a climate of limited freedom of thought and under democratic forms possessing some residual substance. Through a variety of bureaucratic structures this oligarchy sought to manage a great deal that went on in Soviet society, but substantial areas of activity still lay outside its direct administration.

The only trouble with this picture is that it is too static. For the oligarchy had hardly consolidated its power before it began to break up. And as it broke up the constituent elements of the regime assembled and reassembled themselves in a kaleidoscopic succession of patterns. Without attempting to trace these patterns here, we should note some underlying consistencies. First and most obvious, the divisions within the oligarchy intensified the elements of bureaucratic pluralism in the system. Their effects on freedom of speech and intra-party democracy were more complex and contradictory. As the contending leaders sought to outdo each other in getting supporters elected as committee members and congress delegates and in securing favorable resolutions from local conferences, they in effect revived the very factionalism they had united to suppress a few years earlier. And since their struggles were fought out in terms of issues, there was a sharp stimulus to policy debate, which overflowed from the party conclaves into the press and scholarly institutions. Controversy largely centered around such central economic problems as how to handle the peasant and strategies of industrialization, but erupted at various times on a surprising range of other issues. Moreover, since the divided leadership was rarely able to provide agreed guidelines in specialized fields like the arts and sciences, law, education, and so on, each of these tended to become a battleground of ideas and rival groups and personalities in its own right. From a liberal-democratic viewpoint all this may seem normal enough, but in terms of Bolshevik traditions the constant fever of policy debate, the public displays of party disunity, and the recurrence of "factionalist" tactics within the party were decidedly pathological. Which is why those in the dominant faction of the movement could usually count on widespread support within the party when they resorted to the same measures to crush their opponents as had been employed against the anti-oligarchy oppositions of 1920–21: to use the personnel and disciplinary powers vested in the party's central executive organs to remove their rivals' supporters from party positions; to get resolutions against them passed by local committees and conferences; to deny their adherents election to party congresses and the Central Committee; to use the party's authority over the other agencies of the regime to remove these from their rivals' control; to use the party's authority over the media, scholarly institutions, etc., to deprive their rivals of a public voice; and, finally, if the latter, denied all legitimate platforms, resorted to clandestine meetings, circulation of protest declarations, etc., using the political police to expose them and render them liable to direct disciplinary measures. These methods were used successivly against Trotsky and his supporters, Zinoviev and Kamenev and their supporters, and finally Bukharin, Rykov, and Tomsky and their supporters. Thus while the divisions within the oligarchy activated the machinery of intra-party democracy and stimulated public debate, they simultaneously provoked counter-measures that were fatal to both.

The Soviet Union in the 1920's, then, revealed a strong potential to develop into a mono-organizational society and a similarly strong potential to develop into a personal dictatorship, but substantial obstacles would have to be overcome to realize these potentials. Their realization would thus not occur automatically, but required deliberate acts of human will, acts, moreover, that called for great determination and political skill, and a strong initial power base. This point deserves special emphasis. While circumstances were favorable to the emergence of Stalinism, they by no means fully explain its emergence. A full explanation must also give weight to the deliberate acts of Stalin. We must therefore consider these acts, but in doing so there is one question of particular interest to our analysis: could Stalin have become dictator without taking Russia that extra mile to the full fledged mono-organizational society or achieved the latter without making himself dictator—for it should be reiterated that it was their combination, not the dictatorship alone, that constituted Stalin*ism*. The reader will perhaps guess at my answer to this question from what has gone before: it would have been very difficult to attain the one without the other, and any step towards the one tended to involve a step towards the other.

For the oligarchical structure of power both made for and rested on a relatively dispersed and pluralistic pattern of decision-making and a level of sub-system autonomy that was incompatible with a mono-organizational system. Clearly the oligarchs could never have achieved sufficient mutual trust and unity of purpose to deliberately sacrifice their individual power bases in the interests of creating such a system—even if they could agree on its desirability. The way to both a mono-organizational society and a personal dictatorship, therefore, lay through capturing the oligarchs' power bases, liquidating the limited sub-system autonomy, and concentrating decision-making in a single center. Now this, in fact, was what Stalin's tactics amounted to, and although it is an oft-told tale [16] we shall need briefly to recall these tactics in order more fully to appreciate this point.

It is generally agreed that the crucial resource enabling Stalin to establish his dictatorship was control over the party's organizational machinery, through his being (from 1921) the only Politburo member with a seat (and therefore the key seat) in the Orgburo and (from 1922) general secretary of the party. It is also clear that control of this machinery was essential to undermining the authority of his fellow oligarchs and depriving them of *their* various organizational power bases, both inside and outside the party itself. The transformation of the oligarchy into a dictatorship required that this machinery be in the hands of a man possessing the skill to operate it, the drive to use it to extend his power, and the capacity

---

16. See, for example, Leonard Schapiro, *The Communist Party of the Soviet Union* (New York, 1960), especially Chaps. 15, 16, 21; Robert C. Tucker, *Stalin as Revolutionary, 1879–1929: A Study in History and Personality* (New York, 1973, Chaps. 8–11); and Robert V. Daniels, *The Conscience of the Revolution* (Cambridge, Mass., 1965), Chaps. 7–13.

to retain control of it to a point when the change in the power structure was irreversible. This last aspect is often overlooked. For why was Stalin allowed to *go on* using his control of the machine so as to reward his friends and punish his enemies, to build up compliant majorities in committees and conferences, and to place more and more of his supporters in key positions at the center and in the provinces? After all, Stalin's fellow oligarchs did not need Lenin's "Testament" to tell them that he was "abusing his powers" in these ways.

The answer to this has already been foreshadowed. The successive dominant factions in the Politburo needed precisely such things to be done in order to defeat their opponents in the leadership and get their policies implemented, and Stalin was both willing and manifestly capable of doing it for them. Of course they could see he was benefiting from it, but so, it seemed to them, were they. Playing this role required of him special qualities additional to those of a machine boss: skill in coalition-building, flexibility (or cynicism) in falling in with the policies of the temporary majority, and an acute sense of political timing in changing allies and policies. There is also a further aspect: if Stalin's fellow oligarchs licensed him to manipulate the officials and rank-and-file of the party, the latter still had to comply with such manipulation. That they mostly did so is usually explained by a combination of the party's centralist organizational patterns and careerism. These factors were undoubtedly of great importance. As we have seen, the centralist side of "democratic centralism" was emphatically reasserted with the suppression of the opposition groupings of 1920–21 and the prohibition of factionalism. This latter enabled Stalin's organizers to get their nominees elected simply by labeling as "factionalism" any attempt by party members to consult in putting up alternative candidates. Careerism, evident enough even during the Civil War, notoriously blossomed thereafter, whether due, as variously suggested, to the "petit bourgeois" atmosphere of NEP, to weariness, disillusionment, and the craving for comfort and security, to the greater likelihood of idealists perishing in the war or suffering expulsion through opposition activity, or to the influx of worker and peasant cadres who tended to identify the emancipation of their class with their personal elevation. There was, however, a third factor explaining the compliance of the party's lower echelons to manipulation by the Stalin machine: the widespread disquiet over public displays of disunity and the sense that it was pathological and un-Bolshevik for party meetings and media to be constantly taken up with conflicts of policy and personality. Stalin knew how to harness such misgivings to his cause as well, playing the practical, reliable activist who simply wanted to get on with the job of implementing agreed programs as laid down by Lenin rather than haring off after theoretical subtleties: an image of the party worker, the *partrabotnik,* with which the ordinary Communist making his way in the party could easily identify.

Thus while Stalin's use of the organizational weapon was crucial to his achievement of supreme power, he also needed to employ political skills of a high order, so as to secure and maintain sufficient elite and mass backing and to "legitimate" his organizational measures.

Stalin was most adept at exploiting his organizational strengths and neutralizing his organizational weaknesses. Perhaps the best example is his promotion of the "full" Central Committee vis-à-vis the Politburo, a gambit that had the virtue of appearing in line with both intra-party democracy and proposals of Lenin's shortly before his death, but which also had the special advantage that Stalin, through his control of party congress elections, enjoyed a majority in the Central Committee well before he was able to begin stacking the Politburo with his adherents. Though constitutionally master of the Politburo, the Central Committee had lapsed into a subordinate and dependent position before the death of Lenin, but Stalin worked to revive its authority, employing it—particularly in joint meetings with the Central Control Commission, which was even more heavily dominated by his supporters—as a captive court of appeal from Politburo decisions, as a forum to harass his opponents, and eventually as an instrument to restructure the Politburo membership.

A rather similar maneuver was employed with the Council of People's Commissars, or Soviet "Government." Under Lenin's chairmanship this body enjoyed enormous authority, and even though its subordination to the Politburo had become clear well before Lenin's death and its prestige declined sharply with Rykov as chairman in place of the founder of Bolshevism, its potential role as an alternative focus of power remained considerable. The direct influence Stalin could exercise within the Government through his powers in the party Secretariat was, moreover, quite limited. On the other hand there was the Central Executive Committee (CEC) of the Congress of Soviets, and especially its Presidium, to which bodies the Government was formally responsible. These bodies, also very significant in the early years of the regime, had long been lapsing into a primarily decorative role, but now they began to be revived. Again a crucial consideration was that these "soviet" bodies, through party control over the election of their members, were far more susceptible to direct influence by Stalin than was the Council of People's Commissars. The Presidium of the CEC now began to assume much of the business formerly handled by the Government, to hold joint meetings with it, and to assert its superior constitutional status, thus substantially cutting into the power base of Rykov, a man of independent mind whom Stalin must have regarded as an obstacle to his power even before they came into open conflict at the end of the twenties. The building up of the CEC and its Presidium as a counter-weight to the Government was given an added impetus by the election to the Politburo in 1926 of CEC Chairman Kalinin, a man more pliant to Stalin's will than Rykov. The tactical motivation of these developments is reflected in the fact that once Stalin was in a position to stack the Politburo and Government the Central Committee and CEC (including its Presidium) were both allowed to atrophy as working bodies.

If Stalin's organizational power was instrumental in capturing the citadels of Politburo "outs" on behalf of Politburo "ins," it was also extended by every such capture. Thus when Trotsky lost the Army and Navy Commissariat in January 1925, it was taken over by Stalin's ally Frunze and, on the latter's death, his close supporter Voroshilov. Shortly afterwards, when Kamenev and Zinoviev went into opposition, their power bases in the Moscow and Leningrad party organizations respectively were restaffed with loyal Stalinists. Dzerzhinsky's death in 1926 was a windfall for Stalin, for his authority would have been a serious obstacle to Stalin's penetration of the political police (now the OGPU), which henceforth, under humbler and more compliant leadership, went rapidly ahead. Finally, in 1930, with the defeat of the so-called Right Opposition and the removal of Rykov from chairmanship of the Council of People's Commissars, Tomsky from the chairmanship of the Central Council of Trade Unions, and Bukharin from chairmanship of the Comintern, they were replaced by Stalin's protégés Molotov, Shvernik, and Manuilsky respectively. Such appointments could be recognized by most Communists as proper and legitimate, since the new incumbents were invariably men with distinguished records of service to the party, and who, if not the general secretary, was best placed to make recommendations to such positions? Of course, as the new leaders were installed, more or less extensive staff changes soon followed, consolidating the hold of Stalin's supporters on the organization concerned. The effect of these developments was to liquidate the semi-autonomy of one major bureaucratic structure after another, and *pari passu* the semi-autonomy of the areas of activity they administered, binding them into an ever broader and ever tighter organizational network in which the last word on all important matters was reserved for Stalin himself.

Thus by 1930 the transition to the mono-organizational society and to Stalin's personal rule were both well advanced. And meanwhile the biggest remaining gaps in the mono-organizational pattern were being removed with the replacement of NEP by a "command economy" based on centralized directive planning and administration of industry and distribution, and collectivization of agriculture. We may be tempted to see in Stalin's espousal of these changes a manifestation of his psychological compulsion to maximize control and bend all to his will, but even without invoking such psychological factors it is easy to understand his resort to *organizational* measures to solve the problems of rapid industrialization and peasant recalcitrance, since these were the measures at which he was adept, which were most obviously at hand, and which had served him so well in the past.

All the essential ingredients of the mono-organizational system were now present, and they rapidly shook down into the patterns described at the beginning of this paper. Stalin's personal rule, however, had not yet taken on the unmistakenly "tyrannical" features we associate with mature Stalinism. True, his critics could be deprived of a public voice and centers of independent thought constrained and harassed (as RAPP was licensed to do, for instance, in literature); but there was not yet an official orthodoxy on all matters to which everyone must adhere. True, a leadership cult was well established, but Stalin was not yet ascribed superhuman qualities and the masses were not yet being constantly assembled to give exultant displays of their devotion. Most vital of all, though Stalin's power to punish his critics had been amply demonstrated, and fear was already an important ingredient in his rule, he still lacked that truest hallmark of the fully established tyrant—the unlimited power of life and death over all his subjects. And because he lacked that power those in authority under him could still assert a voice of their own and might still, conceivably, combine against him. Hence vestiges of the oligarchical pattern of power survived, especially in the Politburo and other inner executive bodies, but also, to some extent still, in the Central Committee. The men at these levels, moreover, though loyal supporters of Stalin in the past, and therefore presumably satisfied that "their" man was in the saddle, and satisfied too with the social and political transformations he had effected in getting there, had certainly not bargained on becoming the helpless subjects of an arbitrary despot. They may also have had some sense that while Stalin's dictatorship was a necessary condition of the triumph of "socialism" (or the mono-organizational society in our terms), its perpetuation and entrenchment were not essential, and might be harmful, to the further development of "social-ism": whether it was indeed some such perception or merely fear that provoked the tentative moves in 1934 to replace Stalin by Kirov will perhaps never be known. The outcome, however, we know all too well, and it gave Stalin, by 1937, the power to have anyone he wanted killed. Once that was there the remaining attributes of tyranny bloomed abundantly.

Epilogue

Our subject is Stalinism, and not what followed it. Yet what followed is important for our theme since it showed that the two constituent elements of Stalinism were separable, that you could, in other words, have the mono-organizational society without the personal dictatorship. The contemporary failure to perceive them as separable was perfectly understandable, since they had come into being together and were organically linked in a single "Stalinist" system. Furthermore, other contemporary dictatorships, namely Mussolini's and especially Hitler's had dis-played sufficient tendencies towards the comprehensive centralized management of society to suggest a new sociopolitical type: the "totalitarian dictatorship." Indeed the organic combination of personal absolutism with total social control was a key assumption of the most influential models of totalitarianism until some years after Stalin's death.[17] If the subsequent efforts to salvage the concept of totalitarianism in characterizing the Soviet system have proved singularly unen-lightening, this is primarily because existing models, once the attributes deriving from personal dictatorship are subtracted, can tell us so little about the remaining attributes of the system.[18] As a more general term signifying patterns of thought and action that tend to total social control, "totalitarianism" still deserves a place in the lexicon of the social sciences; in this sense Soviet mono-organizational society is strongly marked by totalitarianism, but then so, too, in various degrees,

---

17. See especially Hannah Arendt, *The Origins of Totalitarianism* (New York: Harcourt, Brace, 1951); and Carl J. Friedrich and Zbigniew K. Brzezinski, *Totalitarian Dictatorship and Autocracy* (Cambridge, Mass., 1956).

18. This view, which cannot be argued here at length, would not, of course, command universal assent. For an excellent discussion of the value of the totalitarian concept, see Carl J. Friedrich, Michael Curtis, and Benjamin R. Barber, *Totalitarianism in Perspective: Three Views* (New York, 1969). Cf. T. H. Rigby, "Totalitarianism and Change in Communist Systems," *Comparative Politics,* Vol. 4, No. 3 (April 1972), pp. 433–53.

have been many other societies quite differently organized,[19] and a quite different concept is required, such as that of the mono-organizational system, if we want to focus attention on the salient defining characteristics of societies like the USSR.

If, as I have argued, personal dictatorship went hand in hand with the establishment of the Soviet mono-organizational system, why was it not needed to maintain it? [20] Here I can do no more than sketch out an explanation. Establishing the system was not simply a matter of extending to all segments of social activity a centralized network of administrative subordination; it involved changing, in myriad ways and various degrees, the attitude and behavior patterns of a whole population. Until these patterns became second nature—and this certainly could not happen overnight—any relaxation of the dictatorship and division of power at the top involved a strong danger of the system falling apart. By the time Stalin died, however, older people had had almost a quarter-century to adapt to the system, and there was a whole new generation socialized, from the kindergarten up, to its roles and expectations. In the period that followed, when none of the old dictator's entourage managed to take sole power, it soon became apparent that the system had put down deep enough roots to be viable without such supports as a leader cult and massive arbitrary repression.

An oligarchical sharing of supreme power painfully established itself and gradually acquired a fairly settled institutional shape. Those features of "Stalinism" that had flowed from and supported the personal rule of the tyrant were now increasingly found to be inconsistent with oligarchical rule as well as costly to societal performance, while the defense of those features that constituted the mono-organizational system became the common ground on which the oligarchical consensus rested. That the system could now tolerate and even profit from a measure of bureaucratic pluralism and freedom of thought and expression also became clear, but so also did the strict limits beyond which the system was endangered by such things: limits indicated as much by experiences in Poland, Hungary, and Czechoslovakia as in the Soviet Union itself.

It might be argued that this analysis ignores the personal dominance enjoyed by Krushchev between 1957 and 1964 and by Brezhnev from about 1970. In neither case, however, was this dominance comparable in degree or character with Stalin's, and it is dubious whether the power of Khrushchev and Brezhnev within their respective regimes was greater than that of many chief executives in liberal-democratic systems. If we further take account of the "interregna" of 1953–57 and 1964–69, the Soviet regime since Stalin must be seen as having a

---

19. Cf. Leonard Schapiro, *Totalitarianism* (London, 1972); Barber, *Totalitarianism in Perspective.*

20. Unfortunately there is no space here for a comparative analysis of the role of personal dictatorship in the USSR and other countries with a fully or partly developed mono-organizational system. Certainly a dominant leader pattern with repressive and obscurantist features resembling those found under Stalinism has been usual in countries "going" mono-organizational, but much more study is required to sort out how far common determinants are at work. On the comparative use of the term "Stalinism," see below. More generally, on the concept of the mono-organizational society as a framework for comparison of Communist systems, see Rigby, "Politics in the Mono-Organizational Society."

relatively weak chief executive role. This probably reflects more than anything else protective measures taken within the oligarchy itself, whose members recognize that a strong chief executive might quickly make himself dictator in a system lacking serious societal checks on the supreme echelon of power. It remains problematical, however, whether the oligarchical structure of power could survive a profound or prolonged crisis situation requiring expeditious and decisive leadership.

Should some future chief executive attempt "to escape from the control of the collective," as Khrushchev was alleged to be doing on the eve of his removal, he will need speedily to assume the powers and methods of a tyrant if he is to escape a similar fate. Such an outcome may now seem improbable but cannot be ruled out. Should it occur, we would again have "a mono-organizational society ruled by a tyrant"—our definition of Stalinism. But would it be *Stalin*ism, with a society so much richer, better educated, and more complex than that of 1953, with a new political elite, and above all a *different* tyrant? For if, as Tolstoy tells us, "all happy families resemble each other, every unhappy family is unhappy in its own way," every tyrant will impose his own particular variant of misery on his subjects. For the same reason, it probably casts more confusion than light to extend the "Stalinist" label even to those other Communist regimes with strongmen at the top; it is confusing in the same way, for instance, as labeling the various fascist dictatorships of the 1930's "Hitlerite." Still, as Stalin was the man whose tyranny was built in tandem with the first mono-organizational society, there is some justice in invoking his name whenever such a society throws up a new tyrant.

Stalinism as
Revolution from Above

Robert C. Tucker

I

Western scholarship has been tardy in fixing analytic attention upon Stalinism. A bulky historical literature on the Stalin period and many biographies and memoirs dealing with the man Stalin coexist with a dearth of interpretive discussion of the "ism," by which I mean not alone the body of thought but the entire Stalinist phenomenon as an historical stage in the development of the Russian and other Communist revolutions and of Communism as a culture.

To some degree, this situation shows the impact of Soviet thought patterns upon our scholarship. From the mid-1920's, it became a firm article of doctrine in the Communist movement that the only legitimate "ism" was Leninism—or Marxism-Leninism, to use the subsequently adopted phrase. Stalin himself never countenanced the use of "Stalinism" because of the deviational implications it would consequently have carried. The forcible mass collectivization, the industrialization drive, and other events of the Stalinist revolution from above of the 1930's were officially described as Marxism-Leninism in action—the natural and logical unfolding of the original Leninist revolutionary impulse and program. There was a strong tendency in the Western sovietological literature of the 1940's and 1950's to give credence to this claim, albeit with a different moral judgment on the process. As a sample of—and perhaps epitaph on—the tendency in question, we may cite the following: "Stalinism can and must be defined as a pattern of thought and action that flows directly from Leninism. Stalin's way of looking at the contemporary world, his professed aims, the decisions he made at variance with one another, his conceptions of the tasks facing the communist state—these and many specific traits are entirely Leninist." [1] From such a standpoint, there was no special problem of interpretive understanding of "Stalinism."

Although Stalin never, not even at the height of his personality cult, tolerated the use of the term "Stalinism," he and his party allies of the mid-1920's employed (or, as Trotsky maintained, concocted) the term "Trotskyism" as the emblem of a system of political heresy against Leninism. For Trotsky and his followers, however, the heresy was the political line that Stalin and his associates were

---

1. Alfred G. Meyer, *Leninism* (Cambridge, Mass., 1957), pp. 282–83.

pursuing and the ideological tenets, like "socialism in one country," which they were using in justification of the line. So it is in the Trotskyist polemical literature that we find the earliest interpretive and critical discussion of Stalinism. In this interpretation, Stalinism appeared as the practice, and its reflection in theory, of a conservative bureaucratic takeover of the Bolshevik Revolution, a Soviet Thermidor, of which Stalin himself was merely the representative figure and symbol.[2]

In contradistinction to the first of the two positions just mentioned, I hold that Stalinism must be recognized as an historically distinct and specific phenomenon which did *not* flow directly from Leninism, although Leninism was an important contributory factor. In contradistinction to the second, I will argue here (1) that Stalinism, despite conservative, reactionary, or counter-revolutionary elements in its makeup, was a revolutionary phenomenon in essence; (2) that the Stalinist revolution from above, whatever the contingencies involved in its inception and pattern, was an integral phase of the Russian revolutionary process as a whole; and (3) that notable among the causal factors explaining why the Stalinist phase occurred, or why it took the form it did, are the heritage of Bolshevik revolutionism, the heritage of old Russia, and the mind and personality of Stalin.

Because of the presence and significant contribution of this last, the personal factor, which may be seen as an historical accident (Stalin, for example, might easily have died, like Jacob Sverdlov, in the great flu epidemic of 1918–19), my thesis that the Stalinist revolution from above was an "integral phase" of the Russian revolutionary process as a whole is *not* meant to imply that the Stalinist phase was an unavoidable one given the nature of the Bolshevik movement, of Russia, and of the historical circumstances which prevailed in the prelude. Given the diversity of currents in the Bolshevik movement of the mid-1920's, we must allow that a different, non-revolutionary form of further Soviet developmental movement was a possibility. That such a possibility did not materialize is a fact, but it could have—given such an easily imaginable difference in the historical situation as the rise of some other political leader than Stalin to power in succession to Lenin. On the other hand, my stress here on the culturalist factors in the Stalinist revolution from above implies that Stalin's personality alone must not be seen as the explanation of why Soviet development proceeded in the revolutionary manner that it did under his leadership in the 1930's.

II

The distinction between a palace revolution or coup d'état and a full-scale sociopolitical revolution is familiar and generally accepted. In the one, a swift and more or less violent change of a society's political leadership takes place without far-reaching inroads into the character of the society itself. In the other, a change

---

2. For Trotsky's thesis on the antithesis between Bolshevism and Stalinism, see his pamphlet *Stalinism and Bolshevism: Concerning the Historical and Theoretical Roots of the Fourth International* (New York, 1937). The thesis is elaborated further in his book *The Revolution Betrayed* (New York, 1937).

of political leadership, which may witness a coup d'état at such a critical point of transition as November 6–7, 1917, in Russia, furthers a radical reconstitution of the sociopolitical community and an attempted break with the social past, an effort to refashion the society's culture or habitual mode of life—its institutions, symbol-systems, behavioral patterns, rituals, art forms, values, etc. In the later aspect, a sociopolitical revolution conforms to Wallace's notion of a "revitalization movement." [3]

A sociopolitical revolution normally takes place, to start with at any rate, both "from above" and "from below." Masses of ordinary people participate in the process, while the new political leadership which the revolution has brought to power espouses the transformation of the society as a program and actively promotes it as a policy. Insofar as the revolutionary leadership's ideology contains a prevision of a transformed society, Wallace describes this as its "goal culture." The methods advanced for completing the transformative process he calls the "transfer culture." [4]

A sociopolitical revolution may, therefore, be an historically protracted process, taking place over years or decades, with intervals of quiescence, rather than only during the short time of spectacular social change when it is universally realized that a revolution is in progress. The Russian case illustrates this point. To many, "Russian Revolution" means the events of 1917 culminating in the Bolsheviks' seizure of power toward the end of that year. From a broader and historically more adequate standpoint, the Russian Revolution was a social epoch comprising the manifold social, political, economic, and cultural transformations during the period of Civil War and War Communism that ensued after 1917 and lasted until the initiation of the New Economic Policy in 1921.[5] And on the still more comprehensive view that is being advocated here, the Revolution extended over slightly more than two decades. Otherwise expressing it, NEP society was an interval of relative quiescence between two phases of the Russian revolutionary process: the 1917–21 phase just mentioned, and the Stalinist phase that ensued in 1929–39. In saying this, I do not mean to suggest that NEP society was condemned by the nature of Bolshevism to be no more than an "interval of relative quiescence." Other outcomes, as already suggested, are readily imaginable. But given *all* the factors that were operative, Stalin's personal role included, the outcome was the one that history witnessed. The NEP, that is, proved in fact to be an interval between two phases of the Russian revolutionary process.

Bolshevik public discussion during the early 1920's reflected a sense of the NEP as an historical pause in the commonly employed description of War Communism as a time of revolutionary "advance" or of the NEP as a time of revolutionary "retreat" and "regrouping of forces." The Bolsheviks were aware—grimly so—of being surrounded by a vast mass of predominantly peasant people whose tempo-

---

3. See p. xv and note 5, above.

4. Anthony F. C. Wallace, *Culture and Personality,* 2nd ed. (New York, 1970), p. 192.

5. Such a view is taken, for example, by W. H. Chamberlin in his classic study in two volumes, *The Russian Revolution 1917–1921* (New York, 1935).

rary willingness to respond to revolutionary leadership in the 1917–1921 upheaval went along with a tenacious underlying resistance to the reshaping of their way of life and thought. The peasants who burned down manor houses in 1917 and parceled out the estates had, for example, little animus against the Russian Orthodox religion and, still more important, no wish to live and work in agricultural communes under the Soviet regime. Whence their eloquently expressive saying, quoted by Lenin on one occasion, "Long live the Bolsheviks, down with the Communists!"—the former being those who had bid them take the landowners' land and the latter those who now wanted to deprive them of it. By early 1921 the Bolsheviks found that their continued tenure of power depended upon the suppression of the Communists inside themselves to the extent of legalizing private production and trade under the NEP in the rural economy, small industry, and commerce. To make peace with the overwhelming majority of the population, to reestablish the link, or *smychka,* between workers and peasants, they had to desist from herculean efforts toward rapid socialist transformation of the country's economic way of life and tolerate, if not actively encourage, that small-scale commodity production of which Lenin wrote in 1920 that it "*engenders* capitalism and the bourgeoisie continuously, daily, hourly, spontaneously, and on a mass scale." [6]

The NEP Russia that emerged from the Bolshevik Revolution of 1917–21 could be described as a society with two uneasily coexisting cultures. There was an officially dominant Soviet culture comprising the Revolution's myriad innovations in ideology, governmental structure, political procedures, economic organization, legal order, education, the intellectual pursuits, values, art, daily life, and ritual. Side by side with it was a scarcely sovietized Russian culture that lived on from the pre-1917 past as well as in the small-scale rural and urban private enterprise that flourished under the NEP. It was a Russia of churches, the village *mir,* the patriarchal peasant family, old values, old pastimes, old outlooks along with widespread illiteracy, muddy roads, and all that Trotsky had in mind when he wrote that: "Essentially the Revolution means the people's final break with the Asiatic, with the Seventeenth Century, with Holy Russia, with icons and cockroaches." [7] The coexistence of cultures was competitive in a one-sided way: it was the declared objective of the new one to transform the old one, so that, as Lenin declared in addressing the Moscow Soviet on November 20, 1922, "out of NEP Russia will come socialist Russia."

Doubts of this existed in some quarters, including the émigré Russian intellectuals associated with the symposium *Smena vekh* (Change of Landmarks). For Ustrialov and his fellow *smenavekhovtsy,* the NEP was the beginning of the end of Russian Communism as a revolutionary culture-transforming movement, its incipient deradicalization, and Russia's imminent return to national foundations. On the Bolsheviks' behalf, Lenin anathematized that perspective. And replying

---

6. "Left-Wing" Communism—An Infantile Disorder, in *The Lenin Anthology,* ed. Robert C. Tucker (New York, 1975), p. 553.

7. Leon Trotsky, *Literature and Revolution* (Ann Arbor, Mich., 1960), p. 94.

to those Menshevik-minded Marxists ("our European philistines") who argued, like Sukhanov, that it had been a mistake for socialists to seize power in so culturally backward a country as Russia, Lenin defiantly replied in one of his last articles, "Why could we not first create such prerequisites of civilization in our country as the expulsion of the landowners and the Russian capitalists, and then start moving toward socialism?" If a definite level of culture was needed, as they said, for the building of socialism, "Why cannot we begin by first achieving the prerequisites for that definite level of culture in a revolutionary way, and *then,* with the aid of the workers' and peasants' government and the Soviet system, proceed to overtake the other nations?" [8]

While upholding the historical correctness of the Bolshevik decision to take power in 1917 and to pursue the revolutionary political course that it did subsequently, Lenin in 1921 and after redefined the movement's objective and strategy in the new situation marked by retreat at home and delay of other Marxist revolutions abroad. The transcending of the NEP was to take place within the framework of the NEP, by evolution not revolution. Lenin could not have been more explicit on this point. Revolution, he explained, "is a change which breaks the old order to its very foundations, and not one that cautiously, slowly and gradually remodels it, taking care to break as little as possible." War Communism, with its forcible food requisitioning, had represented a "revolutionary approach" to the building of a socialist society; it had sought to break up the old social-economic system completely at one stroke and substitute for it a new one. The NEP signified an abandonment of that in favor of a "reformist approach" whose method was "not to *break up* the old social-economic system— trade, petty production, petty proprietorship, capitalism—but to *revive* trade, petty proprietorship, capitalism, while cautiously and gradually getting the upper hand over them, or making it possible to subject them to state regulation *only to the extent* that they revive." [9]

The transfer culture, as Lenin now envisaged it, was the "cooperating *(kooperirovanie)* of Russia" along with the development of a popularly administered, non-bureaucratized society with a large-scale, advanced machine industry based heavily on electrification and operating according to plan. The cooperating of Russia meant the involvement of the entire population in cooperative forms of work. This would realize the utopian dreams of the "old cooperators" like Robert Owen, whose error had been not the vision of a cooperative socialism but the belief that it could be put into practice without a political revolution such as the one that the Bolsheviks had carried out. To achieve the cooperated Russia through the NEP, by the reformist methods that now defined the transfer culture in Lenin's mind, would be the work of "a whole historical epoch" comprising

---

8. "Our Revolution (Apropos of N. Sukhanov's Notes)," in *The Lenin Anthology,* pp. 705–6. For Lenin's anathema on the *Smena vekh* tendency see his report to the Eleventh Party Congress in 1922, in *The Lenin Anthology,* pp. 525–26. Ustrialov was the intellectual leader of the *smenavekhovtsy.*

9. All quotations in this passage are from "The Importance of Gold Now and After the Complete Victory of Socialism," in *The Lenin Anthology,* p. 512. The essay was written in November 1920.

one or two decades at a minimum. The methods themselves would consist very largely of "culturalizing" *(kul'turnichestvo)*, the remaking of the popular mentality and ethos by educative means starting with the overcoming of illiteracy. Only through such a gradual, long-range "cultural revolution" would it be possible to gain the population's voluntary acceptance of cooperative socialism.[10] It was the position taken by Lenin in "On Cooperation" and other last articles that Bukharin subsequently elaborated as his contribution to the theory of building socialism in one country which he defended against the Left opposition in the intra-party controversies of the early post-Lenin period.[11]

History, as we know, did not go the way that Lenin charted; it went the Stalinist way. This was radically different from the path delineated in those Lenin articles of the final period that Bukharin, in the essay that he published in *Pravda* in January 1929 for the fifth anniversary of Lenin's death, described as "Lenin's Political Testament." Stalinism in its time of self-assertion and triumph, the 1930's, was a revolution in exactly the sense that Lenin had defined it in warning against a revolutionary approach to the further building of Soviet socialism: "a change which breaks the old order to its very foundations, and not one that cautiously, slowly, and gradually remodels it, taking care to break as little as possible." Instead of transcending the NEP evolutionarily, Stalinism abolished it revolutionarily, by decree and by force. Instead of proceeding gradually and by means of persuasion, it proceeded at breakneck speed and wielded state power coercively to smash popular resistance by terrorizing the population. Instead of taking care to break as little as possible, it broke the spirit along with the bodies of a great proportion of the generation that had come of age during the first phase of the Revolution a decade before. It also consumed a very heavy proportion of those party leaders and members who had, in the 1920's, been Stalinists in the simple sense of supporters of the general secretary and his "general line" in the fight with the oppositions.

The rural revolution called "mass collectivization" illustrates these points. In the space of a few years and at the cost of untold suffering and a famine whose toll of lives ran into many millions, a countryside with about twenty-five million peasant farmsteads functioning on nationalized land was transformed into one in which the great majority of those peasants were organized into some 200,000 collective farms *(kolkhozy)* while many more were employed as hired workers on state farms *(sovkhozy)*. In the *Short Course* of party history (1938), which Stalin edited personally, the collectivization is described as "a profound revolu-

---

10. All quotations and the ideas summarized in this paragraph are from "On Cooperation," in *The Lenin Anthology,* pp. 707–13. The essay was dictated by Lenin in January 1923.

11. For Bukharin's thought in this period, see Stephen F. Cohen, *Bukharin and the Bolshevik Revolution: A Political Biography* (New York, 1973), Chap. VI; and Moshe Lewin, *Political Undercurrents in Soviet Economic Debates: From Bukharin to the Modern Reformers* (Princeton, 1974), Chap. 3. Earlier treatments of enduring importance include Alexander Erlich, *The Soviet Industrialization Debate, 1924–1928* (Cambridge, Mass., 1967), Chaps. I and IV; Moshe Lewin, *Russian Peasants and Soviet Power: A Study of Collectivization* (Evanston, 1968), Chap. 12; and N. Valentinov, *Doktrina pravogo kommunizma* (Munich, 1960).

tion, a leap from an old qualitative state of society to a new qualitative state, equivalent in its consequences to the revolution of October 1917." The *Short Course* goes on: "The distinguishing feature of this revolution is that it was accomplished *from above,* on the initiative of the state, and directly supported *from below* by the millions of peasants, who were fighting to throw off kulak bondage and to live in freedom in the collective farms." [12]

It was indeed a state-initiated, state-directed, and state-enforced revolution from above—as was the Stalinist revolution as a whole—but the *Short Course* lied when it spoke of mass peasant support from below. Historical evidence available to us now in great abundance attests that not alone the ones classified in kulaks, whose "liquidation as a class" was proclaimed as the banner of the collectivization drive, but the mass of middle peasants and even some of the rural poor were sullenly opposed to the rural revolution and joined the *kolkhozy* only under duress or because of fear. The claim in Soviet publicity of Stalin's time and after that the collectivization was Lenin's "cooperative plan" in action is groundless. Not only was there no patient, long-drawn-out educational effort ("cultural revolution") to prepare the peasantry's mind for voluntary acceptance of cooperative farming, and no antecedent industrialization sufficient to produce the hundred thousand tractors that Lenin had foreseen as a powerful inducement to the peasants to farm cooperatively; still more important, the *kolkhozy* were (and are) socialist cooperatives only in their formal façade.

The rural revolution from above of 1929–33 proceeded simultaneously with the heroic phase of the Stalinist industrial revolution from above: that state-directed, frantic, military-oriented industrialization drive whose very slogan, "Fulfill the Five-Year Plan in Four," reflected the gap between what actually happened and the Plan as officially adopted in 1929.[13] The relationship between these two processes presents a highly complex problem on which scholarly opinion has evolved as new factual information has become available in the recent past. It was at one time widely believed that the forcible mass collectivization was a necessity for the desired high-speed super-industrialization in that the *kolkhoz* system enabled the Soviet state to extract otherwise unobtainable (or uncertainly obtainable) agricultural surpluses to finance such basic needs of industrialization as the importation of foreign machinery and technicians and to supply the urban population with food and industry with raw materials.[14] Such, indeed, appears to have been the underlying conception on which Stalin acted

---

12. *History of the Communist Party of the Soviet Union (Bolsheviks) Short Course* (Moscow, 1945), p. 305.

13. On the disparity between plan and practice, involving also the "wild target increases issued in 1930 and 1931," see Holland Hunter, "The Overambitious First Soviet Five-Year Plan," and the comments on Hunter's article by Stephen Cohen and Moshe Lewin in *The Slavic Review* (June, 1973). Hunter's reference to the wild target increases appears on p. 239.

14. For a representative statement of this belief, see E. H. Carr and R. W. Davies, *Foundations of a Planned Economy 1926–29,* Vol. One, Part I (London, 1969), pp. 269–70, where the authors write, *inter alia,* "If industrialization was a condition of collectivization, collectivization was a condition of industrialization."

at the time; collectivization was envisaged as the presupposition of a form of industrialization geared to the priority of heavy industry and war industry over the consumer-goods industries whose greater development would have been a *sine qua non* of a Soviet industrialization within the frame of a continued rural NEP. In the event, however, the economic consequences of collectivization were so catastrophic that recent researches by Western scholars, supported by archival data published in 1968 and 1969 by the Soviet historian A. A. Barsov, have reached the conclusions that (1) "mass collectivization of Soviet agriculture must be reckoned as an unmitigated economic policy disaster," and (2) "the oppressive state agricultural procurement system, rather than serving to extract a net contribution from agriculture as a whole, should be credited with preventing the collectivization disaster from disrupting the industrialization drive." [15]

III

Only two major aspects of the Stalinist revolution from above have been discussed here. Any adequate account, even of fundamentals, would have to consider also the state-building process which went on *pari passu* with mass collectivization and industrialization: the expansion of the bureaucratic state apparatus, the huge growth of the system of forced labor, the concomitant growth of the politico-economic police empire which administered it, and the extreme centralization of the state power. Something more will be said about this below. Concentrating for the present on collectivization and industrialization, I want to ask why they took place in the Stalinist way.

According to a view which draws part of its inspiration from Trotsky's thinking and which achieved wide influence owing to its espousal by Isaac Deutscher, Stalinist industrialization-cum-collectivization (which Deutscher calls "the second revolution") was a necessitated response to a "grave social crisis" of the later 1920's. Citing Stalin's statistics, Deutscher states that in January 1928, in particular, government grain purchases fell short by two million tons of the minimum needed to feed the urban population.[16] Emergency measures were applied by the government to extract grain that was being withheld from the market. The peasants were not, for the most part, politically motivated against the Soviet regime, but were driven by economic circumstances, in that the small farms produced only enough to meet the peasants' own food needs while the "big farmers" with surpluses were charging prices beyond the ability of the town population to pay and also were demanding concessions to capitalist farming. In this dilemma, yielding to the peasants would antagonize the urban working class, and refusal to yield would also bring a threat of famine and urban unrest. A "radical solution" was demanded, and Stalin, having until the very last mo-

---

15. James R. Millar, "Mass Collectivization and the Contribution of Soviet Agriculture to the First Five-Year Plan: A Review Article," *The Slavic Review,* December 1974, pp. 764, 765.

16. Isaac Deutscher, *Stalin: A Political Biography,* 2nd ed. (New York, 1967), p. 313. The phrase "a grave social crisis" appears on p. 312.

ment shrunk from an upheaval, acted "under the overwhelming pressure of events" and embarked upon the second revolution in an "unpremeditated, pragmatic manner." He was "precipitated into collectivization by the chronic danger of famine in 1928 and 1929." [17]

Such, in Deutscher's classic version, is the "circumstantial explanation" (as we may call it) of the initial phase of the Stalinist revolution from above. It is followed by Carr and Davies with specific reference to the collectivization drive. Having shown that party policy, including that of the Lefts such as Trotsky and Preobrazhensky, had always envisaged a gradualistic approach in collectivization, Carr and Davies find the explanation for the abandonment of gradualism in favor of "direct assault" in "the now chronic and irremediable crisis of the grain collections" and "the dire need for grain to feed town and factories." They go on: "In this desperate impasse, the leaders snatched eagerly at the growing belief in the prospects of collective agriculture and in its capacity to meet the needs of a planned economy." And, echoing Deutscher, they declare that "the sudden decision reached at the end of 1929 was neither preconceived not premeditated." [18] This restates Carr's earlier argument (likewise an echo of Deutscher's) that in the summer of 1929 the system of official grain collections had effectively broken down, and: "A third successive annual crisis of the grain collections loomed ahead. The problem of supplying town and factories had become completely intractable. Gradualism was not enough." Then, too, Carr had referred to "the haphazard and impulsive character of the final decision." [19] Elsewhere, referring to the industrial revolution from above, Carr mentions the so-called war scare of 1927 after the severance of diplomatic relations with Soviet Russia by Great Britain, and goes on to say that "the security motive in the drive to catch up with the west by rapid industrialization should not be overlooked." [20]

The circumstantial explanation has been offered in a still more extreme form by Alexander Gerschenkron in his thesis that the economic crisis at the end of the NEP era was also a "political crisis of the first magnitude." He explains: "Inability to maintain the food supplies to the cities and the growing resistance of the millions of the peasants, strong in their intangible diffusion, seemed to spell the doom of the Soviet dictatorship." A threat existed to the continuation of the

---

17. Ibid., pp. 318, 322. Deutscher repeats this interpretation in briefer form in *The Prophet Outcast: Trotsky, 1929–1940* (New York, 1965), pp. 67–68. For a somewhat different attempt to explain the Stalinist revolution by economic necessity, see Maurice Dobb, *Soviet Economic Development Since 1917*, rev. ed. (New York, 1966), p. 244.

18. Carr and Davies, *Foundations of a Planned Economy*, pp. 264, 268, 269. Apropos Trotsky and Preobrazhensky, the authors point out (p. 265) that in 1925 Trotsky wrote of "the gradual transition to collective farming" which would be possible when the necessary technical base had been created; and that "Preobrazhensky's drastic analysis had been conducted within the framework of NEP and on the assumptions of a market economy." Further, "Preobrazhensky afterwards spoke of 'the rapid conversion of millions of small peasant holdings to collective farms' as 'a thing none of us foresaw.' " The latter statement was made at the Seventeenth Party Congress in 1934.

19. E. H. Carr, "Revolution from Above: The Road to Collectivization," in *The October Revolution Before and After* (New York, 1969), pp. 104, 109. The cited essay was first published in 1967.

20. E. H. Carr, "Reflections on Soviet Industrialization," ibid., p. 121.

Soviet regime in these conditions, Gerschenkron asserts, and "it was under the pressure of that threat that Stalin underwent a radical change of mind and embarked upon the gamble of the First Five-Year Plan." [21]

In Deutscher's version of the circumstantial explanation, as has been noted, Stalin, the political leader of the revolution from above, appears as a great improviser who responded to the pressure of extremely adverse national circumstances in "an unpremeditated, pragmatic manner." In consonance with this view, Deutscher calls Stalin a man of "almost impersonal personality." [22] All this received later elaboration in Carr's characterization of Stalin as "the most impersonal of great historical figures." To show what he calls "the essentially impersonal character of Stalinist policy," Carr states that no element of personal conviction, nor any originality of conception, was involved when Stalin took leadership of the industrial revolution from above. The aims he ruthlessly pursued were those "dictated by the dynamic force inherent in the revolution itself." His qualities, like his convictions, were those of his milieu; they "mirrored the current stage of the historical process." His role in Soviet history was that of "the great executor of revolutionary policy" with "no vision of where it would lead." [23]

In seeming inconsistency with the image of an all but mindless political improviser conjured up by the description of Stalin cited above, Deutscher does allow that the man who led Soviet Russia in the revolution from above acted on certain ideas. But he maintains that these were borrowed from others. "The ideas of the second revolution were not his," Deutscher writes. "He neither foresaw it nor

---

21. Alexander Gerschenkron, *Economic Backwardness in Historical Perspective* (New York, 1965), pp. 144–45. Gerschenkron further states (p. 145): "Viewed as a short-run measure, the purpose of the First Five-Year Plan was to break the disequilibrium through increase in consumer-goods output based on increase in plant capacity," although once the peasants had been forced into the *kolkhozy,* "the hands of the government were untied. There was no longer any reason to regard the First Five-Year Plan as a self-contained brief period of rapid industrialization, and the purpose of industrialization was no longer to relieve the shortage of consumer goods" (p. 146). It does not appear accurate to say that the main purpose of the first Plan was to increase consumer-goods production; in any event, the thrust of the industrialization drive in 1929–33 was toward the building up of heavy industry, and consumer-goods supply declined in Russia upon the termination of the NEP.

22. *Stalin: A Political Biography,* p. 273. Trotsky's influence is reflected in Deutscher's portrait of Stalin as a pragmatist and improviser who would act without premeditation under pressure of circumstances. See, for example, Trotsky's characteristic description of Stalin as "a man in whom energy, will and resoluteness are combined with empiricism, myopia, an organic inclination to opportunist decisions in great questions, personal rudeness, disloyalty and a readiness to abuse power in order to suppress the party." Leon Trotsky, "A Contribution to the Political Biography of Stalin," in *The Stalin School of Falsification* (New York, 1962), p. 198. The book was originally published in 1937.

23. E. H. Carr, *Socialism in One Country 1924–1926* (New York, 1968), Vol. I, pp. 177, 185. The characterization is repeated with only very slight modification in *Foundations of a Planned Economy* (Vol. II, p. 448) where Carr and Davies describe Stalin as "the representative figure of the period," adding: "Stalin's personality, combined with the primitive and cruel traditions of the Russian bureaucracy, imparted to the revolution from above a particularly brutal character, which has sometimes obscured the fundamental historical problems involved." The authors do not say what they mean by "the fundamental historical problems involved," but invite the inference that they are invoking what we have called the circumstantial explanation of the revolution from above.

prepared for it. Yet he, and in a sense he alone, accomplished it." [24] Whose ideas were they, then? Deutscher does not directly say, although some pages later he notes that Yuri Larin, "a second-rate economist, once a right-wing Menshevik," had propagated the idea of a "second revolution" in the countryside as early as 1925.[25] We are left to infer that the ideas in question were those of representatives of the Left opposition like Preobrazhensky, who had propounded in the early 1920's the idea of "primitive socialist accumulation," i.e., industrialization through exploitation, chiefly, of the rural economy. Yet Deutscher also declares, and rightly so in this instance, that "there was no question, in the view of the left Bolsheviks, of driving the peasants into collective farms by force. The switchover from private to collective farming was to be carried out gradually, with the peasants' own consent." [26] The strange upshot is that Stalin is treated both as a leader who acted under relentless pressure of circumstances *without* preconceived ideas, and as one who acted *with* or *on* certain ideas which, however, were not his own. But those whose ideas these presumably were did not think, in the Stalinist way, of collectivization as a revolutionary leap which the state would accomplish by coercive means. In short, whatever ideas Stalin took from the erstwhile Left oppostion, the idea of a coercive revolution from above was not one of them.

IV

It is a central thesis of the present essay that the circumstantial explanation, notwithstanding a certain specious plausibility, is fatally flawed, and that we shall not attain a tenable view of Stalinism in its fundamental aspect as revolution from above until this is understood. The circumstantial explanation is flawed, first, in the utterly unproven nature of its assumption that collectivization in the terroristic form that it took was the only realistic alternative for the Soviet regime in 1929, much less a *sine qua non* of its survival as Gerschenkron suggests. Even allowing that the regime was faced in 1927–28 with something like a peasant "grain strike" (to use the loaded *Short Course* terminology), there is no serious evidence of incipient political rebelliousness in the countryside at that time; and there is evidence of general peasant acceptance of the Soviet regime, whatever the specific grievances that caused peasants to grumble or to withhold grain from the market in expectation of more return. Nor, as already indicated has it been shown, nor is it true, that the terroristic collectivation was a necessity for the

---

24. *Stalin: A Political Biography*, p. 295.

25. Ibid., p. 319. Stalin, Deutscher observes, at that earlier time dismissed Larin's notion as a "cranky idea."

26. Ibid., p. 303. Elsewhere Deutscher expands on the relation of the Stalinist course to the Lefts' program as follows: "The Opposition wanted industrialization and collectivization to be carried out in the broad daylight of proletarian democracy, with the consent of the masses and free initiative 'from below'; whereas Stalin relied on the force of the decree and coercion from above. All the same, the Opposition had stood for what he was doing even if the way he was doing it was repugnant to them." *The Prophet Outcast*, p. 70.

results achieved in the industrialization effort during the Plan years. As for the
security motive to which Carr referred, growing out of the external tensions of
1926–27, a recent and careful scholarly review of the facts, while it indicates that
the war scare was more than a mere sham and contrivance of intra-party conflicts
of the time and probably enjoyed a certain credence on the part of various Soviet
leading figures, also concludes that "the war scare was in fact grossly and crudely
manipulated by Soviet politicians in 1927." [27] There were, as I would put it,
grounds for Soviet concern about external relations in Europe, although not, at
that time, for serious fear of an oncoming coalition war against the USSR; but
the *possibility* of war was brandished as a justification for the developing Stalinist
orientation in internal policy.

The circumstantial explanation of forced mass collectivization hardly squares
with the now demonstrated conclusion, cited earlier from Millar, that this course
proved in practice an "unmitigated economic policy disaster," nor is it cogent
that a policy which directly and indirectly produced the worst famine in Russia's
famine-plagued history, that of 1932–34, which cost a conservatively estimated
five million lives,[28] was necessitated by the need to avert a famine. Although
historical "might-have-beens" are just as difficult to establish as are arguments
of the "there-was-no-other-possible-course" type, the insistently emerging conclusion from scholarly researches based on the more abundant data now available
from Soviet sources is that "a continuation of the New Economic Policy of the
1920s would have permitted at least as rapid a rate of industrialization with less
cost to the urban as well as to the rural population of the Soviet Union." [29] In
effect, informed and thoughtful historical hindsight is confirming the basic economic realism of the program for a balanced industrialization policy within the
frame of a continuing NEP that Bukharin presented in his *Pravda* article of
September 30, 1928, "Notes of an Economist." [30] The Bukharinist non-revolutionary alternative for Soviet industrialization policy at the close of the twenties,
an alternative inspired in large part by the Leninist thinking of 1921–23 discussed
earlier here, was real. Had it been adopted, it could well have worked; had it
worked poorly, the cost to the Soviet economy could not have compared with

---

27. John P. Sontag, "The Soviet War Scare of 1926–27," *The Russian Review,* January 1975, p.
77. See also Leonard Schapiro, *The Communist Party of the Soviet Union* (New York, 1959), p. 383,
where it is stated: "There was little prospect of any kind of invasion in 1928."

28. Dana G. Dalrymple, "The Soviet Famine of 1932–34," *Soviet Studies,* January 1964, p. 261.

29. Millar, op. cit., p. 766. One of the sources cited by Millar in this review essay is an article
by Karz, who writes that "the damage done to agriculture within the first three years of the industrialization drive was so severe that it affected adversely its ability to contribute significantly to further
economic development." Karz concludes that "there is a significant probability" that the Soviet
dilemma in agrarian policy toward the end of NEP" was not one that *had* to be resolved by
collectivization and the associated compulsory procurement of farm products or by the abandonment
of a sensible and fruitful industrialization drive." See Jerzy F. Karz, "From Stalin to Brezhnev: Soviet
Agricultural Policy in Historical Perspective," in *The Soviet Rural Community,* ed. James R. Millar
(Urbana, 1971), pp. 41, 51.

30. For recent arguments to this effect, see Cohen, *Bukharin and the Bolshevik Revolution,* Chap.
9 and Epilogue, and Lewin, *Political Undercurrents,* pp. 52–61.

that which had to be paid for the Stalinist solution. Such, also, is the position of an influential school of contemporary post-Stalin Soviet politico-economic thought whose "scarcely veiled endorsement of Bukharin's industrialization strategy" has been persuasively argued and documented by Moshe Lewin.[31]

At this point, a modification of the circumstantial explanation might suggest itself: if Stalinism was not the necessary or sole practicable course that it once seemed to be, it was nevertheless so *perceived* at the time by the decision-makers, who after all had to act without foreknowledge of the whole sequence of effects, including catastrophic consequences, which their decisions would bring about. The difficulty with such a hypothetical fallback position (and this may explain why still-living adherents of the circumstantial explanation have not taken it) is that numerous Bolshevik minds in Moscow and around the country, including some and possibly even a majority in the Politburo, *did not perceive the Stalinist course as the only possible action to take in the circumstances then obtaining.* Bukharin, in a clandestine conversation of July 1928 with Kamenev which became widely known in party circles, clearly foresaw the catastrophic consequences of Stalin's contemplated rural revolution from above. It was, he said, a ruinous policy course signifying a return to War Communism, a course leading to civil war, to an uprising that would have to be drowned in blood.[32] His prevision proved well founded in essence if not in specific detail.

The hypothetical fallback position cannot save the circumstantial explanation because it leaves open and unexplained the fact that the ruling party was divided in its appraisal of the circumstances in 1928–29 and that an influential section of Soviet political opinion opted for a course in agrarian policy and industrialization that would have been evolutionary, in accordance with the later Lenin's counsel, rather than revolutionary. The inevitable next question—why did the evolutionists go down to defeat in the party struggle, or why did Stalinism win?—cannot be answered by reference to the socioeconomic circumstances over which the quarrel raged in Bolshevik circles. It can be answered only by reference to the factors that determined the *Stalinist response* to the circumstances and its political victory. The circumstances as such cannot furnish the explanation of the revolution from above.

V

One of the forces conducive to a Stalinist revolutionary response among Bolshevik politicians was the other Lenin—the still very influential revolutionary Lenin of the War Communism period and the heritage of Bolshevik revolutionism that the other Lenin symbolized. It is understandable that Bukharin, involved

---

31. Lewin, *Political Undercurrents,* Chap. 12.

32. The Bukharin-Kamenev conversation is Document T1897 in the Trotsky Archives at Harvard University. Further historical testimony to the effect that the disastrous consequences of the Stalinist course were foreseen by some well-known Soviet economists in the later 1920's is given by N. Valentinov, "Iz proshlogo," *Sotsialisticheskii vestnik,* April 1961, pp. 68–72.

as he was in a political struggle against Stalin and the policies he was advocating in 1928–29, treated Lenin's last writings as his "political testament," and that is certainly what Lenin himself intended them to be. But for the Bolshevik movement and party, Lenin's political testament was the entire corpus of his thought and writing, the whole record of his revolutionary leadership of the movement up to, during, and after the October Revolution; and Lenin's political testament in this more comprehensive sense, or Leninism as a whole, contained very much that Stalin and Stalinism had good claim to as an authoritative text and warrant for the policies followed in the revolution from above.

The very idea of a process of "revolution from above," taken in the most general terms, has a Leninist pedigree. Even in one of his last articles cited above, Lenin spoke of overtaking other nations "with the aid of the workers' and peasants' government." But the idea of revolution from above has a deeper place in Lenin's thought. When he contended in *The State and Revolution* in 1917, and in such subsequent works as *The Proletarian Revolution and the Renegade Kautsky,* that the doctrine of proletarian dictatorship was the core idea of Marxism and that Marxism called for a seizure of power followed by dictatorial rule by violence against the internal bourgeoisie and associated social forces, he was saying: The revolution does not end with the party's taking of power; that is only a momentous point of historical transition beyond which the party continues its revolutionary destruction of the old order from above, i.e., by wielding the coercive instruments of state power against the revolution's class enemies. Leninist revolution from above meant the use of state power for the continuation of class war *after* the revolutionary party has achieved such power and formed its government under the title of "proletarian dictatorship." [33] This basic idea found its sharpest, though by no means its only, later expression in Lenin's prospectus of 1919 for a work (never completed) on the proletarian dictatorship. Two passages are especially notable: "The dictatorship of the proletariat is the *continuation* of the class struggle in *new* forms. That is the crux of the matter; that is what they do not understand." And: "The state is only a *weapon* of the proletariat in its class struggle. A special kind of cudgel *(dubinka),* rien de plus." [34] Whether Lenin ever used the phrase "from above" in arguing this notion of the proletarian dictatorship as a continuing revolutionary struggle from the vantage-point of state power is of no consequence; the idea was unmistakably present in his thought.

It is true that as early as 1919, at the height of the Civil War and War Communism, we find intimations in Lenin of the transition to the later reformist approach to the building of socialism that has been described earlier in these pages. This

---

33. For an argument by the young Stalin along these lines, see his essay of 1906, "Anarchism or Socialism?" in I. Stalin, *Sochineniia* (Moscow, 1954), I, 345–46. He cited as his authority here not Lenin but the passage in *The Communist Manifesto* about the proletariat's becoming the ruling class and using its political power to deprive the bourgeoisie of its capital step by step, etc.

34. *The Leninn Anthology,* p. 490. The prospectus was first published in 1925 in *Leninskii Sbornik III.* The "they" who "do not understand" were not identified; Lenin may have had in mind such people as Kautsky and the Russian Mensheviks.

transition was associated with the idea that the fundamental obstacle to socialism was the body of habit left over from the past and that the revolutionizing of habit—in other words, of culture—was *au fond* an educational task rather than one to be resolved by coercive means. In his article of May 1919, "A Great Beginning," Lenin hailed a workers' initiative of voluntary unpaid Saturday work (the Communist *subbotnik*) as a development of enormous historical significance, and observed in this connection that "the dictatorship of the proletariat is not only the use of force against the exploiters, and not even mainly the use of force." [35]

But it would not be proper to discount on this evidence the Lenin for whom revolution was, in his own later words, "a change which breaks the old order to its very foundations, and not one that cautiously, slowly and gradually remodels it, taking care to break as little as possible"—and for whom state power, once in the hands of the revolutionary party, should be used as a cudgel against the class enemy. When Stalin in December 1926 rhetorically asked the Comintern Executive what the building of socialism meant in class terms and answered that "building socialism in the USSR means overcoming our own Soviet bourgeoisie by our own forces in the course of a struggle," he was simply drawing upon the Lenin and Leninism of the Civil War period and earlier, the Leninism in which the fundamental question for a Marxist seeking to create socialism was *Kto-kogo?*, or who will vanquish whom in the class war? To this Leninism of *Kto-kogo,* he did subsequently add one proposition that was original with him: that the internal class struggle intensifies with the society's advance toward socialism. He was drawing upon the Leninism that had stood during 1918–21 for forcible food requisitioning from the peasant *(prodrazvërstka),* for stirring up of class war in the villages by means of the committees of the poor *(kombedy),* for the belief (to cite Lenin) that the proletarian dictatorship should mean "iron rule" and not a "jellyfish proletarian government," and for the ruthless resort to terror as an instrument of dictatorial rule. *This was Stalinist Leninism,* and the authenticity of Stalinism's claim to it is not seriously diminished by the important fact that what Leninism stood for in Lenin's own mind, as a conception of how to build socialism in Russia, underwent great modification in 1921–23.

Nor was this Stalinist Leninism Stalin's only. A considerable proportion of his generation, men who had become Bolsheviks when Bolshevism was still an anti-regime revolutionary movement and who politically came of age, as Stalin himself did, during the era of War Communism, shared his outlook to one or another degree. I am not speaking here about general ideas alone or about Leninism simply as a system of political belief, but likewise about the ingrained habits of mind, ways of defining and responding to situations, styles of action, common memories, mystique, etc., that collectively constitute the culture of a political movement insofar as a given age cohort of its membership (and leadership) is concerned. As its name indicates, War Communism had militarized the revolutionary political culture of the Bolshevik movement. The heritage of that forma-

---

35. *The Lenin Anthology,* p. 478.

tive time in the Soviet culture's history was martial zeal, revolutionary volunta-rism and *élan,* readiness to resort to coercion, rule by administrative fiat *(adminis-trirovanie),* centralized administration, summary justice, and no small dose of that Communist arrogance *(komchvanstvo)* that Lenin later inveighed against. It was not simply the "heroic period of the great Russian Revolution," as Lev Kritzman christened it in the title of the book about War Communism that he published in the mid-1920's, but above all the *fighting* period, the time when in Bolshevik minds the citadel of socialism was to be taken by storm.[36]

War Communism had given way to the NEP in 1921 as a matter of official party policy, and in the ensuing new period there emerged, again under Lenin's political and ideological leadership, something that could be called "NEP cul-ture." This NEP culture comprised a many-sided new way of Soviet life which found expression in institutions, ideas, habits of mind, and conduct. Among its elements were the restored monetary economy, the emergent system of Soviet legality, the new stress on a voluntary *smychka* between workers and peasantry, the primacy of persuasion and educative methods in the regime's approach to the people, the previously mentioned Leninist notion of gradualism and cultural revolution as the transfer culture, and a general atmosphere of relative social normalcy. But we must beware of inferring from the familiar history-book linear scheme of development from War Communism to NEP society that NEP culture *displaced* the culture of War Communism in the minds of the generation of Bolsheviks who were moving into political leadership in the later 1920's. It certainly did in some, indeed many, instances; NEP culture had its powerfully persuasive proponents not only in Lenin but also in Bukharin, Rykov, and numer-ous others, some representing the gifted party youth. But we have the weighty testimony of such men as Valentinov, Piatakov, and Stalin himself that the militant, voluntarist political culture and mystique of War Communism lived on among very many Communists. And from about 1927 on, some sensitive minds among the exponents of NEP culture became apprehensively aware of an impend-ing new social cataclysm, a second storming of the citadel as it were.[37] To this it needs to be added that Lenin himself had provided possible cues for such a response in the military imagery that he had used more than once in speaking of the NEP itself: as a forced "retreat" which would in good time be followed by a "subsequent victorious advance." [38]

---

36. For the argument that War Communism brought about a militarization of the revolutionary political culture of Bolshevism, the correlative argument that we must distinguish two Leninisms—that of War Communism and that of the NEP, and the further view that Stalin was a representative of the War Communist strain, see Robert C. Tucker, *Stalin as Revolutionary, 1879–1929: A Study in History and Personality* (New York, 1973), pp. 208–9, 395–420.

37. See *Stalin as Revolutionary,* pp. 402–3, 413, 415–16, for documentation on the survival of the War Communist spirit during the NEP. According, for example, to Valentinov, who was a resident of Moscow in the NEP years, "the party, particularly in its *lower cells,* was instinctively, subcon-sciously, antagonistic toward the NEP." As for the apprehensive awareness of the imminence of a social cataclysm, see the above-cited article by Valentinov, "Iz proshlogo."

38. For example, in "The Importance of Gold Now and After the Complete Victory of Socialism," *The Lenin Anthology,* p. 517.

In seeking to refute the "circumstantial explanation" of the initial phase of the Stalinist revolution, it is not the intent of this essay to deny historical significance to the circumstances facing the Soviet regime in 1927–29, most notably the grain-collection difficulties. The point is that these circumstances did not carry a single unmistakable definition of the situation and implicit prescription for policy. That widely different definitions of the situation and widely different policy prescriptions were possible is proved by the fierce debates and deep policy differences that emerged at the time. Our argument is that the Stalinist definition of the situation in terms of class war with the kulak forces and the Stalinist policy response in the form of "Uralo-Siberian methods" of forcible grain requisitioning and then mass collectivization represented, in part, an appeal to the Bolshevik mores of War Communism, and that this orientation proved potently persuasive largely because of the surviving strength of those mores among the Bolsheviks and not by any means only, as some have thought, because of Stalin's formidable organizational power as General Secretary. From this viewpoint, the great struggle over party policy in 1928–29 between Stalinism and Bukharinism was a fight between policies conceived in the spirit of the revolutionary culture of War Communism and the evolutionary NEP culture—and the former prevailed.

It must be added that Stalin himself should not be seen in all this as a man of organizational power only. It is true that the socialism-in-one-country concept originated with Bukharin and that Stalin on numerous occasions in the mid-1920's echoed the Bukharinist version of it, stressing NEP, for example, as the medium of the movement toward socialism and the peasant's amenability to such a movement. This has helped to foster the image of him as an improviser with hardly any policy ideas of his own at that time, or as one whose policy ideas were purely Bukharinist.[39] Against such a view, two points need to be made. First, given the exigencies of the joint Stalin-Bukharin factional battle against the Left opposition, which was pressing the need for rapid industrialization, it was politically impossible for Stalin to take issue openly with the Bukharinist policy position, or even to fail to concur in it, before the vanquishment of the Trotskyist Left at the end of 1927. Secondly, a close reading of the record shows that the Stalinist position, although not brought into the open as a policy platform before 1928, found expression sotto voce in various Stalin pronouncements of the NEP period, at the very time when he gave to many the appearance of being a Bukharinist in theory and policy.

One such pronouncement, the statement of 1926 about building socialism through "overcoming our own Soviet bouregeoisie by our own forces in the course of a struggle," has already been cited as an example of the Stalinist

---

39. Speaking of Stalin's alliance with the Bukharinists, Robert V. Daniels writes: "In matters of policy and doctrine their line was his guide; in matters of organization, his power was their support." "Stalin's Rise to Dictatorship, 1922–1939," in *Politics in the Soviet Union: Seven Cases,* ed. Alexander Dallin and Alan Westin (New York, 1966), p. 27. This statement is favorably cited by Stephen Cohen at the point where he himself writes: "There was, generally speaking, a rough division of labor between Bukharin and Stalin, between policy formulation and theory on one side and organizational muscle on the other." *Bukharin and the Bolshevik Revolution,* p. 215.

Leninism of *Kto-kogo?* Other evidence includes: Stalin's *Pravda* article of November 7, 1925, in which he defined the present period as an *analogue of the pre-October period of 1917,* i.e., the prelude to a new revolutionary storm; and a studied restatement of this theme, with added detail, in 1926. Moreover, there was a significant theoretical difference between Bukharin and Stalin in their ways of arguing the socialism-in-one-country notion. Bukharin dwelt particularly upon the content of this socialism as an "agrarian-cooperative socialism" of the kind projected in Lenin's last articles; Stalin's emphasis fell heavily on the "one country" theme in a spirit of truculent Soviet Russian nationalism reminiscent of his Russocentric "creative Marxism" (as he then called it) of August 1917, when he prophesied that Russia, not Europe, might show the world the way to socialism. A Great Russian nationalist tendency may be seen, moreover, as an ingredient of the Civil War syndrome in Soviet culture, this war having been fought not alone against the Whites but also against their foreign supporters and foreign interventionists.

The upshot is that there were *two* versions of the socialism-in-one-country position in the mid-1920's. Although the Stalinist version had to be muted then because of the aforementioned pressures of the intra-party contest, the great rapidity of its full-scale emergence immediately upon the defeat of the Trotskyist Left further attests to its presence in the wings of the Soviet political scene even during the heyday of Bukharinism.[40] This is not to deny that Stalin showed plenty of political opportunism at that time, or at others. But to treat opportunistic behavior in a politician as incompatible with deeply held beliefs is to.take a simplistic view of political man. The picture of Stalin as a leader who represented organizational power without policy ideas and who embarked upon the revolution from above in an "unpremeditated, pragmatic manner" and with "no vision of where it would lead" is a fundamental misconception.

VI

But if the surviving spirit of War Communism influenced the way in which the drives for collectivization and industrialization were conceived and carried out, it does not follow that the Stalinist revolution repeated 1917–21 or that the new Stalinist order which took shape in the 1930's was a revival of the system of War Communism. To be sure, the start of the new decade saw such reminders of the heroic period as food rationing, and other resemblances appeared. As Moshe Lewin has pointed out, however, the early Stalinist process showed many distinctive traits that differentiated it from its pre-NEP predecessor: the feverish industrial expansion, the emergence of anti-egalitarian tendencies in contrast to the egalitarianism of the Civil War period, the rise of new elites combined with the loss of the relatively independent political role of the lesser leadership ranks at the earlier time, and the political muzzling of the party rank-and-file in relation

---

40. This argument and the documentation of the evidence adduced in its support have been presented in *Stalin as Revolutionary,* Chap. 11.

to the leadership itself.[41] Still other, major differences call for mention: the *kolkhoz* system itself, which bore small resemblance to the agricultural communes initiated during the Civil War period; the use of police terror as a prime instrument of government in a manner sharply differentiated from the Red terror sponsored by Lenin via the original Cheka; and the inter-relationship between internal and external policy. *The basic underlying fact confronting us is that when the Russian revolutionary process resumed in the Stalinist stage, it had a different character from the revolutionary process of destruction of the old order and makeshift creation of the new that had marked the earlier, 1917–21 stage; and this change of character is to be understood in terms of a reversion to a revolutionary process seen earlier in Russian history.*

It has been argued here that the idea of revolution from above had a Leninist pedigree. While that is important for an interpretation of Stalinism, it must now be stressed that the phenomenon of revolution from above has a range of forms, and that the Leninist form—revolution from above as a victorious revolutionary party's violent use of the "cudgel" of state power to repress its internal class enemies—represented only one element in Stalinism as a complex and many-sided revolution from above. Where the Stalinist phenomenon went far beyond the Lenin heritage lay in its constructive aspect. Leninist revolution from above was essentially a destructive process, a tearing down of the old order from the vantage-point of state power; Stalinist revolution from above used destructive or repressive means, among others, for what was, both in intent and in reality, a constructive (as well as destructive) process. Its slogan or ideological banner was the building of a socialist society. But in substance, Stalinism as revolution from above was a state-building process, the construction of a powerful, highly centralized, bureaucratic, military-industrial Soviet Russian state. Although it was proclaimed "socialist" in the mid-1930's, it differed in various vital ways from what most socialist thinkers—Marx, Engels, and Lenin among them—had understood socialism to mean. Stalinist "socialism" was a socialism of mass poverty rather than plenty; of sharp social stratification rather than relative equality; of universal, constant fear rather than emancipation of personality; of national chauvinism rather than brotherhood of man; and of a monstrously hypertrophied state power rather than the decreasingly statified commune-state delineated by Marx in *The Civil War in France* and by Lenin in *The State and Revolution.*

It was not, however, by mere caprice or accident that this happened. Stalinist revolutionism from above had a prehistory in the political culture of Russian tsarism; it existed as a pattern in the Russian past and hence *could* be seen by a twentieth-century statesman as both a precedent and legitimation of a political course that would, in essentials, recapitulate the historical pattern.[42]

---

41. *Political Undercurrents,* pp. 98–99.

42. This argument, along with the view that Stalinism in essence was such a recapitulation of tsarist revolutionism from above, has been presented in my essay "The Image of Dual Russia," in *The Transformation of Russian Society,* ed. C. E. Black (Cambridge, Mass., 1960). The essay is reprinted in Robert C. Tucker, *The Soviet Political Mind,* 2nd ed. (New York, 1971), Chap. 6.

It was not, however, by mere caprice or accident that this happened. Stalinist revolutionism from above had a prehistory in the political culture of Russian tsarism; it existed as a pattern in the Russian past and hence *could* be seen by a twentieth-century statesman as both a precedent and legitimation of a political course that would, in essentials, recapitulate the historical pattern. Confronted in the aftermath of the two-century-long Mongol domination with hostile and in some cases more advanced neighbor-states in possession of portions of the extensive territories that had made up the loosely confederated Kievan *Rus',* the princes—later tsars—of Muscovy undertook the building of a powerful "military-national state" capable of gathering the Russian lands under its aegis. Given the primacy of the concern for external defense and expansion and the country's relative economic backwardness, the government proceeded by remodeling the social structure, at times by forcible means, in such a way that all classes of the population were bound in one or another form of compulsory service to the state. "The fact is," writes Miliukov, "that in Russia the state exerted enormous influence upon the social organization whereas in the West the social organization conditioned the state system. . . . It was the elementary state of the economic 'base' *(fundament)* which in Russia called forth the hypertrophy of the state 'superstructure' *(nadstroika)* and conditioned the powerful counter-influence of this superstructure upon the 'base' itself." [43]

A salient expression of the tsarist pattern of revolutionism from above was the legalized imposition of serfdom upon the Russian peasantry in the sixteenth and seventeenth centuries, the peasant's attachment by law to the soil, together with the system of *barshchina* (the *corvée*) under which the peasant was bound to contribute a certain number of days of work on the landowner's (or state's) land during the agricultural year. The Russian village commune, itself an archaic institution, was transformed by governmental action into a "coercive organization" for ensuring each member's fulfillment of state-imposed obligations under the principle of mutual responsibility *(krugovaia poruka).*[44] The Stalinist rural revolution from above was in essence an accelerated repetition of this tsarist developmental pattern. It has been noted above that the *kolkhoz* as it emerged from the collectivization process was a cooperative only in its formal façade. Underneath, it bore a far from superficial resemblance to the landed estate in the period of serfdom; and it is a highly significant fact that the *kolkhoz* was actually perceived by many Russian peasants as a revival of serfdom. Westerners who traveled in rural Russia in the early 1930's have reported that it was a common peasant practice to refer to "V.K.P." (the initials of *Vsesoiuznaia kommunisticheskaia partiia,* the All-Union Communist party) in the esoteric meaning of "second serfdom" *(vtoroe krepostnoe pravo).*[45] Two features of the *kolkhoz* system

---

43. P. Miliukov, *Ocherki po istorii russkoi kul'tury. Chast' pervaia. 5-e izdanie* (S. Peterburg, 1904), pp. 133–34. For Miliukov's use of the term "military-national state," see, e.g., p. 143.

44. Ibid., p. 238.

45. See, for example, Leonard E. Hubbard, *The Economics of Soviet Agriculture* (London, 1939), pp. 115–16.

gave special point to this perception. One was that the *kolkhozy* came to operate according to arrangements under which the peasant owed the *kolkhoz* an annual obligatory minimum, specified by Soviet law, of "work-day units" *(trudodni);* this was a return to *barshchina.* Second, when the internal passport system, an institution of tsarist Russia, was revived in Soviet Russia by a governmental decree of December 31, 1932, as a means of bureaucratic control over the movements of Soviet citizens, the farm population was not issued passports. The deprivation of passports attached the peasant to the soil of the *kolkhoz* or *sovkhoz* as securely as his serf ancestor had been attached to the soil of the landed estate.

The culminating phase of tsarism as a dynamic political superstructure engaged in the transformation of Russian society and development of its economic base for state-ordained purposes came in the long reign of Peter I, that "crowned revolutionary," as Herzen later called him. Now the pattern of revolution from above emerged most distinctly, one of its prominent aspects being an industrial revolution from above aimed at building a powerful Russian war-industrial base. Intensifying serfdom, Peter employed state-owned serfs along with prisoners of war and others for industrial projects as well as the construction of canals on Lakes Ladoga, Onega, and others; and on occasion moved entire townships of people to the construction sites of the new enterprises in what are described as "Peter's forced labour camps." [46]

Again, the parallel with the Stalinist industrial revolution from above is striking, the major difference being the greatly expanded scale of the use of forced labor in the Stalinist case. To what has been said above about the relation between collectivization and industrialization, something of importance here needs to be added. During the First Five-Year Plan, the slogan about "liquidation of the kulaks as a class" was used as a pretext for deportation of peasant families en masse—a process made all the more massive by the extreme looseness with which the label "kulak" was applied—to remote areas like the Urals, Siberia and the far North where they were set to work in timbering or on the construction of plants, such as the Magnitogorsk iron and steel complex in the Urals. The vast expansion of the forced-labor camp empire dates from this time. To cite Solzhenitsyn, "In 1929–1930, billowed and gushed the multimillion wave of *dispossessed kulaks. . . .* In sheer size this nonrecurring tidal wave (it was an ocean) swelled beyond the bounds of anything the penal system of even an immense state can permit itself. There was nothing to be compared with it in all Russian history. It was the forced resettlement of a whole people, an ethnic catastrophe." [47] But while in size there was nothing in Russian history to compare with it, this mass

---

46. Ibid., pp. 18–19.
47. Aleksandr I. Solzhenitsyn, *The Gulag Archipelago 1918–1956. An Experiment in Literary Investigation I–II,* trans. Thomas P. Whitney (New York, 1973), p. 54. Hubbard (*Economics of Soviet Agriculture,* p. 117) estimates that during collectivization "probably not less than five million peasants, including families, were deported to Siberia and the Far North, and of these it is estimated that 25 per cent perished." More recently, Lewin has written that "what is certain is that several million households, to a total of 10 million persons, or more, must have been deported, of whom a great many must have perished." *Russian Peasants and Soviet Power,* p. 508.

use of deportation and forced labor for industrialization had a definite historical precedent in Petrine Russia. In the Stalinist industrial revolution from above, therefore, just as in the rural revolution from above, there were elements of a revival of the tsarist pattern of revolutionism from above. In this respect, Stalinism showed the influence not simply of the historically recent Witte system of state-sponsored industrialization, but of the much earlier system of direct exploitation of servile labor in the Russian state-building process.[48]

Here a brief comment is called for on the view, sometimes encountered in Western thought, that sees the Stalinist revolution from above under the aspect of "modernization." The difficulty with this position—apart from the nebulous character of the very concept of modernization—is its obliviousness of the strong element of "archaization" in Stalinism, its resurrection of the historic tsarist pattern of building a powerful military-national state by revolutionary means involving the extension of direct coercive controls over the population and the growth of state power in the process. Unless "modernization" is reduced in meaning mainly to industrialization and increase of the urban population (in which case the term becomes superfluous), the use of it to characterize Stalinism is misleading. If a formula for the state-building process is needed, it might best be the one that Kliuchevsky provided in his summation of modern Russian history from the sixteenth to the nineteenth century: "The state swelled up; the people grew lean." [49]

The Russian historical perspective can contribute in still a further important way to our understanding of Stalinism: it helps to make intelligible the relationship between the first and second phases of the Stalinist revolution. Following the phase that took place from 1928–29 to 1933, there was a kind of pause in 1934, after which the revolution from above moved into its second phase. Signalized by the murder of the party leader Sergei Kirov in Leningrad in December 1934—an event conceived and organized from the center of power in Moscow as a pretext for what followed—the mass terror of the Great Purge enveloped the party and country in the later 1930's. The Great Purge destroyed a generation not simply of Old Bolshevik veterans of the anti-tsarist struggle but of very many of their juniors who had joined the movement after 1917 and served as active implementers of Stalinism in its first phase. It virtually transformed the composition of the Soviet regime and the managerial elite in all fields. This in turn was accompanied by still other manifestations of the revolution from above in its

48. Sergei Witte was the Russian minister of finance from 1893 until 1903. On the "Witte system" and its inspiration in Friedrich List's teaching that backward countries could overcome "the peril of remaining behind" by giving priority to the machine-building industries in industrialization, see Theodore H. Von Laue, *Sergei Witte and the Industrialization of Russia* (New York, 1973), especially pp. 58–60.

49. V. O. Kliuchevsky, *Kurs russkoi istorii* (Moscow, 1937), Vol. III, p. 11. This is a Soviet-issue of a pre-revolutionary treatise based on Professor Kliuchevsky's lectures at Moscow University. In support of the modernization hypothesis, Hélène Carrere D'Encausse pointed out during our Bellagio discussion that Stalinism promoted modernity in the following important dimension: an integrated Soviet Russian nationhood. Her argument calls for careful consideration.

second phase, such as the destruction of the Pokrovsky school of Bolshevik historiography, the concomitant re-appoprriation of major elements of the Russian past as part of the official Soviet cultural heritage, the restoration of pre-1917 patterns in art, education, law and the family. In these aspects, which extended into the 1940's, there were distinctly reactionary or counter-revolutionary overtones in the revolution from above.

It has been said, rightly in my view, that "Stalin's revolution in agriculture and industry and his assault on the party which consummated this revolution must be seen as integrated parts of one and the same process." [50] But it remains to explicate the nexus between the two phases. It does not suffice to take the position, as Schapiro does and as Deutscher did after him, that "it was primarily the need to perpetuate the Great Change in the countryside that perpetuated the terror." [51] This line of explanation is strained and in the end simply unsatisfactory, if only because—as the postwar Stalinist years in Russia showed—rule by terror can be effective without being massive. It is not a persuasive argument that terror on the scale of the Stalinist holocaust of 1934–39 was necessary either to perpetuate collectivization or to prevent Stalin from losing power. Yet, the point about the two phases being "integrated parts of one and the same process" carries conviction.

A partial explanation of this linkage can be derived from the thesis that the Stalinist revolution from above recapitulated in essentials its tsarist predecessor's pattern. The latter involved the binding (zakreposhchenie) of all classes of the population, from the lowest serf to the highest noble, in compulsory service to the state. As the Muscovite autocracy grew in power, the hereditary land-owning nobility was transformed into a serving class (sluzhilyi klass, to use Miliukov's terminology again) whose title to the land was made conditional upon the rendering of military service to the state. The Petrine revolution from above reinforced this situation by instituting an aristocracy of rank (chin) based upon the table of fourteen military and corresponding civilian ranks, under which nobility became a function of rank rather than vice versa. In one of its phases, moreover, the reduction of the boyar ruling class of Kievan and early Muscovite Russia to a serving class during the reign of Ivan IV in the sixteenth century, the chief instrument of the process was the anti-boyar terror carried out under Ivan's personal supervision by his private retinue and security police, the oprichnina. Ivan himself was the first of the Muscovite rulers to assume the title of tsar. Tsarism as a system of absolute autocracy was itself in part a product of this sixteenth-century purge, which, from evidence at our disposal, we know that Stalin consciously took as a model for emulation during the Great Purge of the

---

50. Schapiro, *The Communist Party of the Soviet Union,* p. 430.

51. Isaac Deutscher, *The Prophet Outcast,* p. 109. Schapiro's argument *(The Communist Party of the Soviet Union)* is the rather more comprehensive one that, having ruled by terror in the first phase of the revolution from above, Stalin was faced with the strong possibility of losing power if the terror came to an end, hence chose terror as the means of his remaining in command. To explain the colossal scope of the terror in the second phase, Schapiro refers only to a personal characteristic—Stalin's "thoroughness."

1930's; he had come to view Ivan Grozny and not alone Peter the Great as a Russian statesman of socialist formation. With very few exceptions, the independent-minded Old Bolsheviks were cast as his boyars.

The pertinence of this to the problem of the nexus between the two phases is clear. The Great Purge was at once the crucible of the restoration of an absolute autocracy in Russia—under Stalin now—and concomitantly a continuation of the process of formation of Stalin's neo-tsarist version of the compulsory-service state, an entity that may properly be called "totalitarian." The first phase of the revolution from above had seen the binding of the peasantry and working class in servitude to the ever swelling, every more centralized, ever more bureaucratized, ever more police-dominated Stalinist state; and this new *zakreposhchenie* grew still tighter in later years. The second phase brought the party itself and the intelligentsia in that greatly expanded Soviet sense of the term (which embraces managers, officials, specialists, technicians, and professionals of all sorts) into line with the rest of society. They too became a serving class whose status as such was made tangible and visible with the introduction in the later 1930's and 1940's of a Stalinist table of ranks that bore a distinct resemblance—as did the uniforms and insignia—to the corresponding tsarist set-up. Completing the process ideologically, the Stalinist order developed its own ideology of Soviet Russian statism, which was epitomized by Stalin's courtier, Georgi Malenkov, when he said to a party conference in 1941: "We are all servants of the state." Stalin had given the cue two years before, when, at the Eighteenth Party Congress, he corrected Engels' (and by implication Marx's) mistaken idea that socialism meant the withering away of the state.

To what extent was the Stalinist revolution "from below" as well as from above? Not until the social history of the period is written will this question be fully answerable. Undoubtedly, we should avoid two untenable, extreme positions: that taken in the above-cited passage in Stalin's *Short Course,* that the revolution from above was "directly supported from below by the millions . . . ," and the opposite view that the process had no support from below. But given the still fragmentary state of our knowledge, differences of opinion and emphasis are inevitable when we move beyond this obvious starting-point. Perhaps it would be useful, as a setting for analysis and discussion, to observe two distinctions. First, the distinction between the two phases (1929–33 and 1934–39). Second, the distinction between two different possible meanings of "below": persons in low-level roles in the regime or closely associated with it, notably the membership of the Communist Party and the Komsomol; and the population at large. Using Soviet terminology, we may call them respectively the *aktiv* and the *narod.* Although numerically substantial, the former was no more than a relatively small minority of the latter.

The *aktiv,* or large elements of it, including contingents of Soviet youth, was a vitally important instrumentality of the regime in the first phase of the Stalinist revolution. Many participated in the collectivization and industrialization drives not only actively but enthusiastically and self-sacrificingly. But it is not clear whether any considerable portion of the *narod* gave the regime its voluntary support during this phase. As in the time of War Communism, the regime attempted to foment class war in the countryside by making the poor peasants *(bedniaki)* its allies in mass collectivization. To what extent this policy was a success is not entirely plain, as there is evidence, including documentary evidence from the Smolensk party archives, that mass collectivization was not only opposed by the well-off and middle peasants in their great majority, but unpopular as well among no few of the *bedniaki*.[52] Even a *bedniak* could grasp what "V.K.P." meant and not like it. As for worker participation in collectivization, we have the case of the twenty-five thousand industrial workers who were enrolled by the party to go into the villages as collectivizers. But evidence also exists that at least some portion of the "twenty-five-thousanders" joined this movement under pressure of dire family need combined with material incentives to assist in the collectivizing.

In the second phase, the social picture changed significantly. While the *narod* remained basically passive—indeed more passive than in the early 1930's—large elements of the first-phase *aktiv* exchanged the role of implementers of the revolution for that of its victims. Very many of these people died or went to camps during the Great Purge. To a far greater extent than the first phase, the second was a police operation, and the supreme collective victim was the Communist Party itself as constituted in the early 1930's. By this very token, however, a great many who did not actively participate in the second phase, whether they belonged to the *aktiv* or the *narod,* nevertheless became its beneficiaries. For the decimation of the pre-1934 regime, party, and intelligentsia in the Great Purge opened career opportunities on a vast scale to those from below who showed ability combined with the acquiescent, state-oriented, and Stalin-centered attitudes that were hallmarks of the *chinovnik* under full Stalinism. This influx was largely an influx of the peasant-born or of those who had been children of peasants. Citing Boris Pilniak's statement of 1922 that "the dark waters of muzhik Russia have swept and swallowed the Petrine empire," Nicholas Vakar has argued that the Stalinist revolution, by filling the Soviet hierarchy with persons of peasant stock and infusing age-old peasant mores values into the Soviet way, marked the complete *peasantization* of the Russian Revolution.[53]

VII

This essay has advanced a culturalist interpretation of the Russian revolutionary process as one that took place in two main stages with an interval of quiescence

---

52. For collectivization as reflected in the archive, see Merle Fainsod, *Smolensk Under Soviet Rule* (New York, 1958), Chap. 12. In *Russian Peasants and Soviet Power* (p. 488), Lewin implies a more active, positive participation of the village poor: "In order to understand this process of wholesale dekulakization, it is also essential to bear in mind the misery in which millions of bednyaks lived. All too often they went hungry; they had neither shoes nor shirts, nor any other 'luxury items.' The tension which had built up in the countryside, and the eagerness to dispossess the kulaks, were in large measure contributed to by the wretchedness of the bednyaks' conditions, and the hatred which they were capable of feeling on occasion for their more fortunate neighbours, who exploited them pitilessly whenever they had the chance to do so."

53. Nicholas Vakar, *The Taproot of Soviet Society* (New York, 1961). The statement by Pilniak, cited by Vakar on p. 16, comes from his novel *Goly god.*

during the NEP. The first stage, it was held, produced a situation characterized by the uneasy co-existence of two cultures, a new Soviet culture growing out of the Revolution and a still-surviving old Russian culture with its stronghold in the village. The Soviet culture itself underwent considerable change during the NEP. The second, or Stalinist, stage of the Revolution yielded, as has been indicated, an amalgamated Stalinist Soviet culture that paradoxically involved at once the full-scale sovietization of Russian society *and* the Russification of the Soviet culture. The Soviet Union was re-Russified in the very revolutionary process that purported to complete Russia's sovietizing, or to transform NEP Russia into a socialist society. In keeping with the tsarist tradition, this Stalinist Soviet Russian culture bore a pronounced official *(kazënnyi)* character. Not surprisingly, one consequence was the rebirth in Stalin's time of an unofficial, underground body of thought, feeling, and art which was heretical with reference to the Stalinist culture and which, again not surprisingly in view of Russian tradition, emerged among the educated youth and intelligentsia; this was the rebirth of the "dual Russia" phenomenon as seen in the first half of the nineteenth century. In the post-Stalin era, the underground Russia has come into semi-public view via *samizdat* and the like. So now again, in a way which is both new and old, there are two cultures in Russia.

In addition to interpreting the Stalinist revolution in culturalist terms, this essay has attempted to explain it so. The circumstantial explanation of the revolution from above was rejected in favor of one which stressed, first of all, the way in which the circumstances of 1927–28 were perceived and defined by a political leadership many of whose members, including Stalin, had come of age politically in the era of the October Revolution and War Communism and responded to those circumstances in the revolutionary spirit of the earlier time rather than in the evolutionary spirit of NEP Soviet culture. Further, the form taken by the Stalinist revolution, the relation between its two major phases, and the nature of the new Stalinist order that it created have been treated as a recapitulation in essentials of the pattern of revolutionism from above that belonged to the political culture of old Russia and was visible in the tsarist state-building process from the fifteenth to the eighteenth centuries and the sociopolitical order it produced.

But the question inevitably arises, why did history recapitulate itself so in this instance? Cultural patterns out of a nation's past do not repeat themselves in the present simply because they were there. Nor can we explain the phenomenon by reference to like circumstances, such as NEP Russia's relative international isolation and economic backwardness, for we have argued that circumstances do not carry their own self-evident meaning, that what people and political leaders *act upon* is always the circumstances *as perceived and defined by them,* which in turn is influenced by culture. But also, we must now add, by personality. And so we come at the end to what was mentioned at the start as a third important explanatory factor underlying the revolution from above—the mind and personality of Stalin.

To a certain extent the personal factor is covered by the culturalist explanation itself. In general, there is no conflict between culturalist explanations and those that make reference to the special historical role of a leader-personality. As cultural anthropologists have pointed out, "culture" and "personality" are, to a considerable degree, two ways of viewing one and the same phenomenon, culture being something which has its being mainly *within* people.[54] In terms more immediately pertinent to our argument, a leader-personality becomes politically acculturated through his life-experience both in early years and during manhood. Thus, 1917 and the Civil War were a formative acculturating life-experience for Stalin and many others of his party generation, leaving a deep residue of the revolutionary political culture of War Communism within them. On this level of explanation, Stalin's historical role in the late 1920's was to make himself, as effectively as he did, the leader and spokesman of an outlook that he shared with numerous others in the party leadership and not alone the men of his own faction.

The recapitulation of the tsarist pattern of revolutionism from above presents a more difficult problem of explanation in culturalist *or* personality terms, if only because Russian tsarism, in all its manifestations, was what the Bolshevik revolutionary movement had taken originally as its mortal sociopolitical enemy. However, the Russian nationalist feeling aroused in a section of the party during the Civil War years, the revolution-born spirit of "Red Russian patriotism" against which a party delegate from the Ukraine protested at the Tenth Party Congress in 1921, was an element in the culture that *could* predispose a Bolshevik to perceive certain patterns out of the heritage of old Russia as relevant to the circumstances of the present. On the other hand, it did not do so in the generality of instances of which we know. It is true that Bukharin grasped the direction of Stalin's policy thinking in 1928, with special reference to forced collectivization, and alluded to its tsarist inspiration by terming it "military-feudal exploitation of the peasantry." But the party resolution of April 23, 1929, against the Bukharinist group stigmatized Bukharin's charge as "a libelous attack . . . drawn from the party of Miliukov." [55] This was hardly an admission that Stalin's neo-tsarist Marxism (the use of such a phrase may sound monstrous to Marxists, but the Marxist *Weltanschauung* is capable of many metamorphoses) had found favor with a substantial body of party opinion. Hence, in this problem the explanatory emphasis must fall more on "personality" than on "culture."

To put it otherwise, acculturation is not to be viewed simply as a process in which an individual is affected by formative life-experiences and thereby internalizes culture patterns, including patterns out of the past, as dictated by his psychological needs or predispositions. Stalin, the commissar for nationality affairs and as such the presumable protector of the rights of the minority nations in the Soviet federation, was in fact, as Lenin discovered to his horror shortly before dying, one of those Bolsheviks most infected by "Russian Red patriotism." Lenin showed his realization of this in the notes on the nationality question which he

---

54. See, for example, Wallace, *Culture and Personality*, Introduction; and Ralph Linton, *The Cultural Background of Personality* (New York, 1945), Chaps. 4–5.

55. *Kommunisticheskaia partiia sovetskogo soiuza v rezoliutsiakh i resheniakh s"ezdov, konferentsii i plenumov TsK* (Moscow, 1954), Vol. II, p. 555.

dictated on December 30–31, 1922 and in which he characterized Stalin as foremost among those Russified minority representatives in the party who tended to err on the side of "true-Russianism" *(istinno-russkie nastroeniia)* and "Great Russian chauvinism." Unbeknown to Lenin, Stalin's sense of Russian nationality, if not his true-Russianism, had dated from his youthful conversion to Lenin's leadership and to Bolshevism, which he saw as the "Russian faction" in the Empire's Marxist Party, Menshevism being the "Jewish faction." It was on this foundation that Stalin, during the 1920's, went forward in his thinking and appropriative self-acculturation, as the generality of his Russian-nationalist-oriented party comrades did not, to envisage the tsarist state-building process as a model for the Soviet Russian state in its "building of socialism." [56] And it was the great personal power that he acquired by 1929, with the ouster of the oppositions from the party leadership, that made it possible for him to proceed to carry out his design.

If the thesis concerning the recapitulation of the state-building process places heavy emphasis upon personality even in the context of a culturalist approach, a final explanatory consideration concerning the Stalinist phenomenon narrows the focus onto personality to a still greater degree. Unlike any other Bolshevik, to my knowledge, Stalin, as we have noted, defined the Soviet situation in 1925 and 1926 in eve-of-October terms, implicitly presaging thereby a revolutionary assault against the existing order, i.e., the NEP, in the drive to build socialism. Then, looking back in the *Short Course* of 1938 on the accomplishments of the Stalinist decade, he described them, and collectivization in particular, as equivalent in consequence to the October Revolution of 1917. Underlying both the definition of the situation in the mid-1920's and the retrospective satisfaction expressed in the late 1930's was Stalin's compulsive psychological need, born of neurosis, to prove himself a revolutionary hero of Lenin-like proportions, to match or surpass what all Bolsheviks considered Lenin's supreme historical exploit, the leadership of the party in the world-historic revolutionary success of October 1917. The great revolutionary drive to change Russia in the early 1930's was intended as Stalin's October.

In practice it achieved certain successes, notably in industrialization, but at a cost of such havoc and misery in Russia that Stalin, as the regime's supreme leader, aroused condemnation among many. This helps to explain, in psychological terms, the lethal vindictiveness that he visited upon millions of his party comrades, fellow countrymen, and others in the ensuing years. It was his way of trying to come to terms with the repressed fact that he, Djugashvili, had failed to prove himself the charismatically Lenin-like Stalin that it was his lifelong goal to be. If this interpretation is well founded, he was hardly the most impersonal of great historical figures.

---

56. The demonstration and documentation of this thesis is one of the aims of my work in progress, *Stalin and the Revolution from Above, 1929–1939: A Study in History and Personality.* In *Stalin as Revolutionary, 1879–1929,* I have sought to demonstrate the thesis concerning Stalin's Great Russian nationalism and its youthful origins.

VIII

Having sketched here a primarily culturalist interpretation of Stalinism as revolution from above, based on the Soviet 1930's, it remains to conclude with a comment on the historical sequel. I wish to indicate in particular the relevance of the analysis to the Stalinist phenomenon in its subsequent development. We may distinguish two subsequent periods: that of the Soviet-German conflict of 1941–45 and that of postwar Stalinism (1946–53). In this sequence, 1945 forms a sort of historical pause or hiatus, rather as 1934 did between the two phases of the revolution from above of the 1930's.

The Second World War was, in a way, an interim in Stalinism's development. Not that the "Great Fatherland War," as it was called in Stalin's Russia, had no serious impact on Stalinist Soviet Communism as a sociopolitical culture, but that mainly it reinforced tendencies already present before the war began. Thus, the war gave a powerful further impetus to the Great Russian nationalism which had become evident in Stalin's personal political makeup by the beginning of the 1920's and a prominent motif in Stalinist thought and politics in the 1930's. The official glorification of national Russian military heroes of the pre-Soviet past, notably Generals Suvorov and Kutuzov and Admiral Nakhimov, and the opening of special Soviet officers' training academies named after them, were among the many manifestations of this trend.[57] Too, the war intensified the militarist strain in Stalinism, which has here been traced back to the time of War Communism. It strengthened and further developed the hierarchical structure of Stalinist Soviet society as reconstituted during the revolution from above of the 1930's, and augmented the already far-reaching Stalinist hypertrophy of the state machine. There were also covert trends at that time toward the official anti-Semitism which became blatant in the postwar Stalinist campaign against "rootless cosmopolitans," the murder of large numbers of Soviet Jewish intellectuals, and the infamous "doctors' affair" of Stalin's last months in 1953.[58]

In the postwar period after 1945, we see a situation which appears to conflict with a revolutionary interpretation of the Stalinist phenomenon. The dominant note in Soviet internal policy during those years was conservatism, the reconsolidating of the Stalinist order that had taken shape in the 1930's.[59] An example of such conservatism was the early post-war action of Stalin's regime in cutting

---

57. On Stalinism and Russian nationalism after 1939, see in particular the informative account by F. Barghoorn, "Stalinism and the Russian Cultural Heritage," *Review of Politics,* Vol. 14, No. 2 (April, 1952), pp. 178–203; and his *Soviet Russian Nationalism* (New York, 1956).

58. In "New Biographies of Stalin," *Soviet Jewish Affairs,,* Vol. 5, No. 2 (1975), p. 104, Jack Miller has called attention to "Stalin's covert use of antisemitism against Trotsky, Kamenev and Zinoviev, when in coalition with Bukharin he was routing them in 1926–27," and adds: "The extent to which antisemitism appeared in the Party machine during this phase of Stalin's rise to supreme power is of special interest in the 'russifying' of Marxism."

59. In "The Stalin Heritage in Soviet Policy" (*The Soviet Political Mind,* Chap. 4), I have argued that Stalin turned conservative in his post-war internal policies.

back the private garden plots which—for purposes of both war-time morale and the nation's food supply—the collectivized Soviet peasants had been allowed surreptitiously to increase in size during the war years. True, this was a "conservative" action in the special sense of reinstating what had been a revolutionary change at the time of collectivization fifteen years before.

But Stalinism as revolutionism from above did not end with the completion of the state-directed revolutionary processes of the 1930's and the coming of the Second World War. It reappeared in 1939–40 and again in the late war and post-war Stalin years in a new form: the externalization of Stalinist revolution from above. The years 1939–40 are singled out in this connection because they witnessed the Soviet takeover of eastern Poland and the three Baltic countries during the time of Soviet-Nazi collaboration under the Stalin-Hitler pact of August 1939. Under an organized sham pretense of popular demand, the eastern Polish territories were incorporated into the Ukrainian and Belorussian Soviet republics; and Lithuania, Latvia, and Estonia became constituent ("union") republics of the USSR. Meanwhile, under cover of the Red Army occupation of these lands, the Soviet party, police, and economic authorities proceeded with the forcible transplantation to them of Soviet political culture in its Stalinized form, complete with deportation of all suspect elements of the population into the Russian interior. The revolutionary transformations from above, interrupted by the German invasion of Russia in June 1941, were resumed and completed upon the Soviet reoccupation, later in the war, of what had been eastern Poland and the independent Baltic states.

Then the Stalinist revolution from above was carried into the Balkans and much of East-Central Europe in the wake of the Soviet Army's occupation of Bulgaria, Rumania, Hungary, the rest of Poland, and the eastern parts of Germany. Czechoslovakia likewise succumbed to it following the Communist coup of February 1948. Yugoslavia, where a Communist movement had come to power independently through successful partisan warfare during the German occupation, quietly but effectively checked the subsequent efforts of Stalin's emissaries to direct the Yugoslav transformation from above in such a way as to ensure firm Soviet control of the Yugoslav Communist political system; and as a result Yugoslavia was excommunicated by Stalin later in 1948.[60]

In its war-time and post-war externalized form, the Stalinist revolution from above comprised both the takeover (or attempted takeover) of a given country, normally via military occupation, and then the use of a Soviet-directed native Communist party and its subsidiary organizations as agents of the country's transformation into what was called at first a "people's democracy." The establishment and consolidation of Muscovite control over the organs of power in the country concerned was, as indicated above, an essential element of the process. There were variations in the methods and timetables, but in essence the East European revolution, insofar as it took place under Soviet auspices in a number of smaller countries, involved the transfer to foreign lands of much of what had

---

60. The classic account remains Vladimir Dedijer, *Tito* (New York, 1953).

taken place in Russia in the 1930's. The same may be said of the postwar revolutionary transformation in North Korea, which had been occupied by the Soviet Army at the war's end. China, a potential great power in its own right, presented for that very reason a special problem for Stalin—and for Stalinism. Insofar as the Stalinist revolution from above had been aimed at transforming Soviet Russia into a great military-industrial power capable of fully defending its independence and interests in the world, Stalinism was not likely to appeal to the very Russian-nationalist–minded Stalin as a proper prescription for Communism in China, save to the extent that Russia could place and keep China under its control. Very likely it was these considerations, together with the shrewd realization of the impossibility of long-range success in keeping a Communist China under Russian control, which explain Stalin's ambivalence toward— not to say distaste for—the coming of the Chinese Communists to power. By the same token, we can see in all this a key to the attraction that certain aspects of Stalinism, not including its Russian nationalism, had for Mao.

Finally, despite what has been said above about the generally conservative nature of Stalin's post-war internal policy, it may be suggested that in some paradoxical sense Stalinism as revolution from above returned to Russia during 1946–53 within the setting of the conservative internal policies then being pursued. For Stalin's very effort to turn the Soviet clock back to the 1930's after the war carried with it a shadowy rerun of the developments of that earlier decade. In other words, the post-war reaction was a reaction *to* a period of radical change—from above. In his major postwar policy address of February 9, 1946, Stalin placed a series of further five-year plans on Russia's agenda as a guarantee against "all contingencies," i.e., to prepare the country for a possible future war. This meant the re-enactment of the pre-war policy of giving priority to heavy industry over consumer goods, with all the privation that entailed for the Soviet population. A minor recollectivizing campaign was put through following the above-mentioned early postwar decision to cut back the size of the peasants' private garden plots. Furthermore, in the dictator's final period there were increasingly clear indications that he was preparing, if on a lesser scale, a sort of replica of the Great Purge of the 1930's. There would be show trials of the Soviet Jewish doctors, accused of complicity in an imaginary international Anglo-American-Jewish conspiracy to shorten the lives of Soviet leaders; and no doubt other show trials as well. These would provide the dramatic symbolism needed as an accompaniment and justification of the purge, just as the show trials of the Old Bolsheviks of Left and Right did in the earlier version of the revolution from above.[61]

---

61. An interpretation of the show trial as an element of Stalinist political culture has been presented by the present writer in "Stalin, Bukharin, and History as Conspiracy," first published as the Introduction to *The Great Purge Trial,* edited by Robert C. Tucker and Stephen F. Cohen (New York, 1965), and reprinted in *The Soviet Political Mind* as Chapter 3. The transplantation of the Stalinist show trial to post-war Eastern Europe, Czechoslovakia in particular, is discussed by H. Gordon Skilling in his essay below, and also in *Czechoslovakia's Interrupted Revolution* (Princeton, N.J., 1976), Chap. XIII.

Before the first of the new trials could begin, however, the dictator suddenly fell ill and died. So providential was the timing of this death for very many whose lives were threatened by the oncoming new Stalinist blood purge, including men in highest places, that it has aroused a persistent suspicion that Stalin's passing was hastened in one way or another.

However that may have been, Stalin in his macabre way remained to the end a revolutionary, albeit from above. Of few if any of those whom he chose as his associates and executors, and who survived him in power, could the same be said. This helps to explain why, in Russia at any rate, Stalinism after Stalin was going to differ very significantly from the Stalinism of his time. Without its key progenitor alive and in charge of events, Stalinism lost its very Russified revolutionary soul. Then and there it became what it has remained ever since: extreme Communist conservatism of strong Russian-nationalist tendency.

Part Two

DIMENSIONS OF
STALINISM IN RUSSIA

The Social Background
of Stalinism

Moshe Lewin

I

Prerequisites

The examination of social factors that were crucial in shaping or favouring the Stalinist phenomenon can safely begin from a study of the situation in which Bolshevism found itself at the end of the Civil War and the self-perception, or rather the ideological (theoretical, if one prefers) terms in which the leadership analyzed the situation at this point.

The minds trained to think in Marxist terms about social development and policies were accustomed to a framework which provided some safe departing points and certainties. Socialism, even if its appearance demanded conscious effort and a revolution, could nonetheless be perceived in some essential contours in the womb of the developed capitalist system—the more developed the latter, the more precise the former. Even for somebody like Lenin, who clearly liked the quote from Napoleon, "On s'engage et puis on voit," and often acted upon this maxim, voluntarism and idealism were nevertheless built on a sense of historical process that gave the indispensable backing to conscious intervention, and ensured that the revolution was not just a leap into the unknown but was to some extent a continuation of previous trends.

Russia, by general consent, was a backward country. If before the revolution the quick development of industry encouraged some impatient socialists to exaggerate the growing readiness of Russia for a socialist takeover, there could be no illusions about any such "readiness" by the end of the Civil War. The country was devastated, its not too numerous higher and middle classes destroyed or dispersed, its working class depleted or *déclassé*, and its peasantry seething with unrest. At this moment there were no social forces, no discernible trends in Russian reality which could clearly be counted upon to generate an internal dynamic in the socialist direction—except the pure political will of the leadership. The state machinery, as far as the basic mass of its *chinovniki* (top officials, or rather "bureaucrats") was concerned, seemed unreliable; the quickly changing party membership was often raw, soon to some extent purely adaptive in its motivations to join rather than ideologically motivated, and was not fully reliable either; it

111

had to be re-educated and indoctrinated first, as the original ideals of the Bolsheviks were not originally and naturally shared by the newcomers who became soon the overwhelming majority.

The post–Civil War Marxist found himself thus on the entirely unfamiliar ground where there was no visible backing "of a process" for the party's long-term ideological aims. On the contrary, the party found itself in a rarefied atmosphere of unpredictability and contingency, generated by chaotic, socially hostile petty bourgeois tides.

Lenin, in a number of pronouncements, showed that he was perfectly aware of the isolation of the Bolsheviks in the country they had conquered. The working class had almost vanished; the ex-tsarist officials who populated the offices were alien; the peasants were deeply dissatisfied and did not want to hear about *kommuniia;* the party membership needed purging; the top layers and the whole old guard were exhausted and weakened by corrosive factors of wear and tear.[1]

This self-perception among the leaders of "isolation," of the lack of an appropriate social basis, was crucial. With it went an acutely neurotic fear of dangers for the movement, of its being either swept aside or, more perniciously, losing its identity. In fact, in a situation in which the commitment to their basic ideals was not shared by the masses and was confined to a relatively small layer, this layer found itself under inexorable pressures, causing not only physical wear and tear to individuals, but also hesitation and ideological dilution, and thus increasing their vulnerability to dangers inherent in the transformation of dedicated revolutionaries into rulers. They had always known that they might be in power one day—but they had not anticipated that this would occur in social isolation. They hoped and were accustomed to see themselves as leaders, not rulers.

As we shall see, there could be different ways of overcoming, or of interpreting, this essential fact—different leaders would offer different remedies to the basic diagnosis—but one important explanatory factor is worth mentioning here: the sociological dissertations about the class essence and potential of the peasantry, taken *in abstracto,* were probably as true for Russia as they were, e.g., for China. Nevertheless, when Mao took over in 1949, he was certainly not pestered by a sense of isolation from the masses. He took over with the overwhelming support of the peasant multitudes amidst whom he and his party had operated successfully for some decades. When Lenin took over, not in 1917, that is, but after the Civil War, the country, and especially the bulk of the peasantry, were against him.

One of the important factors behind such an outcome, which was rarely analyzed or admitted by the Bolsheviks, was that they never constituted a real political mass movement, and particularly not in the countryside. They were, in fact, and as a matter of strategic preference, an organization of committees, of leaders, professional revolutionary cadres. Although this form was a source of

---

1. Material on the physical and mental stress which caused an accelerated wear and tear of the old Bolshevik cadres is found in, among others, S. G. Strumilin, *Rabochii byt v tsifrakh* (Moscow and Leningrad, 1926), pp. 61–62.

strength and a factor of success in gaining power, it was at the same time a factor of isolation after power was gained and the Civil War won. This does not mean that there was a lack of support from important social forces, including many peasants, during the Civil War. The leadership exhibited great skill in gaining such support, isolating some sections, neutralizing or convincing others. But this was support for tactical moves and on the basis of tactical reasons—not a result of identification with the basic, long-term aims and the ideological framework, as would be the case in a genuine mass movement. The party did gain a membership of millions—but this happened much later, after it was already safely entrenched in power, when the circumstances and reasons for joining were very different. And even then the party would still remain weak in the countryside, and would continue to suffer from this basic deficiency: its quasi-inexistence in and lack of experience of the rural world.

The "Superstructure"... in the Air

Lenin diagnosed the situation, not unexpectedly, in terms of relations between the "basis" and the "superstructure." The baffling thing for the revolutionary leaders was that they found themselves in the reverse position to that of Marx in regard to Hegel. Where Marx had put Hegel's dialectics on its feet, Lenin found himself—but without any reasons for self-congratulation—putting Marx on his head: his "superstructure" came before the "basis." The former was supposedly socialist, but suspended temporarily in a kind of vacuum, and the problem consisted not, as it was hoped, in adapting the recalcitrant "superstructure" to the basis, but in first creating and then lifting up the basis to the lofty heights of the most advanced political superstructure.[2]

As long as hopes persisted that the revolution would spread to the West the problem could be disregarded. But now, in the hungry and anguished years 1920–21, it had to be faced.

The elements of a solution were suggested by circumstances rather than by theoretical anticipation. First, the Civil War brought with it a fully fledged practice and ideology of "statism," which was undoubtedly entirely new to Leninism. Direct and wide-ranging state intervention, mass coercion, a centralized administrative machine as the main lever of action, an enthusiastic apology for statization *(ogosudarstvlenie)*—all were well-known aspects of "war communism" (the other was extreme egalitarianism). Trotsky's statization policy in regard to the trade unions was one example of it. Osinsky's "sowing committees" *(posevkomy),* which became party policy in 1920, grew out of a less known but widespread and characteristic attitude. Direct state intervention was recommended and justified by different party authorities not on grounds of emergency, but as a socialist principle *par excellence.* According to numerous documents from the archives, state takeover, detailed planning, etc., were seen as ways of displacing the capitalist market (and not just speculation), and *ogosudarstvlenie*

---

2. A good example of such reasoning is in Lenin, "O nashei revoliutsii," in *Polnoe sobranie sochinenii,* Vol. 45 (Moscow, 1964), pp. 378–89.

was prescribed as the best measure for overcoming the acquisitive nature *(sob-stvennichestvo)* and capitalist impulses of the peasantry.[3] Thus it was not a social class any more—not the proletariat—that served as the epitome and bearer of socialism through the state, but—imperceptibly, for some ideologists—the state itself was now replacing the class and becoming the epitome and carrier of the higher principle with, or without, the help of the proletariat.

There was here, in embryo, an entirely new orientation and ideology. It certainly was not present in what "Leninism" was before. Although the desirable social backing might be missing, especially because of the whittling away of the working class, the party did not and could not operate in a void: having begun to rely ever more on the state, ever less on the unreliable masses, the state apparatus, whatever the social composition of its officialdom, was gradually taking over the function of principal lever for the achievement of the desired aims.

In such a way, Bolshevism acquired a social basis it did not want and did not immediately recognize: the bureaucracy. This was becoming, quite early in the process, a key factor in shaping the whole system, but it needed some evolution and dramatic internal fighting for this fact to sink in, to become fully acceptable and later extolled. The whole turn of events was, in any case, misunderstood by the Bolsheviks, who were not adequately prepared to comprehend the state they themselves were building. The available theory was very inadequate on this score. It was becoming important to study not only the social potential of the proletariat, or the peasantry, but the potential, interests, and aspirations of the growing and changing Soviet state machinery. It is doubtful, however, whether such an analysis is available in the Soviet Union even today. The idea of "lifting up" the basis to the superstructure fostered not entirely unjustified hopes that this would "normalize" the situation, but missed the point that the state system which presided over the building of the basis could influence deeply the very character of this basis and thus of the whole system. In terms of the metaphorical thinking which pervaded this type of analysis, it might have looked ridiculous that the roof should shape the foundations, and not vice versa. But there was nothing ridiculous in such a supposition. It was, on the contrary, very realistic—as events would prove.

Why the Scale Was Tilted

The statism of the Civil War period had to be abandoned and was soon repudiated as an ideology of extreme administrative and coercive policies conceived as the main lever of social change. The New Economic Policy (NEP) was thus to be introduced on the basis of the negation of what was at the very heart of the previous stage, and it produced a remarkable set of compromises, between plan and market, political monopoly and social and cultural diversity, state and society, ideology and expedient. Once it was set in motion, the new policy soon

---

3. Interesting new material from archives about the *Posevkomy* and the concomitant statist ideology for running the rural economy can be found in Iu. A. Poliakov, *Perekhod k Nepu i sovetskoe krest'ianstvo* (Moscow 1967), pp. 213–30.

turned into an interesting experience and a model, and began to beget appropriate ideologies.[The attitude towards the NEP as a "transition strategy" or "transition period" of a long-term character spread among many of the Bolshevik leaders, who came to believe that they had finally discovered the most appropriate way to overcome the isolation from the masses and to strike deeper roots in the social milieu. The key idea here now became "organic change," reformism, gradualism. War Communism collapsed, it was argued, because it believed stages could be skipped. But the fallacy begot disaster and couldn't but be coercive. Moving more slowly, Lenin's new strategy proclaimed, would mean delaying ambitious aims, slowing down the restructuring, but gaining in social support and avoiding overall statism, with its unpalatable implications.

The alternation in actual historical development of two models—War Communism and NEP—suggested that two main alternatives were available to the party. The NEP variety, as its main spokesman, Bukharin, expressed it, was based on a revision of a set of assumptions inherent in the isolationist syndrome and challenging it.[4] The peasantry was for him more amenable to cooperation with the party than the more alarmist versions supposed; the peasantry, as reinterpreted by him, ceased to be seen as an automatic begetter of capitalism, and the party therefore could be seen as stronger and socially less vulnerable than the isolationist would suggest. There was therefore no need to hurry with imposing on this society the movement's long-term aims.

As this approach was discarded and replaced, finally, by a revised version of the Civil War model, some concluded that things were in any case predetermined and alternatives were not in fact available. The seeds of the new stage and the new extreme model have been seen by some scholars either in Leninism itself, or in the incompatibility of socialist aims with the backward Russian environment, or else as an inevitable outcome in harmony with Russian historical destinies. All these assumptions can be disputed. The factors operating in Lenin's period which are sometimes presented as simple prerequisites and seeds of a further Stalinist stage, (i.e., just much more of the same) could also be interpreted rather as prerequisites for one or another variety of an authoritarian, oligarchic system, of which Lenin's regime itself was already one example. Under him, the strategy was to maintain a strong state but not to engage in "statism." It was a strategy that kept the powder dry but looked seriously for a maximum of social support, not only for the purpose of staying in power but also for the purposes of peaceful transformation and development. The leadership wanted police, but did not engage in building a police state; they felt themselves isolated but did not transform this feeling into "isolationism," etc. Still more traits of the political version of Lenin's days can be listed that warrant viewing it as a species of its own, still open to changes in several directions. Had this not been the case, NEP would not have been possible at all, nor Lenin's conversion to it, nor its wholehearted adoption by quite a squad (though not all) of party leaders. Thus "Lenin-

---

4. On two basic models and their alternation see M. Lewin, *Political Undercurrents in Soviet Economic Debates* (Princeton, N.J., 1974), Chaps. 4 and 5.

ism" had, as it were, even in the harsh Russian conditions, several "potentials." [5]
Why was the NEP, or any modifications thereof, discarded? The answer does
not necessarily lie in its unfeasibility. Nor is it as all obvious that the stamping
out of social autonomies of any kind, refusal to compromise with social groups,
total cultural controls, and other delights of the next version of statism, as well
as the glorification of the state, or the nationalist-isolationist bent of its ideology,
were the only alternative; the idea that the outcome was a result of a set of
circumstantial interactions of different factors is equally plausible. If it could be
argued that Russia was too backward to move up quickly without massive terror
and all that followed, the same premise makes it difficult to dismiss Bukharin's
thinking as unrealistic. How unrealistic was it to assume that Russia was not
ready for socialist objectives there and then, and needed cautious transitional
strategies?

There is sometimes a tendency to mistake the very availability of an alternative
(or alternatives) in the NEP situation with the political conditions or power
relations inside the decision-making structure. These were characterized, broadly
speaking, by a constant narrowing of the apex where the decisions were taken,
making the party dependent on the vagaries of kitchen political maneuvering,
uncontrollable even by the higher- and middle-rank echelons, and hence vulnerable to a significant element of chance in the outcome of political struggles.
Moreover, during the pre-Stalinist period, two important trends inside the party
contributed to such a "narrowing." The first was the disruption (leading to
suppression) of whatever political play there was in the party's upper layers, as
a result of which the ruling group lost its unity, its capacity for action, and its
ability to counteract moves detrimental to its own freedom. As the leaders eliminated each other by denying each other the right to opposition or other institutionalized forms for argument, they ensnared themselves in an ever narrowing
political circle. The second was a parallel phenomenon—the appearance and
development of the party apparatus—which worked in the same direction. It
became ever less important, as it still was in the earlier stages, to win over the
party in order to conduct a policy, and ever more important to win over the
machinery. As the twenties unfolded and this trend asserted itself, the question
of why one group won is not very complex in itself: one has to study the existing
competing perceptions of the situation and the unfolding of events whereby one
group eliminates the other and imposes its own blueprint. But there seems no
need at this state to resort to factors of predetermination, though they can be
useful at some other stages.

The later events in Eastern Europe help clarify this proposition. There was no
internal reason, e.g., in Poland, to stop the "nepien" policies. They could have
continued but were interrupted by the imposition of re-Stalinization by external
intervention. The switch to a fully fledged Stalinist model rather than the continuation of a more relaxed experimentation, resulted from this intervention of

---

5. Stephen Cohen proposed a similar point in his *Bukharin and the Bolshevik Revolution: A Political
Biography, 1888–1938* (New York, 1973), pp. xvi–xvii, 3–5.

a powerful external factor which also ensured the feasibility of the imposed model. NEPien Russia was a relatively underdeveloped country in which an outstanding part was played by a strongly centralized state. It was open to the continuation of the existing model or to the imposition of something different. There was enough in the historical environment, tradition, and social relations to sustain different roads. There is no need to be astonished that a police state could develop in Russia and undertake revolutions from above—this was not a very new thing. But neither is it difficult to imagine a continuation of a NEP situation. In fact, NEP was already there and was quite in line with the character of the country. But, as we have said, the political machinery fell into hands that saw the grain crisis as a bad omen for the model—and it played the same role in regard to the Russian social structure in those years, as it played twenty years later, acting as an external force, in Poland and Czechoslovakia.

II

The "Superstructure" Rushing Ahead

In the social context, already inherited from NEP and characterized first, as we have said, by a relatively modern state facing a basically rural, hence "local" social structure, and, second, by a party as the ruling lynchpin inside the state, with its own machinery ready to be taken over by a resolute small group—the stage was set, we argue, for tilting the scales and engaging the whole country in a very new direction. The initial moves were almost as easy as the act of tilting would be; but soon, in the absence of any countervailing factors, the process turned out to be both irreversible and extremely costly. Haste, the tendency to telescope stages of development and condense them, was both the result of the sense of power of the rulers at the apex of the unchallenged machinery, and the cause of a specific "disjointed" pattern of development, with the state rushing ahead, presiding over and preceding social and economic development. The whole process thus became, above all, one of hectic state-building and expansion of the state administration.

Engels, in a letter from London to C. Schmidt, written on the second of October 1890, had already argued persuasively that the state enjoyed a high degree of autonomy from social and economic factors, and in deploying its potential it might do one of three things: favor development, block it, or engage indecisively in either.[6] In the Soviet case, at its Stalinist stage, the state in many ways did alternately all three; but it also did much more than Engels anticipated. In terms of the ideological metaphor state action was expected to lift the "basis" to the level of the "superstructure," after which the former would impose its influence on the latter. In fact the reverse occurred: the state engaged in a hectic, hasty, and compulsive shaping of the social structure, forcing its groups and classes into

---

6. The letter is in K. Marx and F. Engels, *Polnoe sobranie sochinenii,* Vol. 37, 2nd ed. (Moscow, 1965). The relevant passage is on page 417.

a mold where the administrative-and-coercive machinery retained its superiority and autonomy. Instead of "serving" its basis, the state, using the powerful means at its disposal (central planning, modern communications and controlling mechanisms, monopoly of information, freedom to use coercion at will), was able to press the social body into service under its own *diktat.*

Two phenomena, both resulting from the powerful push of the industrialization drive in its first stages, particularly favored such an outcome. One was the general state of flux into which Russia was propelled by the "big drive"; the other phenomenon, related to the first, was a gigantic turnover of positions, a peculiar social mobility which collectivization and industrialization created. In another text I have used the terms "quicksand society" and "musical chairs" to describe these two processes. In a matter of a few years only the bulk of the population changed their social positions and roles, switched into a new class, a new job, or a new way of doing the same (workers went to offices, peasants became workers or officials, many of them found themselves in schools and universities, millions of peasants suddenly experienced the shocks of the *kolkhoz* system), and everyone was faced in their new environment with unexpected, harsh realities. For a while, before the dust settled, the whole nation became as if *déclassé,* some *déclassé* down, some *déclassé . . .* up.

The state organization that faced the flux, and was itself quite strained and contaminated by it, engaged in strenuous efforts to master the chaos by different devices; to strengthen the administrative and controlling machineries, with a particular stress on the "organs"—the synonym for security police—seemed the obvious way out of chaos.[7]

This was, then, one aspect of the situation which pushed the state into displaying its particular dynamism and inherent tendencies, and encouraged it to go all the way through to a full blossoming of a new model. But yet another aspect had to be mentioned. The coercive acceleration and stage-skipping, by imposing large-scale, supposedly progressive, forms on an unprepared nation of small-scale producers, without allowing for the very concept of "maturing," brought about a state of social warfare against almost the whole nation, but especially against the peasants. This momentous development contributed to the renewal among the leaders of the old sense of isolation from the social base and the tendency and need to lean ever more strongly on the apparently safest social support: the state bureaucracy. In a later, more morbid, evidently pathological stage, if not the rulers, certainly *the* ruler would feel the support narrowed down even further to the only really "secure" part of the machinery: the security services. . . .

The Ruling Serfs

It was already mentioned that the Civil War, the ravages it caused, in particular the weakening of the urban middle classes, constituted a setback from the point

---

7. M. Lewin, "Class, State and Ideology in the Piatiletkas," to be published under the editorship of Sheila Fitzpatrick, in proceedings of a conference held in Columbia University in November 1974 on "The Cultural Revolution in Russia, 1928–33."

of view of social development and a painful gap to fill out. This can be seen from the acute sense of dependence on those bearers of the previous bourgeois culture (and system) whom Lenin tried hard to enlist in the service of the new system. The managerial and professional classes, however depleted and often hostile, were indispensable, and, indeed, turned out to be crucial in building the new state. The acute sense of dependence on those factors is epitomized by the objective of having "our own" intelligentsia, "our own" cadres, etc. The anti-nepien development in the big drive, although characterized by a hectic—one would say furious —activity of raising its cadres, curiously began with a drive against those very forces Lenin thought were indispensable, thus accentuating further, for a time, the loss of some of the vehicles of development inherited from the capitalist period. As the wholesale étatization now on the agenda unfolded, and no expert group or social agents—even when considered "allies"—were allowed any autonomy, the developmental drive had to be organized, supervised, and carried out by the only social force available for the task—the party and state administration. The social composition, values, and aspirations of the bureaucracy would therefore unavoidably, sooner or later, exercise a deep influence on the character of the system. But for the time being the bureaucratic machineries were still quite a new, quickly growing, heterogeneous body. Their social components have been little studied as yet, and only a tentative sketch can be attempted here.

The lower ladders of the now swelling administrations, in the economic, political, and other spheres, were swamped by newcomers from the popular classes, badly prepared for their new positions, in fact for the most part poorly educated, if not semi-literate. Such people, finding themselves in positions which however menial were endowed nevertheless with some kind of power over others, very quickly learned to make the most out of it, not always necessarily in palatable ways. "Petty bourgeois mentality," to use the language of official disapproval, soon permeated the officialdom, and all too often combined greed with incompetence. To visualize the problem, one should only imagine what happens when, say, a service as sensitive as criminal investigation is composed of people who not only have no juridical preparation, but cannot even write properly. But such was the situation in the pre-war period, and the same was going on all over the administrative spectrum, probably also in the middle ranks, not just the lowest; and it is not forbidden to speculate on the social and spiritual climate which such a milieu generated. *Obyvatel'shchina* (best translated as "Philistinism"), another term of official disapproval, became a widespread phenomenon, even among the top brass in the sensitive sectors.[8] Furthermore, the atmosphere of terror, of constant and ever more bloody purges, and the general climate of witch-hunt and search for enemies all over the place couldn't be propitious for a serious job of

---

8. M. Strogovich gives data on the unbelievably low literacy, if not outright illiteracy, of the criminal investigators in *Za sotsialisticheskuiu zakonnost'*, Vol. 7 (1934), p. 21. Vyshinsky's bitter complaint against both the low educational and professional level as well as the spirit of philistinism *(obyvatel'shchina)* among the investigators and the procurators is in the same review, Vol. 7 (1936), pp. 74–76.

re-education and the raising of standards. Improvements would occur in the long run, but in the short run—and so much in Stalinism depended on events and trends triggered off in the short initial period of industrialization—it is possible to suggest that the mass of culturally low-key lower officialdom was certainly a proper milieu—or even a social basis, to some extent—for the flourishing of the "personality cult" and other irrational trends in those years. The party official Rusanov, a product of precisely such a social background as well as of the *apparat* depicted by Solzhenitsyn in his *Cancer Ward,* is an evocative figure and can serve as an illustration of our proposition.

Not less momentous and interesting a factor were the upper layers of the different *apparaty,* now being constituted into a powerful class of bosses *(nachal'stvo)* endowed with power, privileges, and status, but suffering also from considerable handicaps. In the situation of flux in the thirties, such a stratum was an essential scaffolding for running the system and for its stabilization. The top policy-makers were ready to pay them a price, including a system of covert privileges, special supplies, and power over the fate of men, but it was characteristic specifically of Stalin's policy that, although elevated and apparently pampered, they were submitted to a regime of insecurity, controls, and, finally, terror, undertaken against them from above, which allowed them neither security of personal position nor crystallization into a self-confident and competent ruling class. Once more, in a pattern not unfamiliar in Russian history, a ruling layer was created by the state, trained, indoctrinated, and paid by it—exactly as the early tsars, some centuries earlier, created the gentry *(dvorianstvo)* and enserfed the peasantry for them as a prize for their service to the state. The parallel here is not complete, but similarities remain. In a situation of absolutist rule, the dependence of the servants of the state on the arbitrary rule from above finds its indispensable counterpart in the absolutist and arbitrary rule of officials over people below them, or people *tout court.*

Under Stalin, to sum up this point, the network of bosses *(nachalstvo),* allowed and asked to be authoritarian and rude towards subordinates and the masses in order to discipline them, acquired a dual character, or a Janus-like double face: the one looking down, of a despot; the other looking up, of a serf. One is therefore tempted to ask what would be the ethos, values, mentality, interests of such a bureaucracy, and such a *nachalstvo?* Wouldn't it support, at least for a time, its own version of "autocracy, nationality, and orthodoxy"? In any case, what actually happened was something amazingly similar to just this. We will have to return to this point later.

The Muzhik and His Religion

The peasantry, still the bulk of the nation in 1929, and the relations between them and the state—or rather, the violent clash and prolonged hostilities between the two—played a key role in the shaping of the Stalinist phase of the Soviet system, its outlook, and its ideology.

The rural milieu in Russia during the course of Russian history, and still so during the NEP, had all the traits of a distinct social system, set quite apart from the rest of society. The NEP and its policies probably gave to many peasants a sense of social promotion as millions of them became *khoziaeva,* i.e., independent, respected, and self-respecting producers in their communities, even if many if not most of them were still very poor. But this only strengthened for a time the specific traits of the rural world as a system on its own, with deeply inbuilt mechanisms for self-perpetuation and a high degree of conservatism. The essence of this system consisted of: a) the family farm as basic socioeconomic unit; b) the small scale of the farm's operations; c) village life as the basic environment, with its still viable, more or less developed, communal institutions.

Such basic traits were further strengthened by a widely shared culture, mostly pre-literate in character, with a popular religion as its basic spiritual common denominator, even if local differences in beliefs, folklore, ceremonies, and superstitions presented infinite, often picturesque, varieties over the huge territory. Though the peasants' *Weltanschauung* comprised, of course, many perfectly lay assumptions and assertions concerning the reality of rural life or its relations to other classes, it is safe to say that the hard core of their moral outlook and life philosophy were best expressed by the widely shared religious beliefs. Peasant religion, according notably to Pierre Pascal, from whose ideas I borrow liberally in this section,[9] couldn't but be very different from the apparently identical denomination common to city dwellers. Traditionally, in fact, the rural world dissented from official versions of orthodoxy, even if the state approved of them. In fact, it was precisely state approval that encouraged such dissent.

Some of the specifics of the popular religious beliefs are of consequence for the events we are studying. The peasantry, mostly illiterate, were little interested in dogma, and were not at all "clerical," which meant that they were relatively little dependent on the clergy and even on churches. Well in tune with the basic pattern of family centered life in villages scattered on an immense territory, their religion was a homestead cult. The priest had to come to the homestead *(dvor)* to perform different rituals, and even without him simple liturgy could be performed by the head of the family, about the house or before the icon inside it. In fact, as Pascal says, "The icon plays an immense role," [10] as well as the cult of images of saints, relics, processions and pilgrimages.

The ethical world of the peasantry, as expressed in their religion, was influenced by their communal life, which produced social values that emphasized pity and humility, rejected imposed dogmas, and, in particular, tended to reject any hierarchy, clerical or secular—hence any bureaucracy. Traditionally the popular masses in Russia were excluded from participation in government, and even when certain formal rights were granted, peasants remained beyond the pale of politics, retaining a non-political but nevertheless suspicious, even hostile, attitude towards state officialdom and state coercion. From this point of view, among others, the peasant was particularly "anarchistic." It is worth pondering over Pascal's interesting statement, "One shouldn't forget that the revolution in

---

9. Pierre Pascal, *La Religion du Peuple Russe* (Lausanne, 1973).
10. Ibid., p. 23.

1917 was, for those soldiers and peasants who made it, a movement of christian indignation against the state." [11] There certainly is more than a grain of truth in it. Lenin's *State and Revolution,* in which he expressed the hope, in the most anarchistic vein, that the state would wither away as soon as the power was safely lodged in proletarian hands (and this statement was flanked by the acceptance of the peasant's aspiration to his own piece of land), would probably appeal to the sense of social justice and the spontaneous anti-statism felt by the rural masses. The trouble was, as we are well aware, that from the very first steps, especially as the civil war unfolded, the victorious revolutionaries themselves engaged in state-building, with plenty of officialdom, coercion, and all the other trappings of statehood. The NEP interlude contained a promise of some compromise—but with Stalin's drive from above this state-building took a particularly dynamic turn. It was accomplished precisely in a clash, or warfare against the peasants and this particular anti-*muzhik* slant of Stalin's policies deeply influenced—or rather, vitiated—the character of the state. In more than one way it contributed significantly, as will be shown, to the peculiarly "Byzantine" spiritual climate of the Stalinist autocracy.

For the state and its ideologists, the recalcitrance of the peasants to join the *kolkhozy* overnight and go socialist at one stroke was, basically, an expression of their petty-bourgeois essence, with its lust for property, supposedly intrinsic indiscipline and incapacity for cooperation in large-scale organizations, trading mentality, and inherent potential for recreating capitalism.

Such assumptions were based on an analysis which was, to say the least, quite imperfect. Its more important role was to provide an ideology to justify the coercive methods against the "socially alien" essence of the peasantry, or any other social class which did not conform to party policies. Bolsheviks were an urban party par excellence, ignorant of rural realities and showing little patience with this mass, so backward and conservative. Had they understood the peasants better, they might have discovered—as some amidst them came, in fact, to believe, and as other peasant-based revolutionary movements later proved—that, ignorance and conservatism notwithstanding, peasants are not automatically bearers of capitalism and can be interested in participating in important cooperative social experiments and change.

But as things stood in Russia, with the state poised to impose a new way of life and production and the peasant ocean trying to stick to its familiar mode, the clash that occurred was one between what were almost two nations or two civilizations, profoundly different in modes of production and modalities of organization, in *Weltanschauungen,* and in religion (the one stubbornly religious, the other as stubbornly anti-religious).

The installing of *kolkhozy* was supposed to lift the peasantry into a higher, more progressive way of production and life, and this would help close the gap and smooth the basic differences between town and country. The results of the whole operation were quite different.

---

11. Ibid., p. 48.

Kolkhozy: *The Peasants "On Ration Cards"* [12]

The *kolkhozy,* a supposedly higher form of production and social organization, brought to the peasant, first of all, the thing he dreaded most: a wholesale bureaucratization, or, more precisely, an étatization painfully perceived by the peasant as a setback and a fall in status, from the position of an independent master in his home *(khoziain)* to the one of an unwilling servant of state interests. The whole power of the dictatorship was displayed—less than that wouldn't do—to teach the peasants the severe lesson that his first "commandment" should be the delivery of huge amounts of his produce to the state—without adequate remuneration. At the same time, the distrust of the state towards the new "higher" form was such that the main production means were taken away from the *kolkhozy* and entrusted to special state organizations. Detailed instructions and plans from above, perpetual interference by numerous agencies, the dominance of administrations—all contributed to this peculiar socialism without the peasant, a deeply anti-*muzhik* system transforming the whole peasantry into a legally and factually discriminated class, the lowest on the social ladder—the place they traditionally occupied in Russia. Feeling gagged, exploited, and cheated, peasants responded with an age-old weapon: "The lords' abuse of force no longer had any counterweight except the amazing capacity for inertia of the rural masses—often to be sure very effective—and the disorder of the lords' own administration." This statement of the great historian Marc Bloch [13] was intended for the medieval manor, but it fits marvellously our twentieth-century situation. The peasants' passive resistance exacerbated the relation and incensed the leadership even more—and they responded with ever more of the same: controls, pressures, and terror. Quarter was not going to be given in this fight for the strategic good—grain. But stagnation, to say the least, of agricularal production was to be a heavy price for the whole operation. Peasants developed subterfuges of different types, looked for ways of making the best out of their tiny private plot, and shirked, if they could, in the social sector of the *kolkhoz.* After all, the plot did provide a predictable minimum of food for the family, whereas the work in the *kolkhoz,* unlike the worker's salary, was a residual, a non-guaranteed quantity, and hence not too much of an incentive.

The étatization without a guaranteed income, a higher form without higher yields or standards of living, a collective system which could not feed the peasantry without their tiny private plots—all these were results of the imposition of theoretically advanced forms on people who were not ready for them. The huge agricultural sector, with its *kolkhozy, sovkhozy,* and machine-and-tractor stations (MTS), with its numerous but unreliable peasantry, became a heavy liability for the system, a shaky segment within its foundations, socially unstable and

---

12. In Russian, *na paike,* "submitted to rationing." There was an outcry among the peasants against such a prospect, a real mass lament—and this is well documented. We can therefore safely take it as the most genuine expression of peasant feelings.

13. Marc Bloch, *La Société Féodale* (Paris, 1968), p. 347

economically indolent. The function of the state, to squeeze without being able to encourage growth, led to the creation of an array of repressive administrative machinery poised against the bulk of Russia's society. As post-Stalinist writings would show, the system's rural policies were a source of misery, as well as a fertile soil not so much for good crops as for perpetuating the harshest and most self-defeating traits of decaying Stalinism.[14]

This was why, as we just stated, instead of the promised incorporation into the system in an organic way, the peasants found themselves in a position of discrimination and social inferiority: they continued to exist as a separate class and civilization, nursing, as ever, their distaste for officials and for the state, their feelings being amply reciprocated.

No wonder, for the time being, the so-called collectivization broadened instead of bridging the gulf between the traditional "two nations," the official one comprising the rulers and some of the uneducated, and the other composed mainly of peasants.

The peasant, nevertheless, would defend his country in times of great national danger, as he always did, even when he was a serf, unless he was beaten by a superior enemy or badly served by his own indolent rulers. But Stalin was probably not too sure about this loyalty. According to the state's pet theories, it should not have been expected.

The Tsar, the Emperor, the Marshal

The discussion of the peasantry's role offers the appropriate moment to ponder over another significant phenomenon in Stalinism: the return of the modernizing Soviet state under Stalin to the models and trappings of earlier tsardom. The popularity of the tsar-builders, impetuous and despotic industrializers and state promoters: the growing rehabilitation of traditions from the imperial past; the epaulettes of generals and marshals; Stalin's own bemedaled chest and lofty titles during and after the war; the re-costuming of the state bureaucracy, notably the juridical and the foreign services, into a uniformed officialdom complete with titles almost directly borrowed from the "table of ranks" [15]—all these are well-known events. But the more striking is the deeper affinity and sincerity implied in the changeover of historical antecedents from Stepan Razin and Pugatchev, to Ivan the Terrible and Peter the Great, respectively the first tsar and the first emperor.

---

14. The writings of numerous novelists interested in the Russian peasantry, such as Ovechkin, Iashin, Abramov, Stadniuk, Dorosh, and others, paint a picture of desolation and bureaucratic oppression which Soviet social scientists have not yet been able to match.

15. *Vedomosti verkhovnogo Soveta SSSR,* Vol. 39 (1943) carries the decree of September 16, 1943, introducing the following ranks *(chiny)* for the juridical profession: *deistvitel'nyi gosudarstvennyi sovetnik iustitsii,* equivalent to an army general; next, *gosudarstvennyi sovetnik iustitsii,* first-, second-, third-class equivalent, respectively, of the military ranks of colonel-general, lieutenant-general, major-general, etc., etc. His Marxist Excellency Vyshinsky became therefore *deistvitel'nyi gosudartsvennyi sovetnik iustitsii* and thus eligible to be Gogol's hero in *Revizor.*

This spiritual conversion was rooted in a set of striking parallels in the social setting and political situation created in the early thirties.

The first phenomenon already referred to, the gulf between rulers and the basic mass of the ruled, including not only peasants but many of the educated, took on in Stalin's days the form of a forced collectivization and persecution of many of the educated, and recreated for a time a situation already known as "classic" in Russian history. The traits of "Dual Russia" and its interpretations have been succinctly and cogently shown in an article by R. C. Tucker: [16] its traditional "state-society" dichotomy and the seesaw of "revolutions from above," interspersed with recurrent "thaws," were reproduced in Stalin's times with enhanced sharpness. But the parallel goes further: Peter the Great was engaged not only in an effort of modernization but in a more complex set of social and political strategies. He was creating *"de toutes pièces"* [17] a ruling class, preferably composed of foreigners who could be more trusted because of their detachment from local society and dependence on the benefactor; he was building a regular bureaucracy and a modernised governmental machinery; and at the same time he made the dependent status of the peasantry and the regime in which they lived harsher than ever. In very different circumstances and with notable differences in many aspects, Stalin was engaged in a similar project: industrializing forcefully and impetuously, speedily building and expanding a fully bureaucratic rule, producing his *nachalstvo "de toutes pièces"* (though not necessarily from foreign nationals, rather from the lower classes themselves)—and at the same time changing the status of the peasantry into a new, harsher regime of dependence upon the state and its officials.

The taming of the peasantry, which was thought of as the citadel of backwardness and unruliness, a menace to the state, was thus a repetition of an old theme, duplicated also, and characteristically, in several other planes: the figure of an absolutist ruler, the police state, the dependence of the ruling elite on a capricious rule from above, the no less capricious and deeply resented rule below, the upper layers yielding meekly to the autocrat, the masses to the petty bureaucrat. The reproduction in a new garb of this latter feature—the dominance of local potentates—had a particularly old smell to it.

The building of a mighty state facing a weak society, successfully étatized and controlled, is also a remake of an old feature, but on a larger scale. The state was here once more engaged in making and unmaking ruling groups, making them into an appendage to itself, imposing forms of social and economic activity, deeply influencing class relations, running the whole of the economy, transforming rulers and ruled alike into cogs of the state. The state thereby reproduced patterns of the past, although, characteristically, not of the near but rather of the earlier, eighteenth-century, versions. Tsardom, after all, began to mellow down from the mid-nineteenth century on; it engaged, however halfheartedly,

---

16. Robert C. Tucker, "The Image of Dual Russia," in *The Soviet Political Mind,* rev. ed. (New York, 1971), pp. 121–42.

17. See Pascal, p. 10.

in important social and juridical reforms; some groups and classes—entrepreneurs, workers, peasants, intellectuals—emerged and began to evolve autonomous, often anti-tsarist, attitudes and activities. The political structure proved inadequate to reform itself so as to make room for such development and for the further emancipation of social forces, and this is why it was finally rejected, with the hope that more room for social initiative and greater freedoms would be achieved.

The Stalinist development brought about a different outcome: as the country was surging ahead in economic and military terms, it was moving backwards, compared to the later period in tsarism and even the NEP, in terms of social and political freedoms. This was not only a specific and blatant case of development without emancipation; it was, in fact, a retreat into a tighter-than-ever harnessing of society to the state bureaucracy, which became the main social vehicle of the state's policies and ethos. Hence the tendency to borrow so much from the earlier, more despotic antecedents, which were so resolutely rejected and repudiated by the new regime in its earlier, more youthful age.

"The Contamination Effect . . . "

Three factors seem to be crucial in favoring the phenomenon of Stalinism, with its personal rule, extreme dogmatism with strong pseudo-religious undertones, and renewed nationalism—a remodeled "autocracy, nationality, orthodoxy" *(samoderzhavie, narodnost', pravoslavie)* version: (1) the unhinging of the social structures and the flux created by the industrialization effort and its methods; (2) the characteristics of the growing, though as yet far from stabilized and not fully self-conscious, bureaucracy; (3) the historical-cultural traditions of the country, in particular those represented by the peasantry. All three factors, in conditions of a strenuous and hasty industrial development, favored a development in the same direction: a reliance on the might of the state, ending up with idolatory of the state—a particularly important trait in the system. The widespread sense of insecurity throughout the *apparaty,* including the top layers, prompted many of them to hang onto and support the alleged symbols of security and stability in the system—the general secretary and his "cult." Finally, different layers in the leadership, either as deliberate strategy or as a result of a genuine urge to bridge the gap with the masses and to strengthen the system's links with them, encouraged adoption, diffusion, and concessions to nationalist and other spiritual traditions of the urban, but especially of the rural, masses.

Incidentally, the peculiar factor of haste should be underlined and its influence explored. Its role in shaping events in the sphere of economic planning and management has been studied by economists. It is worth venturing, quite tentatively, on the basis of the Soviet experience, the following maxim: The quicker you break and change, the more of the old you recreate. Institutions and methods which seemed to be entirely new, after deeper insight show the often quite astonishing re-emergence of many old traits and forms. This does not apply only to the obvious example of the army, but certainly to many or most ministries and other institutions; probably also (why not?) to the secret police. The *sancta sanctorum* of security, inaccessible by definition to unproletarian elements, certainly employed, as the army did, some (if not many) of the specialists of the tsarist police. And they couldn't but help restore many of the features of the predecessor in the making and functioning of institutions. In any case, whatever the value of this kind of hunch, it is no hunch but hard fact that the more the Stalinist system rushed ahead with its economic development and socialist transformations the deeper it sank into the quite traditional values of authority, hierarchy, and conservatism.

The spiritual climate, one would expect, must also have been influenced by the basic social fact of those years: the remolding of a rural environment or reshaping of recently ruralized cities. The whole system, society and state, rulers and ruled alike, couldn't but become deeply transformed—each often in quite unexpected ways—during this prolonged clash of initially opposed principles and forces operating in such a social milieu. In the process of remolding and combating the "pretty-bourgeois mentality and spirit" and the religious mind of the masses, a "principle of contamination" (a mock law but with some real content behind it) began to operate and display its astonishing results. In the effort to eradicate the peasant mentality, its religion in particular, the not too successful educators or crusaders often reached the obvious conclusion that ceremonies, festivities, and other deeply seated traditional family and village mores should be combated by proposing the same but in a lay form. Actually, the failure of the anti-religious campaign was to some extent a result of a lack of understanding of this so often berated mentality. The attack on churches and clergy, for example, was a wrong choice of target: the popular religion was homestead-based and could easily accommodate itself to the absence of clergymen and liturgy.

But the proposed tactic, which was to offer lay icons instead of the religious ones, turned out to be a double-edged sword. In the course of the supposedly Marxist crusade against the "opiate of the people," the whole spiritual climate of the system showed signs of succumbing to some of the age-old currents of the Russian Orthodox civilization, absorbing some of its not necessarily most inspiring values. The traditional devotion to and worship of icons, relics of saints, and processions was apparently being replaced by a shallow lay imitation of icon-like imagery, official mass liturgy, effigies, and, especially, processions and pilgrimages to a mausoleum sheltering an embalmed atheist.

One telling example of extolling some of the more primitive trends of rural society when state interests seemed to have warranted it, and offering it as a value for the whole nation, is the policy in regard to the family undertaken in the later 1930's. This policy deserves a deeper study, but for our purpose here one point is worth mentioning: it was clearly the large, archaic rural family, with its high demands on the reproductive faculties of women, authoritarian structure, and apparently solid moral stability, that was presented as a model. It is enough to read *Pravda* of 1936, during the campaign for family, fertility, and authority, to discover where the "model" was taken from. The "crusaders" themselves got trapped in some of the least modern, most orthodox and nationalistic elements of their tradition, now put to use as ingredients of a renewed worship of the state and of its interests. Somebody might have tried eventually to rationalize these currents as a premeditated strategy indispensable in a country whose people need to worship. Prostrating themselves in awe and adoration before the splendors and trappings of statehood and its head, as it used to be under the old tsardom, might have looked like a display of a good knowledge of mass psychology. In any case, from the idea of emancipating the masses from the mental structures inherited from an unglorious past, the system moved into a stage of recreating replicas, if not better versions of the same. The cult of Stalin couldn't help begetting demons, agents and saboteurs, sinful criminals, abject and pitiful apostates eager to desecrate all that was sacred. The features of the Russian soul, supposedly balanced between the extremes of downfall and absolute repentance, descent into deepest sin and relief of the fullest confession, were fully catered for in Stalin's "ritual of liquidation."

That many people in Russia took the bait and responded to these outpourings of demonology is beyond doubt. But was this development really a result of Russian mystical-Orthodox leanings or of popular religious beliefs and a *muzhik* mentality? Or was it, as previously suggested, a response to what was *believed* to constitute popular irrational needs? The distortion and misrepresentation by city spokesmen of the popular needs of peasants, the camouflage of one's own idiosyncracies as a response to somebody else's needs, are not uncommon in civilizations where the gulf between the popular masses and the political and educated establishment is deep, especially in times of stress and crisis. It is therefore worth considering also the thesis that the cultural trends of the Stalinist era were not necessarily responses to what the peasants wanted to get, but rather an expression of the psychic and mental tensions and values of the officials and leaders of a state machinery that was rapidly growing within and in conflict with a still age-old rural civilization. There is no way of explaining what was clearly a deep cultural retreat and the demeaning of culture, to say the least, in terms of some direct influence of the peasantry. But the indirect influence of the rural milieu on the peculiar backward way of moving forward, fraught with tensions and distortions inside the ruling *apparaty* engaged in shaping this milieu, is worth exploring. In other words, then, one is tempted to ask whether Stalin projected his personality over the nation because of politico-strategic considerations, on the basis of his understanding of Russian mentalities, or whether this was an expression of his own psychic drives and needs.

Considering the many traits of his system which went as soon as he disappeared, the latter assumption is the more tempting one, in the last analysis.

"The Personal Equation"

"Where the legal tradition is weak, the personality of the ruler becomes of crucial importance," maintained a knowledgeable scholar. One could add: Where the legal tradition is weak and when whatever there is of it is shattered, propitious conditions are created for the very appearance of such a ruler. Obviously, more than the personal factor should be introduced to understand Stalin and his "ism." The broad social background has already been sketched and should be kept in mind when considering a narrower but crucial factor: the processes working inside the ruling party, shaping or unsettling it. Two phenomena are crucial on this score. First, the change of "social substance," in other words, the continuous changes in the social composition in the party, from a bare twenty thousand in March 1917 to the quarter of a million or more at the end of the same year, getting halved and then once more doubled around 1919 alone, with the curve sharply fluctuating till the first million or more at the end of 1928 was reached. At this point there was a pause for a while, but the process then went on unabatedly. This implies a speedy turnover and influx of entrants, and the initial group of founders couldn't but get immersed in large layers of newcomers, constantly pushed by other newcomers from the depths of Russian society. The newcomers entered a party which was not engaged anymore in fighting tsarism, as the founders were. They did not share the values and motivation, the culture and sophistication of the old guard. Now, facing the country and the new party layers, this old guard, as a group of leading politicians, were unable to unite and to create for themselves conditions indispensable for a stable ruling elite. The failure of the old Bolsheviks to constitute such an elite or oligarchy proved the cause of their demise. As they faltered, the party succumbed to the machinery which emerged and took over—and to those who knew how to build and run such machinery. With one important addition: those at the top of the party *apparat* also had under their control the police and the manipulation of ideology and information.

The stage was thus set for a takeover, on a winner-take-all principle. Today, an enlightened party critic would ask sadly: How did it happen that there were no guaranteed or countervailing powers against such a takeover? The fact remains that the pre-1928 history of the party consisted of a set of moves which kept knocking out those countervailing devices that still existed. The last such step was taken by those leaders who preferred Stalin and helped him extinguish the last opposition. They themselves then succumbed to the same mechanism they had used against others. But this story is quite well known by now.

Stalin was the man who took what levers of power the previous period offered (he himself had been instrumental in forging some of them earlier), tilted the scale in a new direction, reworked the whole ideological and political framework, and launched the system not only into speedy industrialization but also, unabashedly, into state-building of a particular kind: the state as the main tool and as an aim in itself, the highest principle, in fact, of his socialism. He also did more. In the framework of his statism he openly espoused overall terror and even identified himself personally with the police state of his making. He was, in brief, a system founder and its ideologist, and did the job of adapting the previous ideological framework to the reality of this new system. But this reality was complex—and so was Stalin's role in it.

Some historians of tsarist Russia point out that in the course of its development the despotic rulers tended to change their roles and the character of their powers, and adapt them to the system they were presiding over, without changing the formal image of the tsar as autocrat *(samoderzhets)*.

Ivan the Terrible and Peter the Great belonged to those who managed to get rid of pretending social groups, and build new subservient elites and machineries instead. Thus Ivan battered the boyars and founded his Oprichnina; thus Peter, too, built "from scratch" a new ruling stratum and a governmental machinery. Founders and modernizers of this kind remain at the top and can preserve the notion of "autocracy" and the reality of it. But a process sets in whereby the machinery and the ruling strata assert themselves, stabilize, and finally change, in substance if not in law, the reality of the "autocracy" itself. Nicholas I was probably the last real autocrat. The later tsars gradually became heads of this bureaucracy, as their despotic power and their freedom of action was reduced and their dependence on the bureaucracy grew. This change from autocrat to top bureaucrat never worked itself out fully, and the tsars still enjoyed enormous power. But the trend was there. Something similar was also happening under Stalin. Under the tsars, however, the trend took two centuries to make itself felt; under Stalin, when historical processes were immensely intensified and compressed, this occurred in one leader's own lifetime.

Unsettled and shaky as the state machinery still was in its speedy growth during the 1930's, pressure for "settling down," for a regularization of their positions and working conditions, and a say in government, began to reassert themselves. Such pressures, emerging from the ruling stratum of the state and the party, certainly began to be perceived by Stalin. We stated that the former found themselves in a situation of powerful serfs. One has only to recollect the description of the atmosphere in the leadership around Stalin, as presented by Khrushchev in his memoirs, to see that here was a textbook case of relations bound to exist between a despotic and powerful ruler, in full control of the job and fate of each of his hand-picked helpers, and even the narrow circle of potentates around him, who are denied the security of their lives, not to say their jobs. A ruling class without tenure—this was the system Stalin created for them, and it was far from palatable. No able man among them could have believed that this was somehow "historically" or otherwise justified.

Quite early, therefore, trends and pressures should have emerged to "normalize" the situation. This did not necessarily mean a desire in the machinery to get rid of Stalin—though many certainly would have welcomed it—but to change his functions so that the whole model could be ruled in accordance with its "logic," i.e., the interests of the bureaucracy and its top layers in particular. This was, in fact, to be achieved—but only after Stalin's death.

Stalin was not ready to accept the role of just a cog, however powerful, in his own machine. A top bureaucrat is a chief executive, in the framework of a constraining committee. The system, in my view, was getting ready for it quite early (the Kirov tendency in 1934 eventually expressed precisely this), and those observers who after Stalin's death were predicting that by the very character of the system a new Stalin must emerge were missing the point. But Stalin had had the power, and the taste for it—for ever more of it—since he had led the early stage of the shattering breakthrough and gotten full control over the state in this process. At this point, the traits of his gloomy personality, with clear paranoid tendencies, become crucial. Once at the top and in full control, he was not a man to accept changes in the pattern of his personal power. He continued to defend his place in the system and to inflate its dependence on him. He assumed the role of a linchpin in the whole structure, "personalized" this pattern to the utmost, and, well in line with his self-image and personal dynamics, he identified the whole with himself, and himself with history. He achieved a position when he would have been fully justified if he had stated: "L'état,c'est moi"—and with a vengeance, because this "identification" of a man with a position and with history, concealed a potential for losing the indispensable sense of proportion between the personal and the historical, and thus opening the gate to madness. Consequently, changes in the essence of his power and role in the system were out of the question for him. He therefore took the road of shaking up, of destabilizing the machinery and its upper layers, in order to block the process fatally working against his personal predilection for autocracy. This is a suggestion which helps to explain the purges and also some broader aspects of Stalin's role as ruler in Soviet history. By fighting for the continuation of his power, he took the system into a damaging, "pathological" direction, began actually to wreck it: the more the arbitrary rule unfolded, the more it displayed its inadequacy in running a rapidly developing country and its emerging new social forces, both at the base and at the summit of the social hierarchy.

Bolshevism and Clause 58⁹ of the Criminal Code

The personal dynamics of Stalin which would not allow him to accept the role of the later tsars, and made him prefer the role of the earlier ones, is a matter, and quite a complicated one, for biographers. Nevertheless, singling out the personal role of Stalin in "Stalinism" from the other factors revealed by sociohistorical analysis, though it has its difficulties, is a crucial task. In response to real pressures, even if often transformed in his mind into misinterpreted mythological phantoms, Stalin used or manipulated three interdependent levers. First, his own "cult" (he certainly was helped by his would-be "priests" in establishing it) as a peculiar method of communicating with the masses, over the heads of the bureaucracy, as well as with the bureaucratic mass itself, over the heads of their bosses in party and state. But this wouldn't have worked without the additional support generated by the re-activation of trends from the past which were still present in the mentality of many Russians; by the industrial dynamism; and by the forces of inertia and conformism, on which some systems thrive better than others.

But an even more important lever, the second in our count, was the "alliance" of the ruler—a powerful institution by now—with the secret police, without or against the party; and then, thirdly, the provision of an appropriate ideological justification for such an alliance. All three are the essential ingredients of the Stalinist trademark. The building up of the secret police as partner in the "alliance" consisted in elevating them above the party, and transforming them from a more or less conventional security force into a powerful economic agency with non-economic methods and means at its disposal. This was at the root of the enormous *univers concentrationnaire* (to quote the title of a well-known book by David Rousset), which was to become yet another "essential" part of the Stalinist system. Without it, the term would have meant something quite different.

Vyshinsky, Stalin's great inquisitor, was probably the best spokesman and interpreter of Stalin's intentions and ideologies relevant to our theme. He certainly knew, not only his master's written word, but also his voice and intentions. The key idea which he quotes from Stalin maintains that the disappearance of classes will come about "not by means of a lessening of class conflict but by means of its intensification." The same applies to the thesis about the withering away of the state, which will occur "not through weakening state power but through a maximum strengthening of the state in order to defeat the remnants of the dying classes and to organize a defense against capitalist encirclement." [25] There is no need to polemicize with such statements. Why should one manage with only a weak state to eliminate the bulk of enemy forces, but need a mighty, ever mightier machine of oppression in order to supress just some remnants? The logic is no object here. The essential thing is that this is Stalin's central strategic *motto*, the very heart of Stalinist strategy. Vyshinsky added more than a touch of characteristic clarification to it and crossed the *t*'s in his attack against Bolshevik jurists (whom, incidentally, he helped to their graves). They reiterated all too often the old Leninist adage about this withering away of the state and of law, but gave it, not unnaturally, a different twist from Stalin's. Vyshinsky's rhetoric against those lawyers is telling: "We have scarcely understood yet what a diversionary character, in the direct sense of this word, i.e., in the direct sense of Clause 58[9] of the Criminal Code of the RSFSR, this word had. . . . " [26] This venom concerned men like Pashukanis and Stuchka, even Krylenko—but, in fact, the passage was more significant than that. This clause, as well as a few others of the same notorious Paragraph 58 of the Criminal Code, defined counter-revolutionary sabotage, diversion, etc., and was used against the bulk of the cadres of the Bolshevik party and against one of the important promises in Leninism, without which it wouldn't have existed at all as a revolutionary force: the promise of more freedom and justice, and the emancipation of the masses. This is the deeper meaning of the "withering away" thesis—but now it became a directly criminal, counter-revolutionary action, with the sinister Clause 58[9] attached to it.

The "remnants of the class enemy" could not have become so dangerous if they engaged in an open fight. But they would act, Stalin taught, surreptitiously *(tikhoi sapoi)* as covert agents of foreign intelligence, and would use the most devilish means of masking themselves [27]—and the only agency able to cope with this kind of sneaky enemy would be the secret police. Hence, it becomes for the

---

25. A. Ia. Vyshinsky, *Voprosy teorii gosudarstva i prava,* 2nd ed. (Moscow, 1949), quotes this passage on p. 62, from Stalin, *Voprosy Leninizma,* 10th ed., p. 509.

26. Vyshinsky, p. 64.

27. The role of "masks" in Stalin's perception of human behavior is shown by Tucker in *Stalin as Revolutionary,* p. 453.

regime its most cherished institution, its symbol. Of course, the diversionist ex-Bolsheviks were so treacherous precisely because their thesis about the "withering away of state and laws" did aim at those very sacred services of the state. Vyshinsky stated this explicitly: the diversionary work of the previous generation of Old Bolshevik jurists "was in essence aimed at suggesting the 'thought' that such state levers and means of struggle as the army, navy, counter-intelligence, NKVD, courts, procuracy were unnecessary, that they had, so to speak, exhausted their historical role." One couldn't have expressed more clearly this defense of the police state, as a principle, against the Old Bolshevik ideas and, specifically, against the "rightists" with their demands to move forward "peacefully and smoothly" *(mirno i plavno).*

This polemic (which, incidentally, may make Vyshinsky's victims more sympathetic to us, if it was true that they paid with their lives for their dislike of repression and police agencies) offers the full formula for unleashing precisely the oppressive functions of the state and extolling its oppressive organs. For Stalin this aspect became not only a matter of politics but, here too, a mark of personal identification. He trusted the secret police and only them: the management of his household, of his numerous identically built and furnished villas, was actually entrusted, after the suicide of his wife in 1932, to Beria's services.[28]

"Legality," "Extra-Legality": Two Models in One
Under the label of "enemies of the people" perished the flower of the Bolshevik party, the old cadres as well as many newer ones of the post-revolutionary period. The baffling thing about this destruction was its wanton character, its utter folly, as it obviously wrecked the very interests of the system Stalin himself was building and presiding over. If it was madness, as it might well have been, there was nevertheless some method behind it. It was political madness of a man with the super-sensitive feelers of a paranoic. He clearly disliked the past of his party and its ethos—and destroyed it. But he also refused, as we have argued, to accept the contours of the pattern emerging under his own post-Bolshevik rule, whereby the new social groups, especially the state and ruling strata, began to take shape and consolidate their positions. Some other ruler might eventually have yielded to the new order, made the best out of it, and accepted an honorary presidency or even a quite effective leadership function.[29] But a man like Stalin might have perceived such tendencies as encroachments by despicable creatures of his own making closing in on him and trying to despoil him. He therefore defended with fury his own power and his own system.

What was in fact emerging and closing in on him was a new political order which he himself helped bring into the world by a Caesarian operation. On the face of it, those years were the ones of full Stalinism, and everything that hap-

---

28. Svetlana Alliluyeva, *Twenty Letters to a Friend* (London, 1967), pp. 138–43, shows this function and role of the secret police in running Stalin's household.

29. This is Adam Ulam's interpretation (which he calls "a plott by adulation") of the efforts in 1934 to get rid of Stalin by making him even more of a god by pushing him up and out of interference with politics. See his *Stalin: The Man and His Era* (New York, 1973), pp. 372–73.

pened was of Stalin's doing. In fact, he was presiding over the creation of two
political models simultaneously, which were not perceptible to contemporaries
but can be discerned today, and were perceived, as we have said, dimly and
gloomily by Stalin himself. Very soon these two models found themselves in an
unhappy and tension-generating coexistence.

The problem of an uneasy if not outright impossible symbiosis of "legality"
and "arbitrariness" in those years can help highlight the issue. The seesaw of mass
transgressions of "socialist legality" and of campaigns to make the "excesses"
good is a well-known trait of Soviet history, especially in the Stalinist period. It
is also very characteristic that at the very height of police terror, in the years
1935–38, the theme of reinforcing legality, rehabilitating the concept of law, was
being voiced and preached. The theme needs some exploration.

The talented Russian scholar N. M. Korkunov, in his study of the Russian
state and law—an equivalent in those days of the modern "political science"—defined "autocracy" and "autocrat" (*samoderzhavie* and *samoderzhets*) as the sover-
eignty of the ruler, the unlimited character of his rule, but at the same time the
need to limit this rule by legal principles, basic laws of his own making. The
reason for such a tendency, he maintained, was twofold: a) legality allows the
masses to identify with the system—otherwise the lawless system is felt as tyrannical and cannot be stable; and b) the ruler, in order to control the state machinery
directly and efficiently, requires a clear legal framework for the smooth working
of state institutions and bureaucracies. Without it they would be acting purely
arbitrarily and would help to destroy the unity of the state instead of serving this
unity and the interests of the ruler himself.[30] These remarks help to highlight
the problems of the 1930's very aptly. The extra-legal massive measures taken
in the process of collectivization, industrialization, and, later, in the search for
"enemies of the people" shattered the social fabric, and there certainly was a deep
craving among the officials as well as in the population for the security that only
a firm legal framework could provide. To regularize, to consolidate, to reinsure,
to ensure a ruly and predictable working of the responsible institutions, some kind
of "constitutionality" was needed. Such was probably the state of mind in the
apparaty by 1934 and later. The interests of the ruling elite as well as of the system
at large, in terms of gaining or regaining popular support and cohesion, and
providing predictable working conditions for the functioning of the state machinery—the two points Korkunov made at the beginning of the century—were
in the deepest interests of the system and of its most important agencies.

But we know that at the same time, and in ever wilder waves from the end
of 1935 on, the opposite tendency was gaining the upper hand: police rule and
the camp system. Obviously, these two inter-related factors are the very negation
of the craved-for rule of law. On the contrary, the essence of the Gulag system—
this will remain the label under the powerful impact of Solzhenitsyn's writing—is
arbitrariness. It would be naïve to think that the fate of the masses of innocent
people crammed into the camps was confined to them and did not concern the

---

30. N. M. Korkunov, *Russkoe gosudarstvennoe pravo,* Vol. I (St. Petersburg, 1901), pp. 204–7.

majority of the population. In terms of a political analysis of the citizen in this particular state, of his rights and his duties, the existence of the camps was a test case. Inside the camps were masses of people who heard the knock at the door and were thereby doomed. Symptomatically, only one category could enjoy there some semblance of legal protection: the hard-core criminals. Not unnaturally, they were the privileged people in the camps and held internal power there, and only they gained a modicum of juridical guarantees and predictability of release at the expiration of their sentences, or possibly a remittal of sentence, for good behavior or otherwise. There was nothing of this kind for the overwhelming mass of the prisoners. It was an important trait of the political system that any citizen, in any position and walk of life, had no guarantee other than luck or his own naïvete against "the knock at the door." Everyone was thus potentially a candidate to become a camp inmate, even if the majority, of course, did not get the sinister call.

That the rulers without tenure should like to acquire tenure, and the subjects-would-be-inmates should want to change their "status" seems unquestionable. We can therefore look for two factors at work: the emerging forces interested in stability and legality, and the factors that blocked them and perpetuated the ruling, "extra-legal" system. It is symptomatic that these contradictory tendencies should have been preached and practiced by the same man—Vyshinsky, the man with the political antennae of a perfect opportunist. He fought as fiercely for the Soviet law, as he blasted the ubiquitous agents and enemies, figments of a sickly imagination and the antithesis of any lawfulness. Thus, two coexisting models, one merging in the shadow of the other, both apparently presided over by Stalin, may be analytically dissociated, and after a certain stage may be seen in collision. The one, still weak, would later evolve into a system of orderly bureaucracy, with an institutionalized oligarchy at its apex, presided over rather than ruled over by a top political management; the other, which we can call the Stalinist system *sensu stricto,* consisted of the ingredients mentioned above—the cult, the police, the ideological manipulation, and the appropriate mentality. Not unexpectedly, most of those did not survive Stalin very long.

Conclusion

The Stalinist model *sensu stricto* was powerful enough, mightily favored as it was by the state of social flux in its early stage, and by the whole pattern of social development to which we have referred. It was a pattern in which the social structure evolved under the influence of an already existing and all-embracing state organization, became subject to a powerful controlling mechanism, and in which state control was to some extent accepted as a fact that was already familiar, though to a lesser degree, from the previous framework.

In the industrialization process, with the superstructure, as it were, rushing ahead of the emerging social basis, all the important social groups found themselves "bureaucratized" and fully dependent on state administrations. The statism is important, as its many traits were there to stay. But its development was a complex and contradictory affair.

On the one hand, it evolved forms and structures of an autocratic power pattern reminiscent in many aspects, even reproducing directly, traits of the imperial past. But the meeting of hearts and the affinity with the past statehood was not a replica of the past, but a new, original creation, a hybrid of Marxism and tsarism, a transitory phenomenon that was confined to the Stalinist stage alone.

As the state developed and the initial tensions and flux began to subside, the étatized structure began to evolve into a stable pattern—but this was not allowed to take definitive shape because of the vigilant counteraction of the power pattern in control, the strictly Stalinist one. The latter found propitious conditions for its development and was offered the opportunity to run out its full course. After the stage of "development without emancipation" of the earlier period, this ushered in a stage of "development with oppression," which soon evolved into a full social and political pathology.

The larger model of a more ruly, oligarchically run bureaucratic system, which emerged after Stalin's death, could already be perceived in the shadows of Stalinist rule, but couldn't shake off the harness as long as the initial stage of the state's warfare against the nation of small producers went on. In order to tame Stalin, it was necessary to stop this warfare and the warfare mentality, and return to social and economic policies of a "normal" character. Stalin and his entourage, on the contrary, were thriving on warfare and seige conditions and mentalities, and did all they could to perpetuate this state of affairs—even by using, as a matter of strategy and ruling method, the hallucinating procedure of inventing hosts of mythical enemies, and destroying masses of people in the process. This was a case not only of the divorce of a "state" from "society" but also of the divorce of a leadership from the interests of the state. For the nation it was an unmitigated catastrophe.

At the same time, it has proved an embarassing legacy for the leaders of our day. They share quite a set of assumptions with the demonic leader and cannot easily explain how they, the party, etc., can be presented as innocent of past practices or immune to the dangers of a repetition of the same.

Be that as it may, their system offers further scope for development and serious improvements. The ruling stratum is presided over, not raped; the system's *pays politique* is larger than before; communications and contact with the popular classes have considerably improved; and the quality of leadership in many walks of life is much higher. Whatever the improvements, though, as far as the social system at large is concerned, political domination, ideological monopoly, and the tight controls of this modernized "statism" continue to generate problems—in particular in those areas where the inheritance from the thirties is concerned. And such areas and principles are still very much present in Soviet policy.

Stalinism and
Marxian Growth Models *

Alexander Erlich

When Trotsky was still a "non-faction" Social Democrat, he once observed that Marxism was reflected in Lenin's writings like Aphrodite in a *samovar*. It will be our contention that this metaphor holds true *a fortiori* for the writings and doings of the man who liked to be called "the Lenin of today," quite particularly—for the very special kind of contribution he made to the theory and practice of economic growth. We shall argue that Marxian models emerge from Stalin's hands badly bruised and disfigured, but still recognizable and not devoid of operational significance. Yet in order to demonstrate this, and to put things in proper perspective, we shall have to take a few steps back and to have a look both at the prototype and at the uses to which it had been put by pre-Stalinist Bolsheviks.

The readers will have noted that we spoke of model*s*. Indeed, Marx had at least *three* of them. The first and most general deals with the interplay between the level of the effectively assimilated technology ("productive forces") and the set of mutual relationships among people in the process of production as well as the way in which labor, produced means of production, and land are appropriated ("relationships of production").[1] When productive forces and relationships of

---

* I am greatly indebted to Włodzimierz Brus, Stephen F. Cohen, Mihailo Marković, and Robert C. Tucker for valuable comments.

1. A few comments may be in order at this point. To begin with, there is a certain overlap between the relationships of production and the productive forces, since both of them include such things as the organization of the work process. (The other part of the relationships of production consists of appropriation of different production agents by sundry individuals, and is not *directly* related to production processes.) More important in the present context is the fact that our shorthand presentation, like the classic Preface to *Zur Kritik der politischen Ökonomie,* which underlies it, does not do justice to the richness of Marx's treatment of specific situations. For instance, in his analysis of the early history of capitalism, the path-breaking role of such a "superstructural" agency as the state is very strongly emphasized, and Marx makes it very clear that in the case of the so-called manofactory, its relationships of production (a large-scale unit based on the cooperation of the workers) were ahead of its technological basis (non-mechanized hand labor); it was this incompatibility which finally led to the creation of modern machinery. It is quite true, however, that in their writings concerning the transition to socialism (with the important exception of the *Manifesto*), Marx and Engels invariably assumed that revolutionary action of the proletariat will come *after* the pressure of the productive forces against their capitalist shell has become unbearable, and with no state intervention being needed to make these forces more mature for socialism than they already are.

production, which form together the "basis" of the society, are mutually consonant, the system is viable. If the productive forces are forging ahead, a clash ensues. The old relationships of production sooner or later must give way, and this sets off a chain of changes also in the political, legal, and ideological "superstructure." By the same token, a new set of relationships of production cannot effectively take hold, unless the productive forces have reached an adequate level of development. With reference to socialism, this was taken to mean that (1) the average production units must have reached a sufficient level of concentration and calculability to be centrally planned; (2) the workers of these units who cannot take control of their means of production except via common ownership must constitute the bulk of the population; (3) in order to be egalitarian and economically dynamic at the same time, a society must have attained high standards of productivity. Only if these prerequisites are fulfilled can the society of the future be "an association in which a free development of each is the condition for the free development of all." [2]

The second and the third models are more limited in scope. The analysis of capital accumulation in Volume I of *Capital* traces the interaction between increase in stock of equipment, growth of the labor force, and technological progress in a developed capitalist economy, as well as a very different way in which things had unfolded during the period of transition to capitalism. In both cases the specificity of the sociohistorical setting and the role of the profit motive as the driving force is powerfully emphasized; but, as will be shown later, much of the argument is relevant also when a modern sector of a non-capitalist economy grows at the expense of the traditional one and when technology, as well as the ratio of the "embodied labor" to living labor, is undergoing rapid changes. This is even more true of the most systematic and most explicit (although unfinished) "reproduction scheme" of Volume II of *Capital,* which overlaps with the implicit accumulation model mentioned above, and which lays down proportions among major subdivisions of the economy that must obtain in order to secure a full-capacity growth at one of the feasible rates of speed. More specifically, the rate of economic growth is shown to be a function of the relative sizes of capital-goods-producing "sector I" and consumer-goods-producing "sector II" (or, to put the same thing somewhat differently, of the excess of the output of "sector I" over the replacement needs of the economy as a whole).

It is a matter of common knowledge that these constructs played a major role in the grand debate between pre-revolutionary Russian Marxists and their Populist and "revisionist" adversaries. It is equally true that they provided the terms in which Bolshevik leaders framed their strategy after their victory in 1917. The victory was "dizzying" in more than one sense. Exhilarating as it was, it at the same time posed the most awesome problem—how to proceed with the socialist transformation in a country the productive forces of which are evidently not strong enough to sustain a system of socialist planning. Lenin tried at first to

---

2. "Manifesto," in K. Marx and F. Engels, *Selected Works in Two Volumes* (Moscow, 1962), Vol. I, p. 54.

bridge the gap on a more *ad hoc* basis, in the hope that this would be done much more solidly by the impending revolution in the industrially advanced West; [3] in these attempts he moved from the circumspection of his early economic program to the extremes of the "war communism" which he deplored later. But as the revolutionary prospects in the West were dimming and the deepening economic debacle ("enlarged negative reproduction," in Bukharin's polished phrase) was generating a full-blown political crisis, Lenin "seriously and for a long time" turned to the NEP in March 1921. He did not spell out the broad doctrinal implications of the new strategy until nearly two years later, in a much-quoted note on Nikolai Sukhanov's *Zapiski o revolutsii* in which he admitted that "the development of productive forces of Russia has not attained the level that makes socialism possible." But his conclusion was highly unorthodox:

> If a definite level of culture is required for the building of socialism (although nobody can say just what this definite "level of culture" is, for it differs in every West European country), why cannot we begin by first achieving the prerequisites for that definite level of culture in a revolutionary way, and *then,* with the aid of the workers' and peasants' government and the Soviet system, proceed to catch up with other nations? . . . Why could we not first create such preconditions of civilization in our country as expulsion of the landlords and the Russian capitalists, and then start moving toward socialism? [4]

On the face of it, this amendment was standing on its head one of the fundamental Marxian propositions which Lenin himself had defended to the utmost in his battles with the Populists and (after 1905) with Trotsky. Yet, a more generous interpretation seems in order. Lenin did not deny that it was most natural and most desirable to start socializing when productive forces of the country in question were "ripe" for public ownership. But if, as a result of a unique combination of external and internal developments, a revolutionary socialist government emerges in a less mature country, then it has to look for a second-best solution, rather than throw in the sponge. In other words, it must reconcile itself to cutting the coat according to the cloth and to accepting the fact that the sector which is ready for public ownership and central planning because of the large size of its units of production or distribution accounts for a much smaller share of the whole economy than in developed countries and hence occupies much less of a commanding position with regard to the small-scale private sector. The link between two highly inequal parts of the economy was to rest on the "bourgeois" device of the market and operate within the framework of the equally conventional fiscal, monetary, and tariff policies, although the nationalized urban sector would send its forays into villages by promoting strictly

---

3. "It was clear to us that without the support of the international world revolution the victory of the proletarian revolution was impossible. Before the revolution, and even after it, we thought: Either revolution breaks out in the other countries, in the capitalistically more developed countries, immediately, or at least very quickly, or we must perish." V. I. Lenin, *Polnoe sobranie sochinenii* (Moscow, 1964). Vol. 44, p. 36.

4. Ibid., Vol. 45, p. 381.

voluntary marketing and credit cooperatives. It was expected that as a result of this operation, as well as of greater modernity and technological dynamism, the collective sector would win out eventually, and thus put an end to the non-Marxist anomaly.[5]

The results of this dualistic strategy by the middle of the decade were impressive. The aggregate production indices went up at a phenomenal rate in industry and quite respectably in agriculture; the allocation mechanism worked reasonably well, thus demonstrating the superiority of a market-cum-planning system over the over-centralization of War Communism. One could almost visualize economists and political leaders of the early Soviet twenties asking each other the Paul Samuelson question of the American fifties: "What went right?" Such a spirit of optimism was indeed reflected in the writings of Bukharin and his school in the years 1924–26. They pointed with pride to the accomplishments of the NEP as compared with the calamities of the preceding period; they confidently extrapolated these upward trends in the future; and they insisted that the worst thing that could happen would be to upset the unwritten "non-aggression pact" between the socialist sector and its non-socialist environment. Yet these views, which reflected at that time the position of the ruling group within the party, met with a withering critique from the Left, more particularly from Preobrazhensky, the leading economist of the group. He did not deny that the War Communist methods of outright confiscation could not be maintained without courting disaster, and that market exchange had to be, for a long time to come, the crucial link between city and village. He recognized that a peaceful coexistence with the peasants was a *sine qua non* for better or worse, and that this implied "satisfying a certain minimum of [their] needs." But to Preobrazhensky this was an added argument for a rapid forward movement rather than for making haste slowly. The Soviet industry in its mid-twenties size and structure was woefully inadequate to meet (at the same time and out of its own resources) the claims of peasant buyers and the needs of much-delayed replacement, not to speak of the long-range tasks of modernizing a huge underdeveloped country, making provisions for defense, and restructuring agriculture along collectivist lines. By the same token, the existing peasant economy was clearly even less able, if left to itself, to generate a surplus which could sustain the satisfactory rate of growth in the urban sector.

---

5. This position, born of defeat and assumed to be valid for the transitional period only, contained important insights which are at present accepted by many Soviet and Eastern European economists with regard to the operation of a fully established socialist economy. These economists firmly believe that the state can effectively plan "big things" such as distribution of income and volume of investment as well as the allocation of the latter among major regions and industries, while letting particular production units obey in their decisions the rule of the market (corrected for "externalities"). See Moshe Lewin, *Political Undercurrents in Soviet Economic Debates* (Princeton, 1974). This would mean that preponderance of big plants would be less of a crucial pre-condition for planning than in the orthodox Marxian view seemed to assume, although a more developed socialist economy, to be sure, was bound to have a much larger share of such plants anyhow. Moreover, and in distinction from their predecessors, the present-day advocates of coexistence of planning and market consider such a set-up more indispensable on high levels of economic development than on lower ones—a point to which we shall return.

(This was another, and perhaps most threatening, aspect of the insufficiency of "productive forces.") The stupendous "tempos" of increase during the early NEP did not disprove this. They reflected an increasingly full reactivation of the pre-revolutionary capacity, an enormous part of which was made idle by the disruptions of the Civil War and by the stifling War Communist regulations; they were bound to peter out after the period of recovery had come to a close, thus adding to the intractabilities of the situation. In order to break out of the multifarious deadlock, it was imperative, in Preobrazhensky's view, to dramatically increase the rate of investment and thus raise the capacity of the industry within the shortest possible time to the level at which it could effectively meet *all* pent-up outside demands as well as the needs of its own self-expansion. The main burden of this operation was to be borne by the peasantry, which was to be contained in its consumption of industrial goods by quasimonopolistic high prices and by an overriding priority assigned to capital goods in planned imports. In the longer run, the peasants would be compensated for this kind of "forced saving" after the mightily expanded industrial capacity had started delivering in a big way.

Preobrazhensky was quite explicit in linking up his strategy to Marx. Much to the indignation of his opponents and to the embarrassment of some of his friends, he christened the process of reshuffling resources from agriculture to industry "a primitive socialist accumulation," thus taking the cue from the Marxian notion of "primitive capitalist accumulation." He invoked the logic of the scheme of Volume II when he argued that in the process of such transfer the two sectors of the economy should be arranged in a "marching combat order," i.e., that the output of producers' goods should grow faster than the output of consumers' goods (although he took strong exception against "mortgaging all resources for development of heavy industry"). Furthermore, in one of his last published articles he enriched and modified the two-sectors model by breaking the outputs of producers' goods and consumers' goods into components coming from socialist, capitalist, and small-scale producing subdivisions of the society, and by introducing in the two last-mentioned sub-groups a feature which constituted a clear departure from the prototype—*unrequited* contributions from one segment of the economy to another. Lastly, although Preobrazhensky never specifically referred to the Lenin formula of 1923, his reasoning, as it were, infused a stronger sense of urgency into it. The achievement of the "definite level of culture [that is] required for the building of socialism" was to be accomplished by a non-violent but vigorous assault against the peasant sector—more specifically, by the use of existing instrumentalities of economic policy in order to bring about "within the limits of the economically possible and technically feasible" a shift of resources from the private to the socialized sector. This would clearly raise the speed of the catching up well beyond the level that would be attainable if rules of the game of the competitive market had been faithfully adhered to.

Bukharin's first response was, as one could expect, strongly negative. Stripped of polemical verbiage, it consisted in pointing out that Preobrazhensky's medicine was worse than the disease. There was certainly no guarantee that the peasants would cheerfully accept the burden of forced saving and patiently wait for future blessings; in fact, there was every reason to expect that they would react even more violently than they had on earlier occasions such as the "scissors crisis" of 1923, or the "goods famine" of 1925, by cutting their supplies to the cities most drastically; this could pull the rug out from under the most attractive industrialization programs, and possibly from the whole Soviet system as well. (In a later statement, Bukharin put it in a more generalized way: "If a certain branch of production systematically does not get back its expenses of production plus a certain mark-up corresponding to a part of surplus labor, it will either stagnate or contract.") [6] Yet the logic of stubborn facts made him accept, albeit belatedly, the essentials of Preobrazhensky's diagnosis of the situation. As Rykov, Bukharin's friend and ally put it, "The country cannot live any longer without capital investments." The problem consisted in reducing the task to manageable proportions. A highly ingenious and novel strategy emerged. The capital-goods-producing sector was to receive a high priority in investment allocation, but not an overriding one. The capital-using modern technology was to be applied in those industries in which its advantages were absolutely striking; in other areas, preference should be given to labor-intensive technology which would economize investible resources and be quicker in generating output—a policy bearing a strong resemblance to the "walking on two legs" policy of present-day China. The agriculture was to come under a three-pronged attack. The increase in marketable output was to be stimulated by assistance to medium-size peasant holdings, tolerance of high-producing rich peasants as well as a stepped-up but still gradual development of collective farming; at the same time the potentially unsettling increase in peasant spending would be kept in check by taxation and by actively encouraged voluntary saving. Lastly, Bukharin had always insisted that he did not intend to entirely renounce the advantages of the monopolistic position of the Soviet nationalized industry on the peasant market. Hence a tilt in the terms of trade in favor of the urban sector would presumably remain; but it would be sufficiently moderate as not to prevent the peasant economy from growing.

The strategy seemed eminently sound and worth trying out. But it was not to be. At the end of 1927 and in early 1928 the Soviet economy was hit by a serious shortfall in grain deliveries, and this crisis tended to polarize views. Moreover, there had been important changes in political "superstructure." The system termed by Lenin "a workers' state with bureaucratic deformation" bore very little resemblance to Marx's "union of free individuals," also during the lifetime of its architect. As time wore on, the "deformation" was growing apace, and it found its incarnation in the steadily growing power of Stalin. Up to the beginning of 1928, he seconded Bukharin on issues of economic policy while enjoying the

---

6. "Zametki ekonomista," *Pravda,* September 30, 1928 (reprinted in N. I. Bukharin, *Put' k sotsializmu v Rossii,* ed. S. Heitman (New York, 1967), p. 387. It may be worth noting that Bukharin, too, made extensive use of the "I"-versus-"II" dichotomy. Indeed, following his propensity to theorize, he mentioned Tugan-Baranovsky's notion of the limitlessly self-expanding "sector I," and went on the argue, none too convincingly, that consumers' demand must not be neglected because investment goods will inevitably "mature" into consumers' goods. Cf. his *Imperializm i nakoplenie kapitala,* 4th ed. (Moscow and Leningrad, 1929), p. 63.

latter's full support in attempts to crush the "super-industrialist" Left; in this endeavor he succeeded by December 1927. Now he could use his strengthened position to deal with the crisis by getting rid of his moderate allies and starting the nation upon a new course which he could truthfully call his own.

Stalin's most eloquent and immediate response to the event came in deeds rather than in words: we have in mind his journey to Siberia in early 1928 and the notorious "Urals-Siberian method" of enforcing grain collections. He was less direct but quite clear on the level of ideological verbalization. His most fundamentalist argument in favor of collectivization was that the Soviet economy could not develop along two different tracts—large-scale production in industry and small-scale production in agriculture. This seems to take us back to some of the old discussions. An orthodox Marxist would indeed insist that productive forces must reach a high level of socialization all over the economy in order to be "ripe" for public ownership. But all post-1921 Bolsheviks, Stalin emphatically included, had been prepared to live with a dualism of the NEP while fully realizing that it was bound to generate tensions; this would end after the development of industry had advanced far enough so that the greatly expanded "sector I" could supply the agriculture with the requisite equipment. Now Stalin evidently felt that the time had come to pour modern technology into the villages in a big way. Yet his statements to that effect must be taken with a grain of salt. He repeatedly acknowledged that small-scale peasant economy still had vast potentialities for improvement within its present framework, and that it would remain the predominant form of Soviet agriculture for a long time. Moreover, when the "big push" got underway in late 1929, the Central Committee obligingly passed his motion to the effect that the collectivization drive must not be inhibited by shortages of tractors and other kinds of modern machinery; Stalin insisted that even a non-mechanized collective farm was superior to individual peasant holdings; and with a touch of Marxological savvy, he spoke of the "manofactory period" of collectivization. (As will be seen later, the peasants failed to appreciate the fine point of theory.)

In short, Stalin did realize that an all-out re-equipment would be a very costly proposition, and that it would powerfully compete for resources with developing industry, which had top priority. But the plain truth was that he was first and foremost interested in collective farms as collection devices (to use the pun of Ragnar Nurkse) which would invest the power of decision about production and disposition of agricultural output in the state and its village agents, rather than in the peasants. This seemed a much more effective way of securing supplies than tinkering with relative prices. The modern technological basis was to be provided, by and large, *ex post* rather than *ex ante*—and acts of peasant resistance only added to Stalin's grim determination to crush the adversary once and for all. To be sure, he admitted that the major proximate cause of the crisis was the rapid increase in the absolute and relative size of the industrial "sector I," which generated a growing urban demand for food without a corresponding rise in amount of industrial goods available to the peasants; and he made no attempt to prove that such a difficulty could not be resolved within the framework of the revised Bukharin strategy which he had heartily endorsed only a short while ago. But Stalin saw in the peasant supply strike only secondarily an economic problem. It was to him a test of wills, a perfect *Kto kogo?* situation; and his "warfare personality" (to borrow Robert Tucker's expression) came through fully. He felt that to compromise under such circumstances means not merely to lose ground but to lose credibility (shades of some people closer to home), to encourage new acts of defiance, and to start downhill all the way. "What is meant by not hindering kulak farming? It means setting the kulak free. And what is meant by setting the kulak free? It means giving him power." [7] ("Kulak" is here clearly a convenient stand-in for "peasant.") It is not important at this point whether he was right or not—he wasn't—but there is little doubt that he believed every word he said. He was equally serious when he repeated Lenin's 1917 dictum, "To perish or to forge full speed ahead," even though he did not hesitate to distort the meaning of the quotation in a most specious manner.[8] In short, an attractive interaction was envisaged: the collectivization was to secure the state's grip on agricultural supplies—the industrialization had to make the collectivization stick, and to reduce the peasants' share in the economy as rapidly as possible.

The rest of the story has been told many times. The grain-collection crisis exploded into a full-scale confrontation between the regime and the peasants. In the course of the escalatory sequence of powerful blows and massive retribution, the collectivization drive went far beyond the initial targets: in 1932 the collective farms and state farms accounted for 77 percent of the total agricultural area. Similarly, the final version of the first Five-Year Plan stymied all the earlier drafts and seemed like a giant-size replica of the composite bridegroom in Gogol's *Zhenit'ba* (Marriage). It proposed to double the national income within less than five years, nearly double the total capital stock, and raise the volume of investment fourfold: this looked like Preobrazhensky raised to the nth power. At the same time, agricultural output was expected to increase by a respectable 55 percent, which seemed to take care of Bukharin's injunction that in a healthy development program industry should develop the American way, on top of the rapidly growing agriculture. Lastly, the impressive 85 percent figure for increase in total consumption would refute the suspicion that human needs were neglected —another point of Bukharin's concern.

All this seemed much too good to be true—and indeed it was. Rudolf Hilferding once called Tugan Baranovsky's theories "a Marxism gone mad." This characterization fully applies here too. It is quite true that, according to the two-sector model of Volume II, an economy which has a higher share of its total output and capital stock in capital goods is bound to grow faster, other things

---

7. I. V. Stalin, *Sochineniia* (Moscow, 1949), Vol. XI, p. 275.

8. Ibid., p. 250. It should be crystal clear to every reader of Lenin's text ("Groziashchaia katastrofa i kak s nei borot'sia," in *Polnoe sobranie sochinenii,* Vol. 34, p. 198), that when he spoke about "overtaking capitalist countries economically" and doing this "with full speed" in September 1917, he had in mind adapting organizational forms of Western "war economy" and improving on them, rather than exceeding the Western level of development which Stalin was referring to and which would have been a ludicrous objective for a backward country in the throes of a devastating war.

being equal, than an economy with a lower share of capital goods. Like all models worth their salt, the Marxian scheme does not actually tell its users what to do: it puts before them, in Oskar Lange's words, the terms on which alternatives are available and leaves the rest to their preferences. But it does tell them (implicitly, if not explicitly) that some alternatives are extremely costly or plainly not feasible. It is impossible to reduce "sector II" below a certain level without getting a drop in productivity of labor and rising social unrest. It is only slightly less obvious that the relative size of "sector I" imposes a constraint not only on the growth of the economy as a whole but also on the growth of this very sector, the other determinants being capital-output ratio, average length of the construction period of the plant, and ability to cut down on investment demand from "sector II." A little bit of simple arithmetic could show that even if we plow back the whole investment into "sector I," it would take us *more* than five years to treble the volume of investment, if we assume some halfway realistic capital-output ratio and average construction periods of plant: but this is not going to bring us anywhere near doubling total output and total capital stock.[9] True, the technological progress has not been accounted for in our argument thus far; and the authors of the plan heavily relied on it. But here, too, wishful thinking took over. Technological progress is no prairie fire. Experimenting and learning take time. Besides,

---

9. A rough calculation based on two key ratios of the First Five-Year Plan (a fixed capital–net output ratio of 2.9 in the base year declining to 2.5 in the final year, and net investment in fixed capital equaling 15.7 percent of the national income in the base year) shows that it would indeed be possible to increase the volume of fixed investment sixfold over five years, while the fixed capital stock would increase by 64 percent instead of the planned 83 percent; the national income would rise by 90 percent instead of the planned 102 percent. But this would be so only on two breathtaking assumptions which were definitely *not* made by the planners: (1) all investment is being plowed back into "sector I"—a proposition which reaches a peak of absurdity with regard to an economy where, on the eve of the big industrialization drive, nearly 40 percent of total investment activity took place in technologically backward agriculture; (2) the average construction period is equal to one year, which is wildly unrealistic; a calculation using very similar numbers (except that the capital–net output ratio was taken to be 3 throughout) showed that if we assume the construction of a plant to last, on the average, three years rather than one year, the volume of investment will a little more than *double* within five years, while the fixed capital stock and the national income will go up by 26 percent. (It is true that, according to Soviet data, the fixed capital–net output ratio in industry stood at nearly 1.5 in 1927–28, i.e., considerably less than the national average. But the net output of industry had to increase by 148 percent, with its more capital-using "sector 1" increasing three times and the industrial fixed capital more than trebling.)

Actually, such an average construction period is a composite of dubious significance in periods of drastic structural changes. To take an example, steel and machine-building are complementary but not fully symmetrical in their relationship. Steel requires machinery inputs in the construction stages of its plant, while machinery needs steel in both the construction stage and daily operation stage. Hence, insofar as new outputs are supposed to come from new plants, it is preferable to start with the steel industry and build the bulk of machine-building industry later. (No doubt, a modicum of steel-making equipment capacity will be needed right at the start, if we assume a closed economy.) But this means that the construction period of new machinery, from the *social* point of view, is close to the sum total of the construction periods of steel and machinery. Obviously, after all industries had adjusted their relative sizes to the new rate of growth and to the "marching combat order" it would require, this sort of totaling would no longer be relevant.

innovations are more often than not associated with investment: new machines must be built and installed, most of them in new plants if the dissemination of innovation occurs on a large scale. (We assume that *all* existing machines that make machines can be used, and are in fact directed to build new and better machines rather than the old ones—a starkly unrealistic assumption). So at best it would take a two-step operation to make the new technology produce—and this would take considerable time. Moreover, this new equipment would require a great deal of extra steel, on both its construction stage and on its operation stage, particularly since much of it would be more steel-using than the old, owing to the Stalinist bias for capital-using technologies; but given the very long construction period in the steel industry, the requisite output flow would not come on time; and much of the newly built steel-using plant, no matter how advanced, would stand idle meanwhile—something that actually happened in 1932–33. No doubt if the existing capital stock could somehow be transmuted into a new one, quickly and without cost (an assumption made by some neoclassical economists and put to deserved ridicule by Joan Robinson), things could work smoothly. The same would be true if construction periods could be, by some miracle, slashed to a fraction of what they were. Stalin, it seems, had hoped that the last-mentioned possibility might materialize as a result of superhuman labor effort, and he must have had some romantic notions of what technological progress can do in a hurry. But the consequences of miracles that did not happen were grave. Construction processes were not reduced in their duration—on the contrary, they were considerably extended because of the shortages of constructional and raw materials, and in view of organizational and managerial difficulties involved in administering a sharply increased number of investment projects. (The last point was made with great force by Michal Kalecki twenty-odd years later.) Lastly, this lengthening of the average construction period had a strong and negative impact on technological progress by tying up an inordinately large amount of investment in incomplete construction and by adding to the overall tension, which was not conducive to time-consuming innovative activities. The authors of the Stalinist plan seemed to have been blissfully ignorant of all this—or else they must have gone by the rule enunciated by the contemporary wiseacres: "It is better to stand up for high tempos than to sit [in jail] for low ones."

At this point the question seems to be not what the Stalin-led economy accomplished in the way of solid progress, but rather how it managed to avoid collapse, or at least major backsliding. Indeed, several solutions were sought. The large-scale industrial sector, which was plagued by all these distortions, was "open" in three important ways. It could get a massive intake of food, which was to a significant extent unrequited—a "tribute" or "super-tax," as Stalin called it in 1928; collectivization was to take care of this. A substantial part of this food, together with timber and oil, could help to buy the much-wanted foreign equipment, and relieve the back-breaking pressure on domestic capital-goods industries. The tremendous influx of peasant and female labor into industry and construction could plug some of the gaps between targets and fulfillment and help to release scarce capital goods to high-priority areas. The unsung exploits of the OGPU certainly had their impact. Last but not least, the dramatic change in the organizational pattern was of major importance. A system of broadly aggregative fiscal and monetary controls and of a largely "indicative" kind of planning would be unable to prevent the economy, riven by formidable disproportions, from getting off the rails: tight-fisted centralized planning, reaching by its commands into every nook and cranny, was more suited to the task. Yet each of these relaxation possibilities had its cost. The furious peasant resistance against the collectivization, climaxing in the slaughter of livestock, forced the planners to divert a much-larger-than-planned part of the precious capital-making capacity to the production of tractors.[10] Heavy exports of food made the situation of Soviet consumers change from bad to worse, and this could not but adversely affect the productivity of labor. A huge increase in the urban labor force aggravated the housing shortage, added to the inflationary pressures, and, through bringing unskilled men and women into abrupt contact with modern technology, caused a great deal of waste and spoilage. Around 1932–33 it became very clear that if the system continued along the same lines as before, it would explode before long. It would be physically impossible to expand the heavy-industrial sector, now nearly twice the size of what it had been in 1928, at the same staggering rate; this would now require much higher exactions from agriculture, which had been stagnating, if not retrogressing. Nor could the widening spread between machine-building and basic industrial materials be tolerated. Lastly, while the over-centralized planning system helped to stave off a major breakdown, it produced a host of smaller distortions, and generated decidedly unhelpful behavior patterns among administrators as well as in the lower echelons. In terms of the basic Marxian model this meant a correspondence not between the level of the productive forces and relationships of production but between attempts to push the

---

10. One should beware of exaggerations, however. There is no doubt that the net contribution of collectivized agriculture to industrialization during the First Five-Year Plan was smaller than expected, and the importance of a gap between real wages and total industrial output in financing the "socialist" accumulation was correspondingly larger. Yet James Millar seems to go too far in minimizing the impact of collectivization when he quotes the Soviet historian Barsov to the effect that urban sales to agriculture in 1929–32, when measured in 1928 prices, had been larger than agricultural sales to the cities. (See his "Soviet Rapid Development and Agricultural Surplus Hypothesis," *Soviet Studies,* July 1970; and "Mass Collectivization and the Contribution of Soviet Agriculture to the First Five-Year Plan," *Slavic Review,* December 1974). As Michael Ellman pointed out, the prices of 1928 were rigged in favor of industry and against agriculture; and this made the industrial sales loom larger as compared with agricultural sales than would have been the case under non-manipulated prices; moreover, the state procurements of grain and the net marketed output measured in physical units sharply increased throughout the whole period both absolutely and as the proportion of the harvest. ("Did the Agricultural Surplus Provide the Resources for the Increase in Investment in the USSR During the First Five-Year Plan?" *Economic Journal,* December 1975). Lastly, to reiterate a point made in the text, it should be kept in mind and made very explicit that the terms of trade between industry and agriculture in 1929–32 were affected by the *exceptionally large* influx of mechanized equipment urgently needed to compensate for the losses of working livestock; they would therefore be untypical of the longer-run relationships between the two areas of the economy.

growth of productive forces beyond the limits of the feasible, and brutally coercive nature of relationships of production as well as of political superstructure, with the latter two being intertwined to the point of near identity.

Stalin took notice. The Second Five-Year Plan deviated from its predecessor in important respects. While the disparity between volumes of investment allocated to "Group A" and "Group B" remained large, it was significantly smaller than under the First Five-Year Plan: in fact, in terms of both planned investment allocation and planned output, "Group B" was supposed to increase faster than "Group A." A major part of investible resources which went into "Group A," by the way, was to be used for belated completion of projects launched under the First Five-Year Plan, rather than for new starts; this, too, helped to take some tension out of the system. When Stalin declared in 1933 that the planned rate of industrial growth could now be lowered from 22 percent to 13–14 percent because "it was no longer necessary to rush," [11] it sounded like a joke. The first draft of the Second Five-Year Plan, released in early 1932, was every bit as "bacchanal" (to use Naum Jasny's expression) in its targets as the final draft of the First, and Stalin's economists at that time kept lambasting Preobrazhensky, who had the temerity to suggest that the present super-high rate of growth would be "of no use" in a fully developed socialist society. The plain truth was that tensions reached a near breaking point immediately afterward, and continuing along old lines would have been the height of folly. But whatever Stalin chose to say or not to say, he knew the score. His speech at the Eighteenth Party Congress made it very clear. He castigated "some members of the old staff of the Gosplan" for planning to set the 1937 output target for pig iron at 60 million tons: "This was a fantasy, if not worse." (Was it much worse than what Stalin did when in 1930 he singlehandedly revised the 1932 target for pig iron from 10 to "15–17" million tons, or when he declared in early 1931 that a 45-percent annual increase in industrial output was entirely feasible because the Soviet Union was rich in natural resources?) And after announcing the new major objective— catching up with and overtaking the capitalist countries in industrial output per capita—he soberly added: "This requires time. Yes, comrades, time. We must build new plants. We must hammer out new cadres for industry. But this requires time, and quite a bit of it." [12] This seemed, of course, not much more than atmospherics. But it sounded quite different from "There are no fortresses which Bolsheviks could not take," or "The reality of the plan—are living people, it's you and I, etc., etc." Lastly, the Third Five-Year Plan, the draft of which was released during the congress, while differing from its predecessor in respect to the relative rates of growth of the two sectors, was less extravagant than the First. The same was true of two subsequent five-year plans completed (or at least started) during Stalin's lifetime. Most analysts agree that while these plans were taut, they were no longer back-breaking. Stalin's last writings, *Dialectical and Historical Materialism* (1938) and *Economic Problems of Socialism in the USSR*

---

11. Stalin, *Sochineniia,* Vol. XIII, p. 186.
12. Ibid., Vol. XIV (1), pp. 352–53.

(1952) confirm this impression. More than that: they allow us a better insight into his views on some basic problems he had not touched upon before—he may have felt uncomfortable about theorizing as long as his intellectually superior adversaries were still alive.

(1) The relation between the productive forces and the relationships of production as well as between both of them and the political superstructure were among the most important problems which Stalin tackled for the first time. On the face of it, he closely followed the conventional approach. Yet, after telling the story about the link between productive forces and the relationships of production, complete with the standard quotation from Marx about the hand-powered mill producing feudalism and the steam-powered mill producing capitalism, Stalin added a paragraph emphasizing the tremendous importance of the political superstructure which could have a powerful feedback effect on the "basis."[13] The point in itself was anything but new—Marx and Engels made it repeatedly. But in this particular case it was certainly meant as a hint at the uniquely decisive role which the Soviet "superstructure," presided over by the author of the essay, had played in transforming the "basis," with no indication of the explosive force and ruthlessness of the process; reticence was the order of the day. Similarly, in *Economic Problems of Socialism in the USSR,* the shift from the orthodox Marxian view to the later Bolshevik attitude is left unmentioned, and the process of pulling up the "basis" toward the "superstructure" is made deceptively smooth, with the fraudulent equation of Lenin's "cooperative plan" and collectivization playing its part.[14]

(2) But while the educational value of this backward glance should not be underestimated, Stalin's disquisition contained two points of more direct significance. He made it clear that he viewed the *kolkhoz* form of socialist ownership as distinctly inferior to the *sovkhoz* form, and indicated that the first would have to yield to the second because it was becoming an obstacle to the development of productive forces. For a modest start he suggested that part of the produce

---

13. Ibid., p. 324.

14. Consider this example of skillful blurring of the edges: "The productive forces of our country, *particularly (!) in industry* were social in nature, but the form of ownership was private, capitalist. Taking guidance from the law of obligatory correspondence of relationships of production and the nature of the productive forces, the Soviet government socialized means of production, etc. etc." "Ekonomicheskie Problemy . . . ," ibid., Vol. XVI (3), p. 194. (My italics.)

The *coup de plume* is still more flagrant in the case of Lenin's "cooperative plan" (ibid., p. 202). Stalin obviously refers to Lenin's article "O kooperatsii" (March 1923). Yet Lenin said not a word about producers' cooperatives of any sort. Instead, he talked at length about "supporting [only] such a cooperative turnover *(oborot)* in which actual masses of the population are actually participating," and he observed that "for a good cooperatist it was entirely sufficient to be a sensible and literate trader" *(torgash). Polnoe sobranie sochinenii,* Vol. 45, pp. 371, 373. In short, Lenin clearly had in mind marketing cooperatives and not producers' cooperatives: he must have felt that the Soviet economy could not yet afford the latter.

In his "Speech to the Voters" in early 1946 Stalin observed that in order to introduce large-scale units in agriculture, the landlords had to ruin the peasants first, and this made it a time-consuming process. *Sochineniia,* Vol. XVI (3), pp. 15–16. Did he mean to say that his regime succeeded in accomplishing both these tasks simultaneously?

of the collective farm, which had been until now purchased by the state, be channeled into direct product exchange between nationalized industry and collective farms. His unrelenting mistrust of every sort of control which was not ironclad and which allowed even the flimsiest kind of autonomy at lower levels came through most strikingly here. A similar attitude, odd as it may sound, apparently underlay his affectionate treatment of the machine-building industry, all the way from the mid-twenties until his last piece. "To put one part of the means of production (raw materials) on the same level as instruments of production is to sin against Marxism, because Marxism assumes the leading role of the instruments of production as compared with all other means of production." [15] This may be true as a broad statement to the effect that the instruments of production are the main carriers of technological change, but it makes no sense in reference to the concrete processes of production. Stalin probably intended to find an excuse for the disparities between the growth of machine-building and the growth of iron and steel output which were endemic to Soviet plans, particularly to the First. Yet he may also have had something else in mind. In the early thirties, in one of his exhortative speeches, he exclaimed, "Each new factory, each new mill is a fortress in the hands of the proletariat." [16] Perhaps he felt that from the viewpoint of control over the greatest possible number of people it might be better to have more such "fortresses" whose men and machines would be poorly supplied with steel rather than fewer "fortresses" with a smaller number of men and machines well supplied with steel; and that a planned economy could minimize the inconvenience of a shortfall in steel output by rationing the produced amount among the most important users.

(3) The points made at the end of the last paragraph are inevitably conjectural: Stalin's observations on the subject in question are rather cryptic. There is, however, no obscurity whatsoever in his well-known remarks on problems of economic growth under socialism. My comments will consist largely in summarizing criticisms to which they have given rise. (Most of them came from post-Stalinist Poland, with Kalecki, Brus and Łaski leading the way.) [17]

Stalin's dictum that there can be no growth ("expanded reproduction") unless

---

15. Ibid., p. 354. Interestingly, Mao Tse-tung expressed serious reservations on this point in his speech of November 1958: "Within the mutual relationship of heavy industry, [Stalin] did not bring out the major aspect of the contradictions. He stressed heavy industry, calling steel the foundation and machinery the heart. . . . When we propose steel as the foundation, there will be raw material, and the machine industry will follow suit." (I am much indebted to Harry Magdoff and Carl Riskin for calling this document to my attention.) In addition, Stalin is criticized for consistently "walking on one leg"—stressing heavy industry at the expense of light industry and agriculture, emphasizing technology and cadres but showing "distrust of the masses."

16. *Sochineniia,* Vol. IX, pp. 156–57, quoted by John D. Bergamini, "Stalin and the Collective Farm," in *Continuity and Change in Russian and Soviet Thought,* ed. Ernest J. Simmons (Cambridge, Mass., 1955), pp. 219–20.

17. See Michal Kalecki, "Dynamika inwestycji i dochodu narodowego w gospodarce socjalistycznej," *Ekonomista,* 1956, No. 5; *Ekonomia polityczna socjalizmu,* ed. Włodzimierz Brus (Warsaw, 1965); Kazimierz Łaski, *Zarys teorii reprodukcji socjalistycznej* (Warsaw, 1965).

"sector I" is growing faster than "sector II" can be right or wrong, depending on circumstances. As can be easily shown, the rate of growth is directly proportional to the share of net investment in national income and inversely proportional to the amount of extra capital per unit of extra output. (This is usually expressed in terms of the Harrod-Domar formula or of its close equivalent designed by Kalecki.) Hence the rate of growth will be constant and positive if the share of net investment in income remains stable, provided that the amount of capital per unit of output likewise remains stable. (To be sure, the rate of investment must in all circumstances be above zero.) In such a case Stalin's proposition is obviously false. It would be, if anything, even more false when the amount of capital per unit of output goes down (e.g., as a result of capital-saving technological progress). But if the capital per unit of output goes up and the rate of growth is to be maintained on the same level as before, the share of investment in national income must rise correspondingly. Lastly, in order to *raise* the rate of growth, the share of investment must go up; and it must do this even more strongly if the capital-output ratio is rising at the same time. This situation is quite realistic in countries in the early stages of industrialization. The rate of growth in such countries must go up by definition; and it is virtually certain that this will involve a shift toward more capital-using sectors of the economy, particularly when the possibilities of foreign trade are very limited. That's why economists of both major groups within the Bolshevik party in the late twenties were fully agreed that, all things considered, the output of "sector I" had to pull ahead of "sector II." But Stalin made his statement twenty-five years later, when the Soviet Union had already gone through four five-year plans and emerged from them as the second strongest power in the world, with a tremendously expanded share of "sector I" in national income. Moreover, the recent trends in technology were not necessarily pointing to an increase in capital requirements per unit of output.

It is therefore hard to see any economic sense in this dogmatic commitment to a rising rate of investment regardless of circumstances. It is much easier to see the drawbacks. A high rate of investment, even if it is constant, must sooner or later cause an exhaustion of the reserves of the labor force. This would happen sooner rather than later if the Soviet economy had obeyed Stalin's injunction and kept raising the share of investment from an already fairly high level. When a critical level is approached, the planners will attempt to switch to more capital-using techniques which require fewer workers per machine. But while they are raising the output per man, they also raise capital requirements per unit of output, and this, as we have seen, would be bad for the rate of growth. Then we get some sort of rat race between growing capital requirements and growing share of investment, with the rate of growth having increasing difficulties in staying at the old level and the share of consumption in the national income going steadily down (a point forcefully made by Abram Bergson).

It could certainly be argued that this is an unduly static approach. A mature industrial economy which is running into labor shortage can be expected to respond by accelerating the rate of its technological progress: [18] the workers could work not only (and not necessarily) with bigger machines, but also, and in the first place, with better machines, and the diffusion of these innovations would be assumed to be rapid. Yet the Soviet economy, for reasons rooted in its growth pattern and institutional setting, was not very hospitable to technological progress. The pervasive over-strain (even if less severe than in earlier years) made experimentation in new technology both difficult and not very attractive in view of the sustained sellers' market. The system of over-centralized planning, with its tortuously slow information-flows and reluctance on the part of managers to risk under-fulfillment of the plan because of inevitable initial disarrays resulting from a switch to new methods or products, had been throwing up additional obstacles. (Here the situation was, if anything, more difficult than before, owing to greater complexity of the economy and to a much larger number of decisions to be taken.) At the same time, owing to tautness of plans and to their frequent upward revisions, the managers of plants were trying to lay their hands on large quantities of familiar equipment as part of a "playing-it-safe" strategy. Hence the seeming paradox of trying to make up for the slowness of technological progress by means of profligacy in the use of capital—an effort which persists and which is at least partly successful, judging by the unceasing complaints of Soviet leaders. As a result, accumulation not only proceeds at very high speed with regard to the available human resources—it is also being pushed hard, even if not quite as hard as before, against the capacity limits. Both the accumulation model of Volume I and the two-sector model of Volume II are getting a tough workout, as it were. What is even worse, they are getting in each other's way; and the rapidity of technological progress is one of the casualties. [19]

One might reply that Stalin was not a "Struvist" and that efficient and smooth economic development was not his prime objective. Every extra bit of power, whether obtained by hook or by crook, was welcome because it increased the strength of the Soviet state with regard to its enemies at home and abroad, and because opportunities for the tightening of controls over society were still far from exhausted. The planned transition from collective farms to state farms was a case in point. The argument that the late-Bukharin way of solving the stupendous

---

18. As Joan Robinson has pointed out, the widely accepted distinction between a shift within the limits of given technological knowledge and a move beyond these limits is of questionable validity because only the actually used technology is fully blueprinted; hence the switch to an allegedly "known" method which has not been used before is hard to distinguish from an innovation. Yet she acknowledges that the situation would be different in a developing country facing a wide range of fully blueprinted technologies in the advanced countries.

19. This does not mean that the rapidity of technological progress in the Soviet Union is lower than it was in the past or even that it is necessarily lower than in advanced capitalist countries, although eminent Soviet spokesmen have been suggesting the latter. It simply means that with "advantages of backwardness" still in existence, and with the impressive amount of effort put into research and development, the rate of Soviet technological progress is lower than it could have been. Moreover, it is also lower than it should have been in order to implement the *dognat' i peregnat'* slogan in conditions of the "scientific-technological revolution" in the West.

tasks of modernization confronting Soviet society might have led to equally momentous economic progress, but at a much lower price in terms of human suffering and wasted resources, would have sounded hollow to him. Stalin must have felt (although it would have been impolitic of him to say so) that the staggering sacrifices which his industrialization pattern had imposed on the society were in an important sense a gain to the system, and he unquestionably would have a strong point here. The hammer-blows of the collectivization drive broke the back of the group which had a measure of economic independence and which constituted the bulk of the population. The overstrain and all-pervading tension helped to create the mood of quasi-mobilization. Such a fortress-under-siege syndrome would make it easier to brand every dissent as treason and to legitimize the dictatorship both as a powerful protagonist of progress and as an avenging sword against enemies who want to capitalize on the discontent—a point eloquently argued by Professor Gerschenkron. On a less exalted level, the system of plan-made shortages helped to atomize the society by wearing people down and setting them against each other, and by accentuating disparities in income levels. It was not the case of the "old crap" coming back, as feared by Marx in *The German Ideology,* but rather of the "new crap" triumphantly emerging in the form of a new privileged stratum (although not a class) which would be of great value to the leadership (and which could be soundly shaken up whenever it started taking itself too seriously). Lastly, the man at the helm gave every indication of thoroughly enjoying the job, including the most sordid aspects of it. Yet toward the end of his career Stalin sensed mounting tensions. He realized that a measure of housecleaning was needed, as when he talked more volubly than ever before about constraints ("laws") in the economy. He chided those who felt that the sky was the limit, and he somberly observed: "It cannot be said that the requirements of this law [of balanced proportionate development] are fully reflected in our annual and five-year plans." [20] Still, in actual fact Stalin hardly yielded an inch. He made it quite clear that in his capacity of the supreme custodian of the "laws" he would enjoy a great deal of discretionary power, and the cavalier way in which he treated the "law of value" was not encouraging. Lastly, the unshakable insistence on the "preponderant growth of sector I," with no qualifications attached and no limits set, was an invitation to mischief. This was a somewhat more circumspect and sobered voluntarism, but it was voluntarism all the same. And in this mood he departed from the scene.

To conclude: what did Marxian models do for Stalin and what did Stalin do to them? Stalin certainly benefited. The models, for all their lack of elegance and operational difficulties, have been very potent in focusing attention on such key factors of economic growth as interaction between investment and technological progress, the varying ability to control and mobilize resources under different forms of ownership, the importance of consistency between technology and social

---

20. "Ekonomicheskie problemy . . .," in *Sochineniia,* Vol. XVI (3), p. 196.

organization, and the sectoral substructure of the expanding economy. Stalin quickly perceived the production-and-growth-oriented nature of the models. He fully sensed, moreover, that to have a (genuine or faked) stamp of approval coming from a respected theory was important for ideological mobilization, particularly in a movement which took pride in the "scientific" nature of its creed. What he very conveniently chose to disregard was that while the models were "for" a rapid forward movement (to the extent that a model can be "for" anything at all), they were also flashing warning signals against excessive speed and were pointing to complementarities which cannot be disrupted without dire consequences. Instead, Stalin used the inherited concepts in an often shrewd but invariably coarse and bludgeoning way, utterly at variance with their internal logic. As a prominent Czechoslovak economist remarked, "Great leaps forward belong in the gym," and the idea of creating a viable basis for full socialism in a predominantly peasant country through a crash program of several years was pathetically un-Marxian in letter and spirit. The results were rapid economic growth, but also untold misery, monumental waste of resources, and perversion of the ultimate objectives: the formally collectivist relationships of production were voided of the egalitarian and libertarian content which the "classics" and their continuators had expected them to have. In the early stages of the process, the productive forces were not equal to the task imposed on them. Now, after having grown bigger and stronger, they require less confining forms of economic organization, but resistances are formidable—a typically Marxian set of "contradictions." Much of the *samovar* is already gone. Yet a disturbingly large part of it still remains.

Stalinism and
Soviet Legal Culture *

Robert Sharlet

Introduction

One of the paradoxes of Soviet history is that a major movement to revive legality occurred at the very height of the great purges of the thirties. Stalin was the "author" of both the impetus to revive law and the most dramatic manifestations of the terror. This essay will address itself to this paradox. Since there is already an extensive literature on terror, I will emphasize the more neglected subject of the revival of legality beginning in the late thirties. However, it is impossible to pass over in silence the inter-relationship of law and terror in Soviet history, so the interface of these two components of the social regulation process in Soviet society will also be briefly discussed within the context of the restoration of legalism.

Soviet legal culture under Stalinism can be most clearly understood within what can be described as a dual system of law and terror in Soviet society between which, as Harold Berman has observed, the "evidence tends to show a surprising degree of official compartmentalization of the legal and the extralegal." [1] This type of distinction has been most effectively articulated in Ernst Fraenkel's concept of the Nazi legal order as a "dual state." [2] If modified, the "dual state" has

---

* The author gratefully acknowledges the support of the American Council of Learned Societies; the Research Institute on International Change and the Russian Institute, both of Columbia University; and the Union College Research Fund in connection with the preparation of this contribution.

1. See Harold J. Berman, *Justice in the USSR,* rev. ed. (New York, 1963), p. 8. For a similar analytic distinction, see Barrington Moore, Jr., *Terror and Progress* (Cambridge, Mass., 1954), pp. 174–78; and N. M. Korkunov's distinction in Lewin, "The Social Roots of Stalinism," p. 134, above.

2. See Ernst Fraenkel, *The Dual State: A Contribution to the Theory of Dictatorship,* tr. E. A. Shils et al. (London, 1941). Several qualifications have to be made in applying Fraenkel's concept to the Soviet system: (1) the German prerogative state was established by decree; the Soviet prerogative state, which of course was greatly strengthened by particular decrees, was basically received from pre-revolutionary Russia. (2) The creation of the German dual state represented a trend from political rationality to political radicalism; the Soviet dual state reflected the constant, dynamic interaction of these tendencies. (3) The Nazi party was the main component within the prerogative state; the Soviet Communist party, in theory and usually in practice, has been outside of, and in control of, the dual state. (4) In the German dual state, the prerogative state was equated with the political sphere while the normative state was equated with the non-political, private sphere of society; except for

155

heuristic value as a theoretical framework within which to analyze the continual tension between legality *(zakonnost')* and party-orientation *(partiinost')* in the administration of justice in the USSR.

In the Soviet context, this is not a distinction between law or force, but the question of how "force," which is used in the regulation of all modern societies, is administered. In this sense, the Soviet "dual state" controlled by the Communist party, a metajuridical entity with "jurisdiction" over jurisdiction, would be divided into a "prerogative state" governed directly by the rule of force, and a "normative state" regulated through a system of sanctioned legal norms prescribing the permissible boundaries of interpersonal relations and citizen-state relations. Corollary to this framework is the necessity of making a distinction between ordinary cases and "political" cases, the latter being a category which has continually expanded and contracted throughout Soviet legal/extralegal history, depending on the party leadership's variable definitions of politically deviant activity. In so-called political cases, whether they concern opposition, deviation, "wrecking," dissent, or merely the desire to emigrate; *partiinost'* has always superseded *zakonnost'*, regardless of the formal indicia of the politically proscribed actions. Practically speaking, this has meant (and continues to mean) in such cases that political expediency and arbitrariness will prevail over the more predictable use of coercion based on an objective interpretation and application of general legal rules.[3]

In reality, however, the great bulk of the cases of civil litigation and criminal prosecutions, past and present, are actually concerned with such mundane matters as family, housing, labor, inter-enterprise, and personal property disputes, along with a much smaller number of garden variety crinimal cases.[4] In these

---

the brief period of NEP, the public/private dichotomy has not been a relevant distinction in Soviet society, therefore the dual state has exercised jurisdiction over different sectors of a fundamentally politicized society. (5) The German normative state was based on private law and was firmly rooted in modern German history; the public/private law distinction has been irrelevant in the Soviet experience, therefore the Soviet normative state, which was very weakly rooted in the pre-revolutionary system, has been based on public law.

3. See my review-article of Solzhenitsyn's *Arkhipelag GULag, 1918–1956,* Parts I–II, in Robert Sharlet, "Gulag: A Chronicle of Soviet Extralegal History," *Problems of Communism,* XXIII (May–June 1974), pp. 65–71. For the contemporary variation, see Robert Sharlet, *"Samizdat* as a Source for the Study of Soviet Law," *Soviet Union,* Vol. I, Part 2 (1974), pp. 181–96. The interconnection, or *partiinost'* and *zakonnost'*, can be illustrated by two reliably reported incidents: (1) In the well-known 1961 case of Rokotov and Faibishenko, Khrushchev apparently intervened personally, urging retroactive application of the death penalty. When Procurator-General Rudenko replied that retroactivity would violate "socialist legality," Khrushchev reportedly asked in very strong language: "What is more important to you, your *zakonnost'* or your *partiinost'?*" The two foreign-currency speculators were subsequently executed. (2) In another, less serious, economic crime case, a judge who acquitted a "swindler" was summoned by the party. When he explained that because of insufficient evidence he had no choice but to acquit, a party official reportedly asked him: "What are you, a Communist or a formalist?" Yuri Luryi, "The Soviet Legal Profession: Notes of an Ex-Soviet Lawyer," lecture delivered to a "Soviet Law" class at Union College, Schenectady, New York, February 10, 1976.

4. Berman has estimated that over 80 percent of all cases are civil cases. See his article "The Educational Role of the Soviet Court," *International and Comparative Law Quarterly,* Vol. 21, Part 1 (January 1972), p. 85.

ordinary cases there has generally been, and continues to be, relatively strong boundary maintenance between the Soviet normative and prerogative states, although in cases reclassified as "political" this boundary is routinely violated.[5]

Within the modified concept of the Soviet "dual state," this essay will utilize the term "legal culture" as a more precise conceptual tool for gaining insight into the development of the Soviet normative state. The concept of "legal culture" is relatively new in the literature of East and West and generally bears the imprint of the behaviorally derived "Western" concept of "political culture." [6] Soviet scholarship on legal culture also tends to be behaviorally oriented. In the most recent Soviet study, the author emphasizes as legal culture the attitudes, beliefs, and sentiments which condition legal behavior.[7]

In contrast to the behavioral approach to legal culture of East and West, I have found Anthony Wallace's contextual approach to culture (as adapted by Robert C. Tucker) more congenial to the study of legal culture in a developing society. In effect, the idea of a *revitalization movement* as " 'a deliberate organized conscious effort by members of a society to construct a more satisfying culture' " by creating a *transfer culture* as a "system of operations that the movement prescribes for transforming the existing culture" into the *goal culture,* or the "image of an ideal society"—seems to work more effectively in mapping out the "complex of real and ideal culture patterns . . ." in the legal culture of the Soviet Union.[8] Essentially, this is a modification of Ralph Linton's distinction in order to better identify and distinguish between the salient characteristics of the real

---

5. Yuri Luryi, "Political Trials in Russia: Notes of an Ex-Soviet Lawyer," public lecture delivered at Union College, Schenectady, New York, February 9, 1976.

6. See Lawrence M. Friedman, "Legal Culture and Social Development," *Law & Society Review,* Vol. 4, No. 1 (August 1969), pp. 29–44; his remarks on "legal culture" in his article "On Legal Development," *Rutgers Law Review,* Vol. 24, No. 1 (1969), pp. 27–30, 60–62; and an application of Friedman's concept in Joseph B. Board, Jr., "Legal Culture and the Environmental Protection Issue: The Swedish Experience," *Albany Law Review,* Vol. 37, No. 4 (1973), especially pp. 605–9, 612 ff. Most recently, see Friedman's book *The Legal System: A Social Science Perspective* (New York, 1975), especially Chaps. VIII and IX.

7. In this connection, Soviet legal scholars may possibly have been influenced by the work of the Polish sociologist of law Adam Podgorecki of Warsaw, who, in turn, has been influenced by American social-science behavioralism. (See his recent book in English, *Law and Society* [London, 1974].) See, for instance, V. Chkhivadze, "Zakonnost' i pravovaia kul'tura na sovremennom etape kommunisticheskogo stroitel'stva," *Kommunist,* No. 14 (1970), pp. 42–53; and the more sophisticated recent study of E. A. Lukasheva, *Sotsialisticheskoe pravosoznanie i zakonnost'* (Moscow, 1973) which synonymously uses the familiar Soviet concept of "legal consciousness," but now with a greater empirical orientation.

8. See Robert C. Tucker, "Culture, Political Culture, and Communist Society," *Political Science Quarterly,* Vol. 88, No. 2 (June 1973), pp. 182, 185–86. Tucker's source for the real-ideal distinction is Ralph Linton, *The Cultural Background of Personality* (New York, 1945) where the terms are defined, respectively, on pages 43 and 52. For two studies in which an anthropological concept of legal culture is used implicitly, see Robert B. Seidman, "Witch Murder and *Mens Rea:* A Problem of Society Under Radical Social Change," *Modern Law Review,* Vol. 28, No. 1 (January 1965), pp. 46–61; and Seidman, "*Mens Rea* and the Reasonable African: The Pre-Scientific World-View and Mistake of Fact," *International and Comparative Law Quarterly,* Vol. 15, Part 4 (October 1966), pp. 1135–64.

or actual legal process in place in Soviet society at a given time, and those characteristics associated with the Marxian ideal of the "withering away" of law.

I

The Legal Cultures of War Communism and NEP

Soviet legal culture, as we generally know it today, is very much a product of Stalinism. Its main characteristics are stability, formality, and professionalism, characteristics of both legal belief and legal behavior familiar to any Continental lawyer as those of the Romanist legal culture of modern Europe. The legal culture of the Civil law systems of Western Europe was received in Russia both before and after the Bolsheviks came to power. As is always the case in the reception of ideas, this was a selective process, mixing the received legal culture with the indigenous legal culture. After the Bolsheviks' brief, unsuccessful attempt to extirpate this Russian legal culture and govern in a near vacuum of legal rules and institutions, Lenin placed in abeyance his doctrinal commitment to the imminent withering away of the state and law. Responding to the urgent impera-tives of ruling a backward country engulfed in civil war, he took up again the "machine called the state" and conceded the need for a transitional legal culture as a bridge to the future Communist society.[9]

Well before the tax-in-kind signaled the end of War Communism, the Bol-sheviks as a revitalization movement began building a legal transfer culture as part of their broad revolutionary process of transforming Russia to achieve their

---

9. The quotation is from Lenin's lecture on "The State" delivered at Sverdlov Communist Univer-sity in Moscow on July 11, 1919, and published for the first time a decade later in *Pravda,* January 18, 1929. See the translation in *Soviet Legal Philosophy,* ed. John N. Hazard, tr. Hugh W. Babb (Cambridge, Mass., 1951), p. 15. On the legal history of War Communism and NEP, see John N. Hazard, *Settling Disputes in Soviet Society: The Formative Years of Legal Institutions* (New York, 1960); Samuel Kucherov, *Courts, Lawyers and Trials Under the Last Three Tsars* (New York, 1953), Chaps. I–III; Kucherov, *The Organs of Soviet Administration of Justice: Their History and Operation* (Leiden, 1970), Chaps. I, II, IV, XI–XXI passim; Vladimir Gsovski, *Soviet Civil Law: Private Rights and Their Background Under the Soviet Regime,* 2 vols. (Ann Arbor, Mich., 1948–49); and Judah Zelitch, *Soviet Administration of Criminal Law* (Philadelphia, 1931). For valuable primary sources, see *Leninskie dekrety, 1917–1922: Bibliografiia* (Moscow, 1974) and *Dekrety sovetskoi vlasti,* Vols. I–VI (Moscow, 1957–73).

On the ideal characteristics of the Romanist legal culture of the Civil law systems of Western Europe, see John Merryman, *The Civil Law Tradition* (Stanford, 1969) for an emphasis on Italian law and Henry P. deVries, *Civil Law and the Anglo-American Lawyer: A Case-Illustrated Introduction to Civil Law Institutions and Method* (New York, 1974), especially Parts Three and Four, for an emphasis on French law. On the contrasting ideal characteristics of a "Marxian socialist" legal system, see John N. Hazard, *Communists and Their Law: A Search for the Common Core of the Legal Systems of the Marxian Socialist States* (Chicago, 1969), especially chaps. 4–6. Although he does not use the term, Hazard concludes that there exists today a distinct (although hybrid) *Communist legal culture* in which "the Romanist base has been remolded to achieve the purposes of a system of Marxist morality" (see pp. 522 and 528). This paper will concentrate on Soviet legal culture as the source of Communist legal culture.

goal culture of a classless society without coercion. Their early efforts to provide the population with a means of settling minor disputes resulted in a hastily improvised complex of real and ideal legal cultural patterns based on the Marxian ideals of flexibility, simplicity, and popularity; and a patchwork reality of legal rules, institutions, and roles. The Bolsheviks believed that laws should be flexibly applied by simplified legal institutions and legal roles, which should be accessible to the masses through popular participation in the administration of justice. During early War Communism, these ideals infused the jerry-built legal order comprised of miscellaneous proletarian principles of jurisprudence, former tsarist laws, an essentially local court system staffed by a lay and often illiterate bench guided mainly by its revolutionary consciousness, blurred and generally indistinguishable legal and social roles, and the vaguely defined rights and duties of both citizen and state.

Gradually, decree by decree, the real legal culture began to diverge from its Marxian ideals as a proletarian jurisprudence developed, new statutes were enacted, the court system stratified, the bench upgraded, related legal roles began to re-emerge, and rights and duties became more explicit for all. As the incongruity between ideals and reality grew, the legal culture of late War Communism began to lose its character as a legal transfer culture; i.e., it became less and less the vehicle of the withering away of law and, instead, began to increasingly "regress" in the direction of a reconstructed legal "superstructure" in Soviet society. However, the strategic retreat of the law began in earnest in 1921, when Lenin and the Bolsheviks adopted an unequivocably affirmative legal policy and explicitly prescribed a fundamental reorientation of the legal culture which was to serve as a framework for their New Economic Policy:

> The immediate task is to introduce strict principles of revolutionary legality into all areas of life. The strict responsibility of governmental organs, governmental agents, and citizens for violating the laws of the Soviet government and the order which it protects must be developed side by side with increased guarantees of the citizens' person and property.
>
> The new types of relations established both during the course of the revolution and as a result of the government's economic policy must now find their expression in the law and must be protected by the courts. Firm rules of civil law must be laid down for the resolution of all kinds of conflicts in the area of property relations. Citizens and corporations entering into contractual relations with state organs should receive an assurance that their rights will be protected. The judicial institutions of the Soviet republic should be elevated to appropriate heights. The jurisdiction and the scope of activities of the VChK and of its organs should be fittingly reduced and the commission itself reorganized.[10]

---

10. Excerpt from "Resolution of the 11th All-Russian Conference of the Russian Communist Party (Bolsheviks), December 1921, 'On the Current Tasks of the Party in Connection with Restoration of the Economy,' " translated in *Ideas and Forces in Soviet Legal History: Statutes, Decisions and Other Materials on the Development and Processes of Soviet Law,* ed. and tr. Zigurds L. Zile, 2nd ed. (Madison, Wis., 1970), pp. 66–67.

The legal culture which flowed from this new legal policy was a composite of the discarded Russian legal culture and the legal culture of bourgeois Europe. As such, it was a legal "counter-culture" [11] in relation to the Bolsheviks' goal culture. Basically Romanist in orientation, the NEP legal culture rested on the premises of stability, formality, and professionalism. For the Continental jurists and their Soviet Russian counterparts, this meant that a legal system should be stable and predictable, its laws formalized in written codes, and its personnel professionally trained in the law. On the basis of these ideals, a fully articulated legal order was constructed during the first years of NEP. The procuracy was restored, the bar re-established, a hierarchical judiciary re-institutionalized, and professional legal education resumed. Legal roles were once again clearly differentiated and to a great extent filled by former tsarist legal personnel and pre-revolutionary law professors. Codification was undertaken, and the new codes, based heavily on European models, were soon in force for civil law and procedure, criminal law and procedure, land law, and labor law. The codes were supplemented by statutes covering special topics such as patents and copyright, as well as exegetic commentaries guiding the judge in applying the various articles of the codes. Finally, perfecting and integrating the legal culture of NEP, the new USSR Constitution of 1924 established the first all-union Supreme Court "in order to maintain revolutionary legality within the territory of the Union of Soviet Socialist Republics. . . ." [12]

II

The Cultural Revolution of the Law

Except for a thin veneer of Marxian flexibility retaining for the Bolsheviks the "commanding heights" of the new codes, and a narrow stratum of legally educated Bolsheviks in leadership positions within the legal profession, the tiny band of Soviet Marxist jurists of the twenties regarded the legal culture of NEP as a "bourgeois" legal culture. These jurists created a Marxist school of jurisprudence during the early NEP period reflecting the Bolsheviks' desire to "contain" the bourgeoisie in Soviet Russia. Through the Marxist jurists, the Bolsheviks had attached the pre-emptive Article 1, limiting private rights to an otherwise conventional civil code,[13] and had incorporated the doctrines of social danger and analogy within a generally standard criminal code in order to restrict the bourgeoisie. However, the main task set for the jurists was the theoretical containment of "the bourgeois juridical world view" to help keep in sight the goal culture of

---

11. On the idea of counter-culture generally, see Tucker, "Culture, Political Culture, and Communist Society," *Political Science Quarterly,* Vol. 88, No. 2 (June 1973), p. 186.

12. Article 43 is translated in *Ideas and Forces in Soviet Legal History*, p. 72.

13. Article 1 of the 1922 RSFSR Civil Code: "Civil-law rights shall be protected by law, except in those instances when they are exercised in contradiction to their social-economic purpose." Ibid., p. 84.

Communism. The Marxist school of jurisprudence based its critique of the bourgeois legal culture of NEP on the assumptions that all law was a class instrument and that it would eventually begin withering away again in Soviet Russia.[14]

Pashukanis' "commodity exchange theory of law" was found particularly persuasive and adopted by the Marxist school. This theory argued that law was a peculiarly bourgeois institution reflecting the economic relationship of commodity exchange and was therefore destined to die out in Soviet Russia after the final elimination of private property relations. By the late twenties, Pashukanis and his school, supported by the party through the Communist Academy, had come to dominate the intellectual apparatus of the legal culture. With the end of NEP in sight, the commodity exchange jurists launched the "revolution of the law" as part of the broader cultural revolutionary assault against NEP, its institutions, and particularly its bourgeois culture. The revolution of the law, armed with Pashukanis' theory, represented a revived and more sophisticated legal transfer culture aimed at displacing the existing bourgeois legal culture of NEP and renewing the deferred process of the withering away of the law on the road to Communism.[15]

The revolutionaries of the law directed their main attacks against the NEP codes as the core of the real legal culture, and against the legal education system as the nexus between the real and ideal legal cultural patterns and the means by which they were transmitted and maintained. They reasoned that if the thicket of bourgeois laws could be gradually thinned out, the ground could eventually be cleared, with the remaining legal structures becoming increasingly superfluous and falling into disuse towards that time when they would be razed. Tactically, this meant the necessity of initially replacing the NEP codes with shorter, simpler models which would compress (and hence eliminate) the finer distinctions of bourgeois justice. The longer-term thrust was towards radically reforming legal education for the purpose of preparing cadres who would be socialized and trained to preside over the transition from the legal realities of NEP to the future idealized society without law.

Their primary target was the idea of "equivalence," which they regarded as the unifying theme of bourgeois legal culture and the factor most responsible for its cohesion. The idea of the equivalent form of the legal relationship reflected the bourgeois economic principle of the equivalent exchange of commodities in the form of private property in the marketplace. Contract law was considered the epitome of the bourgeois principle of equivalence, which Pashukanis and his

---

14. For a detailed analysis of the emergence of Pashukanis, his commodity-exchange theory of law, and the Marxist school of jurisprudence during the twenties, see Robert Sharlet, "Pashukanis and the Rise of Soviet Marxist Jurisprudence, 1924–1930," *Soviet Union,* Vol. I, Part 2 (1974), pp. 103–21.

15. For documentation of all statements made about the "revolution of the law" in this section and for an in-depth study of the movement itself, see Robert Sharlet, "Pashukanis and the Withering Away of Law in the USSR," in *Cultural Revolution in the USSR, 1928–1933* (proceedings of a conference held at Columbia University on November 22–23, 1974), ed. Sheila Fitzpatrick (Bloomington, Ind., 1977).

school attributed to all other branches of law as well. Against the symmetry of economic-legal equivalence, they opposed the asymmetrical principal of political expediency in their radical efforts to recodify NEP law and reform legal education during the First and Second Five-Year Plans.

Expediency as a principle of codification meant that the draft codes of the legal transfer culture were characterized by flexibility and simplicity, in opposition to the stability and formality of the NEP codes based on equivalence. Although only a few of the draft codes of the Pashukanis school were actually adopted (in the emerging Central Asian republics), their re-codification efforts nevertheless had a subversive effect on the administration of civil and criminal justice during the first half of the thirties. The draft codes were widely distributed in the legal profession, while their basic principles were constantly elaborated upon in the legal press and taught in the law schools. The revolution of the law appeared to be winning, creating what was subsequently called an atmosphere of "legal nihilism" throughout the society.

In the legal transfer culture, criminal law became "criminal policy" *(ugolovnaia politika)*, reflecting its extreme flexibility, while many of the procedural and substantive distinctions characteristic of bourgeois criminal jurisprudence were dropped in the interest of maximum simplicity. Similarly, the civil law of equivalent commodity exchange was supplanted by the new category of "economic law," encompassing the economic relationships between production enterprises within the five-year plans, which were enforced as "technical rules" based on the criterion of planning expediency. All of this was taught in the law schools, where the legal cadres of the future were being prepared to preside over the gradual withering away of the law. "Bourgeois" law professors had been purged from the teaching faculties and research staffs, and "bourgeois" legal disciplines had been dropped from the curriculum and were no longer the subject of professional research. What remained of legal education under Pashukanis' aegis reflected his school's strong commitment to the Marxist doctrine of the withering away of law through a curriculum heavily oriented towards legal philosophy, legal history, criminal policy, and economic law, which in turn had subsumed and severely truncated such branches as labor law, land law, and family law, formerly independent disciplines within the field of civil jurisprudence. The legal education of the transfer culture looked to a future without law, and accordingly stressed theory over practice.

The ideological intensity and theoretical intolerance with which Pashukanis and his school waged the revolution of the law is characteristic of a "millenarian movement," a sub-variant of the conception of the Bolsheviks as a revitalization movement which can be distinguished by the millenarians' obsessive "drive for the elimination of law" as the principal source of evil blocking attainment of their utopia.[16] For Pashukanis and his associates, law was a bourgeois phenomenon solely for the purpose of the regulation and protection of private property in a

---

16. Michael Barkun, "Law and Social Revolution: Millenarianism and the Legal System," *Law & Society Review,* Vol. 6 No. 1 (August 1971), p. 130 and passim.

capitalist society and, hence, an instrument of inequality and coercion. Therefore, they saw law as the main obstacle to the realization of their prevision of a classless society without coercion. As millenarians, they actively sought to build a self-liquidating legal transfer culture based on flexible legal rules, simplified legal roles, and popular legal institutions. Although they failed to dislodge the real legal culture, their legal messianism did have the effect of eroding the legitimacy of the law in Soviet society.

Precisely this success was the source of Pashukanis' downfall, for by the mid-thirties Stalin needed law both to stabilize his "revolution from above" and as an instrument for future social engineering. As a result, Pashukanis' school was destroyed, the revolution of the law overthrown, and the legal transfer culture uprooted by his successors. However, before its demise, legal messianism led directly to what could be called the "jurisprudence of terror."

III

The Jurisprudence of Terror

Pashukanis' attack on bourgeois jurisprudence inevitably contributed to the growth of the "jurisprudence of terror." This phenomenon of the inter-connection of law and terror had its roots in the aftermath of the Bolshevik Revolution, but it began to flower only in the late twenties, as the NEP legal culture shriveled up under the impact of Pashukanis' legal transfer culture. This development entailed the expansion of the prerogative state at the expense of the normative state. As Stalin launched his "revolution from above," the sphere of politically deviant activity was greatly enlarged. The use of political terror grew apace within the prerogative state. The most dramatic expression of prerogative action overriding heretofore normative regulation was epitomized in the process of "de-kulakization" in the course of the initial phase of the forced collectivization campaign during the winter of 1929–30.

The supercession of law by terror in the countryside, in normative terms, involved the ignoring or bypassing of stated legal norms without subsequent remedy.[17] By June 1930, the situation had reached the point that Krylenko, the RSFSR Procurator, complained to the Sixteenth Party Congress that the extralegal authorities were not merely commandeering and preempting legal institutions in the rural areas, but were actually interfering with them in their own campaign against the peasantry.[18] Krylenko was implicitly distinguishing between the direct application of political terror and the first flowering of the jurisprudence of terror with which the legal authorities were implementing the policy of collectivi-

---

17. This is Point I-1-A of the framework adopted for the Ford Grant Project on Soviet Law. The project group, which includes the author and ten other American and European specialists on Soviet law, developed the framework at its planning conference, held in New York City on November 21–23, 1975. The citation for this source is a working memo, "Framework for Analysis," prepared for the group by Donald D. Barry and dated December 15, 1975.

18. See M. Lewin, *Russian Peasants and Soviet Power* (London, 1968), pp. 504–5. On de-kulakization, see his Chap. 17 generally.

zation. This fusion of law and terror included such laws as the decree of November 1929, providing compensation to victims of "kulak violence"; criminal sanctions for the "rapacious slaughter of livestock" of January 1930; and the legislative *carte blanche* of February 1930, empowering local administrative authorities "to take all necessary measures . . . to fight kulaks," including complete confiscation of their property and deportation from the district or region.[19]

The jurisprudence of terror flourished rapidly along the interface of the strengthened prerogative and the weakened normative state. The fruit of this development was an especially grotesque species of political justice. Legal forms were coopted for extralegal purposes, judicial process was subordinated to political ends, and law itself was used to legitimize and rationalize terror. The jurisprudence of terror institutionalized and routinized political terror within the context of formal legalism. In effect, terror was "legalized" and the criminal process "politicized." Through the legalization of terror, the concomitant criminalization of a wide range of political (and even social) behavior, and the politicization of the coopted administration of justice; the jurisprudence of terror became a highly effective instrument for what Walter Connor has aptly called "the manufacture of deviance." Speaking in late 1930, Pashukanis articulated the basic premise of the jurisprudence of terror which he recognized as an inevitable way-station on the road to Communism and the ultimate withering away of the law. Rejecting the idea of a stable system of law; he argued for "political elasticity" and the imperative that Soviet "legislation possess maximum elasticity" since "for us revolutionary legality is a problem which is 99 percent political." [20]

The jurisprudence of terror took two forms. First, there was the tendency to posit loosely defined, as against clearly defined, rules, a natural outgrowth of the Pashukanis school's emphasis on simplification and de-juridization of the law as a stage in its withering away. Thus, vague or ambiguous legal norms denied the principle of predictability, leaving open a large area of discretionary space which in turn permitted (and even encouraged) arbitrariness.[21] The draconic Article 58 of the RSFSR Criminal Code of 1926 (more subjective and flexible than its predecessor Article 67 of the 1922 Code) was the purest manifestation of this tendency. In fourteen sections, Article 58 was sufficiently broad and vague enough to provide a formal legal rationale for potentially proscribing virtually any type of real or alleged thoughts or behavior. Or, as Solzhenitsyn puts it, "Wherever the law is, crime can be found." As such, he aptly depicts Article 58 as the "sword" of political justice, forged in 1927, tempered in the "streams" of prisoners flowing into the Gulag Archipelago during the next decade, and applied with full fury in the "attack of the law on the people in the years 1937–38." [22]

---

19. See partial translations of these laws in *Ideas and Forces in Soviet Legal History*, pp. 166–68.

20. Pashukanis, "The Situation on the Legal Theory Front," translated in *Soviet Legal Philosophy*, pp. 278–80. See also Walter D. Connor, "The Manufacture of Deviance: The Case of the Soviet Purge, 1936–1938," *American Sociological Review*, Vol. 37 (August 1972), pp. 403–13.

21. Point I-1-B of the Barry memo. See above, note 17.

22. My translation from A. I. Solzhenitsyn, in "Gulag: A Chronicle of Soviet Extralegal History," p. 67. For a translation of Article 58, see Robert Conquest, *The Great Terror* (New York, 1968),

The second form taken by the jurisprudence of terror was the tendency to make abrupt, undiscussed, or unannounced changes in legal rules (or in their application) which went in the direction of maximizing the power of the state at the expense of the individual, especially in terms of his personal security.[23] The notorious *lex Kirov* and the infamous "special boards" were near perfect specimens of this tendency. The Kirov amendments to the RSFSR Code of Criminal Procedure of 1923, which immediately followed his assassination, further sharpened the sword of political justice. These amendments of December 1, 1934, empowered (even required) the authorities to expedite Article 58 cases of individual (Sec. 8) or group terrorism (Sec. 11).[24] The NKVD special boards (heirs to the Cheka's "extraordinary commissions of investigation" and successors to the OGPU's "judicial collegia"), in turn, greatly exceeded their relentless predecessors in becoming the main conduits through which the torrents of victims struck down by political justice poured into the netherworld of the Stalinist camp system. Formally established in 1934 in the course of the bureaucratic absorbtion of OGPU into the newly created USSR NKVD, the special boards became one of the most formidable weapons of repression in the regime's arsenal. The special boards were exempted from all criminal precedural requirements, unlike the OGPU's collegia but similar to the Cheka's commissions. However, initially, the boards were subject to limited sentencing powers under the substantive criminal law. Sharing jurisdiction over Article 58 cases with the local military tribunals, which, at the outset, exercised exclusive jurisdiction over the more serious cases entailing heavier punishments, the special boards were limited to handing out five-year sentences under their 1934 decree. Gradually, in the late thirties and during the forties, their sentencing powers were increased from five-year to ten-year to twenty-five-year terms as the special boards dispensed with even the diaphanous cover of the jurisprudence of terror.[25]

Appendix G. For Solzhenitsyn's commentary on the article's fourteen sections, see his *The Gulag Archipelago, 1918–1956*, Parts I–II, tr. Thomas P. Whitney (New York, 1974), pp. 60–67. Article 58 of the 1926 Code was amended on June 6, 1927, into the omnibus political crimes article which became a familiar feature of Stalinism. Article 58 had its roots in first RSFSR Guiding Principles of Criminal Law of 1919 (drafted by Stuchka), made its earliest appearance in the first RSFSR Criminal Code of 1922 (which Krylenko helped draft), gained additional strength in the first Basic Principles *(Osnovy)* of Criminal Legislation of the USSR and Union Republics of 1924 (which the Marxist jurists influenced), and fully blossomed in 1926–27 (under Pashukanis' theoretical stimulus). The 1926 Code represented the successful culmination of several years' struggle between "Marxist" and non-Marxist jurists over the politics of codification and symbolized a major turning-point in the increasing Marxist domination of the legal policy-making arena. Pashukanis and the Marxist school regarded the subsequent 1927 amendments as a significant triumph of the principle of political expediency (over the bourgeois idea of formal equivalence) in the direction of the withering away of the law.

23. Point I-1-C of the Barry memo. See above, note 17.

24. Translated in *Ideas and Forces in Soviet Legal History*, p. 274.

25. The OGPU's judicial collegia were abolished in the secret police reorganization of 1934 simultaneously with the legislative action formally establishing the special boards of the USSR NKVD. See *The Soviet Secret Police*, ed. Simon Wolin and Robert M. Slusser (New York, 1957), pp. 15, 48, note 71; M. S. Strogovich, *Kurs sovetskogo ugolovnogo protsessa* (Moscow, 1958), p. 68; and Kucherov, *The Organs of Soviet Administration of Justice* (Leiden, 1970), pp. 72–76. Yet the term

Finally, there was the political "show" trial as the epitome of the jurisprudence of terror. Coopting the legal forms and procedures of a criminal trial, the prerogative authorities brought to political justice selected surrogates for the prevailing demonology whose public persecution was considered to have redeeming value for the regime. Beginning with the Shakhty trial in 1928, the first major political show trial, the Stalinist regime relentlessly perfected this hybrid of law and terror until, with the Bukharin trial of 1938, the jurisprudence of terror achieved full bloom.[26] As the culmination of the Great Purges, the trial was carefully scripted, directed, and staged within the full panoply of legal formalism. Bukharin and his co-defendants were indicted under Article 58 (including the "terrorism" sections) for "crimes against the state"; tried with meticulous attention to the rules of criminal procedure including the presumption of guilt, the special evidentiary force of confessions, as well as a broad conception of complicity; and predictably sentenced without possibility of appeal and executed soon after in compliance with the *lex Kirov* rules.[27]

In spite of the great care Vyshinsky lavished on this triumph of the jurispru-

---

"special board" *(osoboe soveshchanie)* first appeared earlier in Soviet legislation. In Article 10 of the USSR law of April 7, 1930, on corrective labor camps, the OGPU was specifically authorized to sentence people to the camps by "decree of a collegium or special board. . . ." (See *Sobranie zakonov i rasporiazheniia Raboche-krest'ianskogo pravitel'stva SSSR,* 1930, No. 22, text 248.) Although special boards were apparently created alongside the judicial collegia in 1930 (possibly in connection with collectivization and the decision to incorporate forced labor on a major scale into five-year planning), the latter remained preeminent in the OGPU and, in fact, were further strengthened in 1933 until formally superseded in 1934. For an account of the operation of the special boards with references to numerous "cases," see Solzhenitsyn, *The Gulag Archipelago,* Part I, Chap. 7.

26. The "political show trial" is intended here as a sub-type of the "political trial." In the *political trial,* a kind of "adversarial" struggle exists between the real or alleged political opponent and the regime, with the accused defending himself or being professionally defended against the charges, however foreordained the verdict might be. The spirit of this struggle was epitomized by the chief defendant in the 1922 trial of the Socialist Revolutionaries, who, in his final statement before sentencing, said, " 'If we must die, we will die without fear; if we live, we will continue to fight against you in the same way as before' " (Quoted in Bertram D. Wolfe, "Dress Rehearsals for the Great Terror," *Studies in Comparative Communism,* Vol. 3, No. 2 [April 1970], p. 2.) In contrast, the *political show trial* in Tucker's meaning is staged by the regime, with the defendant coerced to play the leading role, the "crux" of which is his pre-arranged confession "in vivid detail to heinous crimes allegedly committed by himself and others as part of a great conspiracy." Therefore, while political trials had taken place in Lenin's time and since, Tucker points out that the show trial is "one of the special hallmarks . . . of Stalinism" (See Robert C. Tucker, "Stalin, Bukharin, and History as Conspiracy," in his *Soviet Political Mind,* rev. ed. [New York, 1972], pp. 49–50.) On the Shakhty trial of 1928 as the "pilot model" and on the subsequent political show trials, see Conquest, *The Great Terror,* Appendix F and passim. For the most recent "evidence" of the use of torture in producing the Shakhty trial, see Roy A. Medvedev, *Let History Judge: The Origins and Consequences of Stalinism,* tr. Colleen Taylor, ed. David Joravsky and Georges Haupt (New York, 1971), pp. 112–13. Medvedev also confirms that charges of "wrecking" *(vreditel'stvo)* (Article 58, Section 7 amended—see above, note 22) greatly facilitated the fabrication, for reasons of political expediency, of an international politico-economic conspiracy by the bourgeois engineers in the Shakhty case (ibid.).

27. For the official transcript of the Bukharin trial, see *The Great Purge Trial,* ed. Robert C. Tucker and Stephen F. Cohen (New York, 1965).

dence of terror, it was marred by imperfections such as Krestinsky's initial repudiation of his confession, and Rykov's occasional failure to provide the necessary corroborating evidence on cue.[28] Most serious, though, was the barely perceptible but utlimately fatal blight of Bukharin's "anti-trial." As a defendant of stature, he esoterically used the trial as a forum for putting Stalin himself "on trial" before the "bar of history" for his crimes against Bolshevism.[29]

Nevertheless, after the war, Communist Eastern Europe provided fertile new ground for the jurisprudence of terror, and, for several years until the death of Stalin, the political show trial became a hardy perennial. With the Bukharin trial as the model, show trials were staged most dramatically in Hungary, Bulgaria, and Czechoslovakia. Directed by "Soviet advisers," these productions were more plausibly scripted, but no less flawed by the failure of certain principals to play their roles as written for them by their interrogators. The Rajk trial in Hungary of September 1949 went off well, but the main Bulgarian political show trial in December of that year was a near disaster for the jurists of terror. Kostov, the principal defendant, repudiated his confession and pleaded not guilty. Neither the prosecutor nor the bench were able to persuade him in open court to return to the script and perform his role as the villain; so they resorted to the unprecedented technique of having Kostov's confession, extracted during his preliminary investigation, read into the record. Despite the fact that Kostov, like Krestinsky earlier, was finally "persuaded" to confirm his confession later in the proceedings, serious damage had been done to the credibility of the jurisprudence of terror.[30]

Since the Czechs mounted their trials later, in the early fifties, they and their Soviet advisers had the opportunity to refurbish the tarnished image of what could now justifiably be labeled Legal Stalinism or Vyshinskyism. With their greater technological sophistication, the Czechs set out to obviate a repetition of Kostov's deviation from role. Unknown to the Czech defendants, their final dress rehearsal for the Slansky trial of 1952 was tape recorded. Should any of the defendants have balked "on stage," their prerecorded testimony would have been played into the record for maximum verisimilitude.[31]

The Czechoslovak show trials of 1950–54 were the culmination of Vyshinskyism, a name befitting the jurisprudence of terror which Stalin and Vyshinsky had so triumphantly codified in engineering the trial of Bukharin in 1938. Paradoxically, Vyshinsky was then simultaneously implementing Stalin's new legal policy of reconstructing Soviet legal culture and strengthening the normative state, both of which had been severely weakened during the previous decade by Pashukanis

---

28. For Krestinsky's "not guilty" plea, see ibid., p. 36. For Rykov's lapses, see ibid., pp. 332, 342–43, 359–60, 363, 371–77 passim.

29. For the "anti-trial" thesis, see Tucker, "Stalin, Bukharin, and History as Conspiracy," pp. 78–86. See also Stephen F. Cohen, *Bukharin and the Bolshevik Revolution: A Political Biography, 1888–1938* (New York, 1973), pp. 372–81.

30. See *The Trial of Traicho Kostov and His Group* (Sofia, 1949), pp. 68–73, 623–24.

31. See *The Czechoslovak Political Trials, 1950–1954: The Suppressed Report of the Dubcek Government's Commission of Inquiry, 1968,* ed. Jiři Pelikán (Stanford, Calif., 1971), p. 111; and Artur London, *The Confession* (New York, 1971), p. 225.

and his school. This paradox, however, can be resolved if one views high Stalinism as a system which accommodated the coexistence of political terror, the jurisprudence of terror, and socialist legality, each with its particular functions and purposes within the Soviet social regulation process. Prior to Vyshinsky's full ascendancy, Pashukanis, as the principal philosopher of law, had served as the regime's "middleman" between the Stalinist party-state and the Soviet legal profession.[32] With the help of his forceful intellectual and administrative leadership, the law as a regulatory agent had been eclipsed by terror and its jurisprudential rationale, but by the mid-thirties the "revolution from above" had been accomplished and Stalin now needed and could afford to revive, in Kirchheimer's words, legality, "the twin but respectable brother of terror to whom a more specific task is assigned: ensuring the regularity and predictability of behavior."[33] For this new task, as he had for others less savory, Stalin turned to Vyshinsky to serve as his lieutenant.

IV

The Stalin Constitution and the Stabilization of the Law
There were earlier signs,[34] but the publication of the draft constitution in June 1936 clearly foreshadowed the impending major change in legal policy. The new constitutional right of ownership of "personal property" and the provisions for

---

32. Pashukanis began his legal theoretical career as a protégé of Stuchka, who very early recognized his abilities and helped pave the way for the younger man's advancement to the leadership of the Marxist school of jurisprudence in the mid-twenties. However, Pashukanis' theoretical advocacy of his extreme position on the withering away of law beyond the field of civil jurisprudence, to criminal and other branches of public law, split the school into radical and moderate wings. As leader of the moderates, Stuchka was Pashukanis' "loyal opposition" within the Marxist school from in the late twenties until his death on January 25, 1932, at the age of sixty-seven. See above notes 14 and 15.

33. Otto Kirchheimer, *Political Justice: The Use of Legal Procedure for Political Ends* (Princeton, N.J., 1961), p. 287.

34. In his last major article, which also was the last of his three major self-criticisms Pashukanis himself acknowledged the earlier signs that Stalin and the party had expressed a more positive, instrumental approach towards the role of the state and law in building socialism and communism than the Pashukanis school. He traced Stalin's views on the necessity of strengthening the dictatorship of the proletariat as the correct means of achieving the ultimate goal of the withering away of the state and law, from the Central Committee's April Plenum in 1929 through the Sixteenth Party Congress in 1930, the Central Committee's and the Central Control Commission's January Plenum of 1933, to the Seventeenth Party Congress of 1934 where Stalin once again reiterated his thesis. See E. B. Pashukanis, "Gosudarstvo i pravo pri sotsializme," *Sovetskoe gosudarstvo,* No. 3 (1936), pp. 3–11, partially translated in *Soviet Political Thought,* ed. Michael Jaworskyj (Baltimore, 1967), pp. 315–23, especially pp. 316–17. In response to Stalin's statements from 1929 on, and to the implications of the Draft Constitution of 1936, Pashukanis executed three self-criticisms, in 1930, 1934, and 1936, each time trying to revise and adapt his commodity-exchange theory of law to the changing requirements of legal policy. Each time, as a loyal party member, he firmly believed that he was on the correct path, that he was following Stalin's "line." (Interview with a Soviet jurist, Moscow, December 1974.) However, it was Pashukanis' final self-criticism in 1936 which became the subject of the first public attack on him in January 1937. (See note 38, below.)

the first all-union civil and criminal codes implied the strengthening rather than the withering of the law.[35] Stalin's famous remark later that year that "stability of the laws is necessary for us now more than ever" signaled the new legal policy, and the promulgation of the Stalin Constitution a few weeks later, in December 1936, formally opened the Stalinist era in the development of Soviet legal culture.[36]

As the symbol of the defeated revolution of the law and as leader of the aborted legal transfer culture, Pashukanis was arrested and disappeared in January 1937. The purging of Pashukanis and his associates cleared the way for the re-articulation of the dormant Romanist legal ideals of stability, formality, and professionalism. The process of rebuilding Soviet legal culture began immediately under the aegis of Vyshinsky, Pashukanis' successor as *doyen* of the legal profession. While Pashukanis had been the theoretician of NEP legal culture, explaining its rise and predicting its demise, Vyshinsky, the practitioner, was its consolidator by reinforcing and converting it into the "Soviet" legal culture.

The legal culture of NEP along with the statutory legislation of the intervening years, so long castigated as "bourgeois," was redefined as a "socialist" legal culture. The need to systematize the legal culture, so long obstructed as inconsistent with its withering away, became the order of the day for the legal profession. Jurists, driven from the law schools, the research institutes, and the legal press by the revolution of the law, reappeared as participants in the reconstruction of legal education and research. Disciplines banished from the law curriculum by the radical jurists were reintroduced beginning in the spring term of 1937. New course syllabi and textbooks for every branch of law, especially those eliminated or suppressed by the legal transfer culture, began to appear with great rapidity. New editions of earlier texts were purged of Pashukanis' influence and quickly re-issued. Carrying out the mandate of Article 14 of the Stalin Constitution, numerous jurists were mobilized to prepare drafts for the all-union civil and criminal codes. Finally, a positivist jurisprudence, largely derived from the Stalin Constitution and even the *Short Course,*[37] replaced the tradition of revolutionary legal theory epitomized by Pashukanis' sociology of law, as legal practice took precedence over legal thought. In effect, Vyshinsky presided over a counter-

---

35. See Articles 7 and 10 on personal property, and Article 14, paragraph "kh," on the codes, in I. V. Stalin, *Doklad o proekte konstitutsii Soiuza SSR/Konstitutsiia (osnovnoi zakon) Soiuza Sovetskikh Sotsialisticheskikh Respublik* (Moscow, 1936), pp. 62, 65.

36. Ibid., p. 45, Point 8.

37. Published in November 1938, *The History of the Communist Party of the Soviet Union (Bolshevik): Short Course* almost immediately became the Stalinist forerunner of what, for Communist China later, Mao's "Little Red Book" was the functional equivalent. The *Short Course* very quickly became a primary "source" for legal education and scholarship on the "Marxist-Leninist Doctrine of the State and Law." Note, for example, USSR NKIu, *Programma po Stalinskoi konstitutsii (dlia pravovykh shkol)* (Moscow, 1939), pp. 3–4, 13; A. I. Denisov, "Voprosy teorii gosudarstva i prava v 'Kratkom kurse istorii VKP (b),' " a paper *(doklad)* read at a national law conference held by the All-Union Institute of Juridical Sciences (Vsesoiuznyi institut iuridicheskikh nauk), January 27–February 3, 1939; and I. P. Trainin, "The Relationship Between State and Law," in *Akademiia nauk SSSR Izvestiia* (for Economics and Law), No. 5 (1945), translated in *Soviet Legal Philosophy,* pp. 452–53.

revolution of the law as the legal counter-culture of NEP was revived and strengthened. Under his leadership, the process of reconstructing and consolidating "Soviet socialist legal culture" proceeded with great speed until halted by the outbreak of the war in 1941. It was left to a later generation to carry through the task begun by Vyshinsky and his associates in 1937.

The first shot of the legal counter-revolution was fired on January 20, 1937, in *Pravda*. Pavel Iudin, a well-known *apparatchik* of the intellectual "front" whose views could be considered reflective of Stalin's, implicitly called Pashukanis an "enemy of the people" (the most serious criminal category) and excoriated him for obstructing the working out of "a system of Soviet socialist law," [38] a prerequisite for a Romanist-type legal culture. In an April issue of *Pravda*, Vyshinsky followed with a general critique of the impact of Pashukanis' "liquidationist line," especially on the branches of civil, labor, state, and collective-farm law; and on legal cadres and legal education. [39] That fall, the class of '38 of the Moscow Juridical Institute, the leading law school, had to re-take the required course on jurisprudence, which they had originally taken with a Pashukanis protégé who had just been purged. [40]

The new course on "The Theory of the State and Law" was first taught during the fall term of 1937 by Professor A. K. Stal'gevich, a moderate within the Marxist school of jurisprudence who had for years been a critic of Pashukanis' radical position. Professionally and systematically, Stal'gevich criticized Pashukanis' theory from the new positions of the legal counter-culture. This course, which became the basis for a new syllabus on jurisprudence for all Soviet law schools for the year 1938–39, followed the style of the day, which was simultaneously to elaborate particular positions of the legal counter-culture and to criticize the legal transfer culture both generally and specifically. Therefore, the syllabus theme on "The Soviet Socialist State and Soviet Socialist Law" included a topic on "The counter-revolutionary character of the 'theory' of the withering away of the state and law in the period of the dictatorship of the proletariat" while the theme on "The System of Law" included a topic on "The unmasking of the wrecking 'conception' of Soviet 'economic law.' " [41]

---

38. P. Iudin, "Protiv putanitsy, poshlosti i revizionizma," *Pravda*, January 20, 1937, p. 4, col. 4. Pashukanis was arrested soon after and explicitly called a *"vrag naroda"* in the version reprinted in *Sovetskaia iustitsiia*, No. 5 (March 15, 1937), p. 1, note 1.

39. A. Vyshinsky, "Protiv antimarksistskikh teorii prava," *Pravda*, April 9, 1937, p. 3, col. 6.

40. Interview with Professor John N. Hazard, New York City, December 22, 1973. Hazard attended Moscow Juridical Institute (which underwent several name changes in the thirties) from 1934 to 1937. Scheduled to graduate at the end of the spring term of 1937, he was urged to retake the first-year jurisprudence course during the fall term of 1937, along with the seniors of the class of 1938. The reason was that Hazard's class (1937) and the class of 1938 had originally taken the course from M. Dotsenko, who was purged along with his mentor, Pashukanis. (Iudin in *Pravda*, note 38, above, also criticized Dotsenko very severely.) The textbook for the course had been *Uchenie o gosudarstve i prave*, ed. E. B. Pashukanis (Moscow, 1932). Since a new text could not be prepared on such short notice, Stal'gevich taught without one.

41. See *tema* III, topic 5, on pp. 3–4, and *tema* VI, topic 2, on p. 6, NKIu SSSR, *Programma po obshchei teorii gosudarstva i prava (dlia iuridicheskikh institutov)* (Moscow, 1938). For the main

In the long run, it turned out to be easier to "unmask" Pashukanis than to create an alternative legal culture. The critical effort took only a few years, while the constructive task took decades. The "most urgent task," Vyshinsky announced in 1938, was the task of "building a system of Soviet socialist law on the basis of the principles of the Stalin Constitution." [42] Creating a stable, integrated legal system was a prerequisite for establishing a Romanist-type legal culture in the Soviet Union, so the revival and development of *civil law* to secure the new right of personal property and to invest the planned contractual relationships of the plan with greater formal legality, had the highest priority. Within a few weeks of Pashukanis' arrest, a course on "Civil Law" was re-introduced at the Moscow Juridical Institute for the spring term of 1937. In the first lecture on "Civil Law in Socialist Society," the instructor declared economic law a dead subject and denounced Pashukanis for his "harmful theories" hindering "the development of the principles of civil law which are now necessary." In subsequent lectures, he revived such standard civil law topics as property rights, form of contract, contractual relations, and damages for injury, among others.[43]

The first compilation of materials on Soviet civil law went to press during the summer of 1937 and included the relevant legislative acts, judicial documents, and arbitrational decisions for the past twenty years. Intended as an aid for law students while the first textbook was being prepared, the editor pointed out in the preface that "there is no need to prove the necessity of publishing a systematic collection of the sources of Soviet civil law since the almost complete absence of a source book of this type is obvious." [44] Pashukanis was blamed. When the first civil law textbook did appear a year later, part of the introductory chapter was devoted to a detailed and generally professional legal critique of Pashukanis' conception of economic law and the consequent suppression of civil law. On the positive side, the main thrust of the text was to re-establish the individual citizen as a "juridical person" with the legal capacity *(pravosposobnost')* to enter into legal relationships *(pravootnosheniia),* and to classify and legally define the types

---

critique of Pashukanis' theory, see Stal'gevich's first eight lectures, and his fifteenth, twenty-seventh, twenty-ninth, and thirtieth lectures (John N. Hazard, class notes, course on "Teoriia gosudarstva i prava," Moscow, fall term 1937). Although the lecture hall was packed with the new first-year law students and the seniors retaking the course, Hazard could not recall any particular student reaction to the day-by-day criticism of Pashukanis, except for one peasant student who, on the way out one day, leaned over to him and said quietly, "Don't believe everything you hear." (Hazard interview. The author would like to specifically acknowledge Professor Hazard's generous permission to read and quote from his class notes for the various courses he took on Soviet law in Moscow.)

42. Vyshinsky was addressing the First Congress on Problems of the Sciences of Soviet State and Law in Moscow in 1938. The quote is from his translated *doklad,* "The Fundamental Tasks of the Science of Soviet Socialist Law," in *Soviet Legal Philosophy,* pp. 340–41.

43. Hazard, class notes, course on "Grazhdanskoe pravo," Moscow, spring term 1937 lectures 1 and 2–6 passim. The course was taught by Professor G. N. Amfiteatrov, a moderate within the Pashukanis school who was arrested after his sixth lecture. He was later released and resumed his work as a research jurist. (Interview with a Soviet jurist, Moscow, December 1974.)

44. Vsesoiuznyi institut iuridicheskikh nauk [hereafter: VIIuN], *Istochniki sovetskogo grazhdanskogo prava (Uchebnoe posobie dlia vuzov),* Vol. I (Moscow, 1938), p. 2.

of property in Soviet society including state property, collective-farm property, and personal property.[45] The same dualism still prevailed in a 1939 syllabus for a special course on civil law for judicial and procuratorial personnel with the topic on the "civil suit" as the basic means of enforcing one's rights under civil law, side by side with the topic on "The unmasking of the wrecking and the anti-Marxist distortions in civil law." [46] By 1940, the teaching of civil law was still sufficiently new that the USSR Commissariat of Justice issued a "methodological" bulletin on how to deliver lectures and prepare practical exercises for civil law courses in Soviet law schools.[47] Finally, the process of re-codifying Soviet civil law was begun, but was not actually accomplished until the 1960's.[48]

Criminal law also had high priority in rebuilding Soviet legal culture under Vyshinsky. Beginning in early 1937, the legal restorationists subjected the radical criminal theories of the legal transfer culture to damaging criticism from standard positions reflecting Continental criminal justice. The critical barrage was opened by Krylenko, the USSR commissar of justice and Pashukanis' erstwhile comrade-in-arms in the revolution of the law, who himself was purged the following year. He had also been a public critic of Vyshinsky. Krylenko systematically compared criminal law theory before and after Pashukanis' fall, placing the new spirit of stability and formality in sharp contrast to the ideals of flexibility and simplicity which had prevailed up to 1937. A central theme was Krylenko's prescription that the new all-union criminal code "must be firmly based on the principle of the exact definitions [of crimes]" as one of the fundamental principles of socialist legal culture, as opposed to Pashukanis' "rejection of the division of the [RSFSR] Criminal Code into special and general parts" as a way of simplifying criminal law by reducing the precision of the definitions of crimes. This was a sharp about-face for Krylenko.[49] As in the case of civil law, re-codification

---

45. For the critique of Pashukanis, see VIIuN, *Grazhdanskoe pravo,* Part I (Moscow, 1938), Chap. 1, Sec. 8.

46. See *tema* I, topics 5 and 6, p. 3, NKIu SSSR, *Programma po grazhdanskomu pravu* (Moscow, 1939).

47. See NKIu SSSR, *Metodicheskoe pis'mo po voprosam prepodovaniia grazhdanskogo prava v iuridicheskikh shkolakh,* comp. G. N. Amfiteatrov (Moscow, 1940).

48. A Civil Law Commission was organized within VIIuN for the purpose of drafting a USSR civil code. Many *doklady* on the theses of the draft civil code were delivered within the institute during the first half of 1939. See NKIu SSSR/VIIuN, *Informatsionnyi biulleten',* No. 1 (January 1939), pp. 7–8; No. 2 (February 1939), pp. 16–21; No. 4 (April 1939), pp. 5–14; and No. 6 (June 1939), passim. However, work on the draft code was not completed, presumably because of the impending war, but also apparently because Vyshinsky eventually stopped the entire recodification process. (Interview with a Soviet jurist, Moscow, December 1974.) I would speculate that Stalin decided against the temporarily destabilizing effect of implementing a series of new codes on the eve of war. S. N. Bratus', a member of the original VIIuN commission, later became one of the principal draftsmen of the 1961 All-Union Basic Principles of Civil Legislation and of the 1964 RSFSR Civil Code, which was generally the model for the other union republics.

49. N. Krylenko, "K kritike nedavnego proshlogo (proekt ugolovnogo kodeksa 1930 g.)," *Problemy sotsialisticheskogo prava,* Issue I, ed. N. V. Krylenko (Moscow, 1937), pp. 6, 7, 21. On p. 6, Krylenko uses the phrase *"printsip sotsialisticheskogo pravovogo byta"* in the spirit of the concept of "socialist legal culture" being used in this paper. Krylenko was purged in 1938, probably for several

was begun, but was not carried out until years afterward, in the late fifties.[50]

To rectify the situation in legal education, the first all-union syllabus on "The Special Part of Criminal Law" was published in the fall of 1937 and included an introductory theme on "The wrecking 'theory' of Pashukanis and his 'school' on the rejection of the Special Part [of the Criminal Code] and the exact definitions of crimes." [51] The same dualism was apparent a year later in the first new textbook on the "General Part" of Soviet criminal Law, which criticized the legal revolutionaries for "rejecting the concept of guilt and replacing it with the concept of social danger." [52] In effect, this had meant the substitution of an ambiguous and hence flexible general doctrine for a specific formal legal category. The textbook restored the concept of guilt as well as the concept of punishment which had been displaced by "measures of social defense."

The new vocabulary of Soviet criminal law, which reflected the underlying changes in legal cultural patterns, was foreshadowed in the first course on "Criminal Law" (as against "Criminal Policy and Law") at the Moscow Juridical Institute during the spring term of 1937. In the opening lecture, Pashukanis was criticized for calling Soviet legal culture a bourgeois culture which would wither away so that "he saw no chance of working out a system of socialist law." From

---

reasons, including the fact that, as a legal radical, he had collaborated with Pashukanis on the above 1930 draft criminal code, among other projects, and, in defense of the radical positions he was now attacking, had subjected Vyshinsky to sharp public criticism in the course of their debate during 1935. The Krylenko-Vyshinsky debate had revealed the first major public signs of the growing conflict within the Soviet legal elite along radical-restorationist lines. Krylenko was then RSFSR commissar of justice and editor of the commissariat's publication *Sovetskaia iustitsiia (SIu)* while Vyshinsky had recently been promoted to the position of USSR procurator-general and edited the procuracy's journal *Za sotsialisticheskuiu zakonnost' (SZ)*. The debate emerged from within the Communist Academy and raged in the pages of their respective periodicals after Vyshinsky, in his June 1935 issue, published his criticism of Krylenko's commentary on the then (1934) current new radical draft criminal code being proposed by the Pashukanis school. In their 1935 debate, Vyshinsky was criticizing the same radical ideas on criminal law which, after the fall of Pashukanis earlier in 1937, Krylenko himself was now criticizing, no doubt in a vain attempt to save himself from the purge. For the main exchanges in the debate, see, in the following order, Vyshinsky, "Rech' t. Stalina 4 maia i zadachi organov iustitsii," *SZ*, No. 6 (June 1935); Krylenko, "Otvet t. Vyshinskomu," *SIu*, No. 18 (1935); Vyshinsky, "Otvet na otvet," *SZ*, No. 10 (October 1935); Krylenko, "Tochki nad 'i'," *SIu*, No. 33 (1935); and, finally, Vyshinsky, "Vopros deistvitel'no ischerpan," *SZ*, No. 12 (December 1935), which he concludes by confidently predicting that Krylenko's attempts to advance the withering away of criminal law "in our time are doomed to obvious failure" (p. 4).

50. A Criminal Law Reform Commission was organized within VIIuN in October 1938 for the purpose of drafting a USSR criminal code, but, as with the draft civil code, there was a great deal of activity but no results until decades later (see note 24, above). For summaries of the *doklady* on the theses of the draft criminal code, see *Informatsionnyi biulleten'* (1939), No. 1, pp. 7–8; No. 2, pp. 6–9; Nos. 3–5, passim, and No. 6, pp. 1–22, passim. Vyshinsky himself was a member of the Criminal Law Reform Commission along with several other criminalists who later participated in the drafting of the 1958 All-Union Basic Principles of Criminal Legislation and the 1960 RSFSR Criminal Code.

51. See *tema* I, topic 4, p. 1, NKIu SSSR, *Programma po osobennoi chasti ugolovnogo prava* (Moscow, 1937).

52. VIIuN, *Ugolovnoe pravo: obshchaia chast'* (Moscow, 1938), p. 11.

this general position, Pashukanis' theory in the field of criminal law "resulted in a refusal to work out socialist criminal law and the desire to depart from [the application] of criminal repression through a court." The instructor concluded, "It is clear that under the Stalin Constitution this is wholly out of step" and went on in the following lectures to restore to the teaching of Soviet criminal law the traditional concepts "known to other legal systems" but redefined as "socialist" rather than "bourgeois." [53]

Another aspect of the rehabilitation of Soviet criminal law heralded the creation of "Soviet socialist" legal history. In 1938, the first systematic compilation of Soviet criminal legislation from 1917 through 1937 was published with the emphasis on studying the history of Soviet criminal law to trace its origins and progressive development within Soviet socialist legal culture, a line of research which, as the preface correctly stated, had been blocked by the Pashukanis school. The compilers of the volume indicated that full-scale monographic research would be undertaken on the legal history of the other branches of Soviet law as well. [54] This was the beginning of a restorationist trend to "manufacture" a stable and orderly legal past out of the actual contradictory patterns of reality by way of conferring the additional legitimacy of history on the emerging "socialist legal culture" under Stalinism.

The related branches of *criminal procedure* and *civil procedure* both barely tolerated but taught as necessary "technical rules" during the revolution of the law, best reflected the abrupt transition within Soviet legal culture beginning in 1937. M. S. Strogovich in criminal procedure and A. F. Kleinman in civil procedure, the leading textbook writers who were on the periphery of the legal transfer culture, not only survived Pashukanis but became principal participants in the restoration and de-radicalization of the law. The editions of their texts before 1937 had kept just within the tolerance limits of the legal radicals, while their post-Pashukanis editions mirrored the spirit and letter of the legal counter-culture under Vyshinsky.

Strogovich, in the 1935 edition of *Ugolovnyi protsess,* had taken a clear position in favor of procedural flexibility against bourgeois stability and formality: "The study of criminal procedure cannot be reduced to the dogmatic consideration of, and commentary on, the norms of the Code of Criminal Procedure (which usually takes place in formal bourgeois jurisprudence), but should be the analysis of the procedural relationships themselves in the form that they take shape in reality as they are changed and reconstructed in a concrete sociopolitical situation, in conformity with the diverse forms in which the class struggle manifests itself and the various means of conducting the fight against crime." [55] In a similar vein,

---

53. Hazard, class notes, course on "Ugolovnoe pravo," Moscow, spring term 1937, lectures 1 and 2. It was in the first lecture of this course that the law students learned that Pashukanis had been purged, when the instructor referred to him as a *"vrag naroda"* (Hazard interview).

54. VIIuN, *Sbornik materialov po istorii sotsialisticheskogo ugolovnogo zakonodatel'stva (1917–1937 gg.)* (Moscow, 1938), p. 3. An early example of "socialist" legal history was B. S. Utevsky and B. Osherovich, *Dvadtsat' let vsesoiuznogo instituta iuridicheskikh nauk* (Moscow, 1946), which was written as if the "revolution of the law" had never occurred.

55. M. S. Strogovich, *Ugolovnyi protsess,* ed. A. Ia. Vyshinsky, 2nd ed. (Moscow, 1935), p. 5.

Kleinman opened his 1936 edition of *Grazhdanskii protsess* by paying obeisance to Pashukanis on economic law as the " ' particular (specific) form of the policy of the proletarian state in the area of the organization of socialist production and Soviet trade' " within which civil procedure as a technical form of policy was included.[56]

After the liquidation of the legal radicals, Strogovich and Kleinman quickly brought out new editions rejecting Pashukanis' classification of procedural law as technical rules and arguing that his campaign for "procedural simplification" had created an atmosphere of "procedural nihilism" which had the effect of "disorienting legal personnel" and eroding their respect for Soviet law. In criminal procedure this had led to "violations of procedural rules and the rights guaranteed by them to the parties in [criminal proceedings]" while in civil procedure it had meant "the denial of the obligatory necessity of observing the procedure for the hearing of civil cases, and consequently to the weakening of the role of our [civil] proceedings, the role of our courts and of all judicial activities." In opposition to these nihilist tendencies, the proceduralists cited Stalin's legal policy of stability and advocated the rebuilding of procedural formality within the legal counter-culture. In a practical sense, the new positions assumed that procedural rules were legal norms created by Soviet legislation and had to be unswervingly obeyed "like all Soviet laws," and that, in particular, civil procedure was needed along with criminal procedure "to strengthen socialist legality," but also "to strengthen in every possible way the defense of the property and personal rights guaranteed to citizens by the Stalin Constitution." [57]

The collapse of the radical conception of economic law in 1937 liberated not only civil procedure but other captive branches of law, including family, labor, land, and collective-farm law. All were restored to the status of independent legal disciplines in the field of civil jurisprudence, which was being re-established within the legal counter-culture. The return to legal orthodoxy in *family law* preceded the definitive end of the revolution of the law and actually served as a harbinger of the dissolution of economic law. The enactment of the well-known restrictive statute of June 27, 1936, on divorce and abortion, intended to stabilize the Soviet family, set in motion the revival of family law as a separate legal discipline. In the fall term of 1936, Professor F. I. Vol'fson reintroduced the family law course at Moscow Juridical Institute with the opening remark: "Family law has been omitted six years because of insufficient appreciation of the importance of civil law in the Soviet Union." Since the draft constitution called for an all-union civil code, Vol'fson apparently felt safe enough to cautiously initiate a line of criticism rarely if ever heard after 1930 under Pashukanis' complete dominance of the legal profession. Vol'fson argued for the revival of the branch of civil law and for the re-establishment of family law as an independent discipline within civil law, following the model of the "bourgeois codes" of

---

56. A. F. Kleinman, *Grazhdanskii protsess*, 3rd ed. (Moscow, 1936), pp. 3–4.

57. The quotations are from: Kleinman, *Grazhdanskii protsess*, 4th ed. (Moscow, 1937), p. 9; VIIuN, *Grazhdanskii protsess* (Moscow, 1938), p. 9; NKIu SSSR, *Programma po grazhdanskomu protsessu* (Moscow, 1937), *tema* I, p. 1; Strogovich, *Ugolovnyi protsess*, 4th ed. (Moscow, 1938), pp. 12, 62–63; and Strogovich, *Uchebnik ugolovnogo protsessa*, 5th ed. (Moscow, 1938), p. 15.

France, Germany, and tsarist Russia. Reviewing a major victory of the revolution of the law, he lamented that economic law had superseded the RSFSR Civil Code after the end of the NEP and the termination of private commercial relations, and tactfully pointed out that the prevailing status of family law within economic law was unsatisfactory: "The old sections remain in the Civil Code but have lost their importance, and, seeing the growth of economic law, some persons thought civil law was entirely to disappear. This was an error and even dangerous in that it saw only a mechanical and not a dialectical development of the Soviet economy. To be sure, the buildings are socialist property, but in them live people who have relations between each other, and economic law does not regulate these." [58]

Vol'fson's law class in the fall of 1936 could not have missed his implied reference to Pashukanis, who was the author or editor of the principal texts on economic law. After the upheaval in the Soviet legal profession, Vol'fson was able to pursue this line of criticism much more pointedly and openly. In his first textbook on Soviet family law he explicitly addressed himself to the radicals of the legal transfer culture: "Civil law dissolved into economic law and economic law [in turn] took on the appearance of a mere body of knowledge about the administration of the socialist economy. The living human being with his daily needs and interests . . . passed out of the purview of these 'theoretical' jurists." He concluded that the problem was "without a doubt rooted in the wrecking 'theory' of Pashukanis," which had prevented the development of "Soviet socialist family law." [59] Vol'fson set about to rectify the situation by including chapters on marriage, divorce, and alimony and such neglected topics as the "Personal and Property Relations Between Spouses" and between "Parents and Children." As a result of this trend, family law and family legal relationships became more stable and more formalized within Soviet legal culture under Stalinism.

Labor law, land law, and *collective-farm law,* however, did have to await the elimination of economic law. In the fall of 1936, law students were still being taught that "the subject matter of Soviet labor law (a part of Soviet economic law with the purpose of developing cadres) is the totality of legal norms regulating the work of workers and employees." [60] Two years later, law students learned that "Soviet socialist labor law is a part of Soviet socialist civil law . . ." and that its subject matter "is the labor legal relationships of citizens of the socialist state, their working rights and working duties, the legal regulation of their labor, [and] social insurance." [61]

---

58. Hazard, class notes, course on "Semeinoe pravo," Moscow, fall term 1936, lecture 1. For a comprehensive study of the 1936 family legislation, see Rudolf Schlesinger, *Changing Attitudes in Soviet Russia: The Family* (London, 1949).

59. See F. I. Vol'fson, *Semeinoe pravo* (Moscow, 1938), pp. 21–22. I have translated part of the quoted material from p. 22 of this text and have quoted from p. 21 from Zile's translated excerpt in *Ideas and Forces in Soviet Legal History,* p. 255.

60. Hazard, seminar notes, seminar for the course on "Trudovoe pravo," Moscow, fall term 1936, seminar 3.

61. See *tema* I, topic 1, p. 3, NKIu SSSR, *Programma po sovetskomu trudovomu pravu* (Moscow, 1938).

The concept of "citizens" was specifically intended to include the millions of collective farmers who had been excluded from labor-law coverage within economic law which was typical of the suppression of land law and the new subject of collective-farm law. Up until 1937, collective-farm law was denied the status of a new field of law "without precedent in the history of the branches of law," and along with land law "excluded from the curricula of the law schools" and prevented from developing "into the independent disciplines of land law and collective-farm law for studying and generalizing about the legal questions of the land system and collective farm construction." [62] However, after the overthrow of Pashukanis, a 1938 syllabus described "land law and collective-farm law as two branches of socialist civil law for the study of the science of land–collective-farm law . . ." [63] and, since then, both disciplines, along with labor law, have flourished and developed into stable branches of the "system of Soviet socialist law."

Finally, the Stalin Constitution made inevitable and imperative the revival of the branches of *state law* and *administrative law,* both banished from the legal curriculum and from legal research during the cultural revolution of the law as representatives of the "bourgeois juridical world view" which were superfluous under the dictatorship of the proletariat. State law *(gosudarstvennoe pravo)* was reintroduced in the spring term of 1937 and a course on administrative law reappeared in the following fall term at the Moscow Juridical Institute. Neither discipline had been taught for the past six years, so no teaching materials were available. As the state law lecturer said in his introductory remarks, "Today, for the first time in the history of the Soviet Union, is the start of a course with no textbook or syllabus." Nevertheless, he continued, the course would be "of the greatest importance in view of the Stalin Constitution which [is the source of] Soviet state law. No person can claim to be a jurist today without knowing this subject." [64]

Vyshinsky himself, although a specialist on criminal procedure, edited the first textbook on state law in 1938.[65] The first administrative law text, laying out the foundations of the subject as the law of "socialist administration" based on "socialist property," appeared in 1940.[66] Both disciplines were primarily derivative of the Stalin Constitution in the form of exegetic commentaries, and the convergence of the two produced the hybrid called "Soviet state and law," a static

---

62. See A. P. Pavlov, *Konspekt kursa zemel'no-kolkhoznogo prava* (Moscow, 1938), *tema* I, topic 5, p. 10; VIIuN, *Kolkhoznoe pravo* (Moscow, 1939), p. 30; and VIIuN, *Zemel'noe pravo* (Moscow, 1940), p. 16.

63. See *tema* I, topic "v," p. 3, NKIu SSSR, *Programma po zemel'no-kolkhoznomu pravu* (Moscow, 1938).

64. Hazard, class notes, course on "Sovetskoe gosudarstvennoe ustroistvo," Moscow, spring term 1937, lecture 1.

65. See *Sovetskoe gosudarstvennoe pravo,* ed. A. Ia. Vyshinsky (Moscow, 1938), translated as *The Law of the Soviet State,* ed. John N. Hazard, tr. Hugh W. Babb (New York, 1948).

66. See Hazard, class notes, course on "Administrativnoe pravo," Moscow, fall term 1937, lecture 17; and VIIuN, *Sovetskoe administrativnoe pravo* (Moscow, 1940), p. 15.

surrogate for legal philosophy which was to have the effect of freezing Soviet legal culture under Stalinism for many years to come.[67]

V

Soviet Legal Culture Under Stalinism

By the outbreak of the war in the USSR, Vyshinsky and the legal restorationists had made substantial progress in de-radicalizing Soviet legal culture, but the more ambitious task of reconstructing it and the normative state was not carried through until the post-Stalin (and post-Vyshinsky) years, and, to some extent, it is still going on. Essentially, Pashukanis' successors revived the NEP legal culture along with its Stalinist additions, purging it of the residual flexibility which Lenin and the Bolsheviks had originally implanted to limit private rights and contain the bourgeoisie. In particular, this meant leaving the real legal culture largely intact while counter-reforming the ideal legal culture, which the legal radicals had made the greatest inroads upon. Therefore, the greatest impact of the legal counter-culture as a restorationist movement was on legal education and on legal research, especially as the latter bore on the judicial application of the codes and statutes. Consistent with Stalin's policy of stabilization, Soviet legal education was re-professionalized while legal research was reoriented towards a return to procedural formality and the strict interpretation of substantive law. This was the crucial beginning of what became the long-term task of rebuilding an integral legal culture representing the congruence of its ideal and real patterns, or of its silent premises and its visible superstructure of legal rules, institutions, and roles. Vyshinsky in the late thirties, like Pashukanis before him, was struggling for the future of law in Soviet society, but towards the goal of strengthening rather than weakening it. However, while rebuilding Soviet jurisprudence in

---

67. On the new "state and law," see A. I. Denisov, *Sovetskoe gosudarstvennoe pravo* (Moscow, 1940), Chaps. I–III; and S. A. Golunsky and M. S. Strogovich, *Teoriia gosudarstva i prava* (Moscow, 1940), translated as "The Theory of the State and Law," in *Soviet Legal Philosophy,* Chap. 10. It was not until after Pashukanis' legal rehabilitation in the wake of the Twentieth Party Congress of 1956, and the posthumous attack on Vyshinsky's "cult of personality" in law beginning with the Twenty-second Congress of 1961, that the "thaw" in Soviet legal philosophy began. The impetus for the attack on Vyshinsky was not just his positions on criminal law and procedure; both branches of law had already been reformed and recodified. The main thrust of the criticism was against Vyshinsky's positivist jurisprudence in general, within which the legal reforms were taking place. Both before and at the Twenty-first Party Congress, Khrushchev had begun to experiment with a limited revival of the legal transfer culture of the past, through such institutions as the anti-parasite's legislation, the comrade's courts, and the *druzhinniki,* all three of which initially aroused the ire of the legal profession, which feared that these institutions would erode respect for "socialist legality." The idea of "withering away" was again in the air, but to de-Stalinize Soviet legal culture a new jurisprudence was required. Just as Pashukanis before him, Vyshinsky became a symbolic obstacle in the path of creating the jurisprudence of new legal transfer culture, "the theory of the all people's state and law." Khrushchev's successors have not been well disposed towards these trends, which have been superseded under Brezhnev by renewed efforts to strengthen the existing Soviet legal culture.

general, Vyshinsky, like Jekyll and Hyde, was also reinforcing the jurisprudence of terror, his evil legacy to twentieth-century jurisprudence.

The development of contemporary Soviet legal culture, and the consequent expansion of the post-Stalin normative state, paradoxically received its major impetus under Stalinism. It emerged as both a consequence of, and a response to, Stalin's "revolution from above." For Stalin in the mid-thirties, a viable legal culture was essential to help consolidate and legitimize the systemic social changes wrought by his revolution from above, by institutionalizing the results of collectivization and industrialization in a stable legal order. For both rulers and ruled alike, a stable legal culture was also needed to help repair the damage to the social fabric, rent asunder by years of violence and uncertainty, by providing a framework for greater regularity and predictability in interpersonal relations and, especially, the relations between the citizen and the state.

The task of systematically rebuilding Soviet legal culture along these lines was begun in the late thirties but suspended during the war, and only actively resumed in the mid-fifties, beginning with the reform of the procuracy in 1955. Since then, the legal reform movement has encompassed nearly every branch and institution of Soviet law, including the re-codification of criminal law and procedure, civil law and procedure, judicial structure, land, labor, family, penal, health, water, and—most recently, in 1973—education law. The ongoing thrust of the legal reforms of the past two decades, with some retrograde motion, has been towards greater stability, formality, and professionalism, in continuity with the Stalinist impetus and in conformity with the post-Stalin legal policy of "socialist legality."

To conclude, Stalin's rehabilitation of Soviet legal culture in the mid-thirties reflected an understanding that the law "was not a luxury but a necessity," along with terror, for governing the Soviet Union as a developing country.[68] However, he left unresolved the relationship of law and terror within the social regulation process. As Barrington Moore observed after Stalin's death, too much reliance on terror "can destroy the minimal framework of regularity and legality necessary to maintain the total system upon which the regime's power depends," while too little use of terror "diminishes control at the center by permitting the growth of independent centers of authority within the bureaucracy." He concluded in 1954: "Whether the new leaders will be able to solve this problem remains to be seen." [69] At this writing it seems clear that Stalin's successors find an unresolved relationship between law and terror advantageous, although, without a doubt, they have greatly strengthened the former at the expense of the latter. Finally, the jurisprudence of terror, although less fatal and severe for its victims, is also still in existence. Like Soviet jurisprudence in general, it too has undergone reforms since the death of Stalin (and Vyshinsky in 1954). The regime's contemporary jurisprudence of terror is far more legalistic and certainly more subtle, but equally effective in suppressing what is deemed "political" deviance by post-Stalin standards.

---

68. Berman, *Justice in the USSR*, p. 64.
69. Moore, *Terror and Progress*, p. 178.

Utopian Anthropology as a Context for Stalinist Literature

Katerina Clark

Western critics of Stalinist literature tend to focus on the history and institutions of political control. And of course one of its distinctive features was the extraordinary degree of hegemony the government exercised over it. But it should be remembered that, however distasteful political repression in literature might seem to those trained in the Western tradition, it did not *merely* reflect a gratuitous and compulsive drive on the part of the powers that be to control every aspect of Soviet life. Under Stalin there was much excess and arbitrariness. But for all the madness of those years there was also method. The central impulse behind the domestication of literature was to preserve its crucial function as generator and repository of myth. Literature provided affirming myths for the new society, myths of maintenance for the status quo. Consequently, both intellectualist tendencies among writers, on the one hand, and the production of countervailing myths, on the other, were equally anathema to those watchmen (both within and without literature) who would guard its purity.

The myths were themselves political, and, furthermore, celebrated the very system of controls which presided over their origins. Indeed, we have here an incipient chicken-and-egg dilemma. Who directed whom—did myth guide system, or system myth? We will not attempt to answer this question, since that would involve deep excursions into etiology into the kind of behind-the-scenes maneuvering about which there is scant documentation. Furthermore, both "myth" and "system" can be seen as representing different sides of the same coin—Stalinist political culture.[1] This paper will attempt to take both sides—direction and expression—into account.

Since we will be looking at myth in both politics and literature, it will be necessary to find terms which are neither exclusively political nor exclusively literary. An obvious place to go for such terms would be anthropology. This choice of methodology is particularly appropriate in this case because *the core*

---

1. It will be noted that I am avoiding the question of whether Stalin was individually responsible for minting this "coin" or whether, within both "system" and "myth," Stalin the man merely assumed the role of absolute leader. In trying to assess the role played by Stalin in the establishment of literary practice, the Western historian has little more than the Soviet official accounts and hearsay to go on, and his conclusions must needs be speculative.

180

myths of Stalinist society have been erected around kinship structures. The official rhetoric of the Stalin years sought to legitimize the state and its leadership by using kinship analogies and to give them a spurious organicity by invoking metaphors from the epic tribal stage of society. This has resulted in a sort of neo-primitivism which can seem a trifle incongruous in speeches about industrialization, for example, but which has served well the needs of a society which had broken with the traditional (tsarist) line of rulers, which was confronted at an early stage by the problem of succession in its own line (i.e., with Lenin's death in 1924), and which resorted to large-scale repression in the interests of state security.

Stalinist society expected of its citizens extraordinarily far-reaching allegiance to the state. The rationalization for this attachment was found in the analogy between the entire Soviet state and a "family" or "tribe." Soviet Russians were urged to jettison their sense of family based on real blood relationships and to replace it with a higher one based on political kinship. In support of this ideology writers and speakers provided an inexhaustible supply of real or mythic examples of people who renounced their own kin in favor of the new society. Perhaps the most famous of these would be the young pioneer Pavlik Morozov (1918–1931), who informed on his own father and denounced him to the court as an enemy of the people and member of a kulak conspiracy.[2] Pavlik died a martyr's death at the hands of the conspirators, but he did not die in vain, for his deeds were celebrated in countless school and pioneer primers, along with the dream that "millions of Soviet children will constantly strive to become as honest and dedicated sons of the great party as he was."[3]

This use of kinship symbolism for political ends is far from unique to Stalinist Russia. For example, in the Russian radical tradition the family has always been a central symbol for political unity, and in Soviet literature of the 1920's a major *topos* was the individual who was attracted to the "familial warmth" of the party and thus came to break his or her political and blood ties and to throw his or herself into work for the new society.[4] However, in the Stalin period this tendency was much more extensively adopted and was affected by some of the characteristic features of Stalinism: extremism, changeability, and rigidity of application.

The prevailing kinship metaphor of Stalinist ideology did not remain the same throughout, but was subject to some of the zigzagging to which many central values and political figures were subject in those times. However, in the case of Soviet literature the situation was more stable. This is partly because Stalinist literature forms a tradition which rests on exemplars, on canonized works which function as models for authors to follow in their later writing (rather as was the case with icons in old Russia). Additionally, although the second half of the Stalin period (the war and post-war years) saw many political and cultural upheavals, these were more confused, rapid, and chaotic than in the thirties, and did not

---

2. E. Smirnov, *Pavlik Morozov: v pomoshch pionervozhatomu* (Moscow, 1938), p. 37.

3. V. Gubarev, *Syn* (Moscow, 1940).

4. E.g., Iu. Libedinskii, *A Week* (1922).

give rise to a coherent, new kinship model. For these various reasons, during the forties Soviet literature seems to have lost its power to generate major new mythic paradigms. The seminal age for the literary tradition was, ironically, the time of the worst purges, i.e., the mid-thirties.

Thus the focus of this paper will be the distinctive kinship models prevailing in the literature and rhetoric of the mid-thirties, and their crucial role in providing supporting myths for the status quo. However, since the ideals of the mid-thirties represent a reaction against the values of the First Five-Year Plan years (which were also under Stalin), the contrasting kinship models of that earlier period will be introduced to provide a context for "high Stalinist" values.

During the first half of the Stalin period Soviet society was mandated, successively, two spectral utopian kinship models. The first (which was dominant for most of the First Five-Year Plan years, approximately 1928–31) was a variety of normative community by which man was to relate to man as brother to brother—and in so doing to follow the "prophet" Stalin; the second (which was most strongly felt during the mid-thirties, from approximately late 1935 until 1937) was based on a different kinship structure, on a hierarchy of fathers and sons with Stalin as the ultimate father.

These patterns are of course heuristic models rather than blueprints for actual political organization. At the same time they represent more than purely symbolic ideals, since they underwrote a great deal of political activity. Each of the two kinship models dominated the culture in turn, and each to the exclusion of the other: the age of fraternalist extremism was replaced by an age of hierarchical extremism. And each defined a mandatory pattern of relationship to be followed in a "family" whose limits were completely defined. All those not standing within the stated limits of the family were interlopers, and little hope was given that the family would ever be expanded to accommodate them. This xenophobia was disastrous in its consequences for those categories among citizens which threatened the normative ethos of the family. It is no accident that during the First Five-Year Plan years those purged were predominantly the non-lowly (i.e., the materially or educationally privileged), while many of the victims of the late thirties can be seen as representing would-be "fathers" (people such as Bukharin, Kamenev, and Zinoviev) and their supporters. Such categories do not, of course, by any means exhaust the list of those purged.

This change in societal ideal (from "fraternity" to "hierarchy") was actually part of a much more far-reaching shift in Soviet values which occurred in the mid-thirties, and which reached even into the philosophical. The cult of fraternalism and the lowly which characterized the plan years went along with a militant positivism (which was in its own way a democratic epistemology to parallel the democratic anthropology). As the kinship model became more vertical in its orientation ("sons" are to look up to "fathers"), so too did epistemology acquire its own hierarchy whereby there were different orders of "knowing," and a higher-order "knowledge" could be found superior to that of the common garden fact.

A second change can be seen in the revival of emphasis on the historical perspective. When the ideal was that all men were to be brothers, this implied that there would be no distinction between generations, and therefore no before and after, only the NOW. As the societal ideal acquired generational layers, there came a new concern for the past and for origins. And it was at this time that Soviet literature evolved its characteristic mythic masterplot whereby a change-over of generations stands in for legitimate political succession.

A capsulized version of the major shifts in values which took place in the thirties would go as follows. Phase one (1928–31): A cult of the lowly man and the common garden fact (i.e., empirical knowledge). The age of the little. Transitional period (1931–35): Greater social differentiation and scepticism about the empirically verifiable. The age of the big-*ger*. Phase two (late 1935–37 and beyond): A hierarchy in the orders of both man and reality. The cult of the *extra ordinary*. The age of the biggest.

Now to flesh out these bare bones.

The First Five-Year Plan period was of course a time when the entire national effort was put behind the campaign for rapid industrialization and collectivization. But the period also had its own distinctive, anti-elitist ethos, which was expressed in such capsulized slogans as "massism" and "proletarianization." Along with the industrial effort was to go a cultural revolution aimed at preparing society for the dawning new age. In its mildest expressions this cultural revolution involved a cult of the masses and their cultural needs—massive literacy campaigns, etc. But a harder-line interpretation of the term "cultural revolution" was widely implemented, what was called "the intensification of the class war on the cultural front." This "intensification" involved persecution of bourgeois professionals and students and their replacement by "proletarians." But what was this movement if not a large-scale process of voluntary and involuntary leveling? If all men were to be brothers, then the much-celebrated gulf between the educated Russians and the masses would have to be eliminated. . . .

During the plan years the blueprint for society was of a host of little men performing little, everyday tasks, but united as brothers to usher in the new day with their modest efforts. No man could be marked as being superior to any other except by virtue of superior service, and even that had to be integrated into the collective effort. The medals given to workers over these years, such as Hero of Labor and Order of the Red Banner of Labor, and the title "shock worker," were awarded on a mass scale. Frequently they were even given to a workers' collective rather than to an individual, and if to an individual then often for sheer length of service rather than achievement.[5]

Soviet writers were infected with the pathos of this "massist" age. They resolved to kill Literature with a capital *L* as a bourgeois institution. They rejected the concept of literature as aesthetic, as the product of individual genius, and as privileged or distinctive language. Instead literature was hastily married to journalism, and writers happily assumed such roles as information officer, tutor to

---

5. Edward Hallett Carr and R. W. Davis, *A History of Soviet Russia: The Foundations of a Planned Economy* (London, 1969), pp. 514–15.

raw (worker and peasant) literary recruits, and ghost-writer of "collectively" written books.

This anti-individualistic climate had its effect on the literary works themselves, where heroization was virtually taboo. So tyrannical was the cult of the "little man" that a writer was liable to be chided if he so much as paid attention to the factory *foreman* rather than the workers.[6] The captains of industry were kept in the background.

As the First Five-Year Plan drew to a close, starting around 1931, Soviet rhetoric began to reflect a major reorientation of values: a shift from the societal ideal of homogeneity to that of differentiation and to a reaffirmation of the value of hierarchy; and from the cult of lowliness (the masses) to reverence for leaders and outstanding achievement. The reasons for this change are no doubt many and complex. Clearly, however, egalitarian extremism runs counter to the interests of both quality and efficient organization. And by 1931 the hour of reckoning for the Five-Year Plan was drawing near. . . .

A major "signal" of the changing times is Stalin's speech to Soviet managers of July 1931. In this speech he proposed a highly differentiated system of wage payment which discriminated against the common, unskilled worker. He also announced a change of policy towards bourgeois professionals—from a policy of "rout" to one of "encouragement and concern." [7]

In effect, then, the days of "proletarianization" and "massism" were now numbered. Over the next five years official speeches repeatedly called for "higher quality," for "expertise" and for "outstanding achievement." The cult of technology was likewise on the wane: in several major speeches of this transitional period Stalin explicitly replaced his late Five-Year Plan formula "Technology is the answer to everything" *("Tekhnika reshaet vsë")* with "Cadres are the answer to everything *("Kadry reshaiut vsë").*[8] Man could now tower over technology rather than vice versa—but note that it was not the little man who was to be the cornerstone of the enterprise now. The ideal for the transitional period was the man who was bigger than his brothers.

In literature the shift in orientation had begun to be felt at the very beginning of 1931. Critics then began to question the standard preference for quantity over quality in literary production, and in themes for technology and the quotidian over human interest and more enduring topics—especially ideology.[9] Writers abandoned their dream of realizing a literature which would be fired by the creative spark in each and every man and called instead for a literature created by trained experts—or, as Stalin was to call them, "engineers of human souls," [10]

---

6. "Na proverku!" (editorial), *Literaturnaia gazeta,* August 5, 1929, No. 16.

7. "Novaia obstanovka—novye zadachi khoziaistvennogo stroitel'stva (rech' na soveshchanii khozaistvennikov, 23 iunia, 1931)," in *Sochineiia,* Vol. XIII (Moscow, 1951), pp. 55–59, 68.

8. "Rech' tovarishcha STALINA v Kremlëvskom dvortse na vypuske akademikov Krasnoi Armii. 4 maia 1935 goda," *Literaturnaia gazeta,* May 10, No. 26, p. i.

9. Cf. I. Makar'ev, "Pokaz geroev—general'naia tema proletarskoi literatury (doklad na sentiabr'-skom plenume RAPP)," *Na literaturnom postu,* December 1931, No. 35–36, p. 59.

10. P. Iudin, "Novaia, nevidannaia literatura (vystuplenie na moskovskoi oblastnoi i gorodskoi konferentsii)," *Literaturnaia gazeta,* January 22, 1934, No. 6, p. 1.

experts in molding human beings, in taking them beyond their petty worlds to greater vistas.

To this end, critics urged writers to abandon such follies of the plan years as the worship of statistics and the machine. Above all, it was said, readers need to be given human subjects whom they could emulate. Thus the "little man" is to be scrapped as protagonist, and even the stock hero of the second half of the plan years, the shock worker. There are already thousands of such people around, it was pointed out, and besides, such heroes are not *big* enough for readers to be inspired by them. One should write of leaders and managers instead.[11] And as time went on writers began to produce heroes who were not merely big, but monumental.

And so as the thirties progressed the model man developed from little to big, to bigger, and finally to biggest. Correspondingly, the fraternalist model for society was increasingly eroded in favor of hierarchy. But for some years no coherent model emerged to replace that of the plan years, which was now rejected.

During these interim years the literary world enjoyed *relative* liberalism and cultural democracy. It was almost as if the fact that there was no new cultural model meant that it was not clear which trends might threaten its purity. The tone of the press at this time was amazingly moderate, especially as compared with the shrillness of 1928–31 or the inflated rhetoric of 1936–37. The *de facto* parameters determining which writers or literary groups might publish were broader than they had been for some years: as late as November 1935, for instance, one can find in print a comparatively positive article on Velemir Khlebnikov written by D. Mirsky.[12] By contrast, the two adjacent periods which were dominated by coherent cultural models (1928–31, and 1936–37) saw massive "witchhunts" of writers.

It was not until the Stakhanovite movement was launched in late 1935 that a coherent cultural model crystallized which was completely antithetical to that of 1928–31. The Stakhanovite movement represented a peak in the reaction to the plan years' lust for fraternity. The Stakhanovite was not merely to be *greater* than all previous model men, but to represent a *qualitative* leap forward in human anthropology, as the rhetoric of the times claimed.[13]

In making this claim that the Stakhanovite represented a radical break with previous production heroes (such as the "shock worker") we must stress that the crucial difference here lies not in the actual achievements of the Stakhanovites, but in the claims made about them in the rhetoric of the times. There are, in fact, significant differences between the way the Stakhanovites *really* overfulfilled their work norms to such spectacular degrees (as per, for instance, their own accounts), and the official interpretation of these events.

In the initial phase of the Stakhanovite movement (i.e., late 1935–37) their

---

11. Ibid. See also A. Erlikh, "Sdvig," *Pravda,* December 25, 1933.

12. D. Mirskii, "Velemir Khlebnikov," *Literaturnaia gazeta,* November 17, 1935, No. 63, p. 5.

13. "Literatura stakhanovskogo dvizheniia," *Literaturnaia gazeta,* October 29, 1935, No. 60, p. 1.

production records were represented as fantastic feats performed by individuals who had to defy pressures at their enterprises in order to perform them. Furthermore, the skills or technological know-how they used were represented as a kind of knowledge they possessed uniquely and intuitively, as part of their "new man"-ness. In reality, of course, most Stakhanovites received a good deal of instruction, direction, and assistance from the collective, without which their "feats" would have been impossible.

The case of the original Stakhanovite, Aleksei Stakhanov, is a good example of this disparity between rhetoric and reality. The night before Stakhanov, a miner, made his record-breaking attempt at "unfettering" the production norms for digging coal, he was visited by two party officials from his factory who "discussed" his plans with him. And when he went into the mines next day he took with him a small team of workers, each of whom performed specialized tasks as auxiliaries to him.[14] But the collective aspect of Stakhanov's achievement was written out of all those speeches which hailed the "new man." Furthermore, the new-order production hero was not given a general title, such as "shock worker," but named after an individual hero, Stakhanov.

The most characteristic epithet used for the Stakhanovite was *bogatyr',* which places him in the tradition of fantastic Russian epic heroes who perform superhuman feats. And indeed the Stakhanovite was billed as capable of achievements of a higher order than even his superiors could attain. Yet at the same time he was in education, station, and political training one of the most lowly among Soviet citizens. In other words, the new hierarchy in anthropology did not correspond to the political or bureaucratic hierarchies, or to any of the conventional hierarchies, in expertise: the Stakhanovite was an extra-systemic figure.

Almost all the biographies of the original Stakhanovites follow the same pattern. All are of humble origins—from worker or peasant families—and had very little education.[15] In the case of Busygin, one of the initial five, for instance, he was "semi-literate" and had never read a book before performing his feat.[16] Indeed, the Stakhanovite was humble not merely in his origins, but also in his aspirations. As Stalin said of him at the first meeting of Stakhanovites: "These are simple, humble people without any pretensions to receiving all-Union acclaim." [17]

Despite the Stakhanovite's lack of formal education, his achievement in raising production norms was quite explicitly *not* by dint of sheer human strength.[18] The secret of his success lay in his *daring* to discount established empirical norms and "scientifically" determined limits of technology. Any man who had the courage to go beyond that threshold, it was claimed, could outdo production norms by "ten to one hundred times." [19] Thus the Stakhanovite stood as an emblem not

14. A. Stakhanov, "Moi opyt," in *Stakhanovtsy o sebe i o svoei rabote. Rechi na pervom vsesoiuznom soveshchanii rabochikh i rabotnits-stakhanovtsev* (Voronezh, 1935), pp. 7–8.

15. I. Gudov, *Put' stakhanovtsa. Rasskaz o moei zhizni* (Moscow, 1938), p. 54.

16. A. Busygin, "Moia zhizn', moia rabota," in *Stakhanovtsy o sebe i o svoei rabote,* p. 24.

17. "Rech' tovarishcha Stalina na pervom vsesoiuznom soveshchanii stakhanovtsev," *Literaturnaia gazeta,* November 24, 1935, No. 65, p. 1.

18. A. Stakhanov, *Rasskaz o moei zhizni* (Moscow, 1937), p. 35.

19. Gudov, *Put' stakhanovtsa,* p. 84.

only in daring and achievement, *but in epistemology as well.* Among the many extravagant epithets coined for him, "Prometheus unbound" [20] suggests precisely that. By dint of this new knowing there was to be a cut-off between the Stakhanovite's ontological status in society and that of all other citizens, including those of higher rank (and most emphatically including the captains of industry, those who would keep the Stakhanovite "bound"). Only Stalin, that father for whom he was a chosen son, stood above him.

The special relationship of the Stakhanovite to Stalin became a standard moment in all these biographies. Typically, the one thing which inspired the production hero to attempt his record was a recent speech by Stalin.[21] Shortly after performing the feat he would be invited to the Kremlin, where, for instance, Andrei Stakhanov found that "I could not take my eyes off him [Stalin]," and "felt a great need to get closer to him." [22] Stalin, for his part, would return the Stakhanovites' awed gaze by "looking down on us with the eyes of a father and teacher." [23]

With the Stakhanovite movement Soviet society acquired a new kinship model. Even though there had been a hierarchy in previous Marxist-Leninist models for Soviet society, i.e., in Lenin's doctrine of the vanguard, this hierarchy was not to be a permanent feature, and the ultimate kinship model was fraternal. But from the mid-thirties on, different systemic goals emerged. While it was true that in future most citizens would relate to each other as brothers, they would also look up to a father (or fathers).

In the various official speeches made to launch the Stakhanovite movement, Stalin and other spokesmen called for all other citizens to make that qualitative leap from their human level to that of the Stakhanovites. They told their audiences that the day would come when the Stakhanovites would be the rule rather than the exception among Soviet men. In so doing these speakers invoked that traditional Russian revolutionary *topos* for the way forward, one which has been in use since at least Chernyshevsky's *What Is to Be Done?* (1863): "Today there are still few Stakhanovites, but who can doubt that tomorrow there will be ten times more, and in the future. . . ." [24] Thus the fraternalist ideal had not so much been abandoned as delimited in scope. Indeed, the early Stakhanovites themselves made many declarations of the bond they felt with their "[brothers and] sisters in labor." [25] But these were bonds of fellow siblings more than anything else. The new anthropology provided for a higher order man than had been envisaged before (with the Stakhanovite as the prime example), but it also implied that a select few men could represent something even higher.

---

20. "Literatura i stakhanoskoe dvizhenie" (editorial), *Literaturnaia gazeta,* October 29, 1935, No. 60, p. 1.

21. Gudov, *Put' stakhanovtsa,* p. 26; Stakhanov, "Moi opyt," p. 6; Kryvonos, *Stakhanovtsy o sebe i o svoei rabote,* p. 27.

22. Stakhanov, *Rasskaz o moei zhizni,* p. 45.

23. Gudov, *Put' stakhanovtsa,* p. 59.

24. "Rech' tovarishcha Stalina na pervom vsesoiuznom soveshchanii stakhanovtsev," *Literaturnaia gazeta,* November 24, 1935, No. 65, p. 2.

25. Stakhanov, *Rasskaz o moei zhizni,* p. 44.

The main thing which set limits to the heights which most Soviet "new men" could attain was their position vis-à-vis the old Leninist dialectic of historical development, the conflict between the forces of "spontaneity" *(stikhiinost')* and those of "consciousness" *(soznatel'nost').* As formulated in Lenin's *What Is to Be Done?* (1902) the measure of human progress consists in the degree to which the individual or society has gone beyond the primitive state of "spontaneity" towards "consciousness." [26] In the context of Soviet Russia the lack of sufficient "consciousness" among citizens has traditionally been used (since Lenin's *The State and Revolution* of 1917 [27]) as the rationale for the institution of the "vanguard" (or select body of cadres which guides society) in a society which is avowedly intent on "building communism." Of course this lack of "consciousness" would have to be made up with all possible speed if the new society's aims were to be realized. Thus it would seem to be incumbent on anyone postulating a "new Soviet man" who represented a *qualitative* leap forward in human anthropology to establish that this man represented some leap forward in "consciousness."

Not so with the Stakhanovite, however. His elevated position in the anthropological hierarchy seemed almost at odds with his position in a Soviet political hierarchy. Not only was he quite explicitly no prodigy in political consciousness, but he was not a party office-holder (and thus potentially a member of the vanguard) or even a party member. Indeed, although several Stakanovites were made party members after the fact, not all were. [28] In the late thirties the standard formula for the "new man" was: "the best people, both party and non-party." [29]

The Stakhanovite not merely had no formal affiliation with the party at the time of his great feat but was also singled out quite explicitly as a representative of "spontaneity" rather than "consciousness." Stalin remarked in his speech to the First All-Union Meeting of Stakhanovites in November 1935: "The thing which strikes us above all is the fact that this movement began, as it were, of its own accord, spontaneously. . . . It was a movement from below, not born of any pressure whatsoever on the part of the administration of our enterprises." He then went on to show (as was also stressed in the hagiographic writings) how in most individual cases Stakhanovite initiative was, on the contrary, strongly resisted by the factory's administration. [30]

Thus, in Leninist terms, the Stakhanovite represented a qualitative leap forward *in spontaneity:* he was a man of superior energy, daring, and initiative. The model guarantees that he will always be son: he will always need some representative of higher "consciousness," some father to guide that "spontaneity."

26. V. I. Lenin, "Chto delat'?" in *Polnoe sobranie sochinenii,* Vol. VI (Moscow 1960), pp. 29–31.

27. V. I. Lenin, "Gosudarstvo i revoliutsiia," in *Polnoe sobranie sochinenii,* Vol. XXXIII (Moscow, 1962), pp. 1–120.

28. Stakhanov, *Rasskaz o moei zhizni,* p. 54.

29. Vas. Lebedev-Kumach, "Liudi stalinskoi epokhi," *Literaturnaia gazeta,* January 20, 1939, No. 4, p. 3; "Pisatel' na fronte" (editorial), *Literaturnia gazeta,* November 26, 1939, No. 65, p. 1.

30. "Rech' tovarishcha Stalina na pervom vsesoiuznom soveshchanii stakhanovtsev," *Literaturnaia gazeta,* November 24, 1935, No. 65, p. 2.

The hallmark of the new man was the *extra*ordinary—not to say super-human—feat. He was a palpable example of human response to the age's cry "Higher!" *("Vyshe!")*. But while the Stakhanovite, that superhuman producer, is in the West perhaps the best-known example of the new man, he is far from representing the only possibility. A typical 1935 list of "new men" comprises "heroes of the stratosphere and the Cheliuskin [Arctic] expedition, the inventor Tsiolkovsky, the *bogatyr'* parachutist, the participant in a 9,000-km. ski marathon and the worker who drives a shaft for the new Metro." [31] It will be noted that only one of those cited had to do with production or construction. If one were to characterize their achievements in general one would say that all had to do with advancing the norms for man's performance in the physical world: "higher," "farther," "deeper." And in truth the "new man" as a representative of a higher order of "spontaneity" was most often marked by his daring exploits in some struggle with elemental forces (what in Russia is rendered as *stikhiia;* cf. *stikhiinost'*, which can be translated either as "elementalness" or as "spontaneity"). Here one can see a further instance of the neo-primitivism of Stalinist political culture.

The most paradigmatic new man of the mid-thirties was not the production giant but the airman who blazed new aviation routes or set records for long-distance flights. There was nothing uniquely Soviet in this. During the thirties most of the major nations were captivated by the romance of high adventure, and derived much of their national pride and inspiration from sending valiant heroes "higher" or "farther," faster than man had ever done it before. Hitler and Stalin were both especially fond of having their young men prove themselves by scaling mountain peaks. And between the U.S. and the USSR there was an ongoing rivalry in long-distance flights: the U.S. had its Lindberghs and so on, the USSR its Chkalovs and Pananins.

As was the case with the Stakhanovite movement, the most telling aspects of the aviation heroes (as "new men") must be sought not in historical reality, but in the rhetoric they occasioned. While with each record-breaking flight the Russian press was bound to make *pro forma* claims for the superiority of Soviet aviation technology, the main thrust of their claims for Soviet supremacy were in terms of *human* superiority. And here the two standard arguments were, firstly, that the Russian fliers (the "sons") were better able to combat the onslaughts of the elements en route than could the fliers of any other nation, and, secondly, that Stalin (the "father") felt the sort of genuine concern for the well-being of his fliers that was impossible in a "capitalist" national leader. Once again twentieth-century Soviet man is judged outstanding by criteria which harken back to the epic tribal stage of society: the ongoing saga of the flights is billed as an arena wherin is enacted "man's struggle with nature," [32] and the Soviet participants are bound to prove "the fittest."

---

31. "Vnimanie cheloveku" (editorial), *Literaturnaia gazeta,* May 10, 1935, No. 26, p. 1.

32. "Pamiat' tridtsati otvazhnykh synov rodiny" (editorial), *Literaturnaia gazeta,* February 10, 1938, No. 8, p. 1.

Among Soviet airmen, a special place was given to those fliers who flew to the Arctic. This was, of course, "higher" on our globe than any other area. But it was also a place where the innate superiority of the Soviet airman would be more truly proven. The Russians have made their ability to survive in extreme cold a point of national pride. It should also not be forgotten that the pitting of man against the cruel world of snow and ice had special significance in Stalinist Russia because biographers of Stalin commonly highlighted his moments of heroism as he repeatedly escaped tsarist exile in Siberia and then spent the last years of the old regime in exile within the Arctic Circle.[33]

Thus, the "father's" mettle had already been proven. What of the "sons?" The iconic attributes of the mid-thirties aviation hero "reaching out into the higher realms" *(ustremiashchiisia vvys')* were energy, reckless daring, and high spirits —i.e., he represented a positive, but childish brand of "spontaneity." The most famous such hero, V. Chkalov, was presented in the various biographies as having been "a madcap daredevil" in his youth, driven to test out his physical strength in daring escapades.[34] One biographer commented, "His stormy nature sought scope for its expression, it sought some occupation which might channel his surging initiative, which might utilize his love of daring and taking risks."[35] When Chkalov became a pilot he found his metier, yet even then he wanted to fly in a way "different from everyone else," and in consequence was forever tempting fate by flying low under bridges, etc.[36] Another famous flier, G. Baidukov (who accompanied Chkalov on his expedition to the Arctic of 1936), was a veritable hooligan in his youth before "finding himself" in aviation, where he nevertheless did not calm down completely and did a lot of unauthorized stunt flying.[37]

These gifted but high-spirited children needed greater discipline and self-control ("consciousness"). And their main source of it was none other than Stalin himself. Stalin played a much more conspicuous role in the ongoing saga of the airmen than he did with the Stakhanovites. He usually bade them farewell on their departure, communicated with them en route, and was there at the airport to welcome them on their return. Whenever a prominent airman was killed in some disaster, Stalin would act as pallbearer at the funeral. He also proved himself to be the father of fathers by forever "cherishing and taking care of" all fliers,[38] by exuding "fatherly warmth" whenever he met them,[39] and by such touches as summoning the wives to sit with the heroes at a Kremlin banquet. (Krenkel', one of the heroes, recalls: "There was only one more joy which could be, and Stalin thought of it. . . . We felt a lump in our throats. . . . How much

33. Institut Marksa-Engel'sa-Lenina, *Iosif Vissarionovich Stalin (kratkaia biografiia)* (Moscow, 1946), pp. 18, 23–24.

34. G. Stalingradskii, *Geroi sovetskogo soiuza Valerii Pavlovich Chkalov* (Moscow, 1938), p. 4.

35. Ibid., p. 5.

36. Ibid., p. 8.

37. V. Chkalov, G. Baidukov, A. Beliakov, *Nash polët na ANT-25* (Moscow, 1936), p. 6.

38. *Geroi sovetskogo soiuza Valerii Pavlovich Chkalov,* p. 15.

39. Iu. Renn, "Uchitel' i ucheniki," in *Letchiki. sb. rasskazov* (Moscow, 1938), p. 567.

care . . . in this great man, so preoccupied with concerns of world-wide significance." [40])

But together with the father's care came his authority. All the pilots testified
in their memoirs to the marked influence Stalin had in tempering their "spontaneity." Chkalov, for instance, reports, "After my meeting with the great leader
. . . the content of my life became richer; I began to fly with greater self-discipline
than before. . . ." [41] In fact it is even said that at a Kremlin meeting on the eve
of Chkalov's historic Arctic flight of 1936, Stalin proposed changing the flight
route completely—to which the pilots readily agreed.[42] As "children" these
aviation desperadoes were clearly very dependent. . . .

Record-breaking long-distance flights by heroic airmen were a feature of the
entire thirties, not just of 1936. But as with all heroes of the thirties, the image
of the pilots which was projected in the press changed from that of a model
brother whom all should emulate to that of a model son. In order to appreciate
the "before" and "after" here one can compare the rhetoric occasioned by the
Cheliuskin Arctic expedition of 1934 [43] and that inspired by the Chkalov Arctic
expedition of 1936. In a June 1934 *Literaturnaia gazeta* editorial about the
Cheliuskin expedition A. Kamenogorskii writes: "In these heroes the country can
recognize itself. They are like us, like the people in the shop room, the factory,
or *kolkhoz.* Admittedly the image of Soviet man is more fully expressed in these
heroes, but it is not changed for all that." Kamenogorskii also reports that the
one thing which inspired the Cheliuskin leader, Shmidt, and gave him strength
to continue his struggle against the elements was the thought of those millions
and millions of class brothers that went with him on his way. At the same time,
the expedition members' heroism was cited as proof of their "Stalinist make-up
(*Stalinskii sklad,* a very common phrase of these transitional years).[44] Thus while
there might be gradations of greatness at the present time, in future all Soviet
Russians would be more or less equally great—by acquiring that "make-up."

For the Chkalov expedition of 1936, however, a corresponding *Literaturnaia
gazeta* editorial calls the expeditions' heroes "fledgling children of Stalin" (*Sta-
linskie pitomtsy,* a phrase which during these years superseded "Stalinist make-
up"). The author goes on to describe them as ". . . the sons of our native land
. . . who triumphed over the elements," and then draws an implicit parallel with
the Stakhanovites by saying that these are "heroic people who have proven that
there are no limits to the heroism of the Soviet people, and no limits to our

40. Geroi sovetskogo soiuza E. Krenkel', "Chetyre tovarishcha," *Znamia,* 1939, No. 10–11, pp.
220–21.

41. *Geroi sovetskogo soiuza Valerii Pavlovich Chkalov,* p. 11.

42. *Nash polët na ANT-25,* p. 12.

43. Actually, the Cheliuskin expedition originally set out for the Arctic by boat. However, the boat
broke up within the Arctic Circle and the expedition was forced to set up camp on an ice floe until
rescued in a series of plane missions. The expedition is generally regarded as representing a triumph
both against the hazardous Arctic conditions and for Soviet aviation—and is hence comparable with
the Chkalov expedition of 1936.

44. A. Kamenogorskii, "Doroga tsvetov," *Literaturnaia gazeta,* June 20, 1934, No. 78, p. 1.

aviation technology." "But," continues the editorial rhetorically, "what was it that inspired our heroes?" "It was the thought of Stalin which inspired us on our entire route," Chkalov informs the reader.[45]

In the editorial for the succeeding issue of *Literaturnaia gazeta,* one entitled "The Heroes of the Soviet *Tribe*" (emphasis added), this thought is expressed even more lyrically: "For over nine thousand miles this steel Soviet bird flew on with a spreading of wings [actually, *"razmakh kryl'ev"*] such as had never before been seen in the history of aviation. The constant steel whirr of its motor was heard [by all the corners of our land]. . . . The steel bird, driven by the pilot heroes, forged its way through cyclones and storms, the crew with Bolshevik tenacity, will and mastery triumphed over all obstacles and completed a flight which is without precedent in the history of aviation and which has been entered in the history of aviation under the title 'The Stalinist Route' [*"Stalinskii marshrut"*;[46] another flight of later that year, by the way, was given the title *"Stalinskaia trassa"*[47]]." Thus the Chkalov fliers were not just bigger brothers—as Orwell would have us believe the paradigm to be. That might have been true of the Cheliuskin men, but the Chkalov pilots were mighty sons of an even mightier, all-providing father.

One is struck by the wealth of kinship metaphors used in these 1936 editorials. But that is completely typical of the period. Even the Great Purge trials of that year are sometimes explained by using kinship analogies. It should not be forgotten that our "peak" year of 1936 was also the year of the trial of the "Trotskyite-Zinoviev counter-revolutionary block." Indeed, to put things in some perspective, in the issue of *Literaturnaia gazeta* where a report appeared about a Kremlin reception for the Chkalov pilots the editorial, entitled "Vigilance," concerned the lessons to be drawn from these trials.[48] In the published scenario (i.e., trial transcript) for the conspiracy surrounding Kirov's murder which was uncovered at these trials, it was stated that the conspirators' real aim was to kill Stalin, but that they felt that—giving a novel twist to the Hegelian metaphor—"in order to destroy the oak one must eradicate its young saplings as well." [49]

It will be noted that this particular metaphor provides for the possibility that some figures other than Stalin may grow to be "oaks" or wise fathers as well. And, indeed, while it could not be questioned that Stalin was the greatest living "father" of them all, in the utopian kinship model "father" was essentially a function rather than a fixed identity, and hence that function or role could be conferred upon others (conferred upon, but certainly not assumed . . .). In reality the role was always, and primarily, fulfilled by the great *vozhd',* but in rhetoric others were sometimes elevated to this status. In such cases they became, as it were, honorific fathers, and of course their range or degree of authority was never as broad as for the great father, Stalin. The main sign that someone had achieved

45. "Slava geroiam!" *Literaturnaia gazeta,* August 5, 1936, No. 44, p. 1.
46. "Geroi sovetskogo plemeni" (editorial), *Literaturnaia gazeta,* August 10, 1936, No. 45, p. 1.
47. "Stalinskaia trassa" (editorial), *Literaturnaia gazeta,* September 15, 1936, No. 45, p. 1.
48. *Literaturnaia gazeta,* August 13, 1936, No. 46, p. 1.
49. "Obvinitel'noe zakliuchenie po delu," *Literaturnaia gazeta,* August 20, 1936, No. 47, p. 2.

father status was when he was given the epithet "father" (which was, incidentally, one of the main epithets used for Stalin); many were so honored, including
selected members of the top political leadership and authority figures in specialized areas, people like Makarenko (for education) and Gorky (for literature). If
the status was to be conferred posthumously (as was often the case) the formula
used was to proclaim that there is a little of the "seed," "spark"—or even
"blood" [50]—of the father figure to be found alive in every Soviet citizen.

   Thus the rhetoric of the mid-thirties provided for a new utopian kinship model
projected on the basis of the very few examples of the "biggest" human being
that were extant in Soviet society at that time. The model posited an ongoing
hierarchy of fathers and sons, the model "sons" being found in the various
superlative examples of positive "spontaneity" (such as the Stakhanovites and
the Arctic fliers), the "fathers" in Stalin and in anyone else with vaguely comparable "wisdom," "care," and "sternness" to guide the chosen "sons." But the sons
would not grow into fathers: rather they should be perfected as model sons. The
burden of paternity was to fall on the very few.

   It will be noted that this fathers/sons pattern represents the most simplified
of kinship structures. Where, after all, are those complex relationships such as
"mother's brother's wife" that are bread-and-butter categories of most anthropological studies? And where is there provision for the many, many layers of the
Soviet hierarchy? It could be argued that the pattern "fathers/sons" represents
a distillation of the multi-layered hierarchy—i.e., A is to B as B is to C as C is
to D, as . . . father is to son. However I would contend that the specific paradigms chosen to illustrate this pattern, i.e., Stalin/Stakhanovites-cum-Arctic-
airmen—represent poles within the spectrum "new man," to the deliberate exclusion of most middle terms. The Stakhanovite as humble worker with a very
rudimentary education and no political training is an obvious candidate for a
lowly position on a Soviet hierarchy. The Arctic flier is more problematical, but
I would suggest that such gestures as Stalin's changing the entire route of the
Chkalov expedition on the eve of their flight served to dramatize the lowly
position the airmen occupied vis-à-vis even their own achievement! Furthermore,
neither the Stakhanovites nor the fliers would rate very high on any scale of
"consciousness," and their achievements were not political in any direct sense.

   Thus the chosen heroes or "sons" of the mid-thirties were relatively inconsequential, extra-systemic people. The public conferral of the status "new man"
on these figures as a response to their overblown exploits must be seen as a sort
of ritual elevation of the structurally inferior. The lionization of the Stakhanovite
was, I would suggest, merely a different expression of the same thirst for radical
change and *renewal* which led to the ritual "leveling" of other segments of society
during the earlier, compulsively fraternalist phase. The aim of the movement was
not only to provide a titanic worker and celebrate national achievement, but also
to revitalize those middle sections of the Soviet hierarchy (or "middle terms")

50. Cf. "Krov' Kirova stuchit v nashe serdtse (sobranie pisatelei Leningrada)," *Literaturnaia gazeta*, February 1, 1937, No. 6, p. 5.

that come between the mighty father and these mighty sons. It is no accident that praise of the "new man's" achievements was interlaced with criticisms of his superiors, of those who, being at least in theory more "conscious," occupied positions on a hierarchy which the Stakhanovite barely qualified to be on at all. And it is also significant that this particular series of status-reversing rituals occurred at the same time as the worst of the purges.

The case of the Stakhanovites is far from being the only instance in Stalinist Russia where status-reversing rituals involving extra-systemic or structurally inferior figures were enacted. This pattern was very commonly felt among academic and scientific circles, and particularly in the 1940's. In those years it almost seemed that the major arena for "revitalization" had moved from the factory and *kolkhoz* to the institute. Here, however, the figures elevated were not only "sons" but also (lesser) "fathers": On the one hand, the Stakhanovites were used once again as model sons and, many academic experts were required to rewrite all, or sections of, their standard textbooks in the light of the "new scientific discoveries" a Stakhanovite had made in their particular field of expertise: [51] on the other, the doctrines of certain cultural authority-figures [52] of humble origins and rudimentary or belated professional training ("fathers" such as Lysenko, Marr, Gorky, and Makarenko) were declared axiomatic for the given field, to the detriment of all other experts who had attained their status by more traditional routes.

Thus even the infamous Lysenkoism can be seen as an outgrowth of those crucial cultural patterns which were born of the radical change in value orientation of the mid-thirities. And in order to understand the ultimate concern of this paper, typical Stalinist literature, we must look at the paradigms generated in these years.

As Soviet society reached "ever higher," its literature could not fail to be affected by this new direction. An initial and symptomatic difference was that imaginative literature, fiction, came back into its own. The novel, which had so long been eclipsed by the journalistic and other non-fictional forms of narrative which dominated the early thirties, came into the limelight again. At almost the exact time the Stakhanovite movement was launched (in late 1935) there came a multiple awarding of the Order of Lenin to Soviet novelists—multiple as if to make up for lost time.

Most famous of the novelists singled out on that occasion was Nikolai Ostrovskii, whose *How the Steel Was Tempered* (*Kak zakalialas' stal'*, 1934) was already an enormously popular novel, but without official recognition. Significantly, certain crucial aspects of Ostrovskii's biography and attributes, and those of the novel's hero, Pavel Korchagin (the novel was semi-autobiographical) correspond

---

51. See Vit. Vasilevskii, "Geroi nashego vremeni," *Literaturnaia gazeta*, June 19, 1948, No. 49, p. 1.

52. For this term I am indebted to the paper prepared for the Bellagio conference by Dr. Sheila Fitzpatrick and entitled "Stalinism and Culture." Professor Fitzpatrick did not specifically have in mind cultural authority figures of humble origins (her list includes Stanislavskii, for instance); however, the degree to which such figures are of humble origins is quite striking.

to the iconic attributes of the "new man," i.e., the Stakhanovite or aviation hero. (Indeed, as if to confirm this identification, when Chkalov was killed in a 1938 plane crash his death was likened in a *Literaturnaia gazeta* editorial to that of Ostrovskii two years earlier [53]). Ostrovskii/Korchagin was humble in origins and poorly educated, and in his childhood and early manhood many found reason to shake their heads at his pranks, his daredevil feats, his anarchic tendencies, and his lack of discipline.[54] Even after he had matured sufficiently to join the party, this hero showed no interest in party studies and usually failed to do his reading assignments or obey directives.[55] To counterbalance all this, however, the hero proved to be a man of unsurpassed energy, will, endurance, and dedication to the right cause. Moreover, he survived (often by dint of sheer will or incredible physical strength) a long series of encounters with death. This true dying and reviving hero made it through one struggle after the other, only to find himself at the end the victim of a terminal disease. Yet even in his final months of debilitation Pavel was not broken or bitter: he was haunted only by the fear that he might have to "leave the ranks" before the mighty struggle was won.[56]

Thus both Ostrovskii/Korchagin and the Stakhanovites stand for the individual hero who is distinguished by his humility and readiness to give his all for the cause, while yet representing a highly childish brand of positive "spontaneity." Incidentally, Ostrovskii was also completely untrained as a writer, and his novel was scorned by the pundits of the literary world. Hence the lionization of him could be construed as a further example of the ritual of status reversal.

In general, however, the revival of fiction can be viewed in a broader context. Imaginative literature came back into prominence because the survivals of the Five-Year Plan positivist craze had now been sloughed off. Indeed, literature went a long way beyond merely reviving fiction in response to the new values. In order to describe *homo extraordinarius* one needed more fabulous forms. Earlier, Gorky at the First Writers' Congress (1934) had called for the Soviet literature to model its subjects on the great heroes of world literature, such as Prometheus, and especially on the heroes of folk literature.[57] Initially the main impact of this admonition had been that vast resources were invested in collecting oral lore: hundreds of people went scurrying around the countryside recording epics and tales, while in the cities, journals, agencies, and institutes were set up to process and publish them. But by the end of 1935 the connection between fabular forms and contemporary literature became quite marked. Heroes became larger than life, their feats ever more fantastic and epic, and the very language of the texts became more folksy and formulaic. This trend even reached as far as that Five-Year Plan stock-in-trade, the sketch written by a worker about his own

---

53. "Geroi stalinskoi epokhi," *Literaturnaia gazeta,* December 20, 1938, No. 70, p. 1.

54. Nikolai Ostrovskii, *Kak zakalialas' stal'. Roman v dvukh chastiakh* (Moscow, 1936), pp. 16, 35, 158–59, 267.

55. Ibid., pp. 215, 253.

56. Ibid., p. 354.

57. "Rech' M. Gor'kogo," in *Pervyi s"ezd pisatelei. Stenograficheskii otchët* (Moscow, 1934), p. 7.

work. The Stakhanovites, for instance, were tutored to write their sketches not with technical manuals and statistical handbooks, as before, but with fairy tales and adventure fiction.[58]

By 1937 the captains of literature had made some advances on getting their fabulous tales of industrialization written at a sort of second remove from the original folk art. A publishing house called "Two Five-Year Plans" invited some genuine singers of *byliny* and folk tales to venture out of their remote northern villages, which they had never before left, and come to Moscow to create new *byliny* and tales about the wonders of the new age. With that concern for legitimacy and origins which was so typical of official bodies in this period, they took special care to invite a certain Kriukova, the granddaughter of the very *bylina* singer used as a source by the great nineteenth-century collector of folklore Rybnikov.

This was no isolated occurrence. Kriukova entered Soviet literature to stay, and in her wake came a whole series of other folk bards (including representatives of the non-Russian peoples such as Dzhambul of Kazakhstan and Suleiman Stal'skii of Dagestan) who were officially assigned major roles in Soviet literature and given many awards (such as the Stalin Prize) for their "folk" epics. The main work done by these people was not in composing long poems about industrialization, but in composing "folksed-up" rewrites of the Lenin-Stalin-Trotsky story of legitimate succession. In one such *opus,* Kriukova's "Tale of Lenin" (*Skazanie o Lenine,* 1937),[59] the protagonists are the "red sun" Vladimir (Lenin), the "magic knight" Klim Voroshilov, Stalin-*svet* (light), the "furious viper" (Lenin's attempted assassin, Kaplan), and "villain Trotsky." The tale, which commences with the terrorist activities of Lenin's older brother, Aleksander, and ends with Lenin's death and Stalin's succession, is punctuated by a (formulaic) three meetings between Lenin and Stalin (the last on Lenin's deathbed) in each of which Lenin sends Stalin out into the world to do his work. . .

It was not only literature which became quite fantastic and fairy-tale in this period. Reality contrived to become fairly fabulous, too. In all areas of public life—meetings, the press, speeches, ceremonial, those incredible carnival processions where "enemies of the people" were born in effigy, the courts, etc.—the bounds between fiction and fact, between literary plot and factual reporting, all became somewhat blurred. But whatever the occasion, one did not have to dig very deeply beneath the surface of the rhetoric to find signs of the age's obsession with legitimacy, with establishing that Lenin was Stalin's legitimate heir, and that his policies—such as, notably, his effectively breaking with the fraternalist ideals for the new society—were truly Leninist.

For all the inspired outpourings of the people's bards, nowhere was this obsession with legitimacy better served than in that mainstay of Stalinist literature, the novel. In the "folk" epic the crudity of the graft of folksiness and the transpar-

---

58. "Strana zhdët knig: o geroiakh sotsialisticheskogo truda," *Literaturnaia gazeta,* November, 1935, No. 61.

59. M. S. Kriukova, "Skazanie o Lenine," in *Krasnaia nov',* 1937, No. 11, pp. 97–118.

ency of the devices reduced its effectiveness as a repository of myth. The novel did not engage the issues head-on but evolved a mythic masterplot whereby the passage of the generations was used to stand in for legitimate political succession.

Similarly, although the public arena—speeches, the trials, etc.—was permeated with myth, it never became as ritualized or as coherent as in the novel. This can be explained in terms of a *de facto* division of functions between the political arena and its media, on the one hand, and literature on the other. Public life under Stalin was in a state of constant flux: the high premium placed on radical change brought forth an endless stream of new policies for which some "transforming" power was claimed; between the constant policy reversals and the "permanent purge" the turnover in administrative personnel was extraordinarily high; and what was going to happen next became increasingly difficult to predict. The more unpredictable public life became, the more, by contrast, the novel reflected a stable, ordered, and tradition-bound world. It chronicled change, but only as linear progress brought about by a combination of "historical inevitability," the maturation of the protagonists and their own achievements. The excesses of the public arena—such as, notably, the purges—did not find their way to a comparable position in the novel's world. And so, too, those rituals of status reversal, the hyperbolic elevation of structurally inferior or extra-systemic categories, found no place in the novel's well-ordered hierarchy.

The crucial factor enabling the novel to depict a stable, well-ordered world wherein so many of the excesses and contradictions of "Soviet reality" would be eliminated, and yet the legitimacy of the Stalinist leadership symbolically enacted, was the matter of scale. The typical Stalinist novel is set in a microcosm which stands in for the greater world of the Soviet state. Usually this is a *kolkhoz,* factory, small provincial town, or military unit. In this context all is much simpler and more familial: the gap between "fathers" and "sons" is relatively slight and the issue of succession a fairly straightforward one. The fact that certain protagonists stand in for the mighty "fathers" of the outside world is normally indicated by highly conventionalized signs (such as their being surrounded by an aura of light, their working late at night, their having seen Lenin or having fought in the Civil War, and by certain stock adjectives such as "stern" and "deliberate" which indicate their quintessential "consciousness") which authenticate their right to preside over political succession within the limited context of the novel's world.

The hero of the Stalinist novel is not a "father," however, but a "son." The plot revolves around his exploits as he makes his individual progress from a state of "spontaneity" to "consciousness." For the bulk of the novel he appears as the stereotypical mid-thirties "son," with all the burning energy, thirst for adventure, physical prowess, etc., of the Arctic flier or Stakhanovite. There is a crucial difference in that most novel heroes occupy an established position on the local hierarchy. But because he is a "son," his various exploits and setbacks en route to maturation can provide the novel with color and suspense. Likewise, the novel can exude fraternalist values as this "son" learns to get closer to his class brothers. The novel's "father" figures are usually more aloof and inspire awe. However, it is not normally until the end of the novel that the hero matures sufficiently to acquire the status himself.

The novel ends with a succession of the generations. Normally the father figure either dies, retires, or is promoted away from the area. This facilitates the transition, and "son" assumes the position formerly occupied by "father" on the local hierarchy.[60] This highly charged event affirms symbolically that the line of Leninist succession is being maintained and also provides a symbolic resolution of the "spontaneity"/"consciousness" dialectic.

A good example of the Stalinist novel would be Iu. Krymov's *The Tanker "Derbent"* (*Tanker "Derbent,"* 1938). This novel is about the Stakhanovite movement among crewmen of the *Derbent,* a tanker on the Caspian. Thus the novel's world is scaled down with rigor. Indeed, it comprises only one model "son" and one "father." The "overflowing-with-energy-and-initiative Stakhanovite on the "Derbent" is also the only party member on the ship other than the political officer. Ineluctably these two assume the roles of father and son.

It is to be noted, however that the hero as Stakhanovite belongs to the hierarchy among workers on the ship and is not a political office-bearer. The plot enables the hero to cross over to the political hierarchy by having the political officer fall so ill with TB that he has to leave the ship—but not before assigning his role as political officer to the Stakhanovite leader.[61] Thus the hero is able to play "son" and yet end up as "father."

More typically the hero is not actually a Stakhanovite, but his exploits are decidedly those of the high-spirited "son": most often he distinguishes himself in battle or against the raging elements, but in the very act of so distinguishing himself he earns the right to the status "father," which is denied his counterparts in real life.[62] Or, in other words, the hero's journey to "consciousness" symbolically closes the gap between "sons" and "fathers." Reality's contradictions, and the disparities between theory and practice, are all mediated in myth.

---

60. This is, of course, an oversimplification. Not all heroes of Stalinist novels are Soviet state employees. Many either are too young or come from a different time or country. But when this is the case, it merely means that the author has presented a more mediated example of the paradigm.

61. Iu. Krymov, *Tanker "Derbent, "Krasnaia nov',* May 1938, No. 5, p. 85.

62. Even the Stalinist historical novels about statesmanship (such as A. Tolstoy's *Peter the First* or V. Shishkov's *Emelian Pugachev*) have their hero-leader pass through a long period of childish exuberance and impulsiveness before donning the austere cloak of supreme responsibility.

New Pages from the Political Biography of Stalin *

Roy A. Medvedev

The Old Bolshevik A. T. P___v, in an essay of his, gives the following definition of Stalinism:

> In the socialist movement in the twentieth century conservative trends and forces arose that acted as a brake upon the further development of the process of socialist revolution and in many cases worked in an anti-revolutionary direction. The most striking manifestation of these forces is Stalinism. Stalinism is not just a bureaucratic distortion of Marxism and Leninism in general and of the theory and practice of socialist construction in particular. It represents an entire system, a whole separate way of managing social, political, governmental, and economic affairs. It is pseudo-socialism.

Stalin Before 1924

In virtually all the political biographies of Stalin published abroad, considerable space is devoted to the question of the young Stalin's supposed ties with the Okhrana. In my book *Let History Judge* I took a very skeptical view of the recorded statements, rumors, and even documents that have been cited in the foreign press on this point. It must be noted, however, that even today, among the few Old Bosheviks remaining alive, the opinion is still maintained, here and there, that Stalin was recruited by the Okhrana in the very first years of his revolutionary career, and that it was precisely his fear of exposure that drove him to carry out mass repression against his own party. The Old Bolshevik G. B___v wrote me:

---

* My book *Let History Judge: The Origins and Consequences of Stalinism* (New York 1971) was written from 1962 to 1968. A significantly revised and enlarged edition, which I worked on from 1969 to 1973, was brought out, but this was published only in Russian (*K sudu istorii* [New York: Alfred A. Knopf, 1974]). Even after 1973, however, various new materials on Stalin and his epoch continued to come my way. Many have never before been published. Since it is not possible to undertake a complete revision of my book at the present time, I consider it expedient to include the new material in this article, which was written in response to a suggestion by the organizers of the conference on Stalinism held in Italy, July 25–31, 1975. Thus, this article should be seen not as an attempt to give duly exhaustive treatment to one or another aspect of the subject, but as a supplement to what I have already published.

199

It goes against your grain, that's all, to admit that for thirty years the party was headed by an agent of the tsarist Okhrana. But your counter-arguments are not convincing. Stalin knew that if he was exposed and removed from office, he would be shot, as Malinovsky was. But precisely in 1935 certain documents that compromised Stalin came into the hands of some prominent people in the party apparatus and NKVD apparatus. However, Stalin forestalled the plans of those who would have exposed him, and they themselves were shot. Everything points to the fact that Stalin, as a former Okhrana agent, remained an adherent of the monarchical form of rule: his tsarist predilections, his contempt and hatred for revolutionists, his ignorance of Marxist and socialist doctrine. He destroyed the entire leading staff of the October Revolution and transformed the entire Soviet system to suit his own Caesarist preferences.

G. B____v cites no evidence in support of the first part of his allegations. He has none. Therefore there is no reason to reply to them here.

According to Solzhenitsyn, a former tsarist police director, V. F. Dzhunkovsky, as he lay dying in Kolyma, asserted that the hasty burning of police archives in the first days of the February Revolution was a joint effort on the part of certain self-interested revolutionaries.[1] Part of these archives escaped destruction, however, and were shipped to France by the ambassador of the Provisional Government to France, V. A. Maklakov. The same Maklakov was a member of the Provisional Committee of the State Duma, who held the post of minister of justice for a few days after the February Revolution. His brother, N. A. Maklakov, was minister of internal affairs in the tsarist government from early 1913 to late 1915.[2]

In the past few years only one document from the archives of the tsarist police having to do with Stalin has come into my hands. I will cite it here in full, since it has apparently never before been published.

> Central State Archives of the October Revolution,
> Collection of the Department of Police,
> Special Section, file 167, 1905.

Records in the case of Simon Abramovich Zil' ban, of the townsman [*meshchanin*] caste. Sheets 4–36. Circular (typed and printed) of the Ministry of Internal Affairs, Department of Police, Special Section.

May 1, 1904. No. 5500.
To all governors of provinces, mayors, chiefs of police, heads of provincial gendarmerie and of railroad police administrations, chiefs of Okhrana units, and to all border posts.

The Department of Police has the honor of sending you herewith, for appropriate disposition, the following: (1) a list of persons being sought in connection with political cases; (2) a list of persons for whom search may be terminated; and (3)

---

1. A. Solzhenitsyn, *Arkhipelag gulag,* Vol. I–II (Paris, 1973), pp. 78–79.
2. *Voprosy istorii,* 1972, No. 10, p. 167.

a list of persons named in previous circulars, still being sought. . . . List 1—Persons being sought in connection with political cases   (Nos. 1 through 185)

Page 20, No. 52.

Dzhugashvili, Iosif Vissarionovich; peasant from the village of Didi-Lilo, Tiflis district, Tiflis province; born 1881, of Orthodox faith, attended Gori church school and Tiflis theological seminary; not married. Father, Vissarion, whereabouts unknown. Mother, Ekaterina, resident of the town of Gori, Tiflis province. On the basis of an order of His Majesty, issued on the 9th day of May, 1903, the subject was banished for three years, under open police surveillance, to Eastern Siberia for crimes against the state, and was placed in residence in Balagan district, Irkutsk province, from whence he disappeared on January 5, 1904.

Description: height, 2 arshins, 4½ vershki (about 5 feet, 4 inches); average build; gives the appearance of an ordinary person; hair of the head, dark brown; mustache and beard, reddish-brown; straight hair, not curly or wavy; eyes, dark brown, of average size; shape of head, ordinary: forehead, flat, not high; nose, straight, long; face, long, swarthy, covered with smallpox marks; in the right lower jaw, front molar missing; a person of moderate size, with a sharp chin, soft voice, ears of average size, normal gait, birthmark on left ear; second and third toes of left foot joined together.

Detain and telegraph Department of Police for further instructions.

In his youth, Stalin wrote a number of poems in Georgian. They were printed in the newspaper *Iveriia* and signed "Sosolo." These poems were subsequently forgotten, for the most part, but one four-line stanza was quoted in one of the first biographies of Stalin, which came from the pen of Emelian Yaroslavsky. Not long before Stalin's seventieth birthday, a well-known Soviet poet was called into the offices of the MGB, where the proposal was made that he translate a selection of Stalin's verse from the Georgian. The text of the original, a phonetic transcription, and everything necessary for the work (including free choice of menu) was offered. The translator was forbidden to leave the room made available for this work. In a short time, under conditions of top secrecy, the job was completed. But the collection of Stalin's verse never did appear.

In early April 1922 Stalin was placed on the Central Committee Secretariat, in the capacity of general secretary. In an unpublished manuscript by the Old Bolshevik L____y, entitled *Socialist Control and the Socialist State System* (1973), the argument may be found that Stalin was actually removed from his post as the head of the Commissariat of Workers' and Peasants' Inspection (Rabkrin) because of his inability to cope with the job, and that the Central Committee plenum, in order to compensate Stalin for this loss, "invented" a post with the honorific title "general secretary" especially for him.

Such an interpretation of Stalin's new assignment is hard to accept. It is true that Stalin did not distinguish himself in any way in the Rabkrin arena. Properly speaking, he took hardly any part at all in the work of this commissariat, delegating the responsibility to his deputies. It is true that Lenin often criticized the work of Rabkrin quite harshly, remarking, for example, that it was "ridiculous to expect anything more than the carrying out of simple instructions" from this commissariat.[3] However, Lenin did not at that time blame Stalin for Rabkrin's poor functioning. Stalin's appointment as general secretary was by no means a form of "honorable retirement" from the work of Rabkrin. On the contrary, Stalin's power and opportunities grew substantially with that appointment.

In 1923–24 the Central Committee Secretariat was expanded to five, but Stalin remained general secretary. As general secretary of the Central Committee and a member of the Politburo, Stalin in fact dominated the Orgburo as well. It was precisely this situation, Stalin's place on all three of these leading bodies of the party, as well as on the All-Russia Central Executive Committee (later the Central Executive Committee of the USSR) and the Council of People's Commissars (until 1923), that allowed him to concentrate what Lenin termed "boundless power" *(neob"iatnaia vlast')* in his hands and made him, even during Lenin's illness, the number one person in the party, even though the post of general secretary, introduced in April 1922, was not thought of then as the chief position in the party. As early as 1922 and the first half of 1923, taking advantage of the new elections of party bodies, Stalin significantly strengthened his influence upon the party apparatus in the center and in the regional committees, putting through a massive reshuffling of cadres in the province committees, regional committees, and central committees of the national Communist parties. L. Kaganovich became the head of the organizational and instructional department of the Central Committee, S. Syrtsov was appointed head of the records and assignments department (Uchraspred), and A. Bubnov was placed in charge of the agitation and propaganda department (Agitprop). These three actively supported Stalin at that time and constituted his first "headquarters staff" within the party apparatus. Stalin's dominant position in the party apparatus quickly made him the key figure in the Politburo as well, although the chairmen of the Politburo (a position introduced after Lenin fell ill) were Zinoviev (1922–24) and Kamenev (1924–25).

Stalin's enormous power disturbed not only Lenin. There is evidence that Lenin's "Testament," or, at any rate, its essential content, was known to many party leaders even before the Thirteenth Party Congress. In the autumn of 1923, in one of the caves near the town of Kislovodsk, a semi-legal meeting was held, with Zinoviev, Bukharin, Evdokimov, Lashevich, Voroshilov, and several others participating. Formally, the question of strengthening collective leadership of the party was discussed, but in fact the main focus was on limiting Stalin's authority and powers. Zinoviev proposed on that occasion that the Politburo be dissolved and that to provide for leadership of the party a special triumvirate be formed, consisting of Stalin, Trotsky, and himself, Zinoviev (in place of his own candidacy he also suggested Kamenev or Bukharin). Opinions differed; Stalin was found to have some defenders; speaking against Zinoviev's plan were, first of all, Voroshilov, but also Bukharin, apparently. The decision was made to solicit the opinion of Stalin himself. In his summary at the Fourteenth Congress Stalin said in regard to this episode: "To a question sent to me in writing from the depths of Kislovodsk I answered in the negative, stating that if the comrades were to

---

3. V. I. Lenin, *Polnoe sobranie sochinenii,* Vol. 44 (Moscow, 1964), p. 369.

insist I was willing to clear out without fuss, without a discussion, open or concealed. . . ." [4] It is quite possible that at that time Stalin might actually have been obliged to "clear out" of his post as *de facto* head of the party. However, a heated debate with Trotsky and his followers soon began, and the situation changed. The personal hostility between Zinoviev and Trotsky was still very great then, and as a result Kamenev and Zinoviev lent their joint support to none other than Stalin, against Trotsky, and they spoke at the Thirteenth Party Congress as Stalin's chief defenders.

The sharpening differences within the Central Committee and the struggle for power, proceeding in both veiled and open fashion and threatening to split the party, were very disturbing to Lenin, whose health improved noticeably in the summer and fall of 1923. He insisted that Krupskaya—who was almost always with him at the country house in the village of Gorki—read the papers to him, and even though such reading was obviously not good for him, refusal to read was even more disturbing to Lenin, and Krupskaya could not deny him. During these months Lenin met with many people, but he did not wish to invite either Stalin or the other members of the Politburo to visit him. According to Krupskaya's account, this would have been "unbearably difficult for him." As E. Drabkina relates in an unpublished part of her memoirs, Lenin would sit alone for hours and often weep, not only from powerlessness, but also from mortification *(ne tol'ko ot bessiliia, no i ot obidy)*. According to Krupskaya, on January 19 and 20, 1924, she read Vladimir Ilyich the just published resolutions of the Thirteenth Party Conference, in which the results of the debate with Trotsky were summed up. Listening to these resolutions, which were very harshly formulated, Lenin again became greatly disturbed. To calm him, Krupskaya told him that the resolutions had been adopted unanimously by the Party Conference. But that was hardly a comfort to Lenin, whose worst fears, as expressed in his "Testament," were beginning to come true. In any event, it was on the very next day, in an extremely disturbed condition, that Lenin died.

Stalin in the Period 1924–33

Stalin's decisive role in carrying out the basic political, administrative, and social transformations of 1924–33 is obvious. Among not only the personnel of the party apparatus but also a substantial proportion of the party rank and file, the desire for democracy was considerably weaker than the longing to discover a new *leader (vozhd')*, someone they could put their faith in and obey without troublesome doubts. And it was precisely Stalin, the "man of action," that the active party membership began to see as such a "leader" as early as the mid-1920's, a fact attested to by the ovations in his honor that erupted so frequently even at the Fourteenth Congress in 1925. It is no accident that by the end of the period under consideration there had arisen in our country and party the phenomenon which

---

4. *XIV s"ezd VKP(b). Stenograficheskii otchet* (Moscow, 1926), p. 506. Zinoviev's plan was also rejected by Trotsky, before the dispute with him began; Trotsky was opposed to the idea of a "triumvirate." See Voroshilov's speech, *XIV s"ezd*, pp. 398–99.

subsequently was given the not very felicitous name of "the personality cult."

For a time, however, Stalin was little known outside of narrow party-apparatus circles and was the Politburo member with the least popularity among the masses. As late as 1925 the KOVUCH publishing house put out a series of postcards in honor of the eighth anniversary of October. One sixteen-item series was devoted to Lenin; another—to the "Leaders of October"—consisted of ten portraits: those of Bukharin, Dzerzhinsky, Zinoviev, Kamenev, Krasin, Lunacharsky, Rykov, Tomsky, Trotsky, and Chicherin. [One reason Stalin had not been widely known was that he had not been one of the mass orators of the party in the revolutionary days—Translator] Not only during Stalin's lifetime but even today, from time to time, one hears references to Stalin as an outstanding orator. It must be said that at Central Committee plenums and sometimes at party congresses Stalin showed himself to be a skilled and resourceful polemicist, and he was quite good at demagogy; but his speeches often evoked protests because of their rudeness and even the flagrant cynicism of his argument. However, Stalin could not by any means be counted as one of the tribunes of the revolution. He had neither talent nor skill in speaking before mass meetings or in the streets and squares. He did not know how, nor did he ever try, to catch the attention of a crowd and to win over to his way of thinking ordinary people whose opinions were wavering. And it is not simply that Stalin did not have a strong voice or that he had a heavy Caucasian accent. His speeches lacked the vividness and imagery required in a time of revolution.

Stalin himself constantly asserted that in everything he had done he had always followed the lines laid down by Lenin, that he was only a loyal disciple who had consistently carried on Lenin's work. The people in Stalin's immediate entourage constantly hammered away at the same theme, adding only that Stalin was the *best* disciple, who carried on Lenin's work *more steadfastly* than any *other*. This kind of camouflage, to cover what was a retreat from, and often a decisive break with, Marxism and Leninism, was one of the chief tactical devices used by Stalin in his fight against his opponents within the party. But it has also been convenient and useful to many Western historians who do not approach the subject objectively to identify Stalinism with Marxism and Leninism and to portray socialism only in its distorted Stalinist forms. The same conception is upheld even more insistently today by Solzhenitsyn, who declares that there never was such a thing as "Stalinism" per se, that Stalin only followed "in Lenin's footsteps," and that he was only "a blind and perfunctory executive force." [5] Such a conception is quite amenable to those who wish to discredit all forms of socialism, in principle, as well as to those who wish to rehabilitate Stalin and Stalinism. But it is a false conception.

Of course, one cannot help but observe a certain degree of continuity between the policies followed in our country for the first six years after the October

---

5. *Arkhipelag gulag*, Vol. I–II, p. 80. Also, the interview with Solzhenitsyn in Stockholm in December 1974, published in *Russkaia mysl'* (Paris), January 16, 1975.

Revolution and those of subsequent years. This pertains, for example, to the limitations in the area of free speech and freedom of the press which began to be imposed almost immediately after the October Revolution and which were continued and extended in the subsequent years of War Communism. Only with the beginning of NEP were some restrictions of freedom of the press relaxed and the establishment of many privately owned printing presses and several non-party journals permitted. Lenin personally came to the defense of the *Smena vekh* magazine *Novaia Rossiia,* which some members of the Central Committee were demanding be closed down. However, it may be recalled at this point that the magazine *Ekonomist* was closed in 1922 by Lenin's very own order, and its chief contributors were expelled from the country. Also in 1922 the magazine *Golos minuvshego* (Voice of the Past) was shut down and its contributors, headed by S. Mel'gunov, expelled from the country. It was then, too, that the Petrograd magazine *Mysl'* (Thought) was closed and its contributors expelled. These included N. Berdyaev, L. Shestov, N. Lossky, and S. Frank, who were Russian philosophers of great prominence, although not adherents of Marxism or materialism.

Stalin and his entourage continued this line in relation to the press. As early as 1926 *Novaia Rossiia* was closed down after all, and in the following year the same fate befell the magazine *Byloe* (The Past), which had been founded in 1900. Among the magazines forced to cease publication in the period 1925–29 were *Russkii sovremennik; Sovremennik; Novaia epokha; Vol'naia zhizn'; Slovo istiny; Vestnik literatury;* the almanacs *Krug, Kovsh,* and *Zhizn' iskusstva;* and many less well known publications. By 1929 there was not a single non-party publication left, nor any privately owned publishing houses that might serve as vehicles for oppositionist views. One might also argue that Lenin himself laid the groundwork for the notorious *spetskhrany* ("special repositories") by signing a decree as early as January 1920 requiring all government offices that had White Guard literature in their possession to transfer such material to the Commissariat of Enlightment to be kept and used in government libraries only.[6]

One could list further the various measures carried out by Stalin that were actually a continuation of anti-democratic trends and measures implemented under Lenin, although it should be said here that we presume Lenin never could have gone so far in this direction.

In most respects, however, there is no continuity between Stalinism and Leninism; only an analogous "Marxist" terminology is perserved. In pursuing a course aimed at abolishing NEP, in putting through a hasty policy of forced collectivization, carrying out mass terror against the well-to-do peasants in the countryside and against the so-called bourgeois specialists in the cities, employing mainly administrative rather than economic methods to carry out industrialization, categorically forbidding any opposition inside or outside of the party, and thus reviving, under other circumstances, the methods of War Communism—in all this, as in so many other ways, Stalin acted, not in line with Lenin's clear

---

6. *Lenin i kul'turnaia revoliutsiia* (Moscow, 1972), p. 187.

instructions, but in defiance of them, especially of Lenin's last writings of 1921–22, where he laid out the path of the construction of a socialist society under the new domestic and international conditions.

The celebrated "Lenin levy" of 1924 was already a violation of Lenin's clearly stated policy of party-building. It is a known fact that Lenin in the last months of his life repeatedly warned the Central Committee against mechanically increasing the size of the central working-class component of the party. Lenin warned against the danger of flooding the party with petty bourgeois elements from the ranks of blue-collar workers who had not been tempered by dozens of years of factory life (and there were no other types of workers to recruit at that time). Even in the period of preparation for the Eleventh Party Congress Lenin considered it one of the most important tasks of the leadership to *erect barriers* against easy entry into the party, in particular by prolonging the period of candidate membership. But soon after Lenin's death, when the "Lenin levy" was proclaimed, some 250,000 workers "from the bench" were taken into the party in a matter of weeks, there being cases in which the party accepted all the workers of one shop or another in their entirety.[7] During the "Lenin levy" the probationary period for candidate members was waived entirely for blue-collar workers. In April 1923, when a purging operation *(chistka)* had just been completed, there were 386,000 party members in the country. But only a year later, in May 1924, there were 736,000 party members represented at the Thirteenth Congress; i.e., the party had doubled its numbers.

In resolving the extremely complex and difficult economic issues of the decade in question, Stalin was not guided in general by any clear or distinct idea. He rushed from one conception to another, basing his decisions, for the most part, on situations and complications of the moment, and sometimes simply followed the logic of the factional struggle within the party. And although in 1925–26 Stalin made use of the economic policy recommendations drafted mainly by Bukharin, Rykov, and Tomsky, in 1928–30 he made use of those worked out by Trotsky and Zinoviev, although in so doing he simplified and distorted them beyond recognition. Consequently, in the late 1920's and early 1930's Stalin followed domestic economic policies that were the direct opposite of those which Lenin would have followed if he had lived but ten years longer. And Stalin's constant reference to the "Leninist general line" of the party was only an expression of the hypocrisy so typical of him.

Vanity and lust for power were, even then, the things that motivated Stalin most strongly. In his reply "To All Organizations and Comrades Sending Me Greetings" on the occasion of his fiftieth birthday, he wrote hypocritically: "Your greetings and good wishes I credit to the great party of the working class, which bore and raised me in its image and likeness. . . . You need have no doubt, comrades, that I am ready in the future as well to devote to the cause of the working class, to the cause of the proletarian revolution and world Communism,

---

7. I. K. Dashkovsky, "Ekskurs v istoriiu partii" (manuscript).

all my strength, all my ability, and if necessary, all my blood, drop by drop." [8]
But these were just words. Stalin was not about to shed his blood for the cause
of world Communism or the working class. He was ready, however, even then,
to shed rivers of blood to preserve and fortify his personal power.[9]

An unexpected action by Stalin at the first Central Committee plenum after
the Fifteenth Party Congress in December 1927 was also characteristically hypocritical. A few days after the leaders of the "United Opposition" had finally been
expelled from the party, Stalin unexpectedly proposed that he himself be relieved
of his duties in the party leadership. "I believe," he said, "that until recently there
were conditions that confronted the party with the necessity of having me in this
post, as a more or less brusque sort of man, to serve as a kind of antidote to the
Opposition. But now these conditions have disappeared. . . . Now the Opposition
has not only been defeated but expelled from the party as well. And all the while,
we have had Lenin's instructions, which in my opinion must be put into effect.
Therefore, I ask the plenum to relieve me of the post of general secretary. I assure
you, comrades, that the party stands only to gain from this." [10] This proposal,
at Stalin's insistence, was put to a vote and rejected unanimously (with one
abstention). Thereby the plenum handed Stalin what amounted to a *carte blanche,*
which he used without delay to make an unexpected new turn in the entire policy
of the party, a turn much more abrupt and sharp than the one proposed by the
"Left" Opposition leaders who had just been expelled.

In 1927 the "Left" Opposition demanded the removal of Stalin from the party
leadership but at the same time demanded that NEP be brought to an end and
an economic policy be followed that in those conditions would have been incorrect. The demonstration of November 7, 1927, organized by the "Lefts" was
carried out under banners saying "Fulfill the Testament of Lenin! " "Let's Turn
Our Fire to the Right—Against Kulak, Nepman, and Bureaucrat! " "Down with
Stalin! Down with Thermidor! Long Live Trotsky! " "Long Live the Leaders of
the World Revolution Zinoviev and Trotsky! " Many who took part in the
demonstration sang a song that contained the words: "Long live Trotsky—leader
of the Red Army! " The demonstration was easily dispersed, but within a month
Stalin himself took the road of liquidating NEP and fighting against the Right.

I have already written, in *Let History Judge,* that there was no organized
"Right Opposition" in the party in 1928–29. There was only the confusion of

---

8. *Stalin: Sbornik statei k 50-letiiu so dnia rozhdeniia* (Moscow and Leningrad, 1929), p. 271.

9. In the early 1930's Stalin began by roundabout methods to seek some prominent writer of the
day to do a biography of him. Discussions with Gorky, Lion Feuchtwanger, and André Gide were
held on this subject. In the end the well-known French Communist writer Henri Barbusse agreed
to do a book on Stalin. It was called *Stalin, A New World Seen Through One Man,* and published
in 1935. In the introduction to this book, based on Soviet materials placed at Barbusse's disposal,
the author wrote: "Deception, machinations, bribery, police measures and crimes . . . the murder
of political opponents by night . . . through such methods one can become king, emperor, Duce,
or Chancellor, and even hold on to such a post. But one cannot become secretary of the Soviet
Communist Party this way."

10. From an unpublished stenographic record of the plenum.

a considerable section of the party membership and of many Central Committee members, who did not understand why they should carry out an even worse variant of the "Left" Opposition program against which they had just fought so bitterly. But Stalin intensified his pressure on the party and the Central Committee, as if to provoke them into opposition. Stalin himself introduced more and more adventuristic, maximalistic proposals for the Central Committee's consideration. After disputes had already occurred in the Politburo, though without leading to a split in the leadership, Stalin suddenly proposed, in February 1929, that the Politburo make a drastic upward revision in the control figures for the optimum variant of the Five-Year Plan. At the same time he proposed to force the pace of collectivization and to increase the "tribute" exacted from the peasants in order to provide for more rapid rates of industrialization. These proposals of Stalin's, unsupported by any economic calculations and beyond the reach of the country's resources, were nevertheless adopted by a majority of the Politburo. Only at this point, in the vote on Stalin's proposals, did Rykov, Bukharin, and Tomsky abstain and ask to be relieved of their posts. When, at the April plenum of the Central Committee in 1929, Stalin accused Bukharin and his co-thinkers of a Right deviation, Bukharin answered by accusing Stalin of Trotskyism. Bukharin quite rightly accused Stalin of abandoning NEP and condemned the thesis that Stalin had already put forward, that the class struggle grows steadily more intense, the nearer we come to socialism. "This strange theory," said Bukharin, "elevates the actual fact that the class struggle is now intensifying into some sort of inevitable law of our development. According to this strange theory, it would seem that the farther we go in our advance toward socialism, the more difficulties will accumulate, the more intense the class struggle will become, so that at the very gates of socialism, apparently, we will have to either start a civil war or perish from hunger and lay down our bones to die." [11]

There is already a great deal of literature on Stalin's crimes and errors in collectivization. A chapter analyzing those crimes and errors holds an important place in my book *Let History Judge.* I should, however, acknowledge the justice of many of the comments on that chapter made in M. A. Agursky's long review of *Let History Judge,* which bears the title "New Assessments of Stalinism." [12] In 1928, as Agursky correctly notes, a rather shrill anti-religious campaign was resumed in the USSR after a five-year lull, a period of calm in relations between church and state. In the fall of 1928 this campaign began to assume the characteristics of a wave of terror against the church. Persecution struck not only the Russian Orthodox Church but all religious organizations and groups without exception. The beginning of accelerated industrialization and collectivization thus coincided with attempts to root out "religious superstition" by force. In this

---

11. From the unpublished stenographic record.

12. Agursky's review was written in Moscow in May 1973. At present the author has taken up permanent residence in Israel. He has informed me that his review was published, but I do not know in what magazine or newspaper.

sphere, among anti-religious organizations and local authorities at various levels, undoubtedly supported by the higher party and government organizations, there prevailed the psychology of the "great leap forward" which would supposedly solve all the basic economic and political problems of the country in two to three years. By the end of 1928 all the monasteries functioning at the time as model agricultural cooperative (artels) had been closed down. Thousands of monks were sent to Siberia. Orthodox churches began to be torn down, regardless of their cultural and historical value, the example being set in Moscow. Dozens of synagogues and mosques were also destroyed.

The Central Committee held an anti-religious conference in the middle of 1929, and several days later the Second All-Union Congress of the "Militant Godless" was convened. After that the anti-religious terror increased noticeably, but the focus shifted from town to countryside. Religion was apparently regarded as one of the chief brakes upon collectivization. Therefore the resolutions on collectivization adopted in various villages were usually supplemented not only by decisions to deport many of the families of kulaks and "kulak accomplices" *(podkulachniki)* but also by decisions to close local churches, the implementation of which was more often than not accompanied by forcible confiscation and destruction by fire of icons and other objects of religious value. In the process, many peasants, by no means of the better-off layers, attempted to resist the destruction of the churches and were also arrested and deported. Thus, during collectivization hundreds of thousands suffered not because of social criteria but because of their religious beliefs. By early 1930 the terror against the church had acquired a particularly great ferocity. In that situation the frightened Academy of Sciences passed a special resolution removing most of the historic monuments connected with "religious cults" from protected status. Churches and monasteries were torn down not only in ancient Russian towns such as Tver, Nizhnii Novgorod, Pskov, Novgorod, Samara, and Viatka, but in the Kremlin itself. Many church cemeteries were also vandalized, especially ancient cemeteries of the nobility, where a good many of the monuments were of great artistic value.

"The anti-religious terror assumed such a scale," reports Agursky, who has made a special study of the history of anti-religious persecution in the USSR, "that in January 1930, Pope Pius XI appealed to all Christians for a world-wide day of prayer on March 16, 1930, in behalf of the persecuted faithful of Russia. This appeal was joined not only by most Christian churches but by Jewish religious circles, alarmed by the news of terror against Judaism, especially the report that twenty-five members of the Jewish clergy had been arrested in Minsk. The protest campaign outside the USSR reached the point where it began to threaten the political and economic interests of the USSR. Demands for breaking diplomatic relations with the Soviet Union were heard on all sides." [13]

Undoubtedly it was this mass protest campaign that impelled Stalin not only to halt the anti-religious terror but also to disavow it to some extent by attributing it to local "excesses." In his article "Dizzy with Success," published in *Pravda*

---

13. M. Agursky, "Novye izmereniia stalinizma" (manuscript), p. 10.

on March 2, 1930, Stalin wrote: "And what about those 'revolutionaries'—save the mark—who begin the work of organizing an artel by removing the church-bells—how r-r-revolutionary indeed!" [14] On March 15, i.e., one day before the world-wide observances called for by Pope Pius, our newspapers published the Central Committee resolution "On Distortions of the Party Line in the Collective Farm Movement." One of the main points in this resolution was its acknowledge-ment, presented as an error of the local authorities, that churches had been closed down by administrative action. Such excesses were condemned, and in very harsh terms besides. The resolution threatened severe punishment for anyone who should thereafter offend the religious sensibilities of believers. All this was un-doubtedly a concession to world public opinion. However, the temporary cessa-tion of the anti-religious terror was not accompanied by any steps to restore the ruined churches or to return most of those who had been deported to Siberia for religious reasons. Yet it turned out that some 80 percent of all Russian village churches were closed in 1930, and a substantial proportion of the clergy were among those hit by "de-kulakization."

The way "de-kulakization" was carried out in 1930–31 is fairly well known, even on the basis of Soviet literature. M. Sholokhov gives a completely truthful picture in the dramatic scenes of *Virgin Soil Upturned* in which he depicts the deportation of the well-to-do Cossack families of Gremyachy Log. Frightful episodes in this barbaric campaign of terror are also described in F. Panfyerov's novel *Bruski*. In the 1960s, S. Zalygin also wrote on this subject, though in quite a different tone. Nevertheless we shall present here one of the episodes of "de-kulakization" as found in an unpublished short novel by A. M.——n, who took part in the collectivization drive. In 1930, still quite a young man, he was one of the workers sent to the countryside in special brigades to help carry out collectivization, and he also engaged in the work of deporting to the east not only prosperous peasants but even poor peasants who refused to join the collective farm.

> The door opened. The brigade burst into the house. The GPU chief of operations was in front, brandishing a revolver.
>
> "Hands up!"
>
> Morgunov was barely able, in the gloom, to make out the frail figure of the class enemy. He was wearing white underdrawers, and a dark undershirt, and was bare-foot. The tangled beard on a face long unshaven stuck out a little to the front. The eyes, wide with terror, glanced from place to place. The deeply lined face winced; the coarse brown hands were trembling. On the bare chest, hanging by a worn, old cord, was a little cross grown dark with age.
>
> "Oh Lord Jesus! Save us, have mercy on us. . . . "
>
> Freezing air swirled into the well-heated peasant hut. The members of the de-kulakization brigade were already at each window; their expressions were stern; they all expected something terrible to happen, were ready to rush into battle for their own cause, for Soviet power, for socialism. But the kulak-accomplice Terent'ev

---

14. I. Stalin, *Sochineniia.* Vol. 12 (Moscow, 1952), p. 198.

never dreamed of resisting. He kept blinking and crossing himself, shuffling his feet about as though he were standing on live coals, and suddenly be began to sob. Convulsive gasps doubled up his whole body. He bent over in an unnatural position, as his body shook and small gleaming tears followed one another down the calloused, weatherbeaten face. His wife, not a young woman, jumped down from the high sleeping bench and began to wail at the top of her voice. The children began crying. A calf lying beside the stove, apparently not in very good health, began to bawl. Morgunov looked around, aghast. He saw that the hut consisted of nothing but the main room and the big Russian stove. In the guest area, beneath the icons, were two simple wooden benches and a crude table fashioned out of boards. No chest of drawers, no beds, no chairs. On the shelves were some simple wooden bowls, worn by long use, and some wooden ladles of equal vintage. By the stove were some oven forks and buckets of water, and to the left, by the wall, was a large old-fashioned trunk.

The class enemy!

The representatives of authority had already announced to Terent'ev that he was under arrest. He was being de-kulakized and deported right away. All his property was being confiscated. His family would follow him shortly, but where they were going was not known. He could take with him only the clothes he could wear.

Terent'ev trembled and wept: "What kind of kulaks are we? What for? What did I do?"

No one answered him. Rudely breaking the locks, they threw open the trunk and the food cupboard. They dragged out some foot-gear, sack cloth, and foodstuffs.

"What for? What did I do? . . . "

"Nothing! You're a kulak, a *podkulachnik!*. . . You're against the kolkhoz!. . . You don't want to join and you're disrupting the work! That's all there is to it!"

They set about making a list of his goods and possessions. . . .[15]

According to official statistics, 115,200 kulak families were deported to remote regions in 1930, and 265,800 in 1931, i.e., 381, 000 families in all over a period of two years.[16] These figures are significantly larger than those cited in 1933 at the January plenum of the Central Committee. Official Soviet sources also report that the deportation of kulaks and "kulak supporters" was continued in 1932 and that, in addition to families sent to remote regions, there were quite a few kulak families resettled within the same region. There is every reason to believe, nonetheless, that even these "more exact" official statistics are understated. But the deportation of hundreds of thousands of peasant families to remote regions of the country should not be thought of as implying the total annihilation of those families. Although the mortality rate among deportees was quite high, many of them managed to survive in their new locations, and the children and grandchildren of the deportees, when granted freedom of movement, went to work, for the most part, in the cities.

A significantly larger number of peasants died from the terrible, artificially created famine in the winter of 1932–33, which affected primarily the southern Ukrainian areas but also the northern Caucasus, the Volga region, and Central

---

15. A. M——n, "K viashchei slave gospodne" (manuscript), p. 71.
16. *Voprosy istorii KPSS,* 1975, No. 5, p. 140.

Asia. The statistics on the number of Ukrainians in the USSR, given in the book *Population of the USSR,* are, for 1926, 31.2 million, and for 1939, 28.1 million. The actual decrease in population over a period of thirteen years amounted to 3.1 million. But during the same period the number of Russians and Byelorussians in the USSR grew by between 11 and 12 percent.[17] Even if one allows for a reduced birth rate in many parts of the Ukraine, one must assume that the number who died of starvation was no less than four or five million. Moreover, the peasants in other parts of the country as well died by the hundreds of thousands.

"In the early 1930's," wrote Boris Pasternak in his unpublished memoirs, "there was a movement among writers to travel to the collective farms and gather material about the new life of the village. I wanted to be with everyone else and likewise made such a trip with the aim of writing a book. What I saw could not be expressed in words. There was such inhuman, unimaginable misery, such a terrible disaster, that it began to seem almost abstract, it would not fit within the bounds of consciousness. I fell ill. For an entire year I could not write."

Stalin in the Period 1934–39

In 1934 a new stage began in Stalin's sinister career, one in which the cutting edge of terror was directed more and more against the party itself, against the basic cadres of the Communist party, the Soviet government, the Red Army, the economic agencies, and all the other public and social organizations.

The groundwork for this terror was laid with the murder of S. M. Kirov. In the first issue of the so-called *Bulletin of the Opposition,* which Trotsky began to publish outside the country in 1929, one of the very first articles stated that Stalin, in order to crush the Opposition completely, "absolutely must connect the Opposition with assassination attempts, preparations for armed insurrection, etc. . . . The impotent policy of tacking and weaving the mounting economic difficulties and the party's growing distrust of the leadership have made it necessary for Stalin to stun the party by staging something on a big scale. A blow is needed, a shake-up, a disaster. . . . This is the kind of thing—and the *only* kind—that Stalin will think through to the end." [18]

In this instance Trotsky was wrong only about the timing. The blow to stun the party came not in 1930 or 1931 but on December 1, 1934. Stalin did indeed link the assassination with the ability of the Opposition, which was said to be continuing its work deep underground. It was Stalin himself who drew up the list of the former Zinovievists of Leningrad who, at a secret trial in December 1934, were called the "Katalynov terrorist group." They had, for the most part, been Komsomol activists in the 1920's. Working in various government offices, they maintained contact with one another and met from time to time. Most of them were still of an oppositionist frame of mind, but they did not have any organizational structure, much less any idea of engaging in terrorism. It is also

17. A Gozulov and M. Grigor'iants, *Narodaselenie SSSR* (Moscow, 1969).
18. *Biulleten' oppozitsii,* No. 1–2 (1929), p. 2.

known that at the staged trial where all the members of this "group" were condemned to death V. Levin gave a major speech denouncing Stalin and his policies.

In 1935, as is generally known, the first trial of Zinoviev, Kamenev, and a group of their former supporters was held. Arrests of persons formerly active in oppositionist currents continued throughout the year, but this was only a special kind of preparation for the decisive blow against the party. Several laws were passed at the same time which facilitated the terror soon to come. Among these was the decree of the Central Executive Committee of April 7, 1935, which made children aged twelve or over subject to criminal charges; all penalties up to and including being shot were extended to include them.

M. P. Tomsky, a man of prominence in our party, and for many years the president of the All-Union Central Council of Trade Unions, committed suicide in August 1936, when the "public" trial of Zinoviev, Kamenev, and the others began in Moscow. According to Tomsky's son Yuri (the only surviving member of the Tomsky family), his father's suicide occurred immediately after a visit by Stalin, who came to M. P. Tomsky's apartment with a bottle of wine and shut himself in with Tomsky in the latter's study. At first they talked quietly about something, then Yuri heard his father shouting, calling Stalin unprintable names, accusing him of murder. Flinging open the door of the study, Tomsky demanded that Stalin get out. Stalin left, shaking with anger, and a few minutes later a shot rang out in the office. Rykov, too, wished to shoot himself in those days, but his family literally tore the gun out of his hands, something they greatly regretted having done, later, during the Bukharin-Rykov trial.

In 1936, after the second trial of Zinoviev and Kamenev, the commissar of internal affairs, G. Yagoda, who had been of such great assistance to Stalin up until then, was removed from his post and soon arrested, being replaced by N. Yezhov. Yezhov, it should be noted, was by no means some sort of demonic individual. Of working-class origin, he had been orphaned early in life, and, from the age of twelve, was raised by the Shliapnikov family. In his youth he did not manifest any especially malicious or perfidious qualities or other notable failings, such as were evident in the case of Beria, for example. Those who knew Yezhov in the days when he worked in the Komsomol, or for the party in the eastern regions of the country, or during his brief tenure as commissar of agriculture, have told me that Yezhov seemed to them at the time a very ordinary sort, not at all a cruel person, even rather a pleasant one. But from the moment he first met Stalin, he fell completely under the total, unconditional, almost hypnotic influence of the general secretary. Stalin took note of this, and began to push Yezhov rapidly up the ladder. In the fall of 1936 Yezhov and Stalin began to make preparations not only for new arrests and public trials of former Opposition leaders but for the annihilation of the central party leadership as well.

In *Let History Judge* I listed the names of *approximately a thousand* such leaders, the best-known figures in the central party, government, and economic bodies; leaders of regional party committees and central executive committees, of trade-union and Komsomol organizations; the most prominent commanders of the Red Army and Soviet Navy, of the NKVD, the judiciary, and the procuracy; prominent foreign Communists; and leading scientists, writers, and personalities of the art world.

Even adhering to this principle and naming only the best-known and most prominent people, the list of the victims of 1937–38 can be expanded significantly. At present my private "dossier" contains a list of secretaries of territorial committees, regional committees, city committees, and municipal district committees in the larger cities, on which there are 206 names, and this, of course, is far from a complete list of party personnel who died in 1937–38. A list (also incomplete) ·of presidents of regional executive committees, of councils of people's commissars and central executive committees of the national republics, and of municipal soviets in the larger cities contains 129 names. In my possession is a list of the most prominent Komsomol personnel arrested, most of whom perished. This includes members of the Kosomol Central Committee, secretaries of regional Komsomol committees, of the RSFSR Komsomol, and of the Komsomols of the national republics, and secretaries of the municipal Komsomol committees in the larger cities; it contains 126 names. The martyrology of the foreign Communists who died in the USSR could also be added to substantially. Thus, for example, the weekly organ of the Union of Communists of Yugoslavia, *Kommunist,* published on April 3, 1969, a list of eighty-five Yugoslav Communists who fell victim to the Stalin terror. A similar list prepared by the Italian Communist party numbers over 120 names. In my book I failed to mention many famous scientists, writers, and personalities of the art world who fell victim to the punitive organs in 1937–38. Among the great many that could be mentioned are the president of the Academy of Sciences of the Byelorussian Republic, I. Z. Surt; the outstanding linguist E. D. Polivanov; the highly knowledgeable expert on Tibet, Vostrikov; the aerodynamics expert K. I. Strakhovich; the historian M. A. Savel'ev; the poets Nik. Kliuev and Vl. Smirensky; the conductor E. Miloladze; and the artists O. Shcherbinskaia and Z. Smirnova.

In reviewing the lists drawn up by Yezhov, of various well-known cultural or party figures slated for arrest, Stalin sometimes struck out a name here or there, with no concern whatsoever about the charges brought against them. Thus, from the list of literary figures to be arrested Stalin deleted the name L. Brik. "We won't touch the wife of Mayakovsky," he told Yezhov.

Altogether, by my calculations, from 1936 to 1939, about one million party members, or slightly more than that, were struck by the repression. But we must add to that number those who were expelled from the party in the purges of 1933–34 but who still considered themselves Communists. And in 1933, some 800,000 members were "purged," while in 1934, more than 300,000 were. Of course there were also arrests among non-party people in 1937–38 but these were mostly relatives, friends, or co-workers of arrested Communists. The fact that the "great terror" of the late 1930's was directed mainly at the party itself was obvious even to most ordinary people, who slept far more peacefully by night than the Communists did in those years. In 1937–38 someone made up the following "anecdote" and passed it along in a whisper:

> A knock comes on the door at night, and a voice bellows out roughly, "NKVD! Open up!"
> "But we're non-Party people," they answer from behind the locked door. "The Communists are the next flight up."

As is generally known, Solzhenitsyn in his *Gulag Archipelago* and in his publicistic statements has repeatedly declared that he prefers not to regard the Communists arrested in 1936–39 as *victims* of the terror. For most of these Communists engaged in Red Terror in the years 1918–22, directly or indirectly contributed to the violence against the peasantry in 1929–1933, and failed to oppose the persecution of the Trotskyists and Zinovievists. "The question arises," says Solzhenitsyn, "when a victim helps the executioner up until the last moment, and has brought others to him to be slaughtered, and has held the axe—whether this is a victim at all, and not just another executioner." [19]

I do not by any means wish to try to vindicate those Communists who actively carried out terrorist measures at all of the preceding stages, both against the peasantry and against other party members. I have written in regard to this about such figures as Postyshev, Eikhe, Betal, Kalmykov, Amatuni, Trilisser, Sheboldaev, Krylenko, Sharangovich, and many others who actually did play an active role in implementing the terror before they themselves fell victim to it. One might add the case of V. Antonov-Ovseenko, who took an active part in the extermination of Trotsky's supporters and the anarchists in Spain (in spite of their active role in the fight against fascism). Upon his return to Moscow in 1938 Antonov-Ovseenko was arrested and shot. The secretary of the Komsomol Central Committee, A. Mil'chakov, until his own arrest, was one of the most prominent "exposers," and many people had been arrested on the basis of "materials" he provided. Even at the February-March plenum of the Central Committee in 1937 no one decisively objected to the intensification of repression within the party, although Yezhov's report to the plenum contained threats clearly aimed at members of the Central Committee. When Molotov, in his report on "wrecking" in industry, referred to cases of this in light industry, Vareikis yelled at Liubimov, the commissar of light industry: "There, you see! And you said no wrecking was going on in light industry!" Both Vareikis and Liubimov were arrested within the year and shot as "wreckers." Arrests of members of the Central Executive Committee of the USSR were normally sanctioned by Kalinin himself. During one session of the Central Executive Committee in 1937, Kalinin's secretary personally summoned four members of the committee to Kalinin's office, one after the other, and Kalinin, sobbing, signed the statement sanctioning their arrest, which was put into effect immediately by an NKVD operations group stationed in the adjoining room. [20]

---

19. *Russkaia mysl'*, January 16, 1975.
20. Testimony of P. Aksenov, member of the Central Executive Committee of the USSR and president of the Municipal Soviet of Kazan, who was one of those arrested in Kalinin's office.

Even after they had landed in prison or camp, some Communists continued to make justifications for Stalin and his policy of terror. "To be sure, I never believed that Bukharin and Trotsky were agents of the Gestapo," writes the Old Bolshevik K——v in his memoirs, "or that they wanted to kill Lenin; moreover, I was sure that Stalin knew that very well himself. But I thought that the trials of 1937–38 represented a far-sighted political tactic on Stalin's part, that he was right in deciding to discredit all forms of opposition once and for all by using such fearful methods. After all, we were a besieged fortress; we had to close ranks, and not have any doubts or wavering. What did all the theoretical disputes mean to the 'broad masses'? Most 'ordinary people' could not even understand exactly what the differences were between the Rights and the Lefts. . . . So all deviationists, all those of little faith politically, had to be portrayed as such scum that everyone would steer clear of them, that people would grow to hate them and curse them. . . .

"In prison," K——v admits openly, "I became a far more thoroughgoing Stalinist than ever before. . . . I was convinced that even if most of the NKVD personnel were indifferent careerists, ignoramuses only looking out for themselves, nevertheless, in the final analysis, the causes and purposes of their arbitrary activity were absolutely just and virtuous, and for that reason I believed that all the particular mistakes, miscalculations, and injustices, no matter how many, could not change the overall picture, could not halt the victorious development of our socialist society." [21]

But of course in the camps and prisons people like K——v were isolated cases. On the whole I regard Solzhenitsyn's point of view as incorrect. Only in regard to a small number of those who died in the terror is he right. Neither Yagoda nor Yezhov can be regarded as a "victim" of the terror, nor can the other chief executioners and their *immediate, conscious* accomplices. But among the one-to-two million (depending on what estimates are used) who died in the 1930's there were people who were by no means all of the same kind, either in their personal qualities or in the degree of responsibility they bore for the crimes of the preceding years. There were quite a few who were sincere but mistaken or who were victims of another kind of cult—the cult of party discipline. Among them were many honest, self-sacrificing people who, too late, came to understand a great deal. There were many who thought about what was happening in the country and were tormented by it but who nevertheless believed in the party and in the party propaganda. There were also those who had stopped believing the official propaganda but who did not know how to go about altering the situation. Therefore, we simply cannot lump all these people together indiscriminately as criminals who got what they deserved, although it is possible from today's vantage-point to speak of the general historical and political responsibility of the active party membership as a whole for the events of the 1920's and 1930's. By no means do I praise such Chekists as Latsis or Peters, a position Solzhenitsyn ascribes to me in the statement by him quoted above. But I cannot help regarding

---

21. "O moei zhizni" (manuscript).

a certain Chekist named Artuzov, for example, as a victim of the terror. Before he was shot, Artuzov wrote on the wall of his death cell, in blood, "The duty of an honest person is to kill Stalin!"

We would cite innumerable instances of Stalin's hypocrisy toward his erstwhile comrades-in-arms. Thus, for example, at the first session of the Supreme Soviet of the USSR in 1938, M. D. Bagirov suddenly began to criticize the people's commissar of justice of the USSR, N. V. Krylenko, "for not upholding Soviet laws properly."

Bagirov declared:

> Comrade Krylenko concerns himself only incidentally with the affairs of his commissariat. But to direct the Commissariat of Justice, great initiative and a serious attitude toward oneself is required. Whereas Comrade Krylenko used to spend a great deal of his time on mountain-climbing and traveling, now he devotes a great deal of time to playing chess. I am a great advocate of developing all kinds of sporting activities to the maximum in our country, including vacation travel, mountain-climbing, and chess. But I cannot in any way agree to the slightest slacking off either in the management or the functioning of such a highly important commissariat as the People's Commissariat of Justice, nor to such an unserious attitude as Comrade Krylenko's toward the work of the commissariat he heads. We need to know what we are dealing with in the case of Comrade Krylenko—the commissar of justice? or a mountain climber? I don't know which Comrade Krylenko thinks of himself as, but he is without doubt a poor people's commissar. I am sure that Comrade Molotov will take that into account in presenting the slate of nominees for the new Council of People's Commissars of the Supreme Soviet.[22]

One need have no doubt that such "audacious" criticism of a people's commissar could be leveled by a Bagirov only at Stalin's prompting. For sure enough, the post of commissar of justice in the new Council of People's Commissars went not to Krylenko but to N. M. Rychkov. It took Krylenko five days to fill the new commissar in on the affairs of the commissariat. After that Krylenko went to his dacha outside Moscow, where he gathered all his family together. Suddenly the phone rang; it was from the Kremlin. Stalin was asking for Krylenko. "Don't be upset," Stalin said. "We have confidence in you. Continue the work you were assigned to on the new legal code." That very night a special NKVD operations group surrounded Krylenko's dacha and arrested him and part of his family.[23] Half a year later Krylenko was shot, of course with Stalin's authorization.

Mass repression began to subside in the fall of 1938. At that time Stalin, true to his hypocritical tactics, appointed a special commission to investigate NKVD activity—with Beria and Malenkov on the commission. In order to gain access to all NKVD materials, Beria was appointed, on a motion by L. Kaganovich, as first deputy to the people's commissar of internal affairs. The commission found many "irregularities" in the work of the NKVD. The outcome was that a letter appeared, signed by Molotov, Vyshinsky, and Beria, on excesses that had

---

22. *Pervaia sessiia verkhovnogo soveta SSSR. Stenograficheskii otchet* (Moscow, 1938), pp. 142–43.
23. *Partiia shagaet v revoliutsiiu* (Moscow, 1964), p. 236.

occurred in the work of interrogation and in the reviewing of cases. Within several weeks the Central Committee passed two resolutions: (1) "On Arrests, Supervision by the Procuracy, and the Conduct of Investigations"; and (2) "On the Recruitment of Honest People for Work in the Security Organs." Half a month after these resolutions were adopted, N. I. Yezhov was removed from his post as people's commissar of internal affairs. However, he was allowed to retain the post of people's commissar of water transport for several months more. As a member of the party's Central Committee Yezhov attended the Eighteenth Party Congress in March 1939, but his name was dropped from the list of members proposed for the new Central Committee. In late 1938 and early 1939, E. G. Feldman was performing the duties of first secretary of the Odessa Regional Committee of the party. He was a delegate to the Eighteenth Congress and as head of the Odessa delegation attended the Council of Elders at the congress. He left his friends the following notes concerning that session of the Council of Elders.

As the congress was coming to a close, the Council of Elders gathered in one of the halls of the Kremlin, where the congress was being held. At the front of the hall at a long table, as though on stage, sat A. A. Andreev, V. M. Molotov, and G. M. Malenkov. Far to the rear, in a corner, to the left of the area where the Council of Elders were seated, Stalin took a seat, puffing on his pipe. Andreev said that since the congress was finishing up its work, it was necessary to propose a slate of candidates for the voting on the upcoming Central Committee. First, people from the outgoing Central Committee were nominated, excluding, of course, those who had fallen by the way. Yezhov's name came up. "Any opinions?" asked Andreev. After a moment of silence, someone remarked that Yezhov was a good Stalinist commissar, known to all, and should be kept. "Any objections?" Everyone was silent. Then Stalin asked for the floor. He got up, walked to the table, and, still puffing on his pipe, called out:

"Yezhov! Where are you? Oh, there you are. Come on up here!"

From the back rows Yezhov emerged and came up to the table.

"Well, what do you think about yourself?" Stalin asked him. "Can you be a member of the Central Committee?"

Yezhov turned white; his voice breaking, he replied that he did not understand the question, that he had devoted his whole life to the party and to Stalin, that he loved Stalin more than his own life, and knew of nothing in his record that could inspire such a question.

"Is that so?" Stalin asked ironically. "Then who was Frinovsky? Did you know Frinovsky?"

"Yes, certainly, I knew him," Yezhov answered. "Frinovsky was my deputy. He . . . "

Stalin interrupted him and began asking who Shapiro was, who Ryzhova (Yezhov's secretary) was, who Fedorov was, and so on. (At that time all these people had been arrested.)

"Iosif Vissarionovich! But you know it was I—I myself! who exposed their plot. I came to you and reported that . . . "

Stalin did not let him continue.

"Yes, yes, yes! When you thought you were going to get caught, then you came all in a hurry. But what happened before that? Did you organize a plot? Did you want to kill Stalin? Top people in the NKVD were hatching a plot, and you supposedly had nothing to do with it!

"Do you think I don't see anything?" Stalin went on. "Well, let me refresh your memory. Who was it you sent to stand guard over Stalin one day? Who? Did they have revolvers? Why be near Stalin with revolvers? To kill Stalin? And what if I hadn't noticed? What then?"

Then Stalin accused Yezhov of running NKVD activities too frantically and feverishly, of arresting many innocent people, and of covering up for others when necessary.

"Well? Get going! That's all! I don't know, comrades, can this man be left as a member of the Central Committee? I have my doubts. Of course, you think it over. . . . It's up to you, as you wish. . . . But I have my doubts!"

Yezhov, of course, was unanimously voted off the slate, and after the break he did not return to the hall, nor was he seen at the congress after that.

However, Yezhov was not arrested for several days. He was arrested right in the middle of a session of the collegium of the People's Commissariat of Water Transport. From the moment Yezhov was put in charge of the additional commissariat on April 8, 1938, the work of the Commissariat of Water Transport went on in an atmosphere of subdued terror. For his part Yezhov hardly even visited his new commissariat. After his removal from the NKVD, Yezhov attended collegium meetings at the Commissariat of Water Transport but did not interfere; he sat silently, or sometimes made paper airplanes or paper birds and flew them around and retrieved them, even crawling under a chair or table now and then—but always in silence. When he saw the NKVD agents enter the hall of the collegium he stood up with an almost inspired glow on his face and uttered the words, "How long I have waited for this!" He put his gun down on the desk and was led away.[24]

As is generally known, a small number of earlier victims of repression were freed and rehabilitated in 1939–41. The treatment of those under investigation became more courteous, but torture was still used, although not on the same scale as previously. Indicative of that time was the fact that the higher courts and various investigating commissions vindicated more people than the NKVD desired. For that reason, not all of those who had been cleared were released from prison, and the investigations into their cases were begun anew. However, in order not to sow doubts and dissension, such "exonerated" zeks (convicts) were all placed in a single cell. Thus in many prisons, in addition to the death-row cells, there were for a time special cells for the "exonerated" as well, and the prisoners who had been cleared were usually held under conditions just as bad as before.

No one has inquired with any special interest into the question of why Stalin carried out mass terror in Tsaritsyn in 1918 or even why he did so in the countryside in 1930–32. But the mass terror of the late 1930's, aimed primarily

---

24. Testimony of V. M——v, a former member of the collegium of the People's Commissariat of Water Transport.

at the basic cadres of the Communist party itself and at Stalin's former close associates, has given rise to a great variety of alternate explanations—that Stalin deceived the NKVD organs, that Stalin was psychologically unbalanced, and that he allegedly feared exposure of his ties with the tsarist Okhrana. In *Let History Judge* I was critical of all these interpretations. I am certain that Stalin was fully cognizant of his actions. The terror against the party was premeditated and carefully planned. I still think that the main motives for this terror were Stalin's inordinate vanity and lust for power. He aspired to autocratic one-man rule, with no restraints whatsoever; he wished to take undeserved credit for building up the Soviet state and Communist party, and to those ends he promoted a personal cult of himself. And when the basic cadres of the party and state were found to be obstacles to the achievement of these goals, Stalin did not hesitate to destroy this layer of people, just as he had not hesitated in dealing with the well-to-do peasantry or the "bourgeois specialists."

In recent years, however, yet another interpretation of the 1936–39 "purges" has appeared. This was presented most fully in a series of articles by M. Agursky. In Agursky's opinion the 1917 Revolution was not only a social revolution but a national one as well. It represented above all the victory of the outlying national regions over Great Russia, the metropolis. Consequently the leadership that took shape in the new government consisted overwhelmingly of non-Russian elements—Jews, Latvians, Poles, Caucasians, etc. In the mid-1930's, however, a new trend developed. The causes of the purges, writes Agursky,

> were much deeper. Under the purges' mantle there took place a profound social and (no less important) national transformation, as a result of which there came to power a new stratum of people, mostly of peasant origin, among whom there were virtually no aliens any more (Jews, Latvians, Lithuanians, Poles, etc.). This was the reaction of a vast Slavonic country to the internationalist, cosmopolitan experiments of the 1920's and 1930's, which ignored the national factor. Stalin merely summoned the new stratum to power: he did not create it. Without exaggeration, the purges of 1936–38 can be regarded as one of the final stages of the Civil War in Russia. To replace the old elite—which need not be idealized—there came a new stratum which had no continuity with its predecessors, for the purges took place in different phases, and in the end liquidated the entire body of activists who had taken any direct part in the Revolution and Civil War, or had participated in party life and knew the party's structure before 1937. Evidently, an indispensable condition for the formation of the new elite was also the fact that until 1937 its members were only on the lowest level of public life.[25]

In Agursky's interpretation there is undoubtedly an element of truth. However, Agursky makes an absolute out of the only one aspect of the events of those years, an aspect that is far from the most essential or important. It is quite obvious that there was a certain degree of continuity between the party leadership as constituted in 1934 and the new one formed after the Eighteenth Party Congress in 1939. Remaining on the Politburo were not only the Russian V. Molotov but

---

25. "The Birth of Byelorussia," *Times Literary Supplement,* June 30, 1972, pp. 743–44.

the Armenian A. Mikoyan and the Jew L. Kaganovich. And of course Stalin himself was a Georgian, as every knows. Added to the Politburo was another Georgian, L. Beria (in place of the Russian Yezhov). Keeping their places on the Politburo were A. Andreev, K. Voroshilov, and M. Kalinin. A. Zhdanov and N. Khrushchev (a candidate member since 1938), who joined the Politburo for the first time in 1939, had not been on the "lowest level of public life," each having been a member of the Central Committee previously.

It is generally known that there were quite a few Jews, Latvians, Poles, Finns, and members of the various nationalities of the Caucasus, as well as many other "aliens," in the membership of the revolutionary parties. This was natural, since, in addition to the various forms of social oppression, these peoples of the Russian Empire also suffered from national oppression, something that most people are particularly sensitive to. Nevertheless, it would be wrong to refer to the 1917 Revolution as the victory of the national borderlands over Great Russia. The core of the political army of the October Revolution was made up of Russians. Its nucleus was the Russian working class in alliance with the Russian soldiers, i.e., peasants in uniform. And although, after the revolution, the percentage of non-Russians in the leadership of the party and government was significant, Russians were always in the majority. I will cite only the national composition of the Twelfth Congress of the Russian Communist party, i.e., the first party congress after the conclusion of the Civil War and the formation of the USSR.[26]

Russians	60.8%	Armenians	2.4%
Jews	11.3%	Byelorussians	1.2%
Latvians and		Kirghiz	1.7%
Estonians	7.1%	Tatars	1.0%
Ukrainians	4.7%	others	7.1%
Georgians	2.7%		

These figures do not fit in at all with Agursky's scheme, especially in view of the fact that at subsequent congresses Russians were invariably in the majority and the number of Jews, Latvians, and Estonians steadily declined, while the number of Ukrainians and Byelorussians grew. Although the reports of the credentials committees at the Eighteenth and subsequent congresses no longer gave exact figures on the national composition of the congress delegations, in-direct evidence nevertheless suggests that there were no essential changes in the relative number of Russians and members of other nationalities, either among congress delegations or in the higher echelons of the party and state. The repres-sion of 1936–39 noticeably reduced the number of Latvians, Estonians, Finns, Poles, and Hungarians in the national composition of the Soviet elite. That is quite understandable since Latvia, Estonia, Finland, and Poland did not belong to the USSR, and it was not possible to develop new cadres from among those nations. The number of Jews also declined. The author of a major study on "The Russian Jew Yesterday and Today" writes on this question:

---

26. *XII s"ezd RKP(b). Stenograficheskii otchet* (Moscow, 1968), p. 420.

The repression of the 1930's struck the Soviet intelligentsia and the people in the party and state apparatus to a greater extent than it did the workers. Among the intellectuals and apparatus people, as a group, the Communists, in turn, were hit far harder than non-party people. Lastly, among the Communists themselves, repression fell upon the older members of the party with considerably greater force than on those who had joined recently. And it was precisely among the Jews that there were more intellectuals and office workers than industrial workers; the percentage of Jewish Communists was two, three, four times greater than the percentage of Communists of other nationalities; and lastly, if we look at the composition of the party, we see that among older members, Jews were also found in disproportiately large numbers. The combination all the disproportionate elements here mentioned had the result that the repression, while not especially aimed at the Jews, accidentally injured them "on the rebound" more severely than it did other peoples, cutting down the most advanced elements of the Jewish people, and those most devoted to the revolution.[27]

This point of view is much closer to the truth than the reasoning of Agursky. One cannot fail to note, moreover, that after 1938 the number of persons of Caucasian origin, especially Georgians, Armenians, and Azerbaijanis, in high positions in the NKVD increased markedly. More people of Central Asian and Kazakh origin were found in the leadership as well. Russian great-power chauvinism was indeed promoted by Stalin and was reflected in his policy of cadre selection. But that happened somewhat later, during the war and in the period 1948–53.

It is appropriate to add a few remarks here on Stalin's personality. In one of my articles I wrote that one may find in Stalin's behavior and criminal actions not only the pragmatic attitude held by many revolutionaries toward violence and the use of extreme measures but also the dogmatism, casuistry, intolerance, and other qualities which undoubtedly were to a certain extent the product of his five years in an Orthodox school and three in an Orthodox seminary. These remarks provoked a polemic on the pages of the Russian émigré press. My view was supported by Dm. Bezrukikh, who wrote an article that more or less sums up the debate on the influence of the church on Stalin's character formation.[28]

In his article Bezrukikh quoted a passage from the book *Only One Year* by Stalin's daughter, Svetlana Alliluyeva, arguing that his early education was a decisive formative influence on Stalin's character.[29] But of course Stalin's chief personality trait was his extreme cynicism, his unscrupulousness, his contempt for people. In an interesting essay, *Certain Organizational Conclusions of Social Genetics,* a leading Soviet biologist, N. P——v, writes:

> There can be no doubt that great success on the part of an individual has often been based on energy, concentration on a goal, and talent. However, while all these

---

27. B. D——y, *"Russkii evrei vchera i segodnia"* (manuscript), p. 55.

28. *Russkaia mysl',* December 26, 1974.

29. Unlike *Twenty Letters to a Friend,* Alliluyeva's book *Only One Year* gives an incomparably more precise portrait of Stalin from the psychological point of view, and provides us with important factual information on his behavior and activities.

qualities are necessary, they are not decisive. Unscrupulousness has always been a virtually indispensable quality, providing an extremely important advantage over people of ideas, genuine specialists in their fields, inventors, innovators. What is there in common between the hardened professional criminal, often simply a poorly educated type, a primitive with easily satisfied passions, and the masters and rulers of nations who rise over mountains of corpses? What is there in common between professional criminals and the great military commanders, conquerors, feudal lords, captains of industry, and political gangsters, with their great organizational abilities that carry them so rapidly to the heights of the social pyramid? What they have in common is lack of scruple; that is their special characterological feature which facilitates their rise in society to an extraordinary degree—something not possible for ordinary criminals, because of limited intelligence, retentive capacity, education, or aptitude.[30] This characterization may be applied in full to Stalin.

Stalin During the War and the Postwar Period

Nearly all of the army commanders, marshals, and people's commissars of the 1930's fell victim to the Great Terror; none of them left memoirs other than those already written in the 1920's, dealing with the October Revolution and the Civil War. The generals, marshals, ministers, and other highly placed persons who made up Stalin's entourage during the Great Patriotic War and the early post-war years, as a rule, survived Stalin. And when the situation in the USSR began to change, especially after the Twenty-Second Party Congress, many of these people published their memoirs, telling a good deal about their encounters with Stalin. The quality of the memoirs on Stalin published over the past fifteen years has been, and continues to be, uneven. But on the whole, even these memoirs add substantially enough to the source material for the political biography of Stalin. Avoiding, as much as possible, repetition of what has already been published, I shall touch in this section only upon certain episodes relating to the last thirteen years of Stalin's life.

It is well known that Hitler Germany's attack on the USSR on June 22, 1941, came as a complete surprise to Stalin, who was sleeping peacefully in his dacha on the night of the attack (late on the night of June 21 and in the early hours of June 22). This was Stalin's greatest and most fundamental miscalculation, costing our country millions and millions of unnecessary casualties and causing terrible destruction. Of course Stalin could not help but be aware of the danger of German aggression. Even in *Mein Kampf* Hitler had written, with rare candor: "Germany . . . sees the destruction of France merely as a means by which our people can ultimately increase our *Lebensraum* in another area. . . . Nothing will prevent me from attacking Russia after I have achieved my aims in the West."[31]

For us the first phase of the war was a terrible drama. The German troops, having essentially shattered the main forces of the Red Army, broke through to the Don River at Rostov and reached the gates of Leningrad and Moscow. By

---

30. *"Nekotorye organizatsionnye vyvody sotsial'noi genetiki"* (manuscript), p. 41.
31. Quoted in D. M. Proektor, *Agressiia i katastrofa* (Moscow, 1972), p. 45.

early autumn the Germans had lost 800,000 killed and wounded on the Russian front (their losses in all their Western campaigns having been only 300,000). But during the same months the Red Army lost no less than five million killed, wounded, and above all, captured.

There are many reasons for the defeats we suffered in the early period of the war, but not the least factor was the incompetent leadership provided by Stalin, in whose hands all military and civil power in the country was concentrated. Marshall A. M. Vasilevsky—a man who held the post of chief of the General Staff for a long time during the war—has written about this quite recently in his memoirs. Vasilevsky writes:

> The General Staff had been made the working body of the High Command [Stavka], which had no other special apparatus for that purpose. The General Staff supplied the necessary information, processed it, and prepared suggestions which the Stavka subsequently used as the basis for orders it issued. From the start, Stalin expressed extreme dissatisfaction with the work of the General Staff. Moreover, I will not hide the fact that Stalin did not always make the best decisions, and did not always show an understanding of our difficulties. . . . In Stalin's work at the time, there were miscalculations, sometimes of a serious nature. He was at that time unjustifiably self-assured and self-reliant, operating too much on his own and over-estimating his knowledge and abilities in regard to directing a war. He relied very little on the General Staff, and did not by any means make sufficient use of the knowledge and experience of its personnel. Often, without any reason, he would make hasty changes in the top military cadres. Under such conditions the General Staff could not develop to top working capacity and it did not carry out its functions as the working body of the Stavka to the extent it should have. . . . J. V. Stalin rightly demanded that the military cadres abandon outdated concepts of warfare. But he himself did not do this as quickly as we would have liked. He was more inclined to engage in more or less head-on operations. Here, of course, in addition to everything else, he was influenced by the situation on the front, the nearness of the enemy to Moscow, and his penetration deep into the country. . . . The battle of Stalingrad was an important milestone. But he probably did not fully master the new forms and methods of armed combat until the battle of Kursk.[32]

Some memoirs that have appeared in recent years take issue indirectly with the assertion of N. S. Khrushchev, in his secret speech to the Twentieth Party Congress, that Stalin shut himself up in his dacha on the second day of the war and for several days would see no one and took no part in the governing of the country or the direction of the armed forces. In the *Memoirs of Marshal G. Zhukov* (G. K. Zhukov, *Vospominaniia i razmyshleniia*), the author says he met with Stalin at sessions of the High Command on June 26 and June 29, 1941, for example. Other books refer to telephone conversations with Stalin during the first few days of the war. In this case, however, we are dealing with deliberate falsification, or misrepresentation through omission. Earlier, several years before his book appeared, Zhukov made detailed transcripts of his memoirs with the use of a tape recorder; on the basis of these transcripts the first draft of his memoirs—some four hundred pages long—was produced. In this first and, needless to say, more

---

32. A. M. Vasilevsky, *Delo vsei zhizni* (Moscow, 1974), pp. 126–27.

accurate version Zhukov confirmed the fact that Stalin had deserted his post in the first days of the war and discussed many of Stalin's other serious errors in greater detail.

In October 1941 the Germans broke through the Red Army front lines on the outer approaches to Moscow and surrounded four armies (the Nineteenth, Twentieth, Twenty-fourth, and Thirty-second). There were no serious obstacles between the fascists and Moscow, during those days. According to Vasilevsky, this severe defeat was also the result of an incorrect determination by the High Command of what direction the enemy's attack would take. As a result, the Red Army defenses were not deep enough along the main line of the enemy's advance, where his heaviest blows fell. The advance of the German troops created a panic in Moscow, especially on October 16, when rumors spread, after the evacuation of the main government offices, that Moscow was soon to be surrendered. There was evidence that Stalin also left Moscow on that day and went to Gorky or Kuibyshev. Some recently published memoirs contain refutations of this. For example, A. Shakhurin, the minister for aircraft industry, describes this very day, October 16, in detail. On the morning of that day he was at one of the aircraft factories that was to be evacuated, when he was notified to come immediately to Stalin's suite in the Kremlin. Shakhurin writes:

The Kremlin looked deserted, Having entered the vestibule, I took off my coat and proceeded down the hallway. Meetings were usually held in the dining room. As I entered that room, J. V. Stalin appeared from the bedroom. As always, he was smoking and pacing up and down. Directly in front of the entrance to the dining room was a table, and to the left a buffet. To the right, along the wall, were bookcases, but there were no books in them now. Stalin was dressed as usual, in a jacket (kurtka), with his trousers tucked into his boots (it was later that he began wearing a military uniform). The Politburo members came in. Stalin greeted them all, and continued to smoke and pace. We all stood. Then he stopped and, addressing no one in particular, asked, "How are things in Moscow?" Everyone remained silent; they glanced at one another. Without holding back, I stated:

"I was at the factories this morning. At one plant they were amazed to see me. One of the women workers said, 'But we thought everyone had left.' At another, the workers were angry that not everyone had been paid; someone had told them that the director of the State Bank had shipped out the paper money and there wasn't enough left at the bank."

Stalin asked Molotov, "And where is Zverev [the commissar of finance]?"

"In Gorky," Molotov answered.

"Have the money sent back by plane immediately."

I went on: the streetcars were not running, the subways were not working, the bakeries and other stores were closed. . . .

Stalin turned to Shcherbakov and asked why things were in such a state, but without waiting for an answer he turned and again began to pace back and forth, then said, "Well, really, it isn't so bad; I thought it would be worse." And he added, addressing Shcherbakov, "You must get the streetcars and subways running properly immediately. Open the bakeries, stores, and restaurants—and the medical facilities, with whatever doctors are still in the city. You and Pronin go on the radio today and appeal for calm and stability and announce that the normal operation of transport, eating places, and other public services will be guaranteed." The meeting was brief. After several minutes, Stalin said, "All right, that's it." And we went our separate ways, each on his own assignment.[33]

The meeting that Shakhurin writes about undoubtedly took place. But the whole tone of the meeting and Stalin's rather unusual manner and remarks force one to conclude that it occurred, not on October 16, but two days later, when Stalin had returned to the suite in the Kremlin after his sudden departure. Otherwise, how is one to explain his lack of familiarity with the situation in the city and his comment, "I thought it would be worse"? As if someone could stop the Moscow subways and streetcars and close the bakeries and stores without first clearing the matter with Stalin!

It deserves to be mentioned that during the entire four years of the war Stalin visited the front lines only once, in early August 1943, when preparations were being made for the Smolensk offensive by the troops of the Kalinin and Western fronts. On August 3 Stalin visited the command post of the Western Front, and on August 5 the command post of the Kalinin Front, at the village of Khoroshevo, near Rzhev. The rest of the time Stalin directed the war from Moscow, even when military operations, as in 1944, had moved far to the west. This was not particularly convenient for the front-line commanders, who frequently had to fly from their fronts to Moscow in order to coordinate operations and have their plans approved.

After the dissolution of the Comintern in 1943 the *Internationale* ceased to be the official hymn of the USSR. A competition was announced for a new national anthem. By mid-1944 the text of the hymn and the music for it had been selected. However, it seemed impossible to arrive at a satisfactory orchestration. Over a period of several months, eight editing committees were set up and 155 orchestrations were arranged. Usually these were heard by K. E. Voroshilov, who for some reason was considered the connoisseur of music among Politburo members. Stalin, too, attended many trial performances of different orchestrations. Success fell at last to D. M. Royal'-Levitsky, the 231st composer to be asked to orchestrate the hymn. His work was accepted and approved by Voroshilov and Stalin. After the new hymn of the USSR had been performed by the orchestra of the Bolshoi Theater and recorded for radio, a grand dinner was held, also in the Bolshoi Theater, attended by all the members of the Politburo, Stalin, the heads of the Committee on the Arts, leading figures in the world of music, and the arranger D. M. Rogal'-Levitsky. The dinner lasted late into the night. And all this took place in time of war. In the middle of this holiday feast came the news that the Soviet army had broken through to the former state boundaries of the USSR.[34]

---

33. *Voprosy istorii,* 1975, No. 3, pp. 142–43.

34. Stalin generally gave a great deal of time and attention to matters of surprisingly little importance. He personally approved, for example, the project for a new suburban settlement of dachas for writers in the Pakhra district, giving his permission for the maximum size of wooded or cultivated lots on which the dachas would be built to be increased to one hectare.

In the Western press it is usually said that during the war Stalin followed a relatively "mild" and conciliatory policy within the country, in an effort to unite all forces around the party and the army. Reference is made in this connection to the glaringly nationalistic slogans of defense of Russia against age-old German expansionism and to Stalin's reconciliation with the Orthodox Church. There is a certain amount of truth in these assertions. For example, in 1943 the persecution of the church in this country was suspended, and hundreds of churches that had earlier been closed down were opened, many bishops freed, church schools and a Russian Orthodox academy allowed to open, etc. Not only were many children of Communists previously subjected to repression inducted into the army; this was also done in the case of young people from former kulak families deported to Siberia, the Urals, or the north in 1930–32 and denied freedom of movement until the beginning of the war (in every "special settlement" there was a commandant's office of the military). Through the secret services of the NKVD, contacts were made with that section of the émigré community which opposed Hitler. There is evidence that even Miliukov and Denikin provided information useful to the USSR during the war. In all this, of course, some credit was due to Stalin. But he performed certain other "creditable services" as well. During the war the camps of the "Gulag Archipelago" were overflowing with prisoners, many of whom eagerly desired to go fight on the front lines. Here were thousands of former commanders and commissars, so badly needed in the army, which was being bled white, but they were kept under guard by thousands and thousands of strong and healthy troops of the Internal Guard Service (VOkhR) and NKVD divisions, who could also have been of no little service at the front.[35]

During the war years political repression continued, often being applied on pretexts that were completely trivial. And in every district, urban or rural, an NKVD office was maintained, although the militia units by themselves were sufficient for the preservation of order. And how costly were Stalin's policies in relation to Soviet prisoners of war, condemning hundreds of thousands of them to die of hunger and driving two or three hundred thousand into the arms of the Vlasovites and other military or seni-military formations that collaborated with the fascists. But Stalin's most serious crime during the war was the deportation of many small nationalities from their home territories. These people could have made a contribution to the common cause of defeating the fascist foe, but instead they were shipped off by the trainload to the east, to uninhabited places, where as many as 40 percent of the deported Chechens, Ingush, Crimean Tatars, Kalmyks, Volga Germans, and others perished from hunger, cold, and epidemics.

A friend of mine, while vacationing in August 1949 at the Armkhi sanatorium

---

35. After the Soviet army had cleared the Baltic region of German troops in 1944–45, our party found that it was woefully short of cadres to manage the various vital sectors in Estonia, Latvia, and Lithuania. Then the Communists from the Baltic region who had been arrested in 1937–38 and in 1940 came in mind. On Stalin's personal orders, the Baltic Communists who were still alive were released from the camps (although not all were, to be sure) and assigned to government and economic work in the Baltic republics. As a rule, these party members had maintained their loyalty to Stalin and accomplished a good deal in the work of rebuilding the ruined economies of their republics.

in the hills of the Chechen-Ingush region (which had been incorporated into Georgia at that time), at a location not far from Larsi on the Georgian Military Highway, noticed and wondered about a totally uninhabited and somewhat dilapidated village on the slope of Mount Stolovaia. A few days later, having made the acquaintance of a militia colonel from Sverdlovsk, my friend heard and noted down the following candid account of what had happened.

We were brought together [the militia colonel related] in Beria's office in late July 1943. Emphasizing the absolute secrecy of the meeting, they told us about the forthcoming operation and spelled out our specific tasks. Each of us was to don the uniform of a military commander and take up a position, with a military unit, near the village that had been singled out and assigned to him. We were to establish friendly relations with the inhabitants of the village, winning them over with gifts and flattery, to develop close ties with influential people in the village, demonstrating pronounced respect for their customs and way of life, in short, to become their "blood brothers" and to give them a chance to grow used to having Red Army soldiers stationed alongside their village. The Chechens for the most part understood Russian well; nevertheless we were taught the rudiments of their language and instructed in their customs, habits, way of life, etc. They were all Muslims, still practiced polygamy, and consequently their women were a passive and inert element. During the half year that we officers were supposed to live among them, we were to study them very closely and, without their knowledge, to draw up precise lists of the members of all families, find out where absent members were, and make preparations for a grand celebration of the next Red Army Day, to which all the men of the village in question were to be invited. We told them that the great services of the Chechen people in the struggle against the German aggressors would be celebrated on that day, that prizes and certificates from the Supreme Command would be given out then, etc. We carried out these orders, living at the villages for half a year—I at the very one we see from here—and we made the preparations for the Red Army Day celebration of February 23, 1944, starting at 8:00 A.M. On that day everyone gathered for the ceremony. A presiding committee was elected, consisting of the presidents of the local soviets, who suspected nothing, the heads of the district NKVD sections, and all the local notables; an honorary presiding committee consisting of the entire Politburo with Comrade Stalin at the head was also elected. As the representative of the army I chaired the meeting. We began the speeches, the awards, and the remarks by those who had fought in the war; there were only men at the meeting, naturally, since this was happening in the Muslim land of the Chechens.

Exactly at 10:00 A.M. I stood up, pulled a printed envelope from the side pocket of my tunic, broke the wax seals, and announced that I was going to read a decree of the Presidium of the Supreme Soviet of the USSR. Then I read it to the stunned assemblage. The decree stated that the Chechens and Ingush had betrayed the Motherland during the war, had aided the fascists, etc., and therefore were subject to deportation.

"It is useless to resist or try to escape," I went on. "The clubhouse is surrounded." And turning to the NKVD officer seated next to me and to his deputy, I ordered, "In the name of the party! Guns on the table!"

Unimaginable confusion broke out in the hall. People flung themselves at doors and windows but came up against the barrels of automatics and machine guns. During the ceremonies the military unit had surrounded the clubhouse with a solid cordon several rows deep. And think of it! There was no active resistance, even though everyone was dressed in ceremonial costume and wore their daggers. We disarmed them very easily and led them in small groups, under redoubled guard, to the nearest railroad station at Dzau-dzhikau (formerly Ordzhonikidze, and before that Vladikavkaz), where trains of freight cars modified for the transport of prisoners had been readied beforehand.

And while we were dealing with the men, others arrested the women and children, who had been left leaderless, and took them away. They too were loaded into freight cars, but not at the same station as their men, and sent off, trainload after trainload, to Kazakhstan. Some of the women offered resistance. They would not allow anyone to touch them. One threw a dagger and killed a soldier; in two other cases soldiers were wounded. After the people had been taken away, the livestock and goods that had previously been inventoried were gathered up and carried off. The operation throughout the Caucasus was directed by "the man himself"—Beria.

The relations between Stalin and Mao Tse-tung deserve separate investigation. In his well-known letter to the Soviet leaders, A. Solzhenitsyn asserted that Stalin himself had nurtured a ferocious enemy—Mao Tse-tung's China. "We bred Mao Tse-tung in place of a peaceable neighbor such as Chiang Kai-shek." This assertion is completely incorrect. It has been disputed in detail by the well-known Soviet literary scholar and critic L. Z. Kopelev:

> The thesis of the "nurturing" of Mao Tse-tung is not simply very far-fetched; it is the exact opposite of reality. Mao Tse-tung "grew up" not because of, but in spite of, all Stalin's policies in China—both Comintern policies and military-diplomatic ones. From 1926–27, when Stalin, still in a bloc with Bukharin, demanded that the Chinese Communist Party (CCP) subordinate itself to Chiang Kai-shek, and later, when the not very numerous Chinese Stalinists accused Mao and his supporters of "adventurism," "guerrillaism," "national peasant" deviationism, and other deviations, down to and including 1947–48, when it became clear that the Kuomintang army and government would be defeated, Stalin did nothing but create obstacles for the Maoists, distrusting them and accusing them of Trotskyism and national deviationism.
>
> The Long March of Mao and Chu Teh's armies was carried out in 1931–33 against the instructions of the Comintern. Mao was elected chairman of the CCP in 1935 instead of Wang Ming, the candidate of the Comintern, who was voted down and through whom Stalin was pressing the Chinese Communists to join a "united anti-Japanese front under the leadership of Generalissimo Chiang Kai-shek." Beginning in 1931, when the Japanese seized Manchuria, and continuing right down to 1945, the Soviet Union gave every kind of support to none other than that "peaceable neighbor Chiang Kai-shek," supplying him with arms and strategic goods, and sending him military advisers and pilots, while aid to the Communist-controlled Special Area and the Communist armies (the Fourth and Eighth Armies) was limited to greetings, a few doctors, and some "political" emissaries who were mainly intelligence people keeping the CCP leadership under observation. In 1945, when the Soviet troops occupied Manchuria, they did not allow the Chinese Communist troops to enter the area. And in 1946, when Stalin ordered the hasty evacuation

of Manchuria, as demanded by his Anglo-American allies, Mao Tse-tung was informed of this only after several of Chiang's divisions had been flown into Manchurian cities in American planes. Thus Mao's armies, although situated closer to Manchuria, were able only to seize a few stocks of old Japanese arms "magnanimously" left behind by their Soviet brothers, who, to balance that, quite thoroughly dismantled the railroads, even those adjacent to the areas held by the "fraternal" Communist armies. The weapons of those armies in 1946–48 were primarily Japanese or American, taken from Kuomintang troops. From Chiang's surrendering generals they also captured many artillery pieces and machine guns of Soviet make. The successes of the Chinese Communists disturbed Stalin; they did not make him happy. It was in those very years, after all, that the conflict with Yugoslavia began, and the potential rival in the Far East, the intractable and inscrutable Mao, was undoubtedly stronger and more dangerous than Tito and his potential imitators. Therefore after the definitive victory of the Maoists, which was obviously no longer reversible, under a screen of blustering propaganda, Stalin imposed unequal treaty concessions upon the new China, holding fast to the Chinese Eastern Railway, the naval bases at Port Arthur and Dairen, and Sinkiang. . . . At the same time there was an attempt to implant Soviet military advisers in all major Chinese army units and institutions. Stalin subsequently provoked the Korean War in order, above all, to drag China into a local war with the United States, to weaken it and make it more dependent. Such is the real history of Soviet-Chinese relations.[36]

The population of Gulag in 1944–45, despite everything, was significantly reduced in size, primarily because of the higher mortality rate for prisoners during the war years. Some, it is true, were set free immediately after the war. By then many prisoners had completed their five-year or eight-year terms but had been held "until the end of the war" or "for special orders." Very soon, however, new trainloads of prisoners were hauled off to the camps. Among these were people who had collaborated with the occupation forces and the Vlasovites, as well as ordinary prisoners of war who were first sent to special camps for preliminary processing and screening, the majority of them then being sentenced to prison terms of varying length. Hundreds of thousands of Soviet citizens whom the Hitlerites had forcibly shipped off to work in Germany, Austria, and other occupied countries were repatriated and found themselves in the camps. In addition to the Ukrainian and Byelorussian nationalists and Lithuanian guerrillas who actually fought against the Soviet army, arms in hand, all those who in any way "collaborated" with these nationalists went into the camps. Rapid collectivization in the Baltic region, Western Ukraine, and Western Byelorussia was accompanied by the deportation of tens of thousands of wealthy peasant families to the east. In 1948–49 thousands of party functionaries filled the camps again— people arrested in the so-called Leningrad Affair. Thousands of "rootless cosmopolitans"—or, to put it more simply, Jews from the Jewish cultural organizations which had been smashed—were arrested. And repression struck many Soviet scientists, above all, the biologists. In the prisoner's files, in place of such code letters of earlier times as KRTD (*kontr-revoliutsionnaia trotskistskaia*

---

36. L. Kopelev, "Lozh' pobedima tol'ko pravdoi" (manuscript), p. 6.

deiatel'nost'—counter-revolutionary Trotskyist activity), new acronyms appeared: VAT (*voskhvalenie amerikanskoi tekhniki*—praising American technology), VAD (*voskhvalenie amerikanskoi demokratii*—praising American democracy), and PZ (*preklonenie pered zapadom*—worshipping the West). Also appearing in the camps were the "repeaters," people who had been freed in 1945, only to be arrested again and returned to the camps. In the early post-war years, in the Russian émigré communities that had grown up after the Civil War, a special campaign was conducted for a return to the homeland. Several thousand people responded, mainly children and relatives of White émigrés. Some former Russian officers also returned. Their "Soviet" life did not last long, however. Most of these "re-émigrés" were arrested in 1949–50 on stereotyped charges of "spying" or "anti-Soviet activity while abroad." Among those arrested in this way were not only the Old Bolshevik G. Miasnikov, who had fled in the 1920's and had worked as an ordinary laborer in a French factory, but also I. A. Krivoshein, who had been deputy president of the French Resistance movement. At first he was given Soviet citizenship, but after two years he was arrested and sentenced by a special board to ten years' imprisonment.

Also arrested were "participants in the Opposition" of 1925–27, although one would have thought that there were no former Oppositionists left alive or at any rate still free. Someone in the MGB, however, had the bright idea of looking over the records of the Komsomol gatherings of the 1920's. And so throughout the country arrests began of former Komsomols, not only those who had voted for the Opposition more than twenty years earlier but also those who had abstained.

G. A——v writes in his memoirs:

> The young people, seventeen or eighteen years old, who, in 1927, argued about the possibility or impossibility of building socialism in one country, never dreamed of course that their arguments were being overheard, that they would be "kept in mind," and that twenty and more years later, when they had become heads of families and their children were already Young Pioneers and Komsomols, someone would come for them. . . . But there it was—people who the day before had been loyal Soviet citizens, engineers, teachers, heads of shops, construction superintendents, foremen, were now "enemies of the people." Their distraught wives camped on the doorsteps of the agencies of the judiciary, trying to find out what had happened, why their husbands had been taken. But in vain. They were answered curtly and mysteriously, as my wife was at the Moscow procuracy, "For counter-revolution." It was strictly forbidden to tell the reason for the arrest—both before sentencing and after.[37]

In the second edition of *Let History Judge* I wrote that the post-war wave of prisoners included members of many student circles which had actually taken up certain political aims. One of the members of such a circle, A. Voronel, asserts that he had heard of dozens of such circles in Moscow alone and personally knew members of nine anti-Stalin groups.[38] These were mainly circles having strictly

---

37. "Na ob"ekte p/ia 220." (manuscript), pp. 24–25.
38. A. Voronel', "Trepet iudeiskikh zabot" (manuscript).

Marxist programs. They sometimes put out typewritten bulletins or drew up manifestos. Voronel himself was arrested then, for the first time, in a case involving one of those circles.

All these measures of political repression took place with the knowledge of Stalin, of course, and in most cases at his direct instigation. He continued to rule the country autocratically, following the rule of the despots of old, "Divide and conquer," even in relation to his own immediate entourage.

At the Central Committee plenum after the Nineteenth Party Congress Stalin suddenly asked to be relieved of all his duties, citing his advanced age. An extraordinary outcry arose, with shouts such as "Dear Stalin" and "Our own Father" audible above the din. Some of those in attendance, in the front rows, fell on their knees. They begged Stalin to remain and he "agreed," expressing his dissatisfaction, in passing, with a number of his closest assistants (Voroshilov, Mikoyan, Molotov). The plenum elected an enlarged Presidium of the Central Committee, on a motion by Stalin, with no dissenting votes. This was an obvious preparation for rearrangements in Stalin's immediate entourage.

After eliminating all of his erstwhile opponents, Stalin could not endure having bright or independent people around him. Even men like N. Voznesensky and A. Zhdanov, who aspired to the role of party theoreticians, were removed or destroyed despite their continual manifestation of loyalty to Stalin. Stalin's rudeness toward, and even contempt for, people was displayed in many ways. For example, when he called one of his government ministers or a regional party committee secretary on the phone (as a rule, late at night) he would listen to their replies, sometimes making ambiguous comments, and then would suddenly hang up the phone without thanking the person or saying good-by, leaving his interlocutor wondering and anxious. Exceptions were so rare that even today some of Stalin's intimates write about such occasions with undisguised satisfaction. Thus, one of Stalin's former finance ministers, Zverev, in describing one of his phone conversations with Stalin, writes: "At the end of the conversation Stalin said 'Good-by.' That was an extremely rare occurrence: usually he simply hung up the phone." [39]

This same Zverev cites several examples in his book of how amazingly ill-informed Stalin was about the situation in the country. Although the villages were sunk in terrible poverty and the taxes were suffocating the collective farmers, Stalin was sure that the rural population was quite well off. Stalin proposed that rural taxes be raised still higher, Zverev writes, and "even accused me of not being sufficiently well-informed about the material situation of the collective farmers. Once, half-joking and half-serious, he said to me, 'All a collective farmer has to do is sell one chicken and he can keep the Ministry of Finance happy.'

" 'Unfortunately, Comrade Stalin, that is far from being the case—for some farmers, even selling a cow would not be enough to pay the taxes.' " [40]

---

39. A. Zverev, *Zapiski ministra* (Moscow, 1973), p. 244.
40. Ibid., p. 246.

Almost all the statistics on the situation in agriculture were inflated, sometimes several times over, to please Stalin. This practice of distorting statistics was imposed as early as 1929–30 by Stalin himself, and from then on, the real picture diverged more and more from the "statistical" one. Yet it was Stalin who said, at the Fourteenth Party Congress, "We feel that the Central Statistical Administration must provide objective data, free of any preconceptions—for any attempt to make figures conform to this or that preconceived notion is a crime of a serious nature." [41]

But age and the pressures of the war years took their toll on Stalin. He suffered prolonged illnesses, spending most of his time at his dachas outside Moscow (and in the south) and only rarely stopping by in Moscow. In themselves Stalin's dachas were rather modest, especially the rooms in which he lived. No valuables or expensive paintings were ever kept there. The enormous number of gifts he received on his seventieth birthday, including many unique objects of great artistic value, he had placed in a museum. However, colossal sums of government money were spent on protecting Stalin's person and guarding his dachas. Moreover, the large MVD troop units assigned to guard Stalin were under his personal command. This was his "private bodyguard," and if Stalin had ordered it, General Vlasik, who had headed this guard unit since 1918, would have arrested Beria or any other member of the Politburo without hesitation. With the years, Stalin's suspiciousness grew greater. Even in the late 1920's he still loved to stroll about the Kremlin grounds and had often walked the streets near the Kremlin in the evening without any visible guard, although they were very poorly lit at that time. But now he drove through the Arbat with caution, in one of several government vehicles, following one another in a row.

I do not know whether it was Stalin's own idea or the idea of one of his intimates to have a subway line built from the center of Moscow to Stalin's closest dacha, in Kuntsevo. Even today there is a pecular feature in the Moscow subway system—from the center of the city to Kiev station there are two lines running parallel, although at different depths. The reason for this is that the uppermost line, built earlier, was to be extended to Kuntsevo, and a new line was to be built for the people of Moscow, with very grandiose new stations (the Arbat, Smolensk, and Kiev stations). As we know, Stalin did not live to enjoy the benefits of this subway line, and after his death, the upper line, from Kalinin station to Kiev station, was closed as unnecessary. Only after construction began on new districts (Fili-Kuntsevo) was this line completed and opened to the public.

According to A. V. Khrabrovitsky, a former employee in the manuscripts division of the Lenin Library, among the papers in the A. N. Efros Collection is the original of a 1934 letter by Stalin, addressed to the architects Zholtovsky and Shusev, to Efros (an art scholar), and to several others who had written Stalin about the necessity of preserving the Sukhareva Tower by moving it back from

---

41. Stalin, *Sochineniia,* Vol. 7 (Moscow, 1952), pp. 329–30.

the heavily traveled part of the roadway or diverting traffic away from it by taking
down some buildings of no special value on the corners of Trubnaia Square. Stalin
disregarded the protests of the architects. He wrote to them: "Soviet people know
how to create works of architecture better than the Sukhareva Tower."

After the war several grandiose skyscrapers were erected in Moscow. Stalin
personally approved the designs for them. In the hall where Stalin was to appear
to review them, the designs were hung on the walls, with the architect who had
created each one standing next to it. It was assumed that Stalin would have
questions and that the architects would have to give explanations. Stalin entered
the hall and walked along past the designs. Those that pleased him he simply
pointed to in silence; the rest, which he passed by without any sign, were immediately turned face to the wall. The approval of the designs consumed as much time
as it took Stalin to walk slowly along the walls. Not one question did he ask and
not one word did he utter.[42]

Quite recently, from S. Shtemenko's book *The General Staff in the War Years,*
Book Two, we have learned several more details of Stalin's life and habits, not
so much from the war years as from the post-war period. Writes Shtemenko:

> I. V. Stalin never went anywhere except to the concerts and performances nor-
> mally arranged after ceremonial gatherings. "Theater" at home for him was listen-
> ing to music on the radio or to phonograph records. He personally gave a test
> hearing to most of the new records, which were regularly delivered to him; then
> he would immediately pass judgment on them. Notations in Stalin's own hand
> would appear on the records—Good, Fair, Poor, or Trash. In the chest and on the
> end table, on either side of the massive record player, a gift to Stalin from the
> Americans in 1945, only the records with the first two inscriptions were kept. The
> rest were thrown out. Next to the phonograph was a gramophone of domestic make
> with a hand crank. Its owner took it with him wherever necessary.[43]

Stalin not only liked to play billiards; he also liked to watch the Russian game
gorodki being played, and sometimes would even start to play himself, but he
did not play especially well. In those days Stalin had a great deal of leisure time,
and Shtemenko writes with tender feeling about the things that occupied the
aging despot in those years that weighed so heavily upon the entire country.

> Not far from the house [the reference is to Stalin's "nearest" dacha, where he
> stayed most often] stood several hollow tree trunks—with no twigs or branches—in
> which nests for birds and squirrels had been contrived. This was a veritable song-

---

42. According to the scriptwriter E. G——a, there was a showing of a new film at the Kremlin
(and it was obligatory that Stalin look over every new film) during which Stalin suddenly walked
out of the hall. This was taken as a sign of displeasure, and Molotov ordered the film stopped
immediately. After a few minutes Stalin came back into the hall, demonstratively zipping up his fly.
"Why'd you turn it off?" he asked. "Go on with it." It must be supposed that this was one more
of Stalin's routine psychological "experiments" on his "comrades-in-arms."

43. S. M. Shtemenko, *General'nyi shtab v gody voiny,* Book 2 (Moscow, 1974), pp. 39–40.

birds' paradise. In front of this tree-hollow town were little feeding trays. Almost every day Stalin came here to feed his feathered friends.

In the corner of the verandah to the left of the entrance was an iron spade with a wooden handle shiny from use, and in a large cabinet other garden tools were kept. Stalin loved to look after his roses and apple trees, planted along the edge of the pond; he tended a small grove of lemon trees as well, and even . . . raised watermelons.[44]

It is strange to read such descriptions now, knowing what was going on all over the country during those years. But despots and tyrants have always had such caprices. Hitler, too, had a great love of animals and was, as we know, a vegetarian. It seems that V. Lebedev-Kumach wrote a witty poem on this subject for the "Windows of TASS" poster series. It ended with the words:

"I don't want the blood of the lamb.
What I want is—the blood of man."

This could have been written about Stalin, who was personally responsible for the deaths of many millions of Soviet people, one of the greatest criminals in human history.

October 1–20, 1975

(Translated by George Saunders)

---

44. Ibid., pp. 40, 384.

Part Three

STALINISM IN
EASTERN EUROPE

Stalinism and the "Peoples' Democracies" *

Włodzimierz Brus

The term "peoples' democracies" (PDs) designates here the seven Eastern European countries which throughout the post-war Stalinist era remained in the Soviet sphere of influence (Albania, Bulgaria, Czechoslovakia, German Democratic Republic, Hungary, Poland, Romania). In other words, Yugoslavia is outside the scope of our discussion, although we shall use her example occasionally for the sake of comparison, or rather contrast.[1]

The Significance of the "Peoples' Democracies" for a General Analysis of Stalinism

At a first glance the topic may seem secondary or supplementary to the mainstream of "Stalinology," providing only some additional samples of the same brand in its export variety. Aware of the risk of being accused of attempting to enhance the status of his own paper, this author maintains however that the implications of the PDs' experience are quite significant for the study of Stalinism as such. Several aspects could be pointed out in this respect:

1. The very fact of transplantation of Stalinism to the PDs proves that it has been perceived as a *model* of a socialist structure. The universality of the model has been emphasized by applying it in a practically uniform way to countries on various levels of economic, social, and political development, with different historical pasts, and of diverse "political cultures." Thus, a new problem is posed by the PDs' experience: Stalinism as a model, and not only as a product of concrete historical conditions.

2. Stalinism has been applied to the PDs in a concentrated form, almost at a single stroke, and with all its basic properties appearing simultaneously. Evolved in the USSR in the course of two decades, Stalinism emerged in the PDs in a ready-to-wear pattern, which makes it easier to disentangle the main characteris-

---

* This paper is to a considerable extent based on research undertaken in the framework of the East European Economic History Project at St. Antony's College, Oxford, on a grant from the (British) Social Science Research Council.

1. The author wishes to make it clear that the term "peoples' democracies" is not being used in any theoretical sense, and certainly not as a definition of a particular political and socioeconomic system (transitory between capitalism and socialism).

239

tics of the model itself from the impact of particular historical circumstances. The fact that Stalinism in the PDs was a reflection of the latest stage of its development in the USSR doesn't undermine the general validity of the model. In the present author's opinion, this rather enhances its usefulness, because it helps us to understand the end-product of evolution in the course of which the system's responses to changing circumstances brought its very nature more clearly to the surface.

Neither point 1 nor 2 should be understood as denial or underestimation of some differences between the USSR and the PDs, as well as between each of our seven countries during the Stalinist period; these differences were, however, hardly large enough to warrant separation in a general analysis.

3. Because Stalinism in the PDs lasted a much shorter time than in the USSR, and because it appeared in a different international setting, the question "Was Stalin really necessary?" posed *inter alia* for the Soviet Union by Alec Nove [2] seems easier to answer here. And if so, this can provide a valuable clue to answering the more difficult question for the Soviet Union; it is quite frequent that the Eastern European experience is invoked for this very purpose.[3] In both instances, the actual problem is to assess the "necessity of Stalinism" in terms of alternatives open to a Communist regime pursuing Communist strategies.

4. The study of Stalinism in the PDs may also take us further in the extremely complex discussion of the links between Stalinism and the Communist (in the sense of Communist political movement) concept of socialist society in general. If we limit ourselves to the Soviet Union only, the question usually boils down to the relation between Stalinism and the Soviet-type political, social, and economic system. It is rather widely accepted that the term "Stalinism" applies to a peculiar form of this system, a form which historically doesn't cover the whole period of its existence. As Robert Tucker says, "Communism differs from Fascism as Leninism (or Bolshevism) differs from Stalinism. And a clear recognition of this is an essential prerequisite for the advancement of theory in comparative politics as it affects Russia and numerous other countries." [4] This must not necessarily lead to exoneration of Stalinism or to denial of its links with the previous stage (to quote Tucker again, "The pre-existing regime was a ruthless party dictatorship, and the destruction of it was effected without any official admission or overtly obvious sign that a continuity of political life was being broken," [5] or, for that matter, the link between Stalinism and the post-Stalin era. Quite a number of political scientists, sociologists, and economists combine the above interpretation of the term with efforts to trace these links, to discover whether this particular, extreme form of totalitarian dictatorship can be derived from the nature of Communist takeover and the basic tenets of the Soviet-type etatist model.

---

2. Alec Nove, *Was Stalin Really Necessary* (London, 1964).
3. See, e.g., L. Labedz's rejoinder to Nove's argumentation in the book cited above.
4. Robert C. Tucker, *The Soviet Political Mind* (London, 1963), p. 5.
5. Ibid., p. 41.

From this point of view, the PDs might have been regarded as an important piece of evidence in the affirmative sense: history seemed to have repeated itself, once more leading to Stalinism, despite explicit initial proclamations to the contrary and different real starting conditions. Such a hasty conclusion would, however, overlook the paramount external factor of Soviet Stalinism's expansionary tendencies, its drive for the subjugation and molding of the entire "socialist camp" according to its own image. Were the endogenous "objective needs" —again, in terms of Communist strategies—pushing invariably towards Stalinism? Or did the local Communist leaders—all or some of them—see a different path to and a different concept of socialist structure in their countries? If the latter is true, then the question of the imposition of Stalinism on the PDs arises, which may require a new look at the supposedly intrinsic link between Stalinism and Communist strategic aims.

It is impossible to examine here all of these questions. We shall concentrate mainly on the last problem, although some of the others will be touched upon as well. Our intention is to cover the full spectrum of all the seven countries, but in view of the element of personal experience of the author, Poland will figure most prominently in the discussion. This is to serve also as a warning to the reader against possible bias.

Two or Three Stages of Development of the "Peoples' Democracies?"

The history of the East European countries from the end of the Second World War until their Stalinization *sensu stricto* (1949–50) comprises five to six years only. Taking additionally into account the immense complexity of the political and socioeconomic change intertwined with fast shifts on the international scene, it would seem risky indeed to try to identify more than the usual two stages of development of the peoples' democracies during that period. The question has, however, a very significant bearing on our argument. If we accept the division as given, e.g., by Brzezinski—"The First Phase: 1945–1947. The Peoples' Democracy—Institutional and Ideological Diversity," and "The Second Phase: 1947–1953. Stalinism—Institutional and Ideological Uniformity" [6]—we must almost inevitably accept also the view that the transition from the first stage to the second (which had to be already the Stalinist one) was as much pressed by the Soviet Union as by the internal Communist leadership, except perhaps people like Gomułka, who were in a clear minority in the leadership. Communists of long standing could not be expected to abandon their firm belief in the desirability and inevitability of socialist transformation of the society; if this transformation were identical with Stalinism they should have no reservations whatsoever. Under these assumptions Brzezinski is consistent in stressing the internal factor, and rather underplaying the imposition from outside (although in details the picture becomes less clear—see section 4).

---

6. Zbigniew K. Brzezinski, *The Soviet Bloc: Unity and Conflict*, rev. ed. (Cambridge, Mass., 1967).

The alternative way of looking at the problem would be to divide the development of peoples' democracies until Stalin's death into three stages: the first—until the fundamental (for all Marxist-Leninists) question of state power was finally decided, i.e., the Communist regimes firmly established; the second—the transition to construction of socialism, without, however, autonomous adoption of the features considered today as the main marks of Stalinism; the third stage—Stalinism.

Precise chronological divisions are very difficult to establish not only because of diversity between the countries but also because of the uneven pace of change of different aspects of social life. But by and large the first stage can be described as lasting up to 1947—the year when the peace treaties with Bulgaria, Hungary, and Romania were signed, with the elimination of Ferencs Nagy, Maniu, Petkov and their political forces following; when the condition of Polish "free elections" was formally met, after which Mikolajczyk was eliminated; when the Czechoslovak and Polish governments were obviously forced by the USSR to refuse the Marshall Plan invitation; and, finally, when the Cominform was created. Although the Czechoslovak coup came only in February 1948, it can be accepted that by 1947 the Communist regimes were firmly established and the dominant position of the respective Communist parties nowhere threatened. One may safely disregard the various liberal institutional solutions written into constitutions, and, with the amalgamation with Social Democratic parties pending, define in broad political terms the emerging regimes as totalitarian (despite the obvious distaste of the adherents of the pure-model-totalitarianism approach).

Changes followed in all spheres of social life, including the sphere of ideology (stronger assertion of Marxism, gradually less vague and negative definitions of the "nature" of peoples' democracy, etc.); socialist aspirations were unveiled and a number of tactical gimmicks, strongly resented by many old Communists, left behind. The most tangible changes occurred, as it could be expected, in the economy:

First, the ex-enemy countries were quick to catch up with the level of nationalization of industry (and banking, wholesale trade, etc.): by 1948 the marked difference between them and the ex-allied countries practically disappeared.[7] Except Romania, all countries of the region embarked in 1947 upon multi-annual plans (two years in Bulgaria and Czechoslovakia, three years in Hungary and Poland, five years in Yugoslavia); apart from Yugoslavia all other plans were concentrated on reconstruction, but not without elements of structural change.

---

7. In 1947 the percentage-level of nationalization was 80 percent or above in Yugoslavia, Poland, and Czechoslovakia; under 50 percent in Hungary; under 20 percent in Bulgaria and Romania. By 1948 the 80 percent mark was passed by all countries (figures from various sources, and not uniformly compiled, but reliable enough for presenting the order of magnitudes; see W. Brus, "Post-war Reconstruction and Socio-Economic Transformations in Eastern Europe," *St. Antony's College Papers in East European Economics,* No. 41, April 1974). Of course, we are completely omitting East Germany, which became the GDR only in 1949 and maintained its "anti-fascist, democratic system" (*antifaschistisch-demokratische Ordnung*—as distinct from peoples' democracy) until 1952.

Czechoslovakia made a new step in agrarian reform, and, like Poland, launched a significant offensive against capitalist elements in the trade and distribution sphere, applying drastic fiscal measures (the "millionaires' levy") and administrative pressures to increase the socialist (state and cooperative) share of the market. In Poland a huge political campaign ("the battle for trade") was launched in spring 1947 with the use of extraordinary measures (headed by the Special Commission to Fight Corruption and Economic Sabotage), and directed not only against "excessive appropriation of surplus" by private producers and traders, but also against cooperative associations siding with the private sector and fighting state controls. (As the cooperatives were under the political influence of the Socialist party, PPS, this attack had a particular political significance; after a brief resistance the PPS had to give way, acknowledging thereby the dominant position of the Communist party, PPR.) As important as the campaign itself was the ideological interpretation, which (as a result of the April 1947 plenary meeting of the Central Committee of PPR) abandoned the celebrated "three-sector-approach" (state, cooperative, private) in favor of the Marxist distinction between socialist, capitalist, and small-commodity–producer sectors. This was a clear adoption of the principles of NEP in the "who will beat whom" sense. It is worth noting that, contrary to the widespread belief, Gomulka not only did not resist this new attitude but headed the battle. The same was true of the late 1947–early 1948 assault on the Socialist-dominated Central Planning Board (an official top-level PPR-PPS economic discussion, which led to another political victory for the PPR, the strengthening of central planning on Marxist principles) and of the strategy of "organic union" between PPR and PPS. This seems to prove that Gomulka was opposed not to the "socialist construction" stage as such but only to some of its concepts, and particularly to the latter developments indicating the Stalinist pattern.

It is clear that the second stage must have brought about a greater degree of uniformity between the individual countries than the previous one. This is often taken as a sign of Stalinization, with all its powerful uniforming tendencies. However, first of all, there is the question of what was made uniform, and second of the degree of uniformization, which was by no means identical to that of the 1950s. As far as the first point is concerned, the political and economic system of the peoples' democracies was still far from Stalinism: the Communist parties—despite their dominating position in the state—were still retaining their role as political groupings, to some extent involved in a competition for influence (hence the mass recruitment), and allowing internal disputes. Also, the trade unions maintained some degree of autonomy (in the Polish case, until the amalgamation of the PPR and PPS and the reorganization of their structure). The activities of the security police are difficult to assess, but there was certainly no reign of terror of the Stalinist type: again taking the Polish case, after Mikolajczyk's defeat the police pressure of the state markedly subsided and the internal stabilization was much higher than in all preceding years, when something resembling civil war was going on in many provincial areas. The "old" intelligentsia, including people prominent under the previous regimes, was quite broadly participating in economic and cultural life; in the Polish case there was at that time an evident relaxation in an attempt to win over people (the most remarkable developments took place in the army, where high-ranking Soviet officers were consistently replaced by officers of the old Polish army). Cultural life retained strong elements of pluralism. Also, in the organization of the nationalized economy the elements of commercial autonomy of the enterprises were still alive.

Objections may be raised that everything mentioned above proves only that it is simply impossible to do everything at one stroke: this was the initial phase which smoothly moved into another. I do not share this position: First: the development obviously was not so smooth, as the events of mid-1948 and after showed (the anti-Tito Cominform meeting in June, leading, *inter alia,* to a qualitative reinterpretation of the practical meaning of the Soviet example for the peoples' democracies, with new emphasis on collectivization; this amounted to a sharp strategic turn, requiring, in at least one case, Poland, the crushing of serious opposition inside the Communist party, and the overcoming of some resistance in other parties, notably in Romania (Pâtrâşçanu). Second: even after the new line was adopted and the first shocks of the Yugoslav schism and the Polish "right-wing and nationalistic deviation" overcome, the official pronouncements of some of the leaders of the Eastern European countries showed remarkable restraint in pushing forward the imitation of the Soviet example. The proclamation of the "peoples' democracy" as a new form of dictatorship of the proletariat (the end of 1948, under the influence, so the story goes, of Stalin's direct communication to Dimitrov) on one hand reflected the desired transition to the straightforward class struggle for the construction of socialism, but on the other hand left some room for countering the identification of the socialist way with the Soviet way by emphasizing the *new* element in the formula. The distinction between the Soviet and the popular-democratic system came out quite clearly even in Dimitrov's formulation: "The Soviet system and the popular-democratic system are two forms of the same kind of power: the power of the working-class, which is in an alliance with the urban and rural toiling masses and is leading the masses. There are two forms of the dictatorship of the proletariat." [8] The possible emphasis on *two* forms still left open some chance to prove the point made by Marchlewski to Lenin (and mentioned by Lenin), that "we will do the same, but better."

The distinction suggested here—between acceptance of the socialist strategy and the initial reluctance to implement it in a Stalinist way in Eastern Europe—is very delicate and most difficult to prove without either inside knowledge or an insight into firsthand and undistorted archive material. That is why the argument presented in the next section will be by no means complete and coherent; apart from some economic questions, it will contain personal evaluations and deductions concerning, first of all, the Polish development.

---

8. Dimitrov's speech on the Fifth Congress of the Bulgarian Communist Party in December 1948; quoted from the Polish edition of "Selected Works" (Warsaw, 1954), p. 479 (the author's translation).

The Traces of Reluctance—Can They Be Detected?

Even the most concise characteristics of the economic side of Stalinism must evidently comprise three elements: 1) an industrialization drive at the fastest attainable pace, with absolute priority for heavy industry and relentless mobilization of material and human resources for this purpose, regardless of the level of sacrifice of consumer interests; 2) the collectivization of agriculture in a relatively short time, both for doctrinaire reasons as well as for the interconnections (the supply of agricultural products and of labor, etc.) with rapid industrialization; 3) strict centralization of the system of functioning of the economy. Let us examine the attitudes of the Eastern European Communist leadership towards these three points.

The best evidence can be found with regard to point 1. Here I have in mind the difference between the industrialization plans drafted (and in most cases accepted and put into operation) in 1948–49 and their final versions adopted in 1950–51. There is very good reason to believe that the first versions, although obviously the USSR was consulted, reflected much better the indigeneous, as it were, idea of industrial development.[9] The revisions of 1950–51 sometimes made all the difference between an ambitious, difficult, but not entirely unbalanced plan and a super-taut program relentlessly concentrated on some high-priority targets without a chance to attain an overall equilibrium and, particularly, to meet the (formally kept) objectives with regard to the standard of living of the population.

Except for Romania, where there was practically no first version of the plan and the 1951–55 plan reflected the Stalinist industrialization strategy from the very beginning, all of the five other peoples' democracies (there are no sufficient data for Albania available) have changed their plans: the smallest change took place in East Germany where the total investment bill for five years increased by over 6 percent with the share of industry and transport increased at the expense of housing; in Hungary, overall investment outlays for the 1950–54 period were raised by over 60 percent against the dropping shares of agriculture (from 15.7 percent of investment in the initial plan to 12.9), light industry (from 5.9 to 4.1), housing (from 10 to 7.6). In Bulgaria the revision of the plan took the form of the shortening of the time-span from five to four years.[10]

---

9. This was the claim made explicitly in 1956 by the Polish "economic boss" Hilary Minc. It could be viewed as a convenient excuse, but similar statements were made without suspect motives. E.g., a Czechoslovak economic history textbook published in 1974 states quite simply: "In November 1949 a meeting of the Information Bureau of Communist and Workers' Parties was held. The participants in the meeting came to the conclusion that imperialism was starting direct preparations for war. Taking this into consideration the socialist states . . . agreed to speed up the industrialization process. . . . The concretization of the resolutions of the Informbureau in Czechoslovak conditions was discussed at the Plenary Meeting of the CC KPCz in February 1950. At this meeting the decision about modification of the five-year plan was taken." (V. Prucha et al., *Hospodarske dejiny Československska w 19. a 20. storoci* (Bratislava, 1974), p. 344.

10. Data for the countries mentioned from *Economic Survey of Europe Since the War* (Geneva, 1953), Table 11, p. 30.

The increase of investment in Czechoslovakia compared with the original plan was about 50 percent; the annual rate of growth of national income was increased from 8. 2 percent to 11.2, that of production of the means of production from about 11 percent to well over 18 (and that of the consumer-goods industry only from 8.5 percent to 11.5%).[11] In Poland the acceleration of the rate of growth of national income was from 9–10 percent annually to almost 14 percent (the difference being about 50 percent, probably corresponding to the increase in investment for which comparative figures are not available). The annual rate of increase in industry was raised from less than 12 percent to 17 percent (with much a steeper increase in producer goods); the planned rate of growth of agricultural production was increased from under 6 percent annually to 7 percent; the indicators of increase of the standard of living remained unchanged (50–60 percent, growth in per capita consumption over six years, 40 percent increase in real wage alone!). This extraordinarily complacent attitude towards consumption indicators in a situation of extremely heavy burden of accumulation (up to 40 percent in real terms) in itself throws sufficient light on the genuine intentions of the revised plan; it is not surprising that in the 1953 figures for agriculture, light industry, services, housing, etc., lagged behind schedule by 75 percent or more, and those for the standard of living were in most cases even absolutely lower than in 1950. The new plans, and even more the method of their implementation, were qualitatively different from the original ones, although the latter were certainly conceived as serving the purpose of socialist industrialization. It is interesting to note that H. Minc, in his report to the Unity Congress in December 1948, was at great pains to stress the difference between the Polish six-year plan and the two Soviet five-year plans, "which is fully justified . . . because we are not isolated, being strongly supported by the Soviet Union and the countries of peoples' democracy." [12]

As for *collectivization,* no similarly clear-cut evidence of revision is available (at least, to the author's knowledge, and so far), because plans, figures, etc., have usually not been published, and perhaps even never existed in a precise form. Still, if we look at the speeches and resolutions of the Polish congress in December 1948 with regard to agriculture, there is no doubt that the idea of collective farms is treated with extreme caution.[13] A reflection of this caution can be found also in the multiplicity of forms of collective farms, all but the highest providing for less common and more private peasant ownership; the lower forms played a relatively greater role in Eastern Europe than in the USSR (even in the twenties). In developing the policy of class struggle against the "capitalist elements in the countryside" the stress was at that time on economic measures, and on positive

---

11. Ibid., Table 14.

12. H. Minc, *Osiągniecia i plany gospodarcze* (Achievements and economic plans): report presented to the Congress of the Polish United Workers' Party, December 18, 1948), (Warsaw 1949, p. 66).

13. "Once more it is necessary to remind everybody at this congress that all haste in this field [collective farming—W. B.] would be nothing but harmful, that not quantity but quality is decisive here, and that we are not interested in quantity but in the model and example of the new way of economic organization." Minc on tasks in agriculture in 1949, ibid., p. 53.

help for the poor (and middle) peasants to defend themselves against exploitation by the "kulaks." It is again difficult to prove directly that all this meant reluctance and not simply tactics; however, in conjunction with other elements such an interpretation seems plausible. It is, for instance, significant how eagerly and at how early a stage (May 1951, when the share of collective farms—together with private plots of the members—was well under 1 percent of gross agricultural production!) the Polish leadership embarked upon its own version of the "dizziness from successes" campaign.[14] To some extent a similar conclusion could be drawn from the immediate backpedaling in this respect by the Hungarian Imre Nagy government in the summer of 1953, when the green light to do so was assumed.

Probably the least reluctance could be ascribed to the Eastern European leadership in the field of the *planning and management.* In Eastern Europe, as earlier in the Soviet Union, there was no experience of planning in general and indirect planning in particular; thus planning as such was identified with the Soviet experience of strictly centralized management of the economy, applicable in principle to fully controlled, i.e., practically nationalized, units. That is why the crusade against non-Marxist ("bourgeois," "social-democratic") planning was taken up so wholeheartedly in Poland (the CPB discussion) and in Czechoslovakia as early as 1947.

From personal experience (as a junior member of the editorial board of the Polish United Workers' party's theoretical journal *Nowe Drogi* since the beginning of 1947) I recall numerous instances when every opportunity was being used by the top leaders to stick to a less imitative and violent, to a more thoughtful and indigenous way of building socialism in Poland. And after all, why shouldn't they? On one hand, they were perfectly aware of the tremendous difficulties encountered in the Soviet Union, including the personal risks involved in the Stalinist system. On the other hand, around 1948 the Polish party leadership could feel a glimpse of hope breaking through the blank wall of hostility and non-recognition by the people as a legitimate Polish government. By 1947–48 it became more and more obvious that no chance existed for a non-Communist regime free from Soviet tutelage; on the other hand, the regime has proved its ability to lead the post-war reconstruction (including practical incorporation of the Regained Western Territories), to carry out social transformations recognized as basically beneficial from the national point of view. What is more, the plans for the future promised a dynamic development unknown in the inter-war period, with exciting prospects not only for the technical and economic intelligentsia but also for the large strata of former social underdogs, particularly youth. Apart from some aspects (collectivization of agriculture in the first place) socialism as such could become genuinely acceptable, and even attractive for increasing num-

---

14. "Resolution of the CC of the PUWP Concerning the Violation of the Party Line in Gryfice District of the Voivodship of Szczecin," in *Gospodarka Polski Ludowej: Wybór dokumentów cz.I, 1944–1956* (Warsaw, 1973), Document 31, pp. 189–94. Some private sources maintained that this could be linked to Stalin's reaction to Bierut's complaint about grave problems caused by the policy of collectivization ("There is no need for *you* to hurry").

bers of the population. The blow of Stalinism fell on people in most cases not at all opposed to the socialist perspective, often ready for genuine cooperation. As far as Poland is concerned I share the view expressed by an Oxford political scientist, Z. Pelczynski: "It is inconceivable that, left to themselves, the Polish leadership, for all their isolation from the rest of the nation, would have adopted all the policies and the institutional structure which resulted from them. Rapid industrialization, collectivization, struggle against capitalist elements and bourgeois influences, and so on, although a matter of dogma for Bierut, would have been pursued with caution, as the period *from the middle of 1948 to the end of 1949* suggests. National traditions would have been flouted less ruthlessly and Soviet models copied more critically" [15] (my italics). It is arguable that the Polish leadership—taking into account the tragic past of Polish Communists and the particularly sensitive Polish-Soviet relations—acted more cautiously than their counterparts in other countries (not only on the eve of but also during the reign of Stalinism). Nevertheless, it would be hard to believe that in other countries there were no leaders anxious to pursue policies less damaging internally; some economic evidence has been given above, the history of the ill-fated Balkan federation is another one, and even Gottwald reportedly needed extraordinary pressure to consent to the Slansky show trial.

Awareness of the adverse impact of Stalinist policies on the internal stature of the leadership emerged clearly in Yugoslavia, which was a "special case" from the very beginning: at first, the Yugoslavs—as no one else—copied the Soviet pattern, inevitably with much of its Stalinist ingredients; then—after the 1948 break—they got rid of Stalinism in the (relatively) fullest way. This case deserves, of course, a comprehensive examination which transcends the scope of this paper, but one thing seems certain: strong as they were politically in relation to other countries—on the basis of their war and revolutionary record—Tito and the overwhelming majority of his associates had to raise the banner of anti-Stalinist socialism, *inter alia* in order to gain popular support. We have no (and hardly will ever have) reliable measures of political strength of Eastern European regimes at that time, and all assessments in this respect are guesswork. Nevertheless, some evaluations would seem rather unobjectionable: although one could not claim that the peoples' democracies were completely deprived of political support during the Stalinist era (strata with direct stake in the system, "true believers," etc.), the loss of support compared with 1948 was disastrous and accelerating over time, whereas for Yugoslavia the reverse was true. One is tempted to assume that the difference between the Yugoslav and other Eastern European Communist leaders lay not in the sphere of political wisdom, but in the possibilities (and in many cases willingness as well) to resist external pressures. One should not however, confuse, indigenous *reluctance* with power to *resist;* it is the former which is essential for proving the point about the imposition

---

15. Zbigniew Pelczynski, "Political Change in Post-War Poland" (manuscript, quoted by permission of the author).

of Stalinism on Eastern Europe, whereas the latter belongs more to the question of reasons for success or failure of such an imposition.

External Pressure and Internal Transformers

We would rather not dwell on the reasons for which Stalin opted for Stalinization of Eastern Europe. The matter has been discussed very comprehensively both from the international and from the internal Soviet aspects; historical and socio-psychological aspects have been added as well—Russian imperial traditions, ideological inertia of concepts equating the expansion of socialism with the expansion of Soviet institutions, Stalin's lack of experience with and deep distrust of all but Stalinist forms of control, etc, etc. One thing is certain: if Stalin did not believe in the prospect of winning genuine political support of the population in the foreseeable future, and wanted to rely on the complete dependence of the Eastern European leadership on him, he could not have chosen a better, more diabolically cunning method than that actually chosen: by imposing Stalinism on Eastern Europe he obtained not only a system of direct command over the entire institutional structure but also a double grip on the local leadership—faithful and at the same time sufficiently alienated from their own people. Taking into account that as a rule all alleged plots and conspiracies in the 1949–53 period were "international" in character (and hence investigated not under national but under international, i.e., Soviet, police control, which led from one trial to another by the simple method of "dropping" names of some foreign leaders), the hold was tight and many-sided indeed. The leadership of the peoples' democracies was autocratic by virtue of the Stalinist system, but its autocracy was delegated and circumscribed by the Supreme Leader. To quote Gomułka in 1956: "This cult could be called only a reflected brilliance, a borrowed light. It shone as the moon does." [16]

There seems to be also no need for detailed description of the forms and devices used for the imposition of Stalinism and for keeping the peoples' democracies constantly under control. By and large I would not be able to add anything substantial in this respect to the picture drawn by Brzezinski.[17]

What is most interesting is the question of resistance (which is different from reluctance!) to the imposition of Stalinist patterns. We certainly do not know enough about what happened behind the scenes to establish the facts of informal resistance by those Eastern European leaders who, in some position or another, "stayed on the job" during the Stalinist period, even when they became associated with profound de-Stalinization afterwards (like Imre Nagy in Hungary). What came into the open showed obvious resistance on a broad and rather coherent scale only in one case of the Polish "right-wing and nationalistic deviation,"

---

16. W. Gomułka, "Address to the Eighth Plenary Meeting of the CC PUWP, October 1956, translated in *National Communism and Popular Revolt in Eastern Europe,* ed. Paul E. Zinner (New York, 1956), p. 228.

17. Brzezinski, *The Soviet Bloc,* Chap. 6.

which could be credited, at least *ex post facto,* with some sort of program of socialist construction of a non-Stalinist variety (not only in the socioeconomic but also in the cultural field, where really striking policies were carried out, associated with the name of Jerzy Borejsza).[18] Elements of opposition to Stalinization could be attributed also to Traicho Kostov, who resisted Soviet pressure from the Bulgarian national point of view. To what extent similar traces of resistance to Stalinism were the underlying causes for purging such Communist leaders as Rajk, Clementis, Husák, Merker, and others is not clear; e.g., Spychalski in Poland was obviously willing to cooperate fully with the post-Gomułka policies, and nobody could accuse Slansky of not being sufficiently Stalinist.

What about the sub-Stalins, the top leaders of the people's democracies in 1949–53? Have they produced any signs of transforming reluctance into resistance? There are obviously no such signs in the open. As might be expected, all public statements of the time are thoroughly faithful and enthusiastic, which was easily explicable by a combination of entrenched Communist loyalties, ideological convictions sometimes developed into a fanatical belief in the infallibility of the creed and its supreme exponent, tactics, fear, opportunistic calculations. The proportions of this rather common mixture in every particular case depended on many factors, probably not least on personal ones. Again Gomułka was right, while speaking about the sub-Stalins ("the bearers of the cult of personality" in the respective countries), when he paid attention to personalities: "It was not so bad when a reasonable and modest man was dressed in the robes of the cult. Such a man usually did not feel well in this attire. One can say that he was ashamed of it and did not want to wear it, although he could not completely take it off. . . . But it was worse, and even completely bad, when the honors of power, and thus the right to the cult, were seized by a mediocre man, an obtuse executive, or a rotten climber. Such people buried socialism thoughtlessly and with precision." [19] This factor probably played a role in the differences in implementation of Stalinism between the countries of the bloc, despite the general tendency towards uniformity, although this does not rule out the possibility that Stalin himself remained until the end shrewd enough to discriminate in both objects and force of pressure, taking into account national imponderabilia. The differences between countries may be also accounted for simply by the time element, i.e., the historically short duration of Stalinism in the peoples' democracies: Bierut or Gheorghiu-Dej or even Ulbricht may have been successful in passive resistance against Soviet pressure for closing ranks in the intensity of the purges, but would they have resisted (or avoided) the show trials if the pressure had lasted longer? The March 1953 plenary meeting of the CC of PUWP, commemorating the deceased leader, was again concentrating on vigilance; it was then that Spychalski's name was for the first time mentioned here as that of a traitor, which was to be read by everybody as an announcement of his pending trial.

---

18. Quite typically for some personal Communist destinies, Borejsza's brother, Rózanski, was among the most cruel and hated Stalinist henchmen in the security police.

19. Gomułka, "Address to the Eighth Plenary," pp. 228–29.

The time factor undoubtedly played some role as well in the difference between the Soviet Union and the peoples' democracies in general, as far as the "quality," the depth, of Stalinism is concerned. But again it seems certain that this was not the only factor. Political traditions, or, more precisely, the higher overall level of what may be called civilization in social relations, was obviously an obstacle in the way of full imitation of Soviet Stalinism. International considerations were also not without impact, especially as the peoples' democracies—subservient and subjugated as they might have been—retained the status of formally independent states.[20] If, however, there were some objective conditions which stood in the way of the fullest and technically most rapid possible *Gleichschaltung* of the peoples' democracies with the USSR and between themselves, it must also have meant some slender room for maneuver by the more courageous, more idealistic, more skillful Communist leaders. It is against this background that reluctance could turn into something resembling resistance via manipulation of the boss. This must also have been one of the reasons why the ruling bodies were so anxious to avoid any interference with direct lines of communication with the Kremlin.[21]

To sum up: As a rule, reluctance, which I think existed quite widely, was not transformed into resistance; external pressure could rely on an obedient, in some cases zealous, internal political establishment; nevertheless, delaying or watering-down actions could be and probably were, even in this framework, contributing in some degree to the "less than perfect" shape of Stalinism in the peoples' democracies in general, and in some of them in particular.

Was Stalinism Necessary for the "Peoples" Democracies"?

The discussion so far provides hints as to the kind of answer we may give to the question posed: the answer is negative, and here are some of the arguments which seem to support such a position:

We have already emphasized the lesser "depth" or "perfection" of Stalinism in Eastern Europe compared with the Soviet Union. In the political field it was reflected, among other things, in the preservation of some traditional institutions (which may have had a slight influence on the methods of operation of the power elite), and first of all in a different—despite persecution—position of the Church, particularly in Catholic countries; if it is at all possible to compare the scope and intensity of terror in such circumstances, one should say that the fully fledged police states of Eastern Europe acted in a less comprehensive and less Oriental way. Culturally, the pre-Communist traditions were never wiped out so effectively, and isolation from abroad (the West included) never reached the Soviet

---

20. I can't agree here with Robert Tucker's statement that "the formation of the satellite empire meant the incorporation of the countries concerned into the Moscow command-and-control structure, *their reduction to the status of Soviet 'union republics' in all but name"* (my italics). *The Soviet Political Mind,* p. 48.

21. A case in point—rather little known—was the sudden expulsion from the Polish Central Committee and from the government of the minister of public administration and veteran Communist, Wladyslaw Wolski, in 1949, allegedly for establishing direct information links with the then Soviet ambassador in Warsaw, Lebedev, without the knowledge and approval of the Politburo.

tightness. In the economic field some holes resulted simply from uncompleted construction of the system (e.g., the real degree of centralization in management of the economy could not be so high without completed collectivization and full elimination of small private enterprise); the collectivization drive as such differed also from that in the USSR, and not only in quantitative terms (no "civil war" atmosphere, with physical destruction of the "kulaks," material benefits for peasants joining the collective farms, more investment in agriculture, more flexibility and genuine cooperativeness in organization, etc.); this made it possible to avoid agricultural disaster—despite deeply negative phenomena—which may be attributed to learning the Soviet lesson, but even more so to the obvious impossibility of remaining as indifferent towards the lot of the population as was the case in the U.S.S.R. Real earnings fell absolutely in 1951–53 compared with the reconstruction period, for some categories of workers and employees very considerably, and there were shortages everywhere, etc.; but the situation has never reached anything even resembling Soviet conditions of the early thirties; the same applied to the system of labor relations despite the quite widespread practice of compulsory labor and all kinds of restrictions on freedom of profession and occupation.

In spite of all these—secondary!—specific features of Stalinism in the peoples' democracies, the consequences from the point of view of long-term Communist goals were perhaps even more damaging than in the Soviet case, when evaluated in terms of popular attitudes. Several factors can be invoked in support of such a view:

1. The secondary differences notwithstanding, in all essentials an identical system of institutions, ideology, policies was applied to quite diverse conditions—historical, economic, cultural, political—in individual countries; this by itself must have created maladjustments and tensions.

2. The majority of the peoples' democracies did not have long years of experience of parliamentary democracy behind them, yet the degree of development of democratic institutions—freedom of the press, freedom of coalition, independence of the judiciary, etc.—was higher than it had been in Russia; the cultural links with the West were also stronger. The iron corset of totalitarian dictatorship, coinciding with the peak period of the "cult of personality," terror, and dogmatism, was bound to be more strongly felt in these conditions. At the same time the much shorter period for which the system prevailed limited the effectiveness of "educational" function of ideological mystification and thus permitted the preservation of greater perception of the disparity between slogans and reality.

3. The weakness of the internal roots of the socialist revolution in the majority of the peoples' democracies caused difficulties even in acceptance of the general foundations of the new social order; its Stalinist form must have been regarded by an overwhelming majority of the population as a brutal instrument of foreign domination. There can be no doubt that in relation to the peoples' democracies Stalinism was indeed such an instrument.

4. The factual domination of the Soviet Union over the peoples' democracies, multiplied in some cases—particularly in that of Poland—by historical and psy-

chological factors, made it difficult to use nationalistic ideology as an instrument of political attraction of the masses. Disappointment with the system could not be compensated for by great-power status, and any appeal to national feelings was watched in the USSR with suspicious vigilance. This required the Communist parties to perform a balancing act between unconditional acceptance of the leading role of the Soviet Union in all areas of life—from nuclear physics to soccer—and emphasis on national interests and state integrity (for Poland and Czechoslovakia an alleviating factor could be used: the alleged West German threat).

5. In terms of economic growth the period 1949–53 brought about some spectacular achievements, particularly when measured against pre-war performance: national income (according to official figures and defined as net material product) grew at an annual rate of 11 percent in Albania (1951–55), 9.5 percent in Czechoslovakia, 10 percent in East Germany (1951–55), 8.5 percent, in Hungary (1950–54), 11 percent in Poland (1950–55), 14 percent in Romania (1951–55).[22] Industrial production (but measured by the notorious "gross output") at least doubled compared with the starting point, new industrial centers emerged; employment outside agriculture increased dramatically, causing considerable shifts in occupational structure and the level of urbanization. However, even the overall results must have been less striking in the peoples' democracies than in the USSR in the thirties, because of the generally higher level of past economic development, particularly in Czechoslovakia, East Germany, Hungary, and Poland as well. A more detailed analysis would reveal a whole range of reasons for the much lower political effectiveness of the industrialization drive. (a) Even in Poland, where industrial production—gross output!—was above the planned level, more than half of industrial products in physical terms shown on the official list published by the Planning Commission were well under the planned level, including some most important items. (b) The results reflected clearly the privileged position of heavy industry, and particularly the armament industry, which skimmed all the cream off the economy—material input, skilled workers and technical personnel, wages, benefits in kind, etc; the neglect of the consumer-goods industry was enormous, and agriculture—even in the official gross-output measurements—showed almost no or very negligible rates of growth, in spite of the high expectations written into the plans. (c) As I have already said, real wages fell instead of rising, and although in countries with large labor reserves the increase in employment somewhat made up for this from the point of view of per capita income (but very unevenly, depending on the haphazard impact of family structure), the objective situation was very difficult and the disappointment much greater not only because of earlier promises, but also because of higher habitual levels of consumption. (d) Changes in income distribution did not help as much as might have been expected: compared with the pre-war pattern, income was certainly much more equitably distributed and equality of opportunities much stronger, but after 1949–50 differentials tended to widen, and,

---

22. *Economic Survey of Europe in 1956* (Geneva, 1957), p. 2.

increasingly important material privileges (closed shops, preferential housing, special health service, holiday resorts, etc.) were being associated with political and organizational positions; although these phenomena did not reach Soviet proportions, they caused deep resentment. All in all, the feeling of failure was getting stronger all the time—the overstrained economy coping more and more badly with inflation, shortages of goods, disorganization, incompetent management, etc.; the reaction of the authorities was to increase pressure in both the political and in economic field.[23]

6. The political consequences of economic difficulties were more damaging for the Communist rulers also because of the different external background. In the early thirties not only was the Soviet population more effectively cut off from abroad, but the Great Depression, with tens of millions unemployed and starving in the capitalist countries, helped to present Soviet industrialization in a better light; in the fifties Western Europe was well on its way to an unprecedented boom, and the East European population knew it. What is more, the contrast was seen as between the American Marshal Plan and the policy of the Soviet Union, which not only imposed on the peoples' democracies a disadvantageous industrial and foreign-trade pattern, but clearly exploited most of the countries in a direct way as well, despite the publicity given to long-term Soviet credits.[24]

To sum up: The assertion that the disintegrating effects of Stalinism were stronger in the peoples' democracies than in the USSR, despite less drastic methods and wider recognition of factors limiting freedom of action, seems to be well founded. It was not by accident that the first—at least the first widely known—outbursts of popular revolt came in these countries—Plzen and Berlin in 1953, followed by Poznan and Hungary (an incorrigible economic determinist may even rank the countries in question according to their level of economic development and the "diseconomies" suffered because of Stalinism).

Full-fledged Stalinism, as the term is understood here, lasted in the peoples' democracies hardly more than five years. Soon after Stalin's death, for reasons

---

23. As far as the latter was concerned, the most conspicuous moves were currency and/or wage-price reforms of a brutal deflationary character, wiping out by a single stroke a considerable part of the purchasing power and savings of the population (Bulgaria 1951, Romania 1952, Czechoslovakia 1953, Poland 1953—not much over two years after the currency reform of 1950).

24. Western sources (e.g., Brzezinski, p. 127, based on J. Wszelaki, "Communist Economic Strategy: The Role of East Central Europe" (Washington, D.C., 1959) put "the amount extracted by the USSR from East Europe in the period 1945–56" at about twenty billion U.S. dollars. It is difficult to check the accuracy of this and similar estimates, but considering the absence of a convincing balance sheet presented by the other side (e.g., Artur Bodnar, an official of the CMEA Secretariat and of the Polish Planning Commission, in his book *Gospodarka europejskich krajow socjalistycznych* (The Economy of the European Socialist countries) (Warsaw, 1962), mentioning an overall figure for Soviet credits—seven billion U.S. dollars for 1947–57—is unable to account for more than 50 percent in country-by-country distribution and does not even examine flows in the opposite direction, although these post-Stalin debt annulments are mentioned: Albania, one hundred million dollars; Romania, 150; Poland, 500), one must conclude that, despite repeated claims about Soviet help, a substantial net outflow from the Eastern European countries to the USSR took place until 1956.

which are quite well known and need not be discussed here, a "new course" was inaugurated. In the economic sphere the new disposition of resources and the change in the relative shares of accumulation and consumption in national income in the first place led quickly to a drastic reversal of production proportions, trend in real wages, supply of consumer goods, social consumption, even housing. In agriculture the punitive use of compulsory deliveries was stopped, with an effect on production (at least in Poland) quite comparable to the changeover from surplus confiscation to tax in kind at the outset of NEP; the collectivization drive was relaxed and in some cases (Hungary) a marked retreat allowed, to be followed later by almost complete de-collectivization in Poland (1956). The infallibility of the centralistic system of functioning of the economy gradually came into question. Significant changes began in the political sphere—internally and internationally; slowly at first, and then at an increasing speed (although still varying in different countries), prisons and concentration camps began to release the alleged "enemies of the people," agents, spies, and saboteurs.

The suddennesss of the change in the Soviet Union and in the peoples' democracies invalidated both the mythical-absolutist ("iron laws of socialist development") and the rational-relativist ("necessary in the then existing situation") justifications of post-war Stalinism (I refrain from making such a claim about Stalinism in general because it would go far beyond the scope of this paper); no other element of the situation has changed in 1953, apart from a single one— Stalin's death, and this has been sufficient for such a dramatic turn. Do we need a still stronger proof that no objective necessities whatsoever but a definite type of chosen policy only was the source of Stalinism in the 1949–53 period?

For the peoples' democracies, the "new course" and what followed afterwards, all differences between individual countries and all meandering of policy notwithstanding, meant by and large a return to policies pursued in 1948: the "dictatorship of the proletariat," with its strategy of building socialism, industrialization, even collectivization (the Polish case would require a separate discussion), but all at a more modest pace and without the political excesses of the 1949–53 period. Of course, one could hardly expect that the ends lost in 1949 were picked up after 1953 purely and simply; something has happened in between which made a return much more difficult than if it had been a continuous process. E.g., stepping down the rate of investment (share in national income) is an extremely difficult operation from a long-term point of view when conducted under political stress, and involves losses which could be avoided if the average finally resulting were more or less adhered to from the very beginning.[25] The political and moral losses are even harder to make up, and this explains to some extent why the process of

---

25. A sudden downward turn in an investment program becomes, as a rule, the source of cyclical fluctuations which persist for a long time (the "echo effect," as it was called by Oskar Lange). That's why some Eastern European economists even postulated a close calculation of the overall costs of a change of a macro-program in progress versus costs of continuation of the old one (see J. Beksiak, *Economic growth and indivisibility of investments* (Warsaw, 1965). Of course, with regard to national economic plans no decision of this kind can be taken on economic grounds only, without the sociopolitical aspects.

de-Stalinization was so difficult in Eastern Europe and why it progressed so differently in different countries.[26] Nevertheless, one may say that the general trend was (and is—so far) towards some sort of "Kadarism"—another form of totalitarianism, but quite different from the Stalinist extreme.

The reader is reminded that we have been discussing the role of Stalinism in the peoples' democracies exclusively from the point of view of alternative Communist strategies. It is from this point of view that it seems significant to be able to state the quite distinct probability of following in Eastern Europe the "Kadarism" route, with a lot of Bukharinist traces, all the time without Stalinist discontinuity. But there is another, very tempting, question to discuss (or maybe, more precisely, to speculate on) in this context: "Kadarism" is a child of Stalinism in the sense that it reflects both the need for change and the limits of change, imposed, among other things, by the political and ideological weakness of Communism emerging from Stalinist experience. Would not the chances of transforming "Kadarism" into "socialism with a human face" be greater without this experience? The answer to this question is not only of historical importance.

---

26. No attempt at an analysis of the post-Stalin period in the peoples' democracies is made here. I have done it elsewhere (see my book *Socialist Ownership and Political Systems* (London, 1975).

Stalinism and Czechoslovak Political Culture

H. Gordon Skilling

Stalinism was introduced in Czechoslovakia soon after the Communist seizure of power in 1948 and continued in existence for at least a decade—until 1958— and in somewhat modified form for another decade—until the Prague Spring of 1968. Its essential features are well known: concentration of power in the hands of a small group at the party peak, particularly in those of one man; a command economy in which management and trade unions were reduced to mere tools for the implementation of the plan; a monolithic party characterized by total discipline; party and state control of society in all aspects, including the social and intellectual; and the employment of extreme terror as a means of exacting obedience. It was in essence a duplicate of Soviet Stalinism in its perfected form, in accordance with the "law," enunciated by Klement Gottwald, of "the ever-increasing approximation to the Soviet model." Czechoslovakia had to foreswear the national path to socialism followed from 1945 to 1948 and to accept the Soviet pattern as the only authentic version of socialism. Czechoslovak Stalinism did not differ in substance from its prototype and from the copies made in the other Eastern European Communist countries after 1948 (except Yugoslavia). Right down to 1968 Gottwald's successor, Antonín Novotný, sought, with substantial success, to avoid fundamental changes in the system, yielding only reluctantly and partially to the pressures for reform. It fell therefore to Alexander Dubček and the reformers of 1968 to replace the deeply rooted Stalinist model with a new design—"Socialism with a human face," as it was popularly called. As a footnote, one might note the paradox of the re-introduction of a form of neo-Stalinism, under Gustáv Husák, a kind of counter-revolution against the revolutionary transformations which were underway or on the agenda during 1968.

The purpose of the Bellagio seminar, as described by Robert Tucker, was "an interpretative quest" for the "mystery" of Stalinism. In the case of Czechoslovakia the central question was at once evident: How could a system such as Stalinism, originating in the profoundly different conditions of Soviet Russia and deeply embedded in the pre-Soviet Russian past, come into existence, and last so long, in a country of totally dissimilar traditions and circumstances? How could a system personified by Stalin and in part the product of his personality endure for two decades in the land of Masaryk and Beneš, under the rule of mediocre personalities such as Gottwald and Novotný? How could the Czech and Slovak peoples, accustomed to liberty and having a rich democratic experience during the First Republic—and, in the case of the Czechs, even before that, in more limited form, under the Austro-Hungarian monarchy—permit the introduction, and tolerate for so long the continuance, of a political system devoid of democratic features?

The easiest explanation of this phenomenon, and the most usual, is, of course, that Stalinism, a phenomenon totally alien to Czechoslovak tradition, and even to that of Czechoslovak Communism, was imported into Czechoslovakia from outside and imposed on an unwilling people by force. In this interpretation the origin of the Czech and Slovak response lay in the absence of a tradition of revolution, or of a will to resist by violent means, and a willingness, in accordance with long-standing Švejkian tendencies of passive behavior, to comply, on the surface, with the demands of Stalinism while rejecting it internally. This pattern of action, and inaction, adopted in the past toward hated rulers, was not necessarily the product of personal opportunism and did not always take the form of collaboration, but was often motivated by aspirations for national survival and the eventual restoration of traditional values. As a corollary it has sometimes been argued that the enduring democratic values survived throughout the dark years of Stalinism and were reborn in the political renascence of 1968. The dread fifties were then a temporary interruption in an otherwise unbroken continuity of values, never fully destroyed or abandoned even under Stalinism.[1]

There is, of course, an element of truth, and a substantial one, in this interpretation. It is no doubt true, as Alec Nove has said, that Soviet-style party rule would never have developed out of Czechoslovak circumstances without external coercion.[2] It will, however, be argued in this essay that this is too simple an explanation of a complex historical phenomenon and minimizes the domestic roots of Stalinism. Nor does it help in explaining the extreme forms assumed by the Soviet system in Czechoslovakia, for instance in political trials, or in unraveling the puzzling continuance of Stalinism long after Stalin's death, at a time when the element of coercion, in both domestic and international relations, had declined in importance, and when other countries, including the Soviet Union itself, were dismantling at least some of the worst aspects of the system.

Political Culture

In my search for answers to the questions posed above I shall use the term "political culture," not as a magic formula, nor even as a precise theoretical concept, but as a notion useful in clarifying the meaning of Stalinism and the Czechoslovak setting into which it was introduced. I shall employ it, not in the

1. For an argument along these lines, see David W. Paul, "The Repluralization of Czechoslovak Politics in the 1960s," *Slavic Review,* 33 (December 1974), pp. 721–40. See also his Ph.D. thesis, "Nationalism, Pluralism and Schweikism in Czechoslovakia's Political Culture" (Princeton University, 1973), and his manuscript "Political Culture and the Socialist Purpose."
2. See his contribution to *The Czechoslovak Reform Movement 1968,* ed. Vladimir V. Kusin (London, 1973), p. 346.

"subjective" meaning given it by Sidney Verba and others, but in the broader anthropological usage expounded by Robert Tucker, including therefore not only subjective political values, but also objective political behavior. In Richard Fagan's words, as quoted by Tucker, a country's political culture consists of "patterned ways of life and action as well as the states of mind that sustain and condition these patterns," and that, one should add, may often clash with these patterns. It will be necessary therefore to distinguish, in accord with Tucker's argument, between "an ideal political culture pattern" and "a real political culture pattern" and to regard a political system as "a complex of real and ideal cultural patterns." [3] A fundamental feature of a country's political culture—its heterogeneity—must also be recognized.[4] Even if a dominant pattern may be discerned, the political culture will be fragmented, with more or less important sub-cultures always present. There will be differences not only between the ideal and the real aspects of a political culture, but also within the real culture and within the ideal culture, the whole constituting a variegated admixture of conflicting tendencies of thought and action. Political cultures, it should also be noted, are slow to change, but they *do* change, especially in revolutionary conditions, so that the identification of a country's political culture involves the difficult task of distinguishing elements of continuity and change.

In these terms, Communist revolutions, as Tucker has expressed it, are "attempted transformations of national cultures." [5] The receiving population and its indigenous political culture may, he writes, be more receptive or more resistant to the changes involved in revolution, and may in turn exercise a reciprocal influence on Communism, adapting it to the national cultural heritage. In fact Communism, Tucker argues, tends everywhere to become "national Communism," each country giving what is usually "a Russified product" a national imprint. This is sometimes hindered by the countervailing force of Stalinism, which seeks to prevent the national adaptation of Communism in each country.

Applying this reasoning to Russia and Eastern Europe, we may then regard Communism, in its Stalinist form, as the shape taken by Soviet political culture at a certain stage of its development, containing elements derived from traditional Russian political culture, as well as elements derived from Marxist, Leninist, and especially Stalinist theory and practice—an amalgam which was therefore the product of Russian as well as of Soviet history and which underwent substantial change at successive stages. More than in other Communist countries there was a persistence of some traditional (Russian) values and a certain congruence of

---

3. Robert C. Tucker, "Culture, Political Culture, and Communist Society," *Political Science Quarterly,* 88 (June 1973), esp. pp. 177–82. On political culture and Communist studies, see also Robert C. Tucker, "Communism and Political Culture," *Newsletter on Comparative Studies of Communism,* 4 (May 1971), pp. 3–12; Dorothy Knapp, David W. Paul, and Gerson Sher, "Digest of the Conference on Political Culture and Comparative Communist Studies," ibid., 5 (May 1972), pp. 2–17; A. H. Brown, *Soviet Politics and Political Science* (London, 1974), pp. 89–104.

4. Brown, *Soviet Politics,* pp. 89–90; Knapp et al., "Digest," pp. 3–4, 8.

5. Robert C. Tucker, "Communist Revolutions, National Cultures, and the Divided Nations," *Studies in Comparative Communism,* 7 (Autumn 1974), pp. 235–45.

these and the ideas and practices of Communism.[6] In the countries of Eastern Europe, on the other hand, in the early stage of Communist rule the clash between the imported Soviet or Stalinist culture and the traditional culture was sharp and prolonged. The aim appeared to be to stamp out the indigenous culture or to force it coercively into a Stalinist or Russian mold. At the time this effort at total transformation and the creation of both "a new man" and "a new society" seemed on the road to success.

At a later stage, however, even in countries where the Communist system was largely imposed from outside, the reverse process began to operate. The indigenous culture proved more resilient and less malleable than expected, and in varying degrees modified the imported product, producing, over a period of years, a fusion of the new and the traditional, a distinctive political culture, in each country.[7] Czechoslovakia, for instance, in 1968 was in the process of creating, in embryonic form, its own model of Communism, shorn of its Stalinist features and embodying traditional traits of Czech and Slovak cultures and of Czechoslovak Communism. In each country, however, the emerging political culture was a complex one of many diverse elements, differing between countries and nations as to the relative continuity of the old and the degree of change. Moreover, there was no precise and easily identifiable relationship between the more national Communist culture, say, of Yugoslavia or Rumania, and its pre-Communist past.[8]

There have so far been few efforts to employ the concept of political culture for the study of particular Communist countries and only some initial steps in the case of Czechoslovakia.[9] Even rarer have been attempts to probe the nature and origins of Stalinism in Czechoslovakia, as this volume seeks to do primarily for Russia. During the sixties, especially in 1968, some Czech and Slovak scholars and publicists began to reassess the Stalinist phase of their history and to examine the question of causes and responsibility, but the subject is once again taboo in Czechoslovakia. This essay, which represents part of a broader study of Czechoslovak politics and political culture in the past century and a quarter, can only

---

6. On the influence of Russian traditions on Soviet Communism, see Robert C. Tucker's chapter in this volume; also Brown, *Soviet Politics,* pp. 92–94. For a fuller treatment, see Galia Golan, "Elements of Russian Traditions in Soviet Socialism," in *Socialism and Tradition,* ed. S. N. Eisenstadt and Y. Azmon (Humanities Press, 1975).

7. Tucker, "Communist Revolutions," pp. 241–43.

8. For an analysis of the interplay of socialist culture and Polish traditional culture (using culture in a sense broader than the political), see Jan Szczepanski, *Polish Society* (New York, 1970), esp. Chaps. 7, 9.

9. Note the forthcoming study of the political culture of certain Communist states (including the Soviet Union, China, Cuba, Yugoslavia, Hungary, Poland, and Czechoslovakia) edited by Archie Brown and Jack Gray, *Political Culture and Political Change in Communist States* (London, 1977). On Czechoslovak political culture, see the chapter by Brown and Gordon Wightman in that symposium, and Brown's article, "Political Change in Czechoslovakia," *Government and Opposition,* 4 (Spring 1969), pp. 969–90, reprinted in *Political Opposition in One-Party States,* ed. Leonard Schapiro (London, 1972). See also David Paul, "Repluralization," and his unpublished work cited in note 1.

be tentative in nature, based on a series of hypotheses which will require testing and elaboration in further research.[10]

Some Hypotheses

My initial hypothesis is that Stalinism in Czechoslovakia did not spring full-blown from the events of February 1948, but was a projection of the "Bolshevization" of the Communist party of Czechoslovakia (CPCz) carried through after 1929 by Gottwald, its Moscow-selected leader.[11] His primary task was to divest the party of its Social Democratic heritage and to remold it in the image of the Russian Communist party as designed by Lenin and his successor, Stalin. Although labeled "Bolshevik" by Stalin, the characteristics of the remodeled party were closer to the practice and doctrine of Stalin in the late twenties than of Lenin and the Bolsheviks of the pre-war or early post-war years.[12] The "Bolshevized" party incorporated two of the salient features of Stalinist political culture: the total discipline of its members to its leadership ("democratic centralism"), and the complete subservience of its leaders to Moscow and the Russian party. This introduced into Czechoslovak political life a sub- or counter-culture, derived from foreign sources and modeled on the Soviet pattern, which was antithetical to the dominant democratic aspects of Czech and Slovak political culture, to be discussed below. At least in respect to the inner core of the party, its top leadership, and thousands of devoted cadres, Gottwald was successful in creating a party monolithic in character and devoted to Stalin and to the Russian party which was to endure, through successive stages of development, for the next four to five decades. It became the instrument of Communist rule from 1948 on and the vehicle for the establishment of full Stalinism in the 1950s, and was the embodiment of the Stalinist or quasi-Stalinist systems of Gottwald, Novotný, and Husák.

My second hypothesis is the persistent dualism of Czechoslovak Communism, exhibited in two contradictory tendencies of thinking and action—on the one hand, the essential Bolshevist (Stalinist) tendencies just referred to, and, on the other hand, the more democratic and nationalist tendencies derived from the Czechoslovak party's origin within the Social Democratic movement and from the general political context of Czechoslovakia between the wars, within which it grew and had its being.[13] When it was founded, for instance, in 1921 by

---

10. The long-term project, to be conducted jointly with A. Rossos, is tentatively entitled "Struggle for National Survival: Czechs and Slovaks, 1848–1975." In elaborating the above hypotheses and applying them to Czechoslovakia, I was greatly aided by discussions with several Czech scholars (some of whom had had access to party archives), in Prague and abroad, in 1975.

11. See my articles on the history of the CPCz: *The American Slavic and East European Review,* 14 (October 1955), pp. 346–58; 19 (April 1960), pp. 234–47; *Slavic Review,* 20 (December 1961), pp. 641–55.

12. Stalin's term "Bolshevist" will be used henceforth in this essay as equivalent to "Stalinist" and distinguished from the term "Bolshevik" in its original sense. See Stephen F. Cohen's chapter in this book for a similar distinction between early Bolshevism and Stalinism.

13. On this theme, see my book *Czechoslovakia's Interrupted Revolution* (Princeton, 1976), esp. Chap. II; for fuller treatment, see the unpublished work of David Paul cited in note 1.

Bohumír Šmeral, prominent pre-war Social Democrat, as an offshoot of the Czechoslovak Social Democratic party, indeed as the predominant part of the latter, the CPCz embodied at least some of the democratic, nationalist, and socialist elements of traditional Czech political culture. The seeds of the new Bolshevism were, however, already sown in Šmeral's acceptance, albeit reluctantly, of the Comintern's Twenty-One Points requiring that the CPCz be a disciplined section of the Comintern and model its structure and policy on the Russian party. The initial effect of Gottwald's Bolshevization policy was an enormous loss of membership from the originally massive party, so that it became a small sectarian movement, with an appeal chiefly to the most disadvantaged sectors of the population and to the national minorities, such as the Hungarians and Ruthenians, and to a lesser extent the Slovaks, for whom the dominant Czech political culture had less attraction.

Yet in the changed context of the People's Front policy after 1935, the CPCz, under Gottwald's direction, broadened its appeal as a result of its identification with the national and democratic interests of the Republic; it thus regained a substantially large membership and remained one of the strongest parties in elections. This wide public support was an element of strength for the CPCz but at the same time a source of weakness from the strictly Stalinist viewpoint. Although the inner core of the leadership remained loyal to Bolshevist principles, some persons in the higher ranks exhibited deviationist tendencies which had to be dealt with severely by the Comintern. Gottwald himself remained unsullied in his loyalty to the line of policy pursued by the Comintern, which in any case fully endorsed, and in fact had initiated, the more positive attitude of the CPCz to the Republic and its interests. This tended to obscure, and at least temporarily to resolve, the basic contradiction between the Bolshevist attitudes of the inner core and many ordinary members, and the more democratic and nationalist values of other CPCz members who were less prone to accept the discipline of democratic centralism or subservience to the Soviet Union.

The third hypothesis relates to the general political culture of Czechoslovakia under the First Republic, and its two principal nationalities, the Czechs and Slovaks, and can, in the absence of substantial research, be only tentative and impressionistic.[14] It may be assumed, however, that this culture was, in its values, and in large degree in its practice also, profoundly democratic and national. This manifested itself *inter alia* in freedom of expression and association, a competitive electoral system, a multiplicity of political parties and pressure groups, and a genuine system of justice. Another salient feature was a strong sense of national identity and a desire for national independence, which expressed itself, vis-à-vis the Soviet Union, in an attitude of friendship and alliance, without derogation of Czechoslovakia's own national interests and without detriment to the more basic relationship with France and the West.

This is not to ignore the serious deficiencies of the real as distinct from the

---

14. For a valuable study of the politics of Czechoslovakia from 1918 to 1948, see *A History of the Czechoslovak Republic, 1917–1948*, ed. V. S. Mamatey and R. Luža (Princeton, 1973).

ideal political culture. The Western image of an island of well-nigh perfect democracy under a philosopher-king, Masaryk, needs to be balanced by a recognition of features which marred the quality of Czechoslovak democracy. These included, for instance, the dominant role of the two presidents, Masaryk and Beneš, and the Castle *(Hrad);* the powerful position of the coalition of governing parties *(pĕtka);* the influence of bureaucracy and the "partified" character of the administration; the denial of genuine home rule or even of separate nationhood to the Slovaks; the failure to win the full loyalty of national minorities (in spite of a relatively generous and enlightened nationality policy); and the exclusion of the Communist party, and except for brief intervals, of the German and Slovak nationalist parties from full participation in government (as distinct from their legality and their substantial and proportionate representation in parliament).

A full analysis of Czechoslovak political culture would have to take into account its heterogeneity, with national sub-cultures (German, Hungarian, etc.); religious sub-cultures (e.g., Catholic parties); class differences (e.g., agrarian and workers' parties); ideological cleavages (variations within the dominant Czech political culture as between Left, Right, and Center); as well as more striking exceptions such as Sudeten German fascism. Above all, one must recognize the substantial differentiation between Czechs and Slovaks, especially in regard to the status of the latter, with the Czechs assuming the existence of a single Czechoslovak nation and denying self-government to the Slovaks, and the Slovaks (or a substantial part thereof) asserting a separate Slovak nationhood and demanding home rule within the Republic, or even independence. Moreover, although many Slovaks shared in the general values of Czech political culture, others held quite different values of a strongly Slovak nationalist (even separatist) and conservative (even quasi-fascist) character. Czech political culture was, however, unquestionably dominant in practice, submerging the distinctive cultures of the Slovaks and other sub-cultures.

Differences between Czech and Slovak political cultures had, of course, deeper roots in their entire historical evolution, and in the more recent past, in their different levels of national development and their diverse experiences under the Habsburg monarchy. Prior to 1914 Czech political culture was characterized by democratic and competitive politics, pluralism of parties and groups, national resistance to German predominance, strong orientations toward socialism, open criticism of the imperial system of bureaucratic absolutism, and demands for self-government, but without an explicit program of independence. At the same time, active participation in the Austrian system, from 1879 on, left its mark on Czech values and behavior, for instance, in their acceptance of a bureaucratic and coalition type of politics and the pursuit of a moderate step-by-step *(etapová)* policy, often involving opportunistic bargaining with parties of fundamentally different interests and aims. The Slovaks, on the other hand, hampered by economic and cultural backwardness, and the more ruthless policy of Magyarization pursued by the ruling Magyars behind the façade of Hungarian parliamentarism, were much more restricted in their opportunities of political participation and manifested a less robust nationalism, a greater tendency toward assimilation, and a more conservative orientation to politics. These divergent traditions had a great impact on Czech-Slovak relations during the First Republic and under Communist rule after 1948.

The heterogeneity of Czech and Slovak political cultures and the dualism of Czechoslovak Communism make it difficult to draw hard and fast conclusions concerning the relationship between the dominant cultural patterns and the Communist sub-culture.[15] On two crucial issues a wide discrepancy can be discerned: first, the dominant pluralism of Czech and Slovak traditions as opposed to the strict monism of Bolshevist democratic centralism, and, second, the independent national spirit, whether Slovak or Czechoslovak, in contrast to Bolshevist subservience to Moscow's dictates. Yet the sharpness of the dichotomy was somewhat smudged by the shifting strategy of the CPCz, which brought it sometimes into sharp contradiction, and at other times into greater harmony, with dominant Czechoslovak attitudes. Moreover, the cultural patterns of Czechs and Slovaks were also ambivalent, especially in the post-war years, and, as will be seen in the next section, these were sometimes brought, willingly or reluctantly, or by outright coercion, to accept some of the values of Communist political culture. Within this context of changing and diverse political patterns the evolution of post-war Czechoslovak political culture may be better understood and the ultimate emergence of Stalinism explained.

The Establishment of Communist Rule

The Munich surrender, the Nazi occupation, the Slovak separation, and the experiences of war brought about a profound shift in values, including a substantial discrediting of the First Republic and its traditions, and some disillusionment with capitalism and "bourgeois" democracy, and, at the same time, a rise in the stock of socialism, of Soviet Russia and the Communist party of Czechoslovakia, and, in Slovakia, of nationalism. The formation of the National Front coalition government, under the authority of President Beneš, brought the Communists into close cooperation with the non-Communist parties and produced a certain merging of clashing political values. The CPCz seemed to have abandoned its extreme revolutionary aims and its Bolshevist practices, and to have accepted a high degree of pluralism, both within the party, and in political relations generally. Non-Communists, on the other hand, accepted "socialism," at least with respect to nationalization of industry and planning of the economy, and acquiesced in certain limitations on pluralism, notably the acceptance of the National Front as the sole framework of political activity and the ban on the Czechoslovak Agrarian and Slovak People's parties. The concept of a democratic and national path to socialism was endorsed not only by the non-Communists and by the rank and file of the CPCz, but also by the Bolshevist leading core

---

15. For an early analysis of this problem, see Skilling, "Communism and Czechoslovak Traditions," *Journal of International Affairs,* 20, no. 1 (1966), pp. 118–36; in somewhat revised form, in Skilling, *Interrupted Revolution,* Chap. I. See also Golan, "National Traditions and Socialism in Eastern Europe: The Cases of Czechoslovakia and Yugoslavia," in Eisenstadt and Azmon, eds., *Socialism and Tradition,* pp. 41–55.

under Gottwald, with, of course, Soviet approval of this projection of the pre-war strategy of the People's Front. All coalition parties accepted the idea of a distinctive Slovak nationality and at first agreed to substantial autonomy for Slovakia, but soon shifted to a policy of subjecting the Slovaks to centralist rule from Prague. The absence of a long-standing tradition of hostility to Russia and widespread pro-Soviet attitudes produced a general concensus on the alliance with the Soviet Union (already initiated in 1935) as the central pillar of foreign policy, although not to the exclusion of friendly association with Western powers.

In terms of power, the traditional Czechoslovak institution of a coalition government, combined with a distribution of ministries among the parties, provided a framework for sharing authority and for averting a Communist monopoly of power. Unlike their confrères in other Eastern European countries, the non-Communists were able, for three years, to maintain their political existence and to preserve a substantial degree of democracy, and, it appeared, to exert some influence on the CPCz. The latter, on the other hand, having greatly increased its membership and its electoral support, ceased to be an outsider in the political system and in fact became a leading force, accepted as legitimate by the other parties and by the public. There seemed good reason to anticipate an extended period of political cooperation, within the framework of a relatively democratic system and independence in international relations, and to expect a peaceful transition to a socialism of a Czechoslovak variety, distinct from the Soviet brand.

The Communist seizure of power in February 1948 rudely interrupted this prospect and was the prelude to the introduction of Stalinism.[16] It marked the breakdown of the apparent reconciliation of a somewhat modified traditional Czechoslovak political culture and a greatly changed Communist sub-culture, divested of its Bolshevist features. Omens of the impending failure of the effort to reconcile political values had already appeared in serious conflicts within the coalition over basic policy issues; Communist abuse of their control of certain ministries, such as the Interior; the arbitrary Communist takeover in Slovakia in late 1947; and the withdrawal of Czechoslovakia from the Marshall aid program, at the behest of Stalin and in a reversal of its original acceptance by Czechoslovakia, with CPCz approval. In the February crisis, Gottwald, exploiting and abusing democratic and constitutional processes and employing extra-constitutional means such as the action committees and the people's militia, transformed the National Front into a bogus coalition dominated by the CPCz

---

16. For the crisis and its aftermath, see my articles "The Break-Up of the Czechoslovak Coalition, 1947–48," *The Canadian Journal of Economics and Political Science,* 26 (August 1960), pp. 396–412; "The Prague Overturn in 1948," *Canadian Slavonic Papers,* 4 (1960), pp. 88–114. For an analysis of 1948 in the light of later historical studies, see Pavel Tigrid, "Ve stínu lípy," *Svědectví,* XI, No. 41 (1971), pp. 69–96; in English, in *The Anatomy of Communist Takeovers,* ed. Thomas H. Hammond (New Haven, 1975). The long and complicated process by which the Communists seized power in Czechoslovakia suggests that Robert Tucker's inclusion of Czechoslovakia in his category of revolutions imposed from outside is not fully accurate. Czechoslovakia is perhaps a special case, unlike either the indigenous or the imposed revolutions. See Tucker, "Paths of Communist Revolution, 1917–67," in *The Soviet Union, A Half-Century of Communism,* ed. Kurt London (Baltimore, 1968).

and denied opposing political forces any share in power. The pseudo-democratic features of the capture of power, and of the new constitution introduced thereafter, did not dispel the reality of authoritarian Communist rule, in which the Bolshevist principle of democratic centralism was applied to the entire body politic. The Soviet Union, whose increasing hostility to the West required the tightening of bloc unity through this consolidation of power (and the subsequent expulsion of Yugoslavia), fully supported the CPCz's action, and perhaps proposed it in the first place. The Cominform, already established, and Comecon, soon to be created, were manifestations of the subservience of Czechoslovakia and her allies to Moscow, and the abrogation of independence of action in foreign relations.

February 1948 thus marked the triumph of Bolshevist political culture and the beginning of the application of its cardinal principles to Czechoslovak politics, both domestic and foreign. Yet the Communist victory was due at least in part to the weaknesses of traditional Czechoslovak political culture, especially in its post-war version. Belief in the coalition idea, based on the assumptions of the feasibility and the desirability of working with the Communists, discouraged opposition to Communist pressures and sapped the will to resist when the assumptions proved unreal. Traditional friendship with the Soviet Union and acceptance of the primacy of the Soviet alliance, and the lack of any possible aid from the West, placed the non-Communist leaders in a position of embarrassed isolation, with nowhere to turn for support. Moreover, although they had themselves precipitated the crisis (by resigning from the government on the issue of Communist manipulation of the Ministry of the Interior) they had prepared no strategy of further resistance to the Communists, whereas the latter had anticipated a crisis of some kind and were ready to seize the opportunity presented to them. Their opponents relied on democratic and parliamentary tactics which were inadequate when confronted with naked power and were clumsily employed. The non-Communist leaders also counted on Beneš to stand up to Communist pressures and not to yield, as he did, to the array of forces mobilized against him by the Communists. The democratic and national political culture proved ineffective in meeting the Bolshevist challenge and succumbed in this crucial test of strength.

The non-Communists had foreseen, at least in some degree, the ultimate implications of Communist policy and had tried, unsuccessfully, to prevent their consummation. Rank and file Communists, however, although many of them were not fully Bolshevist in outlook, endorsed with enthusiasm what appeared to be a "democratic" assumption of power carried through with unquestioned skill, with enormous "mass" backing, and without effective opposition. The acceptance of Communist rule by certain non-Communist leaders, including even Jan Masaryk, and the acquiescence of President Beneš (though with scarcely concealed reluctance), spread a democratic and constitutional veneer over the "revolutionary" character of the capture of power, and disguised its essentially Stalinist features, especially in the coercive subordination of other parties to the CPCz. For Communists it was a victory for "their" party, opening the way for a more rapid advance to "socialism" and eliminating forces that stood in the way. Most were imbued with high hopes for a better future under Communist rule and had few, if any, doubts of the correctness of the party's policy. Few could have had an inkling of the eventual meaning of the unrestricted party hegemony that was established in February or could have imagined, in their worst nightmares, the macabre denouement of the fifties.

Stalinism Established

It soon became evident that the capture of power was regarded as "a socialist revolution" comparable to the October revolution in Russia, and was intended to effect a fundamental transformation of society in all aspects. It was "a revolution from above" (in the spirit of Stalin's thesis of the role of the superstructure in changing society)—a consolidation and expansion of power by party leaders already in power and the inauguration of radical changes by dictate of the ruling elite. The "socialism" to be established was socialism on the Stalinist pattern, following the slogans of the time: "The Soviet Union Our Model!"and "With the Soviet Union for All Time!" [17] In terms of political culture the purpose was to expunge all aspects of the traditional culture, and indeed of all sub-cultures (other than that of Communism in its Bolshevized form), and to impose on the country the Stalinist political culture as it had developed in the Soviet Union. As elsewhere in Eastern Europe, this meant telescoping, in a few years, the radical changes that had occurred in the USSR over almost a quarter of a century. It also meant that alternative options of development, involving less speed and less drastic change, perhaps on the lines of the Russian NEP, were foreclosed as definitively as in the case of Russia twenty years earlier.

It may be assumed, although there is no solid evidence to confirm it, that the drastic switch in Czechoslovak policy, including the seizure of power and the introduction of Stalinism, was the result of a decision taken in Moscow by Stalin and the Soviet leaders and was part of a coordinated plan for the whole of Eastern Europe. In broad outline the program to be implemented was essentially identical in all countries (except Yugoslavia, where direct Soviet intervention, although abortive, was revealed in the Stalin-Tito correspondence). The Cominform served as the instrument of coordination, providing guidelines through its resolutions and its newspaper for the member parties, which had not lost the habit of obedience to the Soviet Union acquired under the Comintern. Georgi Dimitrov publicly acknowledged "the aid of Stalin" in elaborating the doctrinal underpinning of the post-1948 model of socialism, which identified the people's democracy with the dictatorship of the proletariat and required that the Soviet path, rather than a national one, be followed.[18]

It is not easy to determine whether the introduction of Stalinism was accepted willingly or reluctantly by the national leaders, or whether it met with some initial

---

17. Skilling, "People's Democracy, The Proletarian Dictatorship and the Czechoslovak Path to Socialism," *American Slavic and East European Review,* 10 (April 1951).

18. Ibid., p. 113.

veiled opposition, as suggested by W. Brus in his chapter in this symposium.[19] In Czechoslovakia, the early steps taken in the economic field were not fully Stalinist, and in some respects, for instance in the staging of major show trials, Czechoslovakia lagged behind the other people's democracies. Perhaps the full meaning of Stalinism, and the pace at which it was expected to proceed, were not fully appreciated by Czechoslovak leaders, let alone by lower cadres and rank and file. Later Czechoslovak sources referred to Gottwald's initial efforts to resist pressures and his "inner struggle," especially concerning the arrest and trial of Slánský, and explained his final acquiescence by his "growing isolation," his declining health, and the "Stalinist traits" which became pronounced in the Cold War period.[20] The evidence was, however, slight, and indicated no principled or adamant resistance to the Stalinist line, or even an indirect evasion of its early implementation. On the contrary, everything suggested that, right down to his death, shortly after that of Stalin, Gottwald persisted in the conformism to Moscow's policies which had characterized him from his assumption of leadership in 1929. The Czech leader's utter devotion to Stalin, coupled in later years with his fear of the personal consequences of going against his will, led him to accept without serious question whatever Stalin required of him, including the execution of Slánský, to be discussed in the following sections.[21]

The Stalinist system, although basically similar in all of Eastern Europe, differed in its timing, and in degree, in the individual countries. Although in some, such as Yugoslavia, Albania, and Rumania, many Stalinist features were introduced in the years 1944–48 (and gradually dismantled in Yugoslavia thereafter), in Czechoslovakia, Poland, and Hungary these changes came later, after 1948, and in full form only in the fifties. Moreover, the duration of Stalinism varied. In some cases it began to crumble from 1953 on, but strong vestiges often lingered or were restored after temporary dislodgment; in other cases it continued hardly changed to the present. The case of Czechoslovakia is particularly paradoxical, since, in spite of the relatively late establishment of Stalinism and the antecedent democratic political culture, it lasted long after the death of Stalin and in many aspects was not basically modified until 1968. Moreover, it may be argued, the intensity of Stalinism was greater here than elsewhere, not only in more drastic

---

19. According to Brus, the Polish leaders would have preferred an alternative course along the lines of Bukharin's ideas. See his chapter in this volume.

20. See the *Commission Report* cited in note 31, below, pp. 261–63; Karel Kaplan, "Reflections on the Political Trials," *Nová mysl,* No. 8, 1968, pp. 1060–61. Party archives, according to Czech historians, documented not only Gottwald's chronic alcoholism (dating back to the war years), but also his serious syphilitic condition. Gottwald's fear of Stalin was so great in later years that he was afraid to go the Soviet Union for fear that he would not return.

21. As one commentator has observed, Gottwald *had* a choice as to whether to accept or to refuse the decision of Stalin to eliminate plurality and diversity within his empire and to impose the Soviet model on the other Communist states. He (Gottwald) chose "to condemn his own policy . . . to liquidate the Czechoslovak road to socialism and to condemn it, not just in words, abstractly, but also in the persons of those who had helped him prepare and implement it, and not just condemn them, but have them killed. . . . Nothing can relieve him of responsibility for the choice he made." (Dušan Pokorný, cited below, note 30.)

economic measures, such as the socialization of retail trade, the speedy collectivization of agriculture, and the acceleration of investment after 1950,[22] but above all in the scope and magnitude of terror.

Terror and the Trials

The most incongruous feature of the Stalinist model as introduced in Eastern Europe were the political trials that were held in some of the Communist countries as a kind of re-enactment, two decades later, of the Moscow "show trials" of the thirties.[23] No major trials took place in Poland, Yugoslavia, or the German Democratic Republic. Elsewhere trials of the Soviet type, in each case involving at least one major political leader, were held: in Albania, Koci Xoxe (May 1949); in Hungary, Laszlo Rajk (September 1949); in Bulgaria, Traicho Kostov (December 1949); in Czechoslovakia, Rudolf Slánský (November 1952); and in Rumania, L. Pâtrâşçanu and V. Luca (April and October 1954). All of these, like their Moscow predecessors, were artificial stage productions based (as was later admitted) on false charges and fabricated evidence, and led to severe penalties of death or long imprisonment.

The trials in Czechoslovakia were, as a Czech expert later wrote, "the greatest political trials in post-war Europe" and were distinguished from the others by "their massive character, the cruelty of the repression, and the extraordinary number of the victims." [24] The main Slánský trial, alone involving fourteen persons,[25] was followed by eight other major trials, most of which took place, paradoxically, after the death of Stalin. These grim performances followed closely the Soviet pattern, not only in the scope and number, and the high rank, of the victims, but in the style of these grotesque sessions. There was the same paranoiac atmosphere of a hostile world, in which domestic agents acted for external enemies, and the same fantastic charges, including plans to overthrow the Gottwald regime, espionage, sabotage, anti-state actions in all spheres, and alliance with foreign imperialism (as well as with Titoism and Zionism). These "theatrical masterpieces" were given the widest publicity, being broadcast live from the courtroom. All of the accused confessed their guilt without reservations, and made no plea for special consideration and no appeal against the sentences. The defense lawyers admitted the guilt of their clients, and no defense witnesses appeared. In some respects the Slánský trial was "more perfect" than those in

---

22. See the unpublished draft paper by W. Brus, "Institutional and Social Change in Eastern Europe Since 1950," for a detailed exposition of changes during the peak of the Stalin era.

23. For the full text of the trial of Bukharin et al., see *The Great Purge Trial,* ed. Robert C. Tucker and Stephen F. Cohen (New York, 1965). This includes an excellent analysis of the trial, and of the reasons for it and for the confessions, by Tucker, in his introduction, "Stalin, Bukharin, and History as Conspiracy." See also Roy Medvedev, *Let History Judge: The Origins and Consequences of Stalinism* (New York, 1973), pp. 168–91; and Aleksandr Solzhenitsyn, *The Gulag Archipelago, 1918–1956: An Experiment in Literary Investigation,* 2 vols. (New York, 1973), I–II, 407–19.

24. Kaplan, *Nová mysl,* p. 1054.

25. For the record of the Slánský trials, see *Proces s vedením protistátního spikleneckého centra v čele s Rudolfem Slánským* (Prague, 1953); in English, in brief form, in Eugene Loebl, *Sentenced and Tried: The Stalinist Purges in Czechoslovakia* (London, 1969).

Moscow. No one tried to defend himself against certain charges, as had Bukharin, or tried, as Robert Tucker has suggested, to conduct a kind of counter-trial of their accusers (in Bukharin's case, of Stalin).[26] No one reneged, as did Krestinsky in Moscow, or Kostov in Sofia, retracting their confessions in open court.

In Czechoslovakia, as elsewhere, the trials were only the tip of the iceberg of a massive reign of terror. Many victims were tried in secret, often because of their failure to make the necessary confessions, or their unreliability for performing their roles in the court drama. The number of death sentences issued by the State Court from 1948 to the end of 1952 was estimated (1968) as 233, of which 178 were carried out. The number of persons imprisoned illegally after trials was said to be over thirty-five thousand. Many others (twenty-two thousand persons) were arbitrarily confined without trials in forced labor camps; peasants and small tradesmen (some twenty-five to thirty thousand and sixteen thousand respectively) suffered from Draconian administrative measures under 1950 laws. The total number of individuals affected was thus about one hundred thousand. Many more, whose numbers cannot be estimated, suffered from other illegal administrative measures (without "benefit" of trial), such as dismissal or transfer from jobs, eviction from living quarters, confiscation of personal property, expulsion from high schools or universities, or induction into the armed forces for compulsory labor.[27]

As in the Soviet case, these monstrous events inexorably raised the questions: Why were the trials held? What purpose did they serve? Who was responsible? In Czechoslovakia these questions took on added poignancy since the trials were out of harmony with the country's traditional political culture (of which a system of genuine justice was an integral part), and the terror was much more extreme than in countries lacking this tradition of legality. As Karel Kaplan noted, the trials represented, in Czechoslovak history, "a unique phenomenon, unorganic and unnatural." [28]

How could this have occurred in a country such as Czechoslovakia? Was it primarily a product of international circumstances and of outside pressures? Or were there domestic forces that facilitated and encouraged it? Was it imposed from above, by a few leaders, or was it accepted (reluctantly, or willingly and even with enthusiasm) from below? Who can be held personally responsible—Stalin and the Soviet leadership? Gottwald and the CPCz leaders? other party officials and functionaries? the ordinary rank and file? or citizens generally, non-Communist as well as Communist? To what extent was it resisted by leaders, lesser officials, party members, and the people?

These difficult questions defy any full or final answer. Scant information is available, and little research has been done on the subject. During 1968 there

---

26. Tucker and Cohen, *The Great Purge Trial,* pp. xlii–xlviii.

27. For the above, and further information, see Skilling, *Interrupted Revolution,* Chap. 13. An additional fifty thousand to sixty thousand persons were tried before district courts. Cf. the total figure of eighty thousand given in V. V. Kusin, *Political Grouping in the Czechoslovak Reform Movement* (London, 1972), pp. 173–75.

28. Kaplan, *Nová mysl,* p. 1054.

was considerable discussion of the trials,[29] and articles, books, and interviews with some of the victims, as well as several perpetrators, of the crimes of the fifties were published.[30] Most revealing were the findings of the CPCz commission, headed by Jan Piller, which was assigned the task of re-examining the major trials and the earlier rehabilitation investigations. Using CPCz archives (but not those of the Soviet Union), a team of scholars headed by the historian Karel Kaplan conducted a thorough study and produced a draft report which even in a deliberately modified form was so explosive that it was not published prior to the occupation. Since then, its publication in Czechoslovakia has been prevented, and any further discussion or research has become impossible. The report, in its more or less final form, was published abroad in Czech and several foreign languages.[31] Kaplan's own book on the subject was forbidden to be printed, and he himself was removed from his position in the Historical Institute. Prior to the occupation, however, his series of articles in the party monthly *Nová mysl,* embodying, in somewhat moderate form, the major contents of the report, constituted a valuable contribution to an understanding of Stalinism in Czechoslovakia and to an explanation of the trials of the fifties.[32]

The Trials: An Explanation

The Moscow trials, in Tucker's view, were the personal conception, and the work, of Stalin, and were designed to satisfy his own psychological needs, but they also served specific political purposes, in particular to rationalize the purges, to solidify Stalin's total power, and to justify Soviet foreign policy.[33] In Czechoslovakia, too, it may be presumed that the trials were in large part Stalin's handiwork, but they reflected current domestic and international politics and fulfilled what were deemed to be certain requirements of internal and foreign policy.

The *Commission Report* documented the direct, personal intervention of Stalin and of other foreign party leaders in the conduct of the trials. In a letter dated September 3, 1949, for instance, the Hungarian party leader, Mátyás Rákosi, warned Gottwald that the names of Czechoslovak "spies" would be revealed in

---

29. See, for instance, D. Hamšik, "Trials That Made History," *Literární listy,* March 28, 1968; A. Jesenská, "The Roots of the Moral Crisis and the Trials," *Kultúrny život,* March 29, 1968; panel discussion, "How Was It Possible?" *Reportér,* April 10–17, pp. i–viii; V. Vrabec, "Mills and Millers," *Reportér,* July 24–31, pp. i–vi.

30. For instance, E. Löbl, *Svedectvo o procese s vedením protistátneho sprísahaneckého centra na čele s Rudolfom Slánským,* foreword by Dušan Pokorný (Bratislava, 1968), in English, in E. Loebl, *Sentenced and Tried;* Artur London, *Doznání* (Prague, 1969), in English, *The Confession* (New York, 1970). For interviews with former ministers of national security, see K. Bacílek, *Smena,* April 28, 1968; *Pravda* (Bratislava), May 15; and L. Kopřiva, *Večerní Praha,* May 7; *Reportér,* June 12–19.

31. *Potlačená zpráva (Zpráva komise ÚV KSČ o politických procesech a rehabilitacích v Československu 1949–68,* ed. Jiří Pelikán (Vienna, 1968), in English, *The Czechoslovak Political Trials, 1950–1954* (London, 1971), henceforth cited as *Commission Report,* with page references to the English translation. See also my *Interrupted Revolution* for further analysis.

32. Kaplan, "Reflections on the Political Trials," *Nová mysl,* Nos. 6, 7, 8, 1968.

33. Tucker and Cohen, *The Great Purge Trial,* pp. xxviii ff.

the forthcoming Rajk trial, and that these people, still "at liberty," would strengthen the hand of the accused by their protests. He expressed distrust of high-ranking CPCz officials, including the minister of the interior (Václav Nosek) and the minister of foreign affairs (Vladimir Clementis), and named as suspects two economists, L. Frejka and Josef Goldmann, and a leading journalist, Vilém Nový.[34] As a result, the Prague regime intensified its search for "a Czechoslovak Rajk," stepped up the arrests of suspects, and requested the sending of Soviet advisers into the security sphere.

There was evidence of Stalin's personal intervention on two occasions. On July 24, 1951, he expressed the belief that the evidence against Slánský was not enough to justify his arrest, but declared that his mistakes required his removal from the post of general secretary. Later, on November 11, 1951, in a message apparently delivered personally to Gottwald by Anastas Mikoyan during a mysterious visit to Prague, Stalin indicated a change of mind. When Gottwald "hesitated," Stalin insisted, in a telephone conversation with Mikoyan in Prague, that Slánský be arrested on the basis of the alleged danger of his impending escape to the West.[35]

In the analysis made in Kaplan's articles and the *Commission Report,* the international context of the trials was the Cold War, which divided the world into two hostile camps and renewed international tension; this "revived the theory and practice of Stalinism which during the war and the post-war period had to some extent been relegated to the background, but had never been forgotten." [36] The "war psychosis" which developed led to a widespread fear of conspiracy and to demands for "caution and vigilance," and to the adoption of more militant policies in each country, including a frantic acceleration of the five-year plans. Although the latter has usually been related to the war needs of North Korea, it may have been connected with general planning for a European war, resulting either from international tensions and the war in Asia or from deliberate offensive action by the Soviet Union.[37] In this atmosphere Moscow and other bloc capitals apparently began to consider Czechoslovakia "the weakest link" in the camp and to accuse her of lagging behind in taking action against internal enemies.[38] In

---

34. *Commission Report,* p. 75. The report referred also to intervention by Warsaw but gave no information on this (ibid., pp. 76–80). On November 28, 1952, B. Bierut requested permission for Polish security forces to interrogate Slánský and others about their contacts with Gomułka, but Slánský was executed on December 3, presumably before this could take place (ibid., p. 114).

35. Ibid., pp. 103, 106–7. The pretext for Slánský's arrest was a letter from abroad addressed to "The Great Road-Sweeper," dated November 9, warning the recipient that he was in danger of meeting the same fate as Gomułka and offering him help in fleeing the country. Apart from false statements extracted from other prisoners, this was the sole document used to justify his arrest. The commission regarded the letter as "a provocation" but found no evidence as to who had fabricated it or who had averred that Slánský was the intended recipient. The latter inference was drawn, according to the report, by a group of security officers and Soviet advisers (p. 107).

36. Ibid., p. 43.

37. According to Czech historians, party archives documented Stalin's plans for war and his concrete military preparations for operations in Europe in 1950.

38. *Commission Report,* pp. 46–50. General Svoboda was dismissed as minister of national defense on Stalin's urgent counsel that he was "not deserving of confidence" (ibid., pp. 47–48).

addition, the campaign against Zionism and Israel in Stalin's declining years led to a special anti-Jewish character in the Czechoslovak trials which was absent from the earlier Moscow ones. Eleven of the fourteen defendants were Jewish in origin and were so identified in the proceedings, and charges of Zionism and treasonable links with Israel bulked large in the indictments.

Another salient purpose of the trials was to discredit the concept of "a national path to socialism," which until 1948 had been sponsored by the Soviet Union, and to make certain leaders other than Gottwald, its chief Czechoslovak advocate, the "scapegoats" for this now condemned theory. The reverse side of the medal was to justify the entire line of policy introduced after 1948 on the basis of the doctrine of "following the Soviet path," including, of course, the emulation of Soviet terror itself. Strict conformism in domestic and foreign policies was to be enforced in all the European Communist countries (with the exception of Yugoslavia).[39] In Slovakia, the trials were to serve the political goals of eliminating so-called "bourgeois national" leaders and justifying the strict subordination of Slovakia and the Slovak party to Prague.[40]

A major factor contributing to the trials was the political system, which, in Kaplan's words, was contrary to Czechoslovak traditions and a product of Bolshevik experience, and was imported into Czechoslovakia as part of the practice of modeling all aspects of life on the Soviet pattern.[41] The extreme concentration of power at the pinnacle of the Communist party, and the usurpation of the authority of the state organs by the party, meant that the Central Committee, and organs such as parliament and the government, were unable to supervise the exercise of power, or to prevent its abuse, thus paving the way for the gross illegalities perpetrated during the fifties. Another element was "the unquestioning obedience" exacted of all party members, so that all decisions relating to the trials were carried out, often in good faith and without knowledge of the falsity of the charges.

A special feature of the system was what the Commission called "the mechanism for the manufacture of political trials." [42] This consisted of the topmost party bodies and other commissions which "gave the necessary directives and ideological justifications"; the security services which escaped control of other organs and produced, through interrogation, the confessions on which the trials were based; and the judiciary, which lost all independence and carried out decisions made elsewhere. A crucial role was played by the Soviet advisers, who introduced investigatory methods, which, as in the Moscow trials, combined physical and psychic torture to break the will of the accused and force them to confess. According to L. Kopřiva, former minister of national security, "Their [the advisers'] authority and influence was greater than that of the minister, not only on the officials of the ministry, but also on the party leadership," to whom

39. Hamšik, "Trials That Made History"; Loebl, *Sentenced and Tried,* pp. 20, 24, 40.

40. Gustáv Husák, in a series of articles (*Nové slovo,* June 13–July 25, 1968) which was a reprint of his letter to the CPCz Central Committee in 1962–63.

41. Kaplan, *Rudé právo,* August 14, 1968; *Nová mysl,* No. 6, 1968, pp. 768–70, 790–92.

42. *Commission Report,* pp. 130–40.

they had direct access. "We all believed in them without reservations, informed them of everything, consulted with them." [43]

Personal Guilt

Soviet complicity, and indeed initiative, in launching and conducting the political trials did not absolve Czechs and Slovaks of their own responsibility. Nor could the individual shift blame to the political system as a whole, or submerge his own guilt in that of society, according to a theory espoused by Novotný that "all were guilty." The burden of guilt, wrote Karel Kaplan, fell on "people—concrete persons, individual organs, agencies, or groups." [44] Each person was personally responsible for his own decisions and for the decisions of the organs of which he was a member; he could not escape accountability by any excuse, whether it was orders from above, external pressure, lack of knowledge, inability to do anything, or belief in the correctness of the decisions. The guilt of the individual varied, however, and was graduated according to the position held and the significance of the organ in the mechanism of power. Although the top leaders bore the primary guilt, others, too, must be held accountable, including all who had any share in the system—whether at the middle or lower levels, and whatever their function: security police, judges, lawyers, prison guards, witnesses, etc.

According to such criteria Gottwald must necessarily be assigned the highest blame for the political trials, both for his submission to Soviet demands and for his own initiatives at every stage. The *Commission Report* confirmed his full complicity in the decision to arrest and to try, and ultimately to execute, his closest associate and friend for a quarter of a century, Slánsky. Gottwald was said to have resisted Stalin's demands briefly, expressing, in a draft letter that was never sent, his faith in Slánsky and even admitting his own responsibility for errors made.[45] He soon yielded, however, to Stalin's pressure to remove his colleague from high office and later to arrest him. "Although he had no facts," said the report, "Gottwald drew the conclusion that Stalin, as usual, had reliable information and that his advice was sound." On November 23, at a meeting of Gottwald with Zápotocký, Kopřiva, and the chief Soviet adviser, the decision was taken to arrest Slánsky, an action approved *ex post facto* by the Political Secretariat and the Presidium, and later by the Central Committee. According to the report, Gottwald "misinformed this meeting [of the CC] by stating that

---

43. Kopřiva, *Reportér*, June 12–19, 19–26, 1968. According to Kopřiva's successor, K. Bacílek, there were advisers in all important ministries, and twenty-six in the Ministry of Public Security alone, working in every department and exerting a great influence, in many cases "positive" (cited above, note 30). On the advisers, see also *Commission Report*, p. 136; Kaplan, *Nová mysl*, No. 6, 1968, p. 793; Loebl, *Sentenced and Tried*, p. 32. On methods used in investigations in the Moscow trials, see *The Great Purge Trial*, Tucker and Cohen, p. xxvi; in the Prague trials, Loebl, *Sentenced and Tried*, pp. 17–19; *Commission Report*, pp. 80–81; Husák, *Nové slovo*, June 20, 27, 1968.

44. Kaplan, *Nová mysl*, No. 8, 1968, pp. 1057–60; Z. Mlynář, *Rudé právo*, April 17, 1968; *Commission Report*, p. 260.

45. Kaplan, *Nová mysl*, No. 7, p. 929. On Gottwald's guilt, see Pokorný, in Loebl, *Sentenced and Tried*, pp. 262–63; *Commission Report*, pp. 261–63.

important new evidence had made the arrest essential. He blocked any attempts by members to ask for details by making the plausible excuse that their publication would hamper the inquiry." [46]

Gottwald's colleagues at the top of the political hierarchy also bore the guilt of approving the decisions that led to the many trials. The *Commission Report* condemned all who had held high posts during the trials, including in its sweeping indictment all members of the Presidium and the Secretariat of the Central Committee, and of the Slovak party organs during the years 1950 to 1954. It accused (by name) four ministers of national security, three ministers of justice, the chairman of the Supreme Court, and the general prosecutor. It blamed all three presidents, including, besides Gottwald, Zápotocký and Novotný. Concerning Zápotocký, the report stated, "No instance is known where his view differed from that of the others." When demands for review were raised during 1955–57, "we have no evidence that Zápotocký disagreed with his colleagues on this matter." Novotný was a member of the Political Secretariat which endorsed Slánský's arrest on November 24, and took part in the preparation and supervision of the trial in 1952. He was first secretary during eight subsequent trials and was to blame for his failure to revise the trials and rehabilitate the victims in subsequent years. Even Slánský was held responsible for his part in elaborating and expounding the Cominform line, for directing the work of the security service, and for arranging the trials of many subordinate leaders.[47]

In the self-critical atmosphere of 1968 it was often recognized that the shadow of guilt fell not only on a wide circle of subordinate officials but also on the ordinary citizen, especially the rank-and-file party member who condoned or acquiesced in the trials, or applauded them, and did nothing to protest against them. "We are all responsible for the political trials," wrote Dušan Hamšik in 1968, "—the nation *as a whole,* as *a continuum.*" "It is a dark stain on our past, a burdening of our history by which we are all determined for good or ill. . . . " [48] The trials, especially the confessions, raised doubts in people's minds, but most stifled them or did not express them out of fear of the consequences. Many joined in the hunt, approving or signing resolutions and appeals for strict punishment of the accused, even calling for the death sentence.[49] The majority displayed a general indifference and callousness to the fate of fellow citizens and even of intimate comrades. In Kaplan's words, society "remained deaf to the fate of people. . . . " "Those who doubted were few, those who protested and fought, fewest of all, perhaps only the closest relations." [50] "The silence of the great and

---

46. *Commission Report*, p. 107.

47. On the personal responsibility of leading Communists, ibid., pp. 249–59, 260–77; on Zápotocký, pp. 263–64; on Novotný, pp. 264–68; on Slánský, pp. 274–76. See also Husák's condemnation of Novotný, *Rudé právo,* June 15, 1968. Cf. Skilling, *Interrupted Revolution,* pp. 384–87, 402–4.

48. "Trials," *Literární listy,* March 28.

49. *Commission Report*, pp. 143, 285, 303. For an analysis of the mobilization of support for the trials, see V. Vrabec, "The Relationship of the CPCz and Public Opinion to the Political Trials at the Beginning of the Fifties," *Revue dějin socialismu,* No. 3, 1969, pp. 363–87.

50. *Nová mysl,* p. 1065.

of the small," wrote Dušan Pokorný, "is the most dreadful testimony as to the state of the society in which all this has been enacted. It is a scream of impotence—coming also from those who perhaps originally were very powerful." [51]

How Could It Happen?

This question, comparable in some degree to the question of "war guilt" and personal responsibility for Nazi crimes in Germany, remains unanswered, gnawing at the conscience of many a Czech and Slovak and baffling the researcher. The phenomenon of Czechoslovak Stalinism can hardly be explained in Švejkian terms, by specifically Czech traits of outward adaptation to alien rule and malingering for the sake of survival and the defense of traditional values. The reactions of Czechs and Slovaks to Stalinism expressed, it would seem, more general human responses which were also manifested, in different form and degree, in other countries of Eastern Europe, and in Russia itself. The reaction was a complex one composed of disparate and often conflicting elements, ranging from a positive identification with the Stalinist system to a reluctant acquiescence supplemented by feelings of guilt.

The triumph of Stalinism, and its apogee in the trials, represented a link in a chain of events from 1921 on—the entry of the CPCz into the Communist International; Gottwald's assumption of leadership; capitulation at the time of Munich; war-time occupation, including collaboration; and the unresisted February coup. Some of these experiences stamped Stalinist (Bolshevist) patterns more and more deeply on Czechoslovak thought and behavior. Others, especially the surrenders of 1938 and 1948, undermined faith in national traditions, which offered perhaps moral support or a source of hope for some, but did not provide a programme of action capable of resisting the evils of the fifties. In the words of the *Commission Report,* "Step by step society became divorced from its cherished traditions and the values inherited from the past, while moving away from the ideals of a humane socialism. The will to resist the illegality weakened. . . ." [52]

For Communists a crucial role in the psychology of acceptance of Stalinism was played by certain key elements of Stalinist political culture: utter devotion to Stalin and the Soviet Union; unlimited confidence in the CPCz and in Gottwald; and unconditional obedience to the party's commands. Victims of the trials, as well as those who conducted them, later admitted that their disciplined faith required them to subordinate reason and conscience, causing the former to confess to nonexistent crimes and the latter to carry out their party instructions without mercy. [53] For the victims in the trials, confession of guilt was often described by the accuser, and accepted by the accused, as a final service to be

---

51. Pokorný, in Loebl, *Sentenced and Tried,* p. 264.

52. *Commission Report,* p. 100.

53. For references to "faith" in the *Commission Report,* pp. 63, 245, 274. See also A. J. Liehm, *Literární noviny,* May 23, 1964, republished in English *The Politics of Culture,* ed. A. J. Liehm (New York, 1967, 1968). Cf. the interview with Eduard Goldstücker, ibid., pp. 300–301. On discipline, see Kaplan, *Nová mysl,* No. 6, p. 791.

rendered to the party.[54] What began as enthusiasm and trust in a kind of "divine community," based on love and comradeship, degenerated, as time went on, into distrust of all, fearful caution, and blind consent born out of fear.[55]

For non-Communists, as well as for some Communists, many factors combined to produce an acquiescence in the system and to foster some credence in the genuineness of the trials. Central was the element of fear, produced by ruthless coercion of dissidents or doubters, which affected all, from the top down, and led to complicity in the grim process of terror, or passivity in the face of injustice. Reinforcing this was a barrage of propaganda which, in Kaplan's words, created "a mass psychosis, which blunted the feeling for legality and the sense of justice. . . ." [56] As a result "the bulk of the population believed every word they were told" and "falsehood replaced truth in their thinking." [57] Selective information, or disinformation, deprived persons, even at higher levels of the party hierarchy, of the facts required for honest judgment, and if it did not produce complete belief, it created uncertainty and doubt. In this corroding atmosphere it was difficult to retain sanity, to maintain moral standards, and still more to display courage. Fear and isolation generated feelings of hopelessness, impotence, and apathy—"What could one do?" These tendencies to silence and inaction were reinforced by the desire to stay alive and free, to keep one's job and offices, and to protect one's family. Due to the economic difficulties and political crises of the time, it was easy to believe in the guilt of scapegoats, such as the accused in the trials, who thus were deprived of sympathy or support. For those bitterly opposed to Communism, and for disillusioned Communists, there was reason to rejoice at the cruel fate of hated leaders or superiors, and no reason to believe in them or give them aid. This was reinforced by anti-Semitic or anti-German prejudices, which made many of the condemned appear even less deserving of sympathy.[58]

Space does not permit the discussion of related questions as to why Stalinism continued so long in Czechoslovakia and why the rehabilitation of the victims of the trials was so slow and incomplete. This would require an examination of the fifteen years of Novotný's rule from 1953 to 1968, during which Novotný made some reluctant and partial concessions to reform but resisted any substantial alterations of the system. While the outer forms of Stalinism, and much of its inner essence, were preserved, the system began to disintegrate under the pressure of reform demands and oppositional trends. Many of the supporting

---

54. Kaplan, ibid., No. 7, p. 936; Goldstücker, *Literární listy,* May 30, 1968. For this in the Moscow trials, see *The Great Purge Trial,* Tucker and Cohen, pp. xli–xlii; Medvedev, *Let History Judge,* pp. 187, 403.

55. J. Blažková, *Kultúrny život,* May 17, 1968. For references to "fear" in *Commission Report,* see pp. 143, 145. See also J. Mucha, in Liehm, *Politics of Culture,* pp. 218–20.

56. Kaplan, *Nová mysl,* p. 1056.

57. *Commission Report,* p. 143.

58. For further discussion, see Skilling, *Interrupted Revolution,* pp. 387–91, 397–99. For efforts to explain Stalinism and the trials in the Soviet Union, see David Joravsky's introduction to Medvedev, *Let History Judge,* pp. xi–xviii, and Medvedev, ibid., Chap. XI.

factors mentioned above, such as fear and faith, weakened, but continued to exercise an influence. As far as the trials were concerned, Novotný yielded to pressures for partial revision, but steadfastly blocked any systematic and complete rehabilitation. Doubtless this was due to his own deep involvement, in the later trials at least, and his awareness that his position, and even his freedom, were at stake. Moreover, as the *Commission Report* emphasized, the mechanism for the "manufacture" of the trials remained almost intact, with few changes in personnel, thus impeding a serious review of past injustices. This led the Piller Commission to conclude that the responsibility for the trials and for their revision was inextricably linked, and that some persons shared responsibility for both.[59] It was thus left for the Dubček regime, in 1968, to seek a definitive solution of the problem.

Conclusion

The movement for radical change in 1968, if not interrupted by outside intervention, would have brought about revolutionary transformations in all aspects of Czechoslovak society and would have replaced the Stalinist system by a model of socialism more in harmony with earlier experiences and values of Czechs and Slovaks, including those of the Communist party itself. In this respect the "interrupted revolution" represented a renascence of deeply rooted national traditions, such as pluralism, national independence, and Slovak nationalism.[60] Exposure of the "judicial crimes" of the fifties produced not only a revulsion against these terrible injustices but also a resurgence of other traditional values, such as respect for legality and for human rights, and led to plans for a thorough rehabilitation of the victims and proposals for the restoration of judicial independence.[61] If the goals of 1968 had been fully achieved, fundamental aspects of the political culture of the First Republic would have been restored, although merged with values derived from socialist and communist traditions. In that sense the events of 1968 expressed a continuity of values stretching back into earlier periods of Czech and Slovak history.[62] It demonstrated the durability of these traditions and documented the difficulty of permanently remolding a political culture, especially by coercion from outside.

Yet one cannot ignore the other side of the medal: the repeated discontinuity of Czech and Slovak development throughout a history full of dramatic crises, often the product of drastic intervention from outside. The events of the fifties, in particular the terror and the trials, were as much a part of Czechoslovak history

---

59. *Commission Report,* on rehabilitation, pp. 148–243 For further discussion, see Skilling, *Interrupted Revolution.* Chaps. II, III.

60. Paul, "Repluralization of Czechoslovak Politics," and other works, cited above, note 1. See also Skilling, *Interrupted Revolution,* pp. 846–51.

61. M. Lakatoš, *Úvahy o hodnotách demokracie* (Prague, 1968), pp. 149, 157, 179–81.

62. Vladimir V. Kusin, *The Intellectual Origins of the Prague Spring* (Cambridge, England, 1971), pp. 16–17; chapter by Brown and Wightman, in Brown and Gray, *Political Culture,* cited in note 9; Golan, "National Traditions and Socialism," in Eisenstadt and Azmon, eds., *Socialism and Tradition,* pp. 52–55.

as was the First Republic and ought not to be ignored in an analysis of the political culture of the two nations. The ultimate rebirth of certain traditional values in 1968 could not annul the fact that for two decades these were, at best, buried deep in the consciousness of some and could exercise no influence on political practice. For almost a generation Stalinist leaders did succeed in suppressing the previously dominant political culture (at least the real culture of overt behavior) and in introducing a largely alien, and previously subordinate, pattern of politics. The attempt to transform the ideal political culture—the values and beliefs of the people, by massive indoctrination and terror, proved more difficult but achieved some degree of success, at least in weakening the hold of older ways of thought on people's minds and in discouraging them from acting on these beliefs, and in eliciting from many a positive response toward newer but more alien values. The more democratic and national aspects of communist tradition were also submerged by the dominant Stalinist patterns of thought and behavior, and communists were torn between conflicting loyalties and clashing precepts.

The concept of political culture cannot fully resolve the mysteries of these events, but helps to explain not only the introduction of Stalinism, and its strength and long endurance, in an unfavorable environment, but also its disintegration and collapse. Traditional cultural patterns, hampered by their very virtues as well as their weaknesses, were unable to prevent the victory of Stalinism, and in some degree facilitated it. This triumph was further aided by the fact that it could draw on significant native support, and, once in power, was able to sink new and deeper roots. Yet the very fact that the Stalinist phenomenon was imported from a foreign country with a vastly different tradition contributed to a growing recognition of its inappropriateness in Czechoslovakia and prepared the ground for the "awakening" of 1968. This was, in some degree, a revival of old values, including the more democratic and national aspects of Communism, which had persisted in the minds of many throughout the years of their outward suppression. Yet it was, in greater measure, a "re-awakening" in the true sense of the word, a rebirth of ideas and values which had been almost destroyed and were but dimly remembered. It was more, too, than a mere resurrection of the old, but represented a fusion of new and old in what was in effect a novel and distinctive political culture, freshly formulating traditional ideas, and embodying newborn ideas appropriate to the Czechoslovakia of the late sixties.

This case study demonstrates that the evolution and the survival of a political culture are bound to be affected by the international context of a nation's life, decisively so in the case of a small country in an exposed position. This was vividly illustrated in the modern history of the Czechs and Slovaks during which external influences—Austro-German and Magyar before 1914; French, British, and American after 1919; and later German and Russian—exerted a powerful impact on the politics of these two small peoples. The very existence of a distinctive culture and of its fundamental traits was threatened by outside forces, and, in the case of Nazi Germany and Soviet Russia, by direct and coercive intervention. In the latter case the threat was aggravated still more by the existence of a native counter-culture—Czechoslovak Communism, which helped to undermine the dominant culture and, once in power, sought to extirpate it. The influence of Soviet political culture was not, therefore, a purely exogenous factor but a domestic factor of cardinal importance in shaping the actions and thinking of Czechs and Slovaks. Hence, in 1968, when an effort was made to free Czechoslovak politics from Soviet thralldom, this faced strong and bitter opposition not only from outside, but also from certain domestic elements, and was ultimately blocked by military intervention. The re-establishment of a kind of neo-Stalinism, under Husák, was facilitated by a similar combination of Soviet pressures and domestic support. The natural and organic development of a genuine national political culture has thus often been distorted or, as at the time of writing, completely thwarted, by an unfavorable international context in which outside influences were aided and abetted by domestic forces.

Part Four

STALINISM versus MARXISM?

Marxist Roots of Stalinism

Leszek Kolakowski

What Do We Ask and What Do We Not Ask About?

When we ask, "How were the Stalinist system of power and the Stalinist ideology related to Marxism?" the main difficulty lies in the proper way of shaping the question. Our problem can be, and in fact used to be, specified in different manners; some of its specifying forms are unanswerable or pointless, and some are rhetorical, as the answers are obvious.

An example of a question that is both unanswerable and pointless is: "What would Marx say had he survived and seen his ideas embodied in the Soviet system?" If he had survived, he would have inevitably changed. If by miracle he was resurrected now, his opinion about which is the best practical interpretation of his philosophy would be just an opinion among others and could be easily shrugged off on the assumption that a philosopher is not necessarily infallible in seeing the implications of his own ideas.

Examples of questions to which answers are obvious and hardly require any discussion: "Was the Stalinist system causally generated by the Marxian theory?" "Can we find in Marx's texts implicit or explicit value judgments which run counter the value system established in Stalinist societies?" The answer to the first question is obviously negative because no society has ever been entirely begotten by an ideology or may ever be accounted for by ideas of people who contributed to its origin; anybody is Marxist enough to admit that. All societies reflect in their institutions many of their members' and makers' ideas—conflicting with each other—about how the society ought to be; but none was simply produced by these ideas as they had been conceived of before its existence, and to imagine that a society could ever spring up entirely out of a utopia (or *kakotopia*) would amount to believing that human communities are capable of getting rid of their past history. This is a commonsense platitude and purely negative at that. Societies have always been molded by what they thought about themselves, but this dependence has always been partial only.

The answer to the second question is obviously positive and is irrelevant to our problem. It is easy to see that Marx had never written anything to the effect that the socialist kingdom of freedom would consist in one-party despotic rule; that he did not reject democratic forms of social life; that he expected from socialism the abolition of economical coercion in addition to, and not by contrast to, the abolition of the political one, etc. If this is true, it still may be true either that there are logical reasons why his theory implies consequences incompatible with his ostensible value judgments, or that empirical circumstances prevented this theory from being practically implemented in a way much different from how it actually was to happen. There is nothing odd in that political and social programs, utopias, prophecies bring about an outcome which is not only different from, but significantly opposed to, the intention of their authors; some previously unnoticed or neglected empirical connections make the implementation of one part of the utopia possible only at the price of denying other ingredients. This again is a commonsense triviality; most of what we learn in life consists of the knowledge about which values are compatible and which exclude each other; most utopians are simply unable to learn that there are incompatible values. More often than not, this incompatibility is empirical, not logical, and this is why their utopias are not necessarily self-contradictory in logical terms, only impracticable because of the stuff the world is made of.

Thus, in discussing the relation of Stalinism to Marxism, I dismiss as irrelevant sayings like: "This would make Marx spin in his grave"; "Marx was against censorship and for free elections"; etc.—whether or not such statements might be validated unambiguously (which is somewhat doubtful in the case of the first saying).

My curiosity would be better expressed in another fashion: Was (or is) the characteristically Stalinist ideology that was (or is) designed to justify the Stalinist system of societal organization a legitimate (even if not the only possible) interpretation of Marxist philosophy of history? This is the milder version of my question. The stronger version is: Was every attempt to implement all basic values of Marxian socialism likely to generate a political organization that would bear marks unmistakably analogous to Stalinism? I will argue for the affirmative answer to both questions, while I realize that to say "yes" to the first does not logically entail "yes" to the second (it is logically consistent to maintain that Stalinism was one of several admissible variants of Marxism and to deny that the very content of Marxist philosophy favored this particular version more strongly than any other).

How Can "Stalinism" Be Identified?

It is of no great importance whether we use the word "Stalinism" to designate the well-located period of one-person despotism in the Soviet Union (i.e., roughly from 1930 to 1953) or to embrace any system that reveals clearly similar features. Nevertheless, the question of how far the post-Stalinist Soviet and Soviet-type states are essentially the extensions of the same system is obviously not a terminological one. There are reasons, however, why the less historical and more abstract concept, stressing the continuity of the system, is more convenient.

We may characterize "Stalinism" as an (almost perfect) totalitarian society based on the state ownership of the means of production. And I take the word "totalitarian" in a commonly used sense, meaning a political system where all social ties have been entirely replaced by state-imposed organization and where, consequently, all groups and all individuals are supposed to act only for goals which both are the goals of the state and were defined as such by the state. In other words, an ideal totalitarian system would consist in the utter destruction of civil society, whereas the state and its organizational instruments are the only forms of social life; all kinds of human activity—economical, intellectual, political, cultural—are allowed and ordered (the distinction between what is allowed and what is ordered tending to disappear) only to the extent of being at the service of state goals (again, as defined by the state). Every individual (including the rulers themselves) is considered the property of the state.

The concept so defined—and, in so defining it, I believe that I am in agreement with most authors dealing with the subject—calls for a few explanatory remarks.

First, it is clear that to achieve the perfect shape, a totalitarian principle of organization requires the state control of means of production; in other words, that a state which leaves some significant parts of the productive activity and of economical initiative in the hands of individuals and which, consequently, leaves segments of society economically independent of the state, cannot reach the ideal form. Therefore, totalitarianism has the best chances to fulfill the ideal within a socialist economy.

Second, it should be stressed that no absolutely perfect totalitarian system has ever existed; we know, however, societies with a very strong, constantly operating, built-in tendency to "nationalize" all forms of human communal and individual life. Both the Soviet and Chinese societies are or were in certain periods very close to the ideal; so was Nazi Germany, even if it did not last long enough to develop itself fully and if it was satisfied with coercively subordinating economical activity to state goals instead of nationalizing everything. Other fascist states were (or are) far behind Germany on this road; nor have European socialist states ever achieved the Soviet level of totalitarianism in spite of an incessant, and still working, drive in that direction.

It is unlikely that the "entelechia" of totalitarianism could ever be actuated in its impeccable shape. There are forms of life which stubbornly resist the impact of the system, familial, emotional, and sexual relationships among them; they were subjected strongly to all sorts of state pressure, but apparently never with full success (at least in the Soviet state; perhaps more was achieved in China). So is individual and collective memory, which the totalitarian system is permanently trying to annihilate by reshaping, rewriting, and falsifying history according to actual political needs. It is obviously easier to nationalize factories and labor than feelings; and easier hopes than memories. The resistance to state ownership of the historical past is an important part of anti-totalitarian movements.

Third, the above definition implies that not every despotic or terroristic system of ruling is necessarily totalitarian. Some, even the bloodiest, may have limited goals and do not need to absorb all forms of human activity within state goals; the worst forms of colonial rule in the worst periods usually were not totalitarian; the goal was to exploit subjugated countries economically, and, since many domains of life were indifferent from this point of view, they could be left more or less untouched. Conversely, a totalitarian system does not need to use permanently terroristic means of oppression.

Totalitarianism, in its perfect form, is an extraordinary form of slavery without masters. It converts all people into slaves and thereby bears certain egalitarian marks.

I certainly do realize that the application of the concept of totalitarianism and the very validity of this concept have been, in the last period, increasingly referred to as an "outdated" or "discredited" theory. Yet I am not acquainted with either conceptual or historical analyses which actually discredited it—as opposed to many earlier analyses which justified it (in fact the prediction that communism would mean the state-ownership of human persons appeared in Proudhon; that this was what actually happened in Soviet society was pointed out and described later on by so many well-known authors—whether or not the word "totalitarianism" was used—that it would be a useless pedantry to quote them here).

The Main Stages of Stalinist Totalitarianism

The Soviet variety of totalitarian society was ripening for many years before reaching its excellence. The well-known main stages of its growth need only to be mentioned briefly.

In the first stage, basic forms of representative democracy were done away with: parliament, elections, political parties, uncontrolled press.

The second stage (overlapping with the first) is known under the misleading name of "war communism." The name suggests that the policies of this period were conceived of as temporary and exceptional measures to cope with the monstrous difficulties imposed by civil war and intervention. In fact, it is easy to perceive from relevant writings of leaders—in particular, Lenin, Trotsky, Bukharin—that they all envisaged this economic policy (abrogation of free trade, coercive requisitions of "surplus"—i.e., of what local leadership estimated as surplus—from the peasants, universal rationing, compulsory labor) as a permanent achievement of the new society and that this policy was eventually abandonned as a result of the economic disaster it had caused, and not because the war conditions which forced it no longer existed. Both Trotsky and Bukharin emphatically assured that compulsory labor made up an organic part of the new liberated society.

Important elements of totalitarian order that were set up in this period persisted, to become permanent components of Soviet society. Such a lasting achievement was, first of all, the destruction of the working class as a political force (the abrogation of soviets as an independent expression of popular initiative; the end of independent trade unions and of socialist parties). Another was the suppression—not yet definitive—of democracy in the party itself (the ban on factional activity). Throughout the NEP era the totalitarian traits of the system were increasingly strong, despite the fact that free trade was accepted and that a majority of the society, i.e., peasants, enjoyed economic independence of the state. Both in a political and a cultural sense, NEP meant the mounting pressure of the party-owned state on all not yet state-owned (or only half–state-owned) centers of initiative, even though it was only the subsequent stages of development which would bring full success in this respect.

The third stage was coercive collectivization, which amounted to destroying the last not-yet-nationalized social class and gave the state the full power to control economic life (which did not mean, of course, that it enabled the state to set up real economic planning; it did not).

In the fourth stage the party itself as a potential (albeit no longer actual) non-nationalized force was destroyed in purges. The point was not that any effective rebellious forces survived in the party but that many of its members, in particular the older ones, kept loyalty to the traditional party ideology. Thus, even if perfectly obedient, they were rightly suspected of dividing their loyalties between the actual leader and the inherited ideological value system; in other words, of being potentially disloyal to the leader. The party was to be taught that ideology is what the leader in any given moment says it is, and the massacres performed this job successfully; they were the work of an ideological *Führer*, not of a madman.

The Face of Mature Stalinism

The upshot of this process—of which all phases were deliberately decided and organized, though not all were planned in advance—was a fully state-owned society which came very close to the ideal of perfect unity, cemented by party and police. Its integration was identical with its disintegration; it was perfectly integrated in that all forms of collective life were entirely subordinated to, and imposed by, one ruling center; and it was perfectly disintegrated for the same reason: civil society was virtually destroyed, and the citizens, in all their relations with the state, faced the omnipotent apparatus as isolated and powerless individuals. The society was reduced to the position of a "sack of potatoes" (to use Marx's phrase applied to French peasants in the *Eighteenth Brumaire*).

This situation—unified state organism facing atom-like individuals—defined all the important features of the Stalinist system. They are all well-known and described in my books. We should briefly mention a few of them, the most relevant to our topic.

First, the abolition of law. The law persisted, to be sure, in the sense of rules of procedure in public matters. It was entirely abolished, however (and never restored), in the sense of rules which could in any point infringe upon the state's omnipotence when dealing with individuals. In other words, the law was supposed to be such as to never restrict the principle that citizens are property of the state. The totalitarian law, in crucial points, has to be vague and imprecise, so that its actual application should hinge on the arbitrary and changing decisions of executive authorities and so that each citizen, at virtually any moment, could be considered a criminal. The notable examples have always been political crimes as defined in penal codes; they are constructed in such a way that it is virtually impossible for a citizen not to commit crimes almost every day; how far these crimes are actually prosecuted, or how much terror is employed, are a matter of the rulers' political decisions. In this respect nothing has changed in the post-Stalinian period: both the transition from mass to selective terror and the better observance of procedural rules are irrelevant to the persistence of characteristically totalitarian law, as long as they do not limit the effective power of the state over the lives of individuals. People may be actually jailed or not for telling political jokes; they may have their children forcibly taken away or not if the parents fail to raise them, as it is their legal duty, in the Communist spirit (whatever this means). Totalitarian lawlessness consists not in the fact that extreme measures are always and everywhere applied but in the fact that individuals have no protection in law against whatever forms of repression the state wants to use at any given moment; in the disappearance of law as a mediating device between the state and people and in its being converted into an entirely malleable instrument of the state. In this respect, Stalinist principle has not been abrogated by now.

Second, the one-person autocracy. It seems to have been a natural, "logical" outcome of the perfect-unity principle which was the driving force in the development of the totalitarian state. This state, to achieve its full shape, called for one and only one leader endowed with limitless power. This was implied in the very foundation of the Leninist party—conforming to the often-quoted prophecy of Trotsky (soon to be forgotten by the prophet) of 1903. The whole progress of the Soviet system in the twenties consisted in the step-by-step narrowing of the forum where conflicts of interests, of ideas, and of political tendencies could be expressed: for a short period, they still were articulated publicly in the society, then their field of expression moved up to the party, then to the party apparatus, to the Central Committee and eventually to the Politburo. Since, however, sources of social conflict could be prevented from being expressed, yet had not been eradicated, it was Stalin's well-grounded contention that even in this narrowest caucus the conflicting trends, if allowed to continue, would convey the pressure of the not-yet-killed conflicting interests within the civil society. This is why the destruction of the civil society could not be consummated so long as different tendencies or factions had room to articulate themselves, even in the supreme party organ.

The changes which occurred in the Soviet system after Stalin—the transition from personal tyranny to an oligarchy—seem to be the most salient in this particular point. They resulted from the incurable contradiction inherent in the system: perfect unity of leadership, as required by the system and embodied in personal despotism, was incompatible with other leaders' need for minimum security; they were degraded, under Stalin's rule, to the same precarious slave status as other people, and all of their enormous privileges did not protect them against sudden fall, imprisonment, and death. Oligarchical rule after Stalin became a sort of mutual security pact of the party apparatus. This contract, to the extent of its effective application, runs counter to the principle of unity. In this sense, the decades after Stalin's death may be properly spoken of as an ailing Stalinism.

It is not true, nonetheless, that Soviet society, even in the worst periods, has ever been ruled by the police. Stalin governed the country, and the party itself, with the police machine, yet he governed as party leader, not as police chief. The party—which for a quarter of a century was identical with Stalin—has never lost its all-embracing sway.

Third, the system of universal spying as the principle of government. That people were both encouraged and compelled to spy upon each other was obviously not how the state defended itself against real dangers but how it forced to the extreme the same principle of totalitarianism. As citizens, they were supposed to live in the perfect unity of goals, desires, and thought—all expressed through the mouth of the leader. As individuals, they were expected to hate each other and to live in never-ending mutual hostility. Only thus could the isolation of individuals from another achieve perfection. In fact, the unattainable ideal of the system seems to have been a situation where all people were at the same time inmates of concentration camps and secret police agents.

Fourth, the apparent omnipotence of ideology. In all discussions on Stalinism this is the point in which more confusion and disagreement appear than in any other. We can see it when we follow the exchange of statements on the subject by Solzhenitsyn and Sakharov, respectively. The former's point, roughly, is: The whole Soviet state, in both internal and foreign policy, in both economic and political matters, is under the overwhelming rule of the false Marxist ideology, and it is this ideology which is responsible for all disasters of the society and of the state. Sakharov replies that the official state ideology is dead and that nobody takes it seriously anymore; consequently, it is silly to imagine that it could be a real force guiding and shaping practical policies.

It seems that both observations are valid within certain restrictions. The point is that the Soviet state has had an ideology built in its foundation from the very beginning as the only principle of its legitimacy. It is true, to be sure, that the Bolshevik party seized power in Russia under ideological banners that had no specifically socialist, let alone Marxist, content (peace and land for peasants). But it could establish its monopolistic rule on the Leninist ideological principle, i.e., as a party which be definition was the only legitimate mouthpiece of the working class and of all "toiling masses," of their interests, will, and desires (would they be unknown to these masses themselves), and it owed its ability to "express" the will of the masses to its "correct" Marxist ideology. A party is supposed to be a voluntary organism tied together with ideological bonds. A party which wields despotic power cannot get rid of the ideology which justifies this power and remains, short of free elections or the inheritance of the monarchic charisma, the only basis of legitimacy. The ideology is absolutely indispensable in this system of rule, no matter by whom, by how many, or how seriously it is believed, and it remains such even if—as is now the case in European socialist countries—there are virtually no believers anymore, among either the rulers or the ruled. The leaders obviously cannot afford to express the real and notorious principles of their policy without risking the utter collapse of the power system. The state ideology believed by nobody has to be binding to all unless the entire fabric of the state is to crumble.

This does not mean that the ideological considerations cited to justify each step in practical policy are real, independent forces before which Stalin or other leaders bowed. Still, it would be unfair to say that they do not limit this policy to a certain extent. The Soviet system, both under and after Stalin, has always pursued the *Realpolitik* of a great empire, and the ideology was bound to be vague enough to sanctify any particular policy—NEP or collectivization, friendship with Nazis or war with Nazis, friendship with China or condemnation of China, support for Israel or for Israel's foes, cold war or detente, tightening or relaxation of the internal regime, oriental cult of the satrap or its denounciation. And still it is true that this is an ideology which keeps the Soviet state and preserves its integrity.

It has been frequently pointed out that the Soviet totalitarian system is not intelligible unless we take into account the historical background of Russia, with its strongly pronounced totalitarian traits. The autonomy of the state and its overwhelming preponderance over civil society was stressed by Russian historians of the nineteenth century, a view that was endorsed with qualifications by some Russian Marxists (Plekhanov, in his *History of Russian Social Thought;* Trotsky, in the *History of the Russian Revolution*). This background was repeatedly referred to—after the revolution—as the genuine source of Russian Communism (Berdyaev). Many authors (Kucharzewski was one of the first) saw in Soviet Russia a straight extension of the tsarist regime, including its expansionist policy and the insatiable hunger for new territories, and the "nationalization" of all citizens and the subordination of all forms of human activity to the state's goals. Several historians have published very convincing studies on the subject (recently, R. Pipes and T. Szamuely), and I do not question their findings. However, this background is not sufficient to explain the peculiar function Marxist ideology has had in the Soviet order. Even if we went so far as to admit (this is how Amalrik would have it) that the whole meaning of Marxism in Russia ultimately consisted in injecting into a shaky empire fresh ideological blood that would allow it to survive for a while before falling apart definitively, we would still have no answer to the question: How did Marxism fit into this task? How could the Marxist philosophy of history, with its ostensible hopes, aims, and values, supply the totalitarian, imperialist, and chauvinistic state with an ideological weapon?

It could, it did; and it did not need to be essentially distorted, just interpreted.

Stalinism as Marxism

In discussing this question, I take it for granted that Marx's thought from 1843 onwards was propelled by the same value-loaded idea for which he was continuously seeking a better and better form of expression. Thus I share the opinion of those who emphasize the strong continuity in Marx's intellectual development and do not believe in any more or less violent break in the growth of his leading ideas. I cannot argue now in favor of this controversial—albeit not original at all—viewpoint.

In Marx's eyes the original sin of man, his *felix culpa,* responsible for both great human achievements and human misery, was the division of labor with its inevitable result, alienation of labor. The extreme form of alienated labor is the exchange value which dominates the entire production process in the industrial societies. It is not human needs, but the endless accumulation of exchange value in money form, which is the main driving force of all productive efforts. It resulted in transforming human individuals, their personal qualities and abilities, into commodities that are being sold and bought according to anonymous laws of market, within the system of hired labor. It generated the alienated institutional framework of modern political societies, it produced an inevitable split between the personal, selfish, self-centered life of people in civil society on the one hand and their artificial and mystified community in political society on the other. As a result, human consciousness was bound to suffer an ideological distortion: instead of affirming human life and affirming its own function as an "expression" of life, it built an illusory separate kingdom of its own, designed to perpetuate the existing split. In bringing about private property and, consequently, the division of the society into hostile classes struggling for the distribution of the surplus product, the alienation of labor finally gave rise to the class which, being the concentration of the entire dehumanization, is destined both to demystify consciousness and to restore the lost unity of human existence. The revolutionary process starts with smashing institutional devices which protect the existing labor condition, and it ends with a society out of which all basic sources of social conflict have been removed and the social process subordinated to the collective will of associated individuals. The latter will be able to unfold all their individual potentialities not against the community but to enrich it, the necessary labor having been step by step reduced to the minimum and the free time exploited for the sake of cultural creativity and high-quality enjoyment.

The entire meaning of both past history and present struggles is revealed only in the romantic vision of the perfectly unified mankind of the future. This unity implies that people will not need mediating devices separating individuals from the species as a whole. The revolutionary act that will close the "pre-history" of mankind is both inevitable and directed by free will, the very distinction between freedom and necessity having disappeared in the consciousness of proletariat, a class which ruins the old order in the very process of becoming aware of its own historical destiny.

My suspicion is that this was both Marx's anticipation of perfect unity of mankind and his mythology of the historically privileged proletarian consciousness which were responsible for his theory's being eventually turned into an ideology of the totalitarian movement: not because he conceived of it in such terms, but because its basic values could hardly be materialized otherwise. It was not the case that Marx's theory lacked any vision of the future society; it did not. But even his powerful imagination was incapable of stretching as far as to envisage the transition from the "pre-history" to "genuine history" and to fancy a proper social technology which would convert the former into the latter. This gap was to be filled by practical leaders, and this necessarily implied that additions and specifications had to be done in the inherited body of the doctrine.

In dreaming of perfectly unified humanity Marx was not, properly speaking, a Rousseauist; Rousseau did not believe that the lost spontaneous identity of each individual with the community would ever be restored and the poison of civilization effaced from human memory in the future. Marx did believe precisely that: not as though a return to the primitive happiness of savagery and the jettison of civilization were possible or desirable, but because he believed that the irresistible progress of technology would ultimately overcome (dialectically) its own destructiveness and offer humanity a new unity based on freedom from wants, rather than the suppression of needs (in this respect he shared the Saint-Simonists' hopes).

Marx's liberated mankind does not need any machines set up by the bourgeois society in order to mediate and to regulate conflicts of individuals between each other or between each of them and the society; and this means: law, state, representative democracy, and negative freedom as conceived of and proclaimed in the Declaration of Human Rights. All these devices are typical of a society ruled economically by the market, made up of isolated individuals with their antagonistic interests, and trying to keep its stability with the help of these instruments. The state and its legal skeleton protect bourgeois property with coercive means and impose rules on conflicts; their very existence presupposes a society where human activities and desires naturally clash with each other. The liberal concept of freedom implies that "my" freedom inevitably limits the freedom of my fellow men, as it is the case indeed if the scope of freedom coincides with the size of ownership. Once the system of communal property replaces bourgeois order, these devices lose their ground. Individual interests converge with the universal ones; there is no need to support the unstable equilibrium of the society with regulations that define the limits of an individual's freedom. Not only "rational" instruments of the liberal society will be done away with: tribal or national ties inherited from the past will disappear soon in the same process, and in this respect the capitalist order paves the way for communism; old irrational loyalties are crumbling anyway, both under the cosmopolitan power of capital and as result of the internationalst consciousness of the proletariat. The end of this process will be a community where nothing is left except for individuals and the human species as a whole, and individuals will directly identify their own lives, their abilities, and their activities as social forces. Thus, to experience this identity they will need no mediation of political institutions or of traditional national ties.

How could this be achieved? Is there any technique of this social transubstantiation? Marx did not answer the question, and it seems that from his viewpoint the question was wrongly put. The point was not to look for the adequate technique of social engineering after having drawn an arbitrary picture of a desirable society, but to identify and to "express" theoretically social forces already at work, forces which tend toward such a society. And to express them meant to reinforce practically their energy, to provide them with indispensable self-knowledge, to let them consciously identify themselves.

Practical interpretation of the Marxian message offered different possibilities, depending on which values were considered fundamental to the doctrine and which formulations were supposed to give the clue to the whole. It does not seem that anything was wrong with the interpretation that would become a Leninist-Stalinist version of Marxism and may be reconstructed as follows:

Marxism is a ready-made doctrinal body which is the same as the class-consciouness of proletariat in its mature and theoretically elaborated form. Marxism is true both because of its "scientific" value and because it articulates the aspirations of the "most progressive" social class. The distinction between "truth" in the genetic and in the current sense of the word has always been obscure in the doctrine; it was taken for granted that the "proletariat," by virtue of its historical mission, has a privileged cognitive position, and thus that its vision of the social "totality" is bound to be right. And so what was supposed to be the "progressive" automatically became "true" whether or not this truth could be validated with universally admitted scientific procedures. This was a simplified form of the Marxian concept of class consciousness. Certainly, the claim of the party to be the monopolistic owner of truth did not automatically follow from that concept; such an equation required in addition the specifically Leninist notion of party. There was nothing anti-Marxist in this notion, however. If it is true that Marx did not work out any theory of party, he had a concept of a vanguard group that was supposed to articulate the latent consciousness of the working class, and he did conceive of his own theory as an expression of this consciousness. That the "proper" revolutionary consciousness of the working class had to be instilled from without into the spontaneous workers' movement was an idea taken up by Lenin from Kautsky and supplemented with an important addition: since in a society torn by the class struggle between the bourgeoisie and the proletariat only two basic ideologies can exist, it follows that an ideology which is not proletarian—i.e., which is not identical with vanguard-party ideology—is necessarily a bourgeois one. And thus, considering that the workers are unable to reach with their own forces their own class ideology, they are bound to produce a bourgeois one; in other words, what the empirical, "spontaneous" consciousness of workers can generate is essentially a bourgeois *Weltanschauung*. Consequently, the Marxist party is both the only vehicle of truth and entirely independent of the empirical (and, by definition, bourgeois) consciousness of workers (except for the fact that the party sometimes has to make tactical concessions in order not to run too far ahead of the proletariat if it canvasses for its support). The same remains valid after the seizure of power. Being the sole owner of truth, the party not only may completely discard (except in a tactical sense) the inevitably immature empirical consciousness of masses, but cannot do otherwise without betraying its historical mission. It knows both the "laws of historical development" and the proper connections between the "base" and the "superstructure"; therefore, it is perfectly able to discern what in the real, empirical consciousness of people deserves destruction as a "survival," a remnant of the past historical epoch. Not only do religious ideas obviously fall into this category, but so does everything that makes people's minds different in content from the minds of the leaders. The dictatorship over minds *is* entirely justified within this concept of proletarian consciousness; the party really knows better than the society which are the society's genuine (as opposed to empirical) desires, interests, and thoughts. Once the spirit of the party is perfectly incarnated in one leader (as the highest expression of society's unity), we have the ultimate equation: truth = proletarian consciousness = Marxism = party's ideology = party leaders' ideas = chief's decisions. The theory claiming for the proletariat a sort of cognitive privilege culminates in the statement that Comrade Stalin is never wrong. And there is nothing un-Marxist in this equation.

This concept of the party being the sole bearer of truth was strongly supported, of course, by the expression "dictatorship of the proletariat," which Marx used casually two or three times without explanation. Kautsky, Martov, or other Social Democrats could well argue that what Marx had meant by "dictatorship" had not been the form of government but its class content, and that he had not opposed "dictatorship" to a democratic state. But Marx did not specifically say anything of this sort in the context, and there was nothing obviously wrong in taking the word "dictatorship" at its face value, meaning precisely what Lenin meant and expressly said: a reign based entirely on violence and not limited by law.

Next to the question of the party's "historical right" to impose its despotism in all domains of social life, the question of the content of this despotism was solved basically in keeping with Marxian predictions. Liberated mankind was supposed to abolish the distinction between civil society and the state, to abrogate all mediating devices that prevented individuals from achieving the perfect identity with the "whole," to get rid of the bourgeois freedom that implied antagonisms of private interests, to demolish the system of hired labor that compelled workers to sell themselves like commodities. But Marx did not say exactly how to achieve this unity except for one indisputable point: the expropriation of expropriators, i.e., the abrogation of private ownership of the means of production. One could and ought to argue that once this historical act of expropriation has been performed, all remaining social conflicts are nothing else but the expression of a retarded (bourgeois) mentality which has survived from the old society. But the party knows what is the content of the correct mentality corresponding to the new relations of production, and it is naturally entitled to suppress all phenomena out of keeping with that content.

What technique, in fact, is appropriate to reach this desirable unity? Its economic foundation has been laid. One could argue that to Marx civil society was not to be suppressed or replaced by the state, but rather the state was expected to wither away; political government was to become superfluous and only the "administration of things" to remain. But once the state by definition is an instrument of the working class on its road to communism, it cannot by definition use its power against the "toiling masses," only against the relics of the capitalist society. And how could the "administration of things," or economic management, not involve the use and distribution of labor power, i.e., of all working people? Hired labor (and this means a free market of the labor force) was to be eliminated, and it was. But what if people do not want to work under the impetus of communist enthusiasm alone? If they do not, this obviously means that they are imprisoned in bourgeois consciousness, which it is the task of the state to destroy. Consequently, the workable way of abrogating hired labor is to replace it by coercion. How are we to implement the unity of civil and political society once only the political society expresses the "correct" will of the people? Whatever opposes that will is again, by definition, the resistance of the capitalist order; thus, the destruction of civil society by the state is the proper way toward unity. Whoever argues that people should be first educated to cooperate freely and without compulsion must answer the question: when and how can such an education be successful? It certainly runs counter to Marx's theory to expect that this education is possible within a capitalist society, where the working people are under the overwhelming influence of bourgeois ideology. (Did not Marx say that the ideas of the ruling class are ruling ideas? Is it not a pure utopia to hope for a total moral transformation of the society in a capitalist order?) And after the seizure of power, education is the task of the most enlightened vanguard of the society; compulsion is used only against the "survival of capitalism." And so there is no need to make the distinction between the production of the "new man" of socialism and sheer coercion; consequently, the distinction between liberation and slavery is bound to be blurred.

The question of freedom (in the "bourgeois" sense) becomes irrelevant to the new society. Did not Engels say that genuine freedom was to be defined as the extent to which people were capable of both subjugating their natural environment and consciously regulating social processes? If so, then, first, the more a society is technologically advanced, the freer it is; second, the more social life is submitted to unified direction, the freer it is. Engels did not mention that this regulation would necessarily involve free elections or other bourgeois contrivances of this sort. There is no reason to maintain that a society entirely regulated by one center of despotic power is not perfectly free in this peculiar meaning.

And there are many quotations from Marx and Engels to the effect that throughout human history the "superstructure" was at the service of the corresponding relations of property in a given society; that the state is "nothing else" but a tool to keep the existing relations of production intact; that the law cannot but be a weapon of a class power. There is nothing wrong in concluding that the same situation prevails, at least so long as communism in the absolute form has not entirely dominated the earth. In other words, the law is an instrument of the political power of the "proletariat," and since law is just a technique to wield power, and, more often than not, its main task is to cover violence and to deceive the people, it makes no difference whether the victorious class rules with the help of the law or without it; what matters is the class content of power and not its "form." Moreover, the conclusion seems quite valid that the new "superstructure" must serve the new "basis," which means, among other things, that cultural life as a whole should be entirely subordinated to political "tasks" as defined by the "ruling class" speaking through the mouth of its most conscious segment. Therefore it is arguable that universal servility as the guiding principle of cultural life in the Stalinist system was a proper deduction from the "basis-superstructure" theory. The same applies to the sciences; again, did not Engels say that the sciences could not be left to themselves, without theoretical philosophical guidance, lest they fall into all sorts of empiricist absurdities? This was in fact the reason many Soviet philosophers and party leaders used to evoke from the very beginning to vindicate for philosophy—i.e., party ideology—the right to control all the sciences (in their content, not only in their scope of interest). In the twenties Karl Korsch had already pointed out the obvious connection between the philosophy's claim to supremacy and the Soviet system of ideological tyranny over the sciences.

Many critical Marxists used to say, "This was a caricature of Marxism." I would not deny that. However, I would add that one may talk meaningfully about "caricature" only insofar as it resembles the original, as it does in this case. Nor would I deny the obvious fact that Marx's thought was much richer, much more differentiated, and much subtler than could be supposed on the basis of a few quotations endlessly reiterated in Leninist-Stalinist ideology to justify the Soviet system of power. Still, I would argue that these quotations were not essentially distorted; that the dry skeleton of Marxism, deprived of its complexity, was taken up by Soviet ideology as a strongly simplified, yet not falsified, guide to building a new society.

It is not Stalin's invention that the whole theory of communism may be summed up in the single phrase "abolition of private property"; or that there can no longer be any wage labor when there is no longer any capital; or that the state has to have centralized rule over all means of production; or that national hostilities are bound to disappear together with class antagonism. All these ideas, as we know, are clearly stated in the *Communist Manifesto*. Taken together they do not simply suggest but actually imply that once the factories and the land are state-owned—and this is what was to happen in Russia—the society is basically liberated; Lenin's, Trotsky's, and Stalin's claim was precisely that.

The point is that Marx really, consistently believed that human society would not be "liberated" without achieving unity. And, except for despotism, there is no other technique known to produce a unity of society; no other way of suppressing the tension between civil and political society but the suppression of civil society; no other means to remove the conflicts between the individual and "the whole" but the destruction of the individual; no other road toward "higher," "positive" freedom—as opposed to "negative," "bourgeois" freedom—but the liquidation of the latter. And if it were true that the whole of human history is to be conceived in class terms—that all values, all political and legal institutions, ideas, moral norms, religious and philosophical beliefs, artisitic creativity, etc., are "nothing else" but instruments at the service of "real" class interests (and there are many fragments to this effect in Marx's writings)—then it is true that the new society should start with breaking violently the cultural continuity with the old one. (The continuity, in fact, cannot be entirely broken, and in Soviet society a selective continuity was accepted from the beginning, the radical quest for "proletarian culture" having been only a short-lived extravagance, never sponsored by the leadership; the stress on selective continuity grew stronger with the development of the Soviet state, mostly as a result of its increasingly national-ist character.)

My suspicion is that utopias (meaning visions of a perfectly unified society) are not simply impracticable but become counter-productive as soon as we try to create them with institutional means; and this because institutionalized unity and freedom are opposed to each other, and a society that is deprived of freedom can be unified only in the sense that the expression of conflicts is stifled, not conflicts themselves, consequently, it is not unified at all.

I do not neglect the importance of changes that occurred after Stalin's death in the socialist countries, even if I maintain that the political constitution of these countries has remained intact. The point is that to admit, however reluctantly, a limited impact of the market on production, and to give up or to loosen rigid ideological control in certain areas of life, amounts to renouncing the Marxian vision of unity. All these changes reveal rather the impracticability of that vision and could hardly be interpreted as symptoms of a return to the "genuine" Marxism—no matter what Marx "would have said."

An additional—certainly not conclusive—argument in favor of the above inter-pretation lies in the history of the problem. It would be utterly false to say that "nobody could predict" such an upshot of Marxism humanist socialism. It actu-ally was predicted by anarchist writers, long before the socialist revolution, that a society based on Marx's ideological principles would produce slavery and despotism. At least in this respect mankind cannot complain that the Great History deceived and surprised it with unpredictable connections of things.

The question we have discussed is a "genetic versus environmental factors" problem in social development. It is very difficult to distinguish the respective role of these factors even in genetic inquiry, when the properties under investiga-tion are not precisely definable or if they are of a mental rather than physical character (e.g., "intelligence"). This is much more true in discussing the respec-tive weight of "genetic" and "environmental" circumstances in social inheritance (an inherited ideology versus contingent conditions in which people try to imple-ment it). It is commonsensical to state that in each particular case both factors are at work and that we have no way of calculating their relative importance and of expressing it in quantitative terms. To say that the "genes" (inherited ideology) were entirely responsible for the actual shape of the child would obviously be as silly as to state that this shape is to be exclusively accounted for by "environ-ment," i.e., contingent historical events (in the case of Stalinism, these two inadmissibly extreme interpretations are expressed respectively as a view that Stalinism was "nothing more than" Marxism in actuality, or "nothing more than" the continuation of the tsarist empire). Unable though we are to perform a computation and to devolve upon each set of factors its "fair share," we may reasonably ask whether or not the mature form was anticipated by "genetic" conditions.

The continuity I have tried to trace back from Stalinism to Marxism appears in still sharper outline when we discuss the transition from Leninism to Stalinism.

Not only was the general tendency of Bolshevism perceived and its outcome pretty accurately predicted just after 1917 by the non-Bolshevik factions (the Mensheviks, not to speak of the liberals); the despotic character of the new system was to be attacked soon within the party itself, long before Stalinism was definitively established (the "Workers' Opposition," then the Left Opposition, e.g., Rakovsky). Trotsky's belated rejoinder to the Mensheviks, who in the thirties saw all their predictions borne out ("We told you so") is pathetically unconvincing; all right, he argued, they did predict what would happen, yet they were entirely wrong; they believed that despotism would come as a result of Bolshevik rule; now it has come, but as the result of a bureaucratic coup. *Qui vult decipi, decipiatur.*

Stalinism and Marxism

Mihailo Marković

Does Stalinism have any roots in Marxism, and, if it does, how strong and significant are they?

This is by no means a purely theoretical, value-free question. "Stalinism" stands for so much political abuse, terror, and criminal regression that one would reasonably expect strong motives both to link it as firmly as possible with Marxism and, on the other hand, to disassociate the two altogether. The more conservative a theoretician is, the more eager he would spontaneously be to transfer a part of this odious emotional connotation from Stalinism to Marxism and to explicate the latter in such a way as to almost analytically derive the view that the former was nothing but its necessary theoretical and practical consequence. On the other hand, radical scholars, who keep considering Marx's thought the theoretical horizon of the whole epoch, will be tempted to see in Stalinism a completely deviating, independent, and irrelevant phenomenon which can be fully accounted for in terms of the very specific conditions of a backward, semi-feudal, semi-Asiatic Russia.

In order to make the issue more rationally debatable and more theoretically interesting, "Stalinism" should be taken in a more general sense—as a phenomenon that transcends the lifetime of the man Stalin and the national boundaries of Russia, as a very widespread and strong tendency of solving ideological and practical questions within the contemporary labor movement and especially after the victorious socialist revolution took place. The concept of Stalinism would lose its informative value if it were generalized so much that it covered any authoritarian form of revolutionary movement, post-revolutionary society, and its political culture. After all, there is hardly any that is non-authoritarian; and yet it would be misleading to identify Chinese, Cuban, or Yugoslav societies and their dominating ideological trends with Stalinism. On the other hand, what the term refers to exists as a more or less strong trend almost all over the world, and in all likelihood would have existed even if the man from whom the name was borrowed and who exemplified the trend in the most complete and drastic form had never lived.

The Concept of Stalinism

I shall take the following characteristics to be necessary and sufficient conditions of Stalinism:

(1) Commitment to a violent anti-capitalist revolution which *does not develop beyond* the replacement of the political power of bourgeoisie by the power of *political bureaucracy* and of private property by *state ownership* of the means of production.

(2) The leading force of the revolution and the backbone of the post-revolutionary society is a *monolithic, strongly disciplined, strictly hierarchical party* which has a *monopoly* of all economic and political power and *reduces all other* social organizations to its *mere transmissions.*

(3) The state tends to exist even after the complete liquidation of a capitalist class. Its primary new function is a *rigid administrative* planning of all production and complete control of all political life. The state is officially a dictatorship of the working class; in reality it is *dictatorship of the party leadership or of one single leader.*

(4) The new society is construed as a *collectivist welfare* society in which most forms of *economic and political alienation* would survive.

(5) As a consequence of the centralist political and economic structure, smaller nations in a multi-national country are *denied self-determination* and continue to be *dominated* by the biggest nation.

(6) *All culture is subordinated to the sphere of politics* and is strictly controlled and censored by the ruling party.

The proper question to be aked whenever someone attempts to define a complex social phenomenon or to build up an "ideal type" referring to a cluster of heterogeneous attitudes and beliefs is: Does the given definition or "ideal type" adequately describe a segment of reality; are there such social forces that could be qualified as "Stalinist" in accordance with the given explication?

The answer would have to be affirmative. A considerable part of the explication fully coincides with the official views of a number of contemporary Communist parties: A most militant critique of capitalism goes together with complete endorsement and uncritical, enthusiastic acceptance of the new forms of political society—of the state, the standing army, political police, centralistic administrative decision-making, ruthless political repression of heretical intellectuals, disillusioned peasants, national liberation activists. That a centralistic authoritarian party should assume an overall control of all social activities is recognized as a necessary feature of socialism.

The purpose of revolution is actually seen in accelerated technological development, increase of the material standard of living, and abolition of *capitalist* exploitation—without any critical consciousness of the existence of *bureaucratic* exploitation. And this is the central element of ideological mystification in Stalinism: the obviously alienated repressive political power of the top party leadership is hailed as the genuinely revolutionary and most democratic political structure in the whole preceding history.

If Stalinism exists in the sense given by the preceding explication, what is the nature of its link with Marxism? There is no controversy about the existence of such a link, obviously mediated by Lenin and Leninism. There is no controversy about the fact that Stalin and Stalinists have been or are participants in revolutionary movements, that to some extent they were inspired by Marx and Engels and more specifically by Lenin, and that some of their activities have been contributing to radical social changes in the twentieth century.

The starting point for all Russian Bolsheviks, including Stalin, was the deep conviction that Russian semi-feudal society was in hopeless stagnation; that the Russian bourgeoisie was not able to overthrow tsardom, to introduce bourgeois-democratic reforms and secure a rapid economic and social growth; that, therefore the relatively small but concentrated and militant Russian proletariat, together with the peasantry, should seize power and make an accelerated industrialization possible. Marxian socialism was the ultimate goal for them, but they knew that this goal was distant. Conditions in Russia were quite different from those that Marx specified as the necessary conditions of socialist revolution: Russia was still a predominantly rural society, ruled by feudal landlords, without any bourgeois-democratic institutions or traditions, with little likelihood that the weak bourgeois liberals (the kadet party) would turn into vigorous fighters for modernization and progress. That is why the Bolsheviks believed that their party had a double historical responsibility: first, the task of securing an accelerated material, political, and cultural development, and, later, the task of building up a new socialist society.

And this still is the paradigm case of revolution in a backward country. The Leninist adaptation of Marxism, with its idea of the two different stages of revolution—with its conception of a centralized, monolithic, highly disciplined cadre party—was and still is a revolutionary alternative for underdeveloped countries. However, any serious Marxist study of this type of historical situation cannot but establish that this kind of revolution has to last for decades, and that it gives rise to a considerably authoritarian, mixed type of society with state ownership of the means of production and rigid bureaucratic control of all social life. This society is not yet socialism but, at best, the ground for its development. Consequently Leninism is not so much a further development of Marxism but rather a theory about the creation of historical conditions in backward semi-feudal societies under which Marxism would be applicable and socialism built up. Stalinism, on the other hand, stops that whole process at a certain point. By destroying the last remnants of inner party democracy, by converting the party and the state into instruments of tyrannical personal power, by freezing all relations of production at an early state-capitalist level it definitely assumes a counter-revolutionary character.

Therefore, the view that Stalinist ideology and practice is *the contemporary form of Marxism* or that it is a *necessary* practical consequence of Marxist theory is utterly untenable. It is quite remarkable that three completely different kinds of people, for completely different motives, hold this view. *First,* Stalinists themselves over-emphasize this connection with both Marxism and Leninism for the purpose of legitimization. They are never tired of quoting passages from the three great classics, whose scrupulous and devoted followers they pretend to be. *Second,* most conservative political scholars insist on an identity or necessary link between the two in order to make Marxism as disreputable and despicable as

Stalinism has been ever since the Great Purges and Khruschev's revelations. Third, former Stalinists, who never understood very much of Marx's humanism, in their efforts to get rid of their past still behave in accordance with their former faith, mixing up all four great classics and treating them equally. It will be easy to show that the whole philosophical background of Marx's critique of capitalist production, of the state, politics, law, and the whole of bourgeois culture was to Stalin and his followers a book with seven seals. The critique of alienation and the idea of universal human emancipation was neither grasped nor taken seriously by them—therefore they missed the whole point of socialist revolution and of the building up of a new communist society. By missing the point they wasted a real possibility of radical liberation and humanization. The realization of that optimal historical possibility, the creation of a society without oppression and exploitation presupposed a high degree of material and cultural development, a high degree of consciousness. Its necessary condition was the existence of a universal emancipatory class *for itself.* What took place in the absence of such a class and such a consciousness was a banal substitution of one ruling elite for the other, of one political society for the other. Stalinism is the product of such an abortive revolution.

However, arguments against the identification of Stalinism and Marxism do not constitute a sufficient ground for drawing the conclusion that the link between the two is altogether contingent or that they are quite disparate phenomena. For several decades Stalinism was able to preserve the appearance of the legitimate heir of Marxism not only because of similar rhetoric but also because it offered easy and simple solutions to some inherent contradictions of Marxism or built up its specific theories on issues where Marx remained vague and ambiguous. To illustrate this point it would suffice to compare Marx's and Stalin's views on the early stage of socialist development.

Both say that in the process of socialist revolution the proletariat becomes the ruling class, the means of production are socialized, and produced goods are distributed according to work.

But Marx considers the seizure of political power only "the *first step* in the revolution," and he calls it, curiously enough, "winning the battle of *democracy.*" The dictatorship of the proletariat is at the same time a "democracy." The state is "the proletariat organized as the ruling class." He speaks about "despotic inroads on the rights of property" in the beginning. But the purpose is to "entirely revolutionize the mode of production." [1] In the new society just as it *emerges* from capitalist society, individuals are regarded only as workers and are remunerated only according to their work—which is still the narrow horizon of bourgeois right. [2] "When in the course of development class distinctions have disappeared and all production has been concentrated in the hands of a *vast association of the whole nation,* the public power will *lose its political character.*

---

1. Marx and Engels, "Manifesto of the Communist Party" in *The Marx-Engels Reader,* ed. Robert C. Tucker (New York, 1972), p. 352.

2. Marx, "Critique of the Gotha Program," in *Marx-Engels Reader,* p. 388.

In place of the old bourgeois society, with its classes and class antagonisms, we shall have an association in which the free development of each is the condition for the free development of all." [3] Then society will inscribe on its banners, "From each according to his ability, to each according to his needs!" [4]

There are a number of unsolved problems and unanswered questions in these famous and indeed brilliant sentences. How is it possible for the whole proletariat to rule, especially taking into account its misery, illiteracy, degradation by the very process of labor? Why ever are words "dictatorship" and "despotic" used? Is the worker's *state* property *eo ipso social* property? How will the state ever be transformed into a free association of the whole nation? How will all human needs ever be satisfied? We shall have to return to some of these problems.

In Stalin everything is quite simple. There are no contradictions because there is no longer any interest in historical development. "The basis of the relations of production in the socialist order, which has so far been realized only in the USSR, is the social ownership on the means of production," which implies that state property is identical with social property. This social ownership of the means of production is "in complete harmony with social character of the process of production"; there is no need, therefore, for any "revolutionizing of the whole mode of production" (as in Marx), and there is no structural difference between the early stage which "just emerged from capitalist society" and a communist society "as it has developed on its own foundations." In this later stage, if one ever reaches it, according to Marx "all production is concentrated in the hands of a vast association of the whole nation" and "the public power loses its *political* character"—whatever this might mean. But when Stalin characterizes human relationships in the process of production he never allows a possibility of worker's participation in decision-making, or their actual running of production and "state" affairs. The only thing he mentions is "comradely cooperation" and "socialist solidarity of producers." The principle of remuneration according to work—which, as we have just seen, is a living contradiction, authorizing a principle of bourgeois inequality as a means to reach communist equality—has been given an utterly simple and vulgar interpretation: "The produced goods are distributed according to work, following the principle: Who does not work should not eat." [5] The riddle—how to reconcile the individual's commitment to his class, to the revolutionary movement, to the interests of society as a whole, with personal freedom, with the basic emancipatory goal of individual self-realization—this riddle no longer exists for Stalin. As early as his youthful work *Anarchism or Socialism* he had decided that the principle of liberation of a person as a condition for the liberation of collectives, of the whole mass, is a key principle of *anarchism.* The key principle of Marxism, on the contrary, says Stalin in 1906, is the mass. Liberation of an individual is not possible before liberation

---

3. "Manifesto of the Communist Party," pp. 352–53.
4. "Critique of the Gotha Program," p. 388.
5. *History of the Federal Communist Party (of the Bolsheviks),* Chap. IV, Sec. 3 ("Historical Materialism").

of the mass, therefore the slogan of Marxism is "Everything for the mass." [6]

The purpose of this comparison of Marx's and Stalin's views is only to illustrate the main thesis of this paper:

Stalinism and Marxism differ essentially both in their critique of capitalist society and in their approach to socialism. However, Stalinism has some roots in Marxism, not only genetically but also in sofar as it offers a simple and invariably conservative, ahistorical interpretation of a number of puzzles present in Marx's theory.

The Critique of Capitalism and the Nature of Socialist Revolution in Marx and Stalin

Marx's critique of capitalism is very deep and radical, embracing structures of different levels of generality and reaching the very basic roots of irrationality and dehumanization present in that system.

The level of critique closest to the surface is constituted by the description of the empirically observable forms of capitalist oppression, exploitation, workers' misery, ideological manipulation, moral corruption, and suppression of revolutionary movements in *individual capitalist countries:* England, France, Germany.

At the next deeper level one finds in Marx's writings the critique of capitalism as *a particular form* of class society. Society is split into "political" and "civil" society. Political society is the sphere of the state, where in the name of apparent general social interest an apparatus of force tries to preserve law and order in the interest of the ruling bourgeois class. Civil society is the sphere of individual and group egoism, of the *bellum omnium contra omnes.*[7] Because of private ownership of the means of production, a vast amount of unpaid workers' product is being appropriated by the capitalist owners, and this constitutes the essence of capitalist exploitation. Under conditions of capitalist domination and production for profit, the productive forces cannot develop beyond a certain limit, and the whole system must break down.

However, capitalism is only one particular form of class society. A deeper level of Marx's analysis is constituted by his critique of every society that is based on *commodity production,* regulation by the *market,* and domination of living labor by *dead, stored-up labor;* every society in which public power has a *political* character. A necessary consequence of all commodity production is *reification* of human relationships: relationships among producers in the process of production and exchange assume the form of relations among products of labor. The social features of human activity assume the appearance of the natural features of the *objects.*[8] In such a way human relationships are mystified and people lose control over their own work. Production is regulated not by human consciousness about their real needs but by blind forces that prevail on the market.

To the extent that market-regulated commodity production survives in the

---

6. Stalin, *Anarchism or Socialism,* Introduction.

7. Marx, "On the Jewish Question," in *Writings of the Young Marx on Philosophy and Society,* ed. Easton and Guddat (Gasden City, N.Y., 1967) p. 227.

8. Marx, *Capital,* Vol. 1, Book 1, Sec. 4.

initial stages of post-capitalist society Marx's critical remarks retain their full relevancy and validity: Marx is critical of the situation in bourgeois society wherein "living labor is but a means to increase accumulated labor," wherein, consequently, "the past dominates the present." [9]

It follows, then, that as long as past, accumulated labor remains at the disposal of just one particular social group—be it bourgeoisie or state bureaucracy—the present living labor, that is, the working class, is dominated by it. And what preserves and reinforces this domination is the fact that the citizens do *not* run society either directly or through their elected, rotatable, and replaceable representatives—public power has a *political* character, i.e., it is mediated by a sphere of professional decision-making and external state control. It turns out, then, that this deeper structure of Marx's critique has preserved its actuality for the entire period of either "state socialism" or "socialist market economy."

This holds even more for the deepest infrastructure of Marx's critique: analysis of *alienated* human activity. All injustices and social evils of either pre-capitalist socioeconomic formations or capitalism or "state socialism" have their ultimate basis in the fact that man has lost control over the products of his own work, that he has been wasting his capacity for creative activity, that due to incessant competition and conflict he has estranged himself from other human beings and from himself. This critique of human condition is the root *(radex)* of all other critique; therefore, only such an anthropologically founded critique is really radical and really far-reaching.

Stalin's critique is very simple and superficial in comparison. It entirely lacks the latter two levels: the critique of the domination of living labor by accumulated labor, and the critique of alienation (alienated labor, alienated politics). Consequently, it lacks precisely those most basic humanist elements of Marx's critique which are still relevant not only for capitalism but also for the Stalinist society of the transition period.

Stalin's critique deals only with those features of capitalism which are associated with private ownership of the means of production, over-emphasizing in such a way the discontinuity between capitalism and the system existing at that time in the Soviet Union.

In addition to commonplaces about the conflict between the productive forces and the relations of production, the pauperization of the vast masses of small producers and crises of hyperproduction,[10] Stalin repeats the basic elements of Lenin's theory of imperialism: (1) The domination of the financial capital increases the exploitation of the workers and their spirit of revolt. (2) Capitalism becomes a world system of colonial oppression. (3) The struggle for the redistribution of the spheres of influence leads to conflicts among the capitalists themselves and makes imperialist wars inevitable.[11]

---

9. "Manifesto," p. 347. ("The rule of capital over the worker is merely the rule of things over man, of dead over live labor." *Marx-Engels-Archiv* [Moscow, 1933] p. 68.)

10. *History of the Communist Party of the Soviet Union (Bolsheviks),* Short Course (New York: International Publishers, 1939), Chap. IV, Sec. 2.

11. Stalin, *"The Foundations of Leninism,"* in *Problems of Leninism* (Moscow, 1945), pp. 15–16.

At the more concrete, empirical level Stalin's critique deals with specific conditions in Russia. Russia has been described as the nexus of all contradictions of imperialism. There the domination of capital went together with the despotism of tsarism and aggressive Russian nationalism. Tsarist Russia was the greatest reserve of Western imperialism in the sense of providing both a huge army for counter-revolutionary interventions and a vast area of economic expansion for the international system of capitalism. In alliance with the Western imperialist countries Russia led aggressive wars and took part in the divisions of Turkey, Persia, and China. The interests of tsardom and Western imperialism were so interlinked that the revolution against tsardom had to grow into a proletarian revolution.[12]

The less profound and radical the critique of capitalism is, obviously the less profound and radical the idea of socialist revolution. If capitalism is seen only as a particular social system and not *also* as an instance of a deeper structure of class domination due to the state's disposal of the total accumulated past labor, and, furthermore, as merely an instance of universal human alienation and reification, then the whole idea of revolution will be very narrow and restrictive.

There are three important aspects in which Marxist and Stalinist conceptions of the socialist revolution are essentially different. These are: (1) the objectives of revolution, (2) the conditions under which revolution is possible, (3) the nature of the negation of capitalism.

(1) The Stalinist conception of revolutionary goals is indeed so narrow that it actually blocks the revolutionary process at a very early stage and transforms what promised to be a profound universal liberation and humanization into a mere substitution of one particular system for another.

In Marx's view, the proletariat will be forced to a revolution "by the contradiction between its *humanity* and its situation, which is an open, clear, and absolute negation of its humanity." [13] Therefore Marx never reduced revolution to a merely political or even economic change. As early as 1843, in his article *On the Jewish Question,* Marx made a sharp distinction between *human* emancipation and *political* emancipation: "Political emancipation is . . . a dissolution of the old society upon which the sovereign power, the alienated political life of the people rests." But at the same time it is "a reduction of man, on the one hand, to a member of civil society, to an *independant* and *egoistic* individual, on the other, to a *citizen,* to a moral person." [14]

However, "human emancipation will be complete only when the real individual man has absorbed in himself the abstract citizen, when, as an individual man, in his everyday life, in his work, and in his relationships, he has become *a social being,* and when he has recognized and organized his own powers *(forces propres)* as social powers, and consequently no longer separates this social power from himself as *political* power." [15]

---

12. Ibid., pp. 16–19.
13. Marx, "The Holy Family," in *Marx-Engels-Gesamt-Ausgabe (MEGA),* Vol. I/3, pp. 205–6.
14. Marx, "On the Jewish Question," *MEGA* Vol. I/1, 1, pp. 596, 599.
15. Ibid.

Although the paradigm of political emancipation for Marx in this early period is French bourgeois revolution, the formulation is broad enough to cover any other purely *political* liberation. It inevitably splits every individual into a *private* person, free to express his egoism in the sphere of private, everday life, and the *citizen,* who in the sphere of public life observes certain *political* norms and has his relationships with other individuals regulated by *law.* This split is very characteristic for a Stalinist society precisely because it has not gone much beyond the political revolution. In his writings in 1844 Marx somewhat changed his vocabulary and made a clear distinction between *political* and *social* revolution: "Every revolution breaks up the *old society;* to this extent it is *social.* Every revolution overthrows the existing ruling power; to this extent it is political." [16]

The worker in capitalism is excluded from political life—he has no say in political decision-making. The overthrow of the political power of the bourgeoisie could make the worker a political subject. But he is also *shut out* of *social* life because he is completely absorbed by a mechanical, degrading labor. "As the irremediable exclusion from this life is much more complete, more unbearable, dreadful, and contradictory than the exclusion from political life, so is the ending of this exclusion, and even a limited reaction, a *revolt* against it, more fundamental, as *man* is more fundamental than the citizen, *human life* more than *political life.* The industrial revolt may thus be limited, but it has a universal significance; the *political* revolt may be universal, but it conceals under a gigantic form a *narrow* spirit." [17]

This description fits Stalinism marvelously: "under a gigantic form a narrow spirit." Marx indicates that any one-sided political thinking brings about the following three detrimental consequences: First: A narrow, purely political approach goes invariably with the view that improvement of the workers' social conditions can be achieved by a mere overthrow of the existing form of government. "Because the proletariat thinks politically it sees the source of bad social conditions in *will* and all the means of improvement in *force* and in the overthrow of a particular form of state." Therefore workers waste their forces "on foolish and futile uprisings which are drowned in blood." [18]

Second: Over-emphasis on political goals conceals more profound and more important social goals. The French workers' "political understanding obscured from them the roots of their social misery; it distorted their insight into their real aims and *eclipsed* their social instinct." [19]

Third and most important: Reduction of a revolution to its merely political aspect leads to the emergence of a new ruling group: "A revolution of a political kind also organizes, therefore, in accordance with this narrow and *discordant* outlook, a ruling group in society at the expense of society." [20] This is an amazing

---

16. Marx, "Kritische Randglossen zu den Artickel: Der König von Preussen und die Sozialreform. Von einem Preussen" (*Vorwärts,* August 10, 1844), in *MEGA,* Vol. I/3, p. 22.

17. Ibid., p. 21.

18. Ibid., p. 20

19. Ibid.

20. Ibid., p. 22

anticipation of the emergence of political bureaucracy after the narrowly conceived twentieth-century revolutions.

The view that socialist revolution must basically have the character of universal human emancipation, that political revolution must only be the first episode of a much more thoroughgoing social revolution which will transcend any political power as such, was altogether absent from Stalin's conception of revolution.

He speaks about the October Revolution as an event of limited duration: as early as 1924 he speaks about it as something finished and belonging to the past.[21] In an article written for *Pravda* on the occasion of the tenth anniversary of the October uprising [22] Stalin gave the following list of its achievements: (1) The means of production were expropriated from the capitalists and landlords and transformed into social property. (2) Political power was seized from the hands of bourgeoisie and given to the soviets. The bourgeois state apparatus was destroyed; bourgeois parliamentarism as the form of capitalist democracy was opposed by the power of the soviets as the form of *proletarian* democracy. (3) The destruction of the old bourgeois society was followed by the building up of a new socialist one—and Stalin's description of this creation of the new society is characteristic: "building up of the party, the trade unions, the soviets, cooperatives, cultural organizations, transportation, industry, Red Army." (4) All oppressed people of the huge Russian state were liberated; new relationships of mutual confidence and brotherhood among workers and peasants of various nations of the USSR were established, in the name of *internationalism.*

That this is only a fragment of Marx's program of revolution is quite obvious. And even this scanty description of the achievements of the first decade of the revolution has very strong ideological elements. State ownership of the means of production has been construed as social property. The soviets, the initial organs of genuine proletarian democracy, by 1927 no longer had any real political power (which at that time was entirely in the hands of the party and state apparatus). The non-Russian nations which were really liberated from the oppression of the Russian tsars found themselves dominated by the Russian political bureaucracy. And the vast project of building up a new society has been reduced to two simple tasks: creation of new institutions (party, trade unions, soviets, Red Army) and accelerated industrialization.

The emphasis on the issue of political power is enormous. According to Stalin, "The question of the dictatorship of proletariat is the question of the *basic content* of the proletarian revolution." [23] And he offers the following interpretation of Lenin's phrase "The basic question of the revolution is the question of power": The main problem is not seizing power but preserving it, solidifying it, making it invincible. This trend of thought is completely opposite from that of Marx.

---

21. Stalin, "The October Revolution and the Tactic of Russian Communists," in *Problems of Leninism* (Moscow, 1945), pp. 94–95, 111–13.

22. Stalin, "The International Character of the October Revolution" (*Pravda,* November 6–7, 1927), in *Problems of Leninism,* pp. 199–204.

23. Stalin, "Foundations of Leninism," p. 39.

Marx thought that the state, the police, the standing army have to begin to disappear immediately after the seizure of power. For Stalin it was necessary to continue to strengthen political power and to conceive the dictatorship of the proletariat as the whole historical "epoch" of "transition from capitalism to communism." [24]

What was the *economic* dimension of the revolution for Stalin and Stalinists? Where Marx thought of profound change of human relationships and of the very nature of economic activity (abolition of alienated labor, abolition of the fetishism of commodities, transcendence of the narrow professional division of labor, reduction of working hours and liberation of time for free, creative, non-economic activity, etc.) Stalinism saw only the need for centralization of all productive powers in the hands of the state, rigid administrative planning, and accelerated technological development. None of this is specifically socialist. The only really socialist element is the abolition of capitalist exploitation as a consequence of the liquidation of the capitalists as a class. But the Stalinist concepts both of revolution and of socialism are quite compatible with the preservation of another concealed form of exploitation: To the extent to which workers retain the status of wage-earners and have no part in economic-decision making, to the extent to which the means of production have not been really socialized but remain at the disposal of a particular social group (the political bureaucracy), although not owned by it, exploitation, in the form of the material privileges of the bureaucracy, remains an ever-present possibility.

(2) As to the conditions of revolutionary change, Marx held that a genuine socialist revolution was possible only after its preconditions were developed within capitalist society. That was by no means a pedantic doctrinaire demand, nor did it imply a passive attitude of waiting until all conditions were ripe. A high level of technological development was necessary for a number of reasons: first, in order to overcome general poverty, to develop a wealth of needs, and to satisfy them on a mass scale and not only for a privileged elite; second, in order to overcome small production, which spontaneously gives birth to bourgeois relations; third, in order to create a modern industrial proletariat, a compact, well-organized, educated class, the only social force objectively interested in radical change of all social relationships; fourth, in order to transform thousands of concrete, personal master-slave relations into very abstract, impersonal forms of class struggle where the oppressor appears in the form of a few all-embracing institutions and the task of liberation no longer involves physical or social "liquidation" of all those little masters, but rather assuming control of institutions. In a comparable way a preceding bourgeois-democratic revolution and a developed political system of bourgeois liberalism is a necessary condition of socialist democracy: it is difficult to be in charge of basic social decision-making if one has not yet even attained the stage of being a citizen and having some elementary civil rights and responsibilities; it is difficult, if not impossible, to organize a democratic revolutionary movement in a country where some basic political

---

24. Ibid, p. 41.

freedoms, no matter how formal, have not been recognized and implemented; it is difficult to reach higher levels of equality in a society which has never practically experienced the most abstract and elementary one: equality before the law.

Marx did not think that human beings are condemned to wait until the blind forces of capitalism grind to a halt. They can make shortcuts, accelerate development, get indispensible experience through revolutionary actions such as the Paris Commune, use some specific old collectivist forms that capitalism has not yet destroyed as points of support in the struggle for the new society (for example, the old Russian community, the *mir*). But Marx did not think that real transcendence of private property and of alienation is possible in a backward society. Backward societies will give rise to "crude, unreflective communism"; there "the domination of material property looms so large that it aims to destroy everything which is incapable of being possessed by everyone as private property." The role of worker is not abolished but "extended to all men; the private capitalist is replaced by "the community as universal capitalist." Further characteristics of such a society are: "universal envy and leveling," negation of man's personality in every sphere, "abstract negation of the whole world of culture and civilization, and the regression to the unnatural simplicity of the poor and wantless individual who has not only not surpassed private property but has not yet even attained to it." [25]

The trouble with Stalin is not so much that he believed that what he called socialism was possible in one relatively backward country. If Marx was able to refer to the primitive collectivist society just described as "communist," why should not Stalin have referred to the Soviet society that had emerged after the First Five-Year Plan as "socialist"? But Marx called this form of communism (and theorizing about communism) "crude, unreflective." Whereas Stalin asserted that socialism (in his sense of the word, as it existed at that moment in Russia) was the most developed existing form of a democratic society. He said that what distinguished the draft of the new Constitution of the USSR from bourgeois constitutions was the fact that it was free from all reservations and restrictions concerning the equality of rights of citizens and democratic freedoms! "The Constitution of the USSR is the only thoroughly democratic constitution in the world. . . . There are no longer any antagonistic classes in society: . . . society consists of two friendly classes, of workers and peasants; . . . it is these . . . laboring classes that are in power; . . . the guidance of society . . . is in the hands of the working class." Workers dispose of the means of production —any possibility of exploitation is precluded.[26] Thus the real trouble with Stalin is that he associated the term "socialism" with both an undeveloped, authoritation society and an apologetic, utterly mystifying description of that society. Whereas, in fact, because of general backwardness:

---

25. Marx, "Economic and Philosophical Manuscripts," in *Marx's Concept of Man,* ed. Erich Fromm (New York, 1961), pp. 124 ff.

26. Stalin, "On the Draft Constitution of the USSR," in *Problems of Leninism,* pp. 550, 557.

• Poverty and great scarcity in material goods went together with elitist material privileges like in the preceding class society.

• Small production continued to generate bourgeois relations, which was the most important excuse for the political bureaucracy to perpetuate its rule under the disguise of the dictatorship of the proletariat.

• The peasants, not the workers, constituted the vast majority of the population, and while they were very eager to get the land, they were never enthusiastic about life and work in *kolkhozy;* there are few cases of passive resistance on such a mass scale in all of modern history.

• Because the master-slave relationship in a concrete, personal form has not been transcended until this very day, there was an immense amount of both revolutionary and counter-revolutionary violence, and only now is Soviet society entering a period when the basic impediments to liberation are abstract impersonal institutions and not tsars, Kerenskys, or Stalins.

• Because bourgeois democracy was declared formal and obsolete before it was attained, the freedom of the citizen has virtually been reduced to finding out and conforming to the necessity imposed by the political leadership.

(3) Marx's negation of capitalism is structurally different from Stalin's. Marx is aware that capitalism is an indispensable step in history: it enormously developed human productivity and human knowledge, and it created a wealth of human needs, although in alienated form. Therefore, whatever its limitations, bourgeois society also carries with it some results of genuine past creativity. While the former have to be abolished, the latter are of universal human importance and have to be preserved in the new communist society. Thus Marxist negation has the character of a genuine transcendence *(Aufhebung)* and of a moment of historical totalization.

Stalin's thinking, on the contrary, is historic in a most superficial way: there is a change from one particular form to the other but there is nothing universally human that evolves and emerges in ever richer specific forms. His contrasts are dualistic, completely lacking mediation. Capitalism is simply evil, oppressive, full of contradictions; socialism is progressive, harmonious, free of any essential inner limitations. Both total negation of the one and unreserved affirmation of the other are purely ideological.

The Roots of Stalinism in Unsolved Problems of Marxism

In the following analysis of the defining characteristics of Stalinism the essential difference from Marxism will only be indicated; the emphasis will be on showing how Stalinism was able to present itself as the legitimate successor of Marxism, emerging on the ground of its unsolved contradictions and ambiguities.

(1) Stalinism, as we have seen, reduces the revolution to the substitution of state property for private property and of bureaucratic political power for bourgeois political power. That is vastly different from Marx's conception. But it seeks its ground in the following two ambiguities in Marx.

First of all, he uses the term "private property" in two different senses. In a most profound philosophical sense, private property is a general human attitude toward the world that is characterized by the desire to *own* an object (or a person reduced to a thing) in order to be able to enjoy it, to appropriate it. A necessary condition of human emancipation is the supersession of that attitude. To be what one *could be* is much more important than to have what one *could have;* full appropriation of an object does not presuppose owning it. Another meaning of the term "private property" is much more widely known; it is ownership of the means of production. To say that abolition of private property is essential characteristic of socialist revolution makes sense from the standpoint of Marxist humanism if the term "private property" is taken in the first, more general, less well-known meaning. If it is taken in the second, more empirical, more widely-known meaning, it coincides with Stalinism; in that case a mere nationalization constitutes a revolution.

There is a comparable ambiguity in Marx's use of the term "politics." In earlier, more philosophical writings all politics was classified as a sphere of alienation; therefore, the great task of revolution is to abolish the *political* character of public power. Beginning with the *Manifesto of the Communist Party* Marx speaks about "the conquest of political power by the proletariat." Either he is here using "political" in a more neutral, descriptive meaning (in the sense of any power to regulate, coordinate, direct processes of general social importance) or the question arises: How will this alienated power in the hands of workers' representatives ever be dismantled? Will not this power gradually alienate these representatives from the people whom they are supposed to represent? Stalin simply accepted the descriptive and eliminated the critical concept of politics, which totally distorted Marx's whole theory of proletarian revolution and of the new communist society.

(2) The Stalinist conception of the party as the unchallenged leading force in the preparation and execution of the revolution as well as in the process of building up a new society has its immediate basis in Lenin but not in Marx. The emphasis in Marx is on the movement of the whole working class, on the international character of the movement, on the autonomy of the individuals within it.

But Marx did not solve the problem: how will the *whole* proletariat form its common will, make the step from a "class in itself" toward a "class for itself," win power and run society "organized as the ruling class." How will this most alienated and degraded class build up a consciousness about essentially new possibilities, a consciousness that requires enormous general culture and far surpasses official academic scholarship? And if a vanguard of the class does the job, how to avoid alienation of the vanguard, manipulation of the class by it? How to secure the necessary inner-party democracy in a revolutionary situation when a scared capitalist establishment increases repression and drives the vanguard more or less underground?

Stalin comes up with simple solutions following Lenin's realism but devoid of Lenin's humanist and democratic perspective. The party will not be the expression and the means of the proletarian movement—it will be the party which will use the movement as a means to conquer and keep power. In order to avoid and survive repression it will be clandestine, disciplined, "monolithic" from the beginning. That basic issue is not inner democracy but efficiency: in order to perform efficiently it will tend to achieve maximum ideological unity and unity of leadership. The common will of the proletariat is the common will of the party—which is the common will of the leader. Lenin's rather one-sided view that it is the intelligentsia which introduces proletarian consciousness from outside, as a mediating link between the workers and universal human science and culture, was made even more one-sided and elitist in Stalin's hands. Even more emphasis was laid on heteronomy without any rational foundation; party theory cannot depend on autonomous and uncontrollable science; it must be created by the leading cadres; intellectuals can only elaborate it, spell it out, justify it. In that way Marx's idea of abolishing the *political* character of the public power was turned into its extreme opposite. All public power became political, and not only separate legislative, economic, scientific, cultural power—all were ultimately unified in the service of one political purpose, all inspired and supervised by one single great, wise, omniscient, omnipotent leader.

(3) For Marx the state is in principle an oppressive institution, an organ of alienated political power. Thus while he was convinced that the class struggle inevitably leads to the dictatorship of the proletariat,[27] a peculiar kind of state in the hands of the vast majority of people, and while he clashed with the anarchists, who resolutely challenged both the necessity and desirability of "the workers' state," he also strongly held that this form of the state must be transcended and replaced by free associations of producers who autonomously, without any mediator, decide all questions of public importance.[28]

Stalin explicitly revised this theory. He quoted it from Engels' *Anti-Dühring* since Engels' authority was smaller than Marx's. Engelsian view on the state was allegedly correct, but only if we abstract from the international situation and if there is no more capitalist encirclement.[29] Because socialism has not yet completely won in the whole world the new Soviet state must stay.

That under those conditions it was necessary for Soviet society to be "strong enough to defend the conquests of socialism from foreign attack" is beyond doubt. What was indeed very doubtful was Stalin's identification of strong *society* with strong *state,* implying that coercive organs of the state were necessary to defend

---

27. Marx, letter to J. Weydemeyer, 1852.

28. Marx and Engels, "Manifesto of the Communist Party," in *Selected Works* (New York, 1968), p. 53.

29. Stalin, "Report to the Eighteenth Congress of the CPSU (b)," in *Problems of Leninism,* pp. 632–38. Stalin's excuse was that classical Marxist writers, separated by a period of several decades, could not have foreseen each and every zigzag of history in the distant future in every separate country. But what was at issue was not an unpredictable "zigzag of history" but a basic principle of Marxism. Also, it was difficult to explain why Lenin in August 1917 fully agreed with Engels' account of the "withering away" of the state. According to Stalin, *The State and Revolution* was only a defense of the classical Marxist doctrine of the state "from the distortions and vulgarizations of the opportunists." Allegedly, Lenin was preparing to write a second volume in which intended to sum up the experience of the Russian revolutions. And who was able to doubt that Lenin would have come up precisely with the doctrine which was now expounded by his loyal disciple? (Ibid., pp. 634–35.)

revolutionary achievements, whereas genuine Soviet power and "armed people" would be too weak for that task. The main changes introduced by Stalin were: (1) The withering away of the state was postponed *ad calendas Graecas,* allowing its survival even in the period of communism.[30] (2) Stalin removed any element of negativity from the idea of the Soviet state. He referred to it as "a completely new state never seen before in history." [31]

How was it possible for such a view to pass as a Marxist one? Because it was never quite clear in Marx's texts what it means to pass from the "dictatorship of the proletariat" to self-government. He never considered the possibility of such a change in one country, nor the possibility of the transformation of a dictatorship of the proletariat into a dictatorship of vanguard of the proletariat. If ever one single word produced enormous confusion it was the term "dictatorship" used by Marx in this context. Under the assumption of Marx that the revolution takes place in a developed society where the proletariat already constitutes the vast majority of the population the term "proletarian democracy" or "self-government" would have expressed Marx's idea much better. Militants in the movement were psychologically prepared for future Stalins from the beginning, due to the expectation of *dictatorial* power in the transition period.

(4) We saw how essential is the difference between Marx's concept of *social* revolution, which radically changes all social relationships and abolishes existing forms of economic and political alienation, and, on the other hand, Stalin's concept of revolution which does not even touch the issue of alienation and reduces the new society to a collectivist welfare state which, within the existing material limits, tends to initiate bourgeois consumerism and to lay more and more stress on the greater rate of material output, on growth as its most important advantage over capitalism.

When taken in totality, Marx's views do not give any ground for such distorted interpretations. However, they were hardly ever taken in totality by revolutionary leaders, partly because Marx and Engels themselves contributed to a fatal under-estimate of their early philosophical writings. Without basic humanist ideas from those writings a political culture was generated among Marxists (even within the Second International) which overemphasized the importance of the growth of productive forces, of material output and abundance of goods. That the poverty of the proletariat was not only material but also spiritual, that true wealth is wealth of human needs and not only of objects owned, that "the overcoming of private property means the complete emancipation of all human senses and capacities" [32] (which have in capitalist society been replaced by the simple alien-ation of them all—the sense of *having*)—these great enlightening ideas were later neglected by their own author and completely ignored by most followers. As a

---

30. "Will our state remain in the period of Communism also?" "Yes it will, unless the capitalist encirclement is liquidated and unless the danger of foreign military attack has dissappeared" (Ibid., p. 637.)

31. "As you see, we now have an entirely new, socialist state, without precedent in history." (Ibid., p. 637.)

32. Marx, "Economic and Philosophical Manuscripts," p. 132.

result, a *better life for all* in socialism came to mean a *materially* richer life. As a consequence the style of life that developed in socialist countries did not, for a long time, essentially differ from the bourgeois style. Some alternatives appeared only with strong anti-Stalinist tendencies within these societies and with emergence of new forms of socialism in China, Yugoslavia, and Cuba. These new communal forms of social life differ among themselves very much; they are to a very considerable extent conditioned by a generally low level of development and by pre-capitalist culture or a rebellious sub-culture generated within bourgeois society. They are not yet the forms of a higher-level style of life that transcends bourgeois culture on its own ground. What is common to all of them, however, is the refusal to reduce socialism to "Soviet power plus electrification" (or also chemization or computerization).

(5) Stalinism has transformed the proletarian internationalism of Marx into a principle that demands that each nation conform to a center.

Within multi-national socialist states this is a demand to fully subordinate to the central state power. But as nations differ very much in size and are unevenly developed, the princple of equality turns out into a rule of striking inequality: the biggest nation drastically dominates the center and represses any resistance, no matter how justified, as a bourgeois-nationalist deviation.

Within the community of socialist states Stalinist ideologues have always interpreted "internationalism" as an obligation to give every political and economic support to the first socialist country and to unconditionally follow the lead of this natural center.

There is nothing in the *basic* theories of Marx from which such an interpretation could follow. There could not be any justification for the privileged position of any nation for the simple reason that what counted in the historical process were not nations but classes—which, of course, was rather one-sided and made the opposite extreme possible later, in 1848–49. The point of Marx's internationalism was much more a denial of nationalism ("Workers have no fatherland"; "National differences and antagonisms between people are daily more and more vanishing"), than a concrete concept of mutual relations among nations in a large socialist community. The real issues were, first, the attitude of the international labor movement toward genuine national liberation movements, and, second, the right of self-determination of weaker, smaller, formerly oppressed nations with respect to bigger, stronger, formerly oppressive ones. The general humanist ideas of Marx imply solutions of these problems: national oppression is only a special case of general oppression and reification; furthermore, it is mediated by double class domination. The workers' movement, which struggles not for its particular class rule but for universal human emancipation, must see a natural ally in each movement if the particular interests of the latter coincide with the universal interests of human emancipation. It was not Marx nor Engels but Lenin who stated these solutions concretely. In the epoch of imperialism, national-liberation and colonial wars become the most important strategic reserve of the international labor movement. After the revolution each nation has the right of self-determination, including separation. And especially the proletariat of the weaker, formerly oppressed nation should advocate staying together in the great community of nations.

Stalinism paid lip service to Lenin's doctrine on the national question but in practice abandoned it completely. The road to it was paved by Stalin's strange doctrine about the existence of revolutionary and reactionary nations. Obviously, if whole nations could be qualified in that way the dictatorship of the proletariat involves a dictatorship of "revolutionary" over "reactionary" nations.

But this dreadful view, opening the road to "revolutionary" chauvinism and genocide, was not Stalin's invention; one finds it in Marx's and Engels' political articles in the *Neue Rheinische Zeitung,* in 1848–49.[33] In some of these texts Marx and especially Engels seemed to have forgotten all their principles. The forces of revolution in 1848 are allegedly four *nations:* Germans, Hungarians, Poles, and Italians. "They have assumed the historical initiative in the year 1848 *as in the previous* thousand years. They represent the *revolution.* "On the other hand, "The South Slavs, who have trailed behind the Germans and Hungarians for a thousand years, only rose up to establish their national independence in 1848 in order to suppress the German-Magyar revolution at the same time. They represent the *counter-revolution.* "[34] It is easy to understand the anger of Marx and Engels: It really was Slavic armies that crushed the revolution. The tragedy of that historical situation was that the forces that led the revolution at the same time were associated with centuries of national oppression, and that the people who used a unique opportunity to liberate themselves rebelled against revolutionaries. What cannot be either understood nor justified is the identification of all classes of a nation, therefore praising German and Hungarian feudal lords and burghers, condemning Slavic serfs, and condemning in a way very reminiscent of Josip Djugashvili. They are, and for a thousand years have been, only barbarians. "They never had any history of their own, they have no future, no capacity for survival, and will never be able to attain any kind of independence"; for that they "lack the primary historical, geographical, political and industrial conditions." "The Germans have taken the great pains to civilize the obstinate Czechs and Slovenes, and to introduce amongst them trade, industry, a tolerable agriculture and education." [35] "The South Slavs would have become Turkish without the Germans and, in particular without the Magyars . . . and this is a service for which the Austrian South Slavs have not paid too dearly even by exchanging their nationality for that of the Germans and Magyars." [36]

This sort of attitude is not merely great-nation chauvinism: Marx and Engels have a record of life-long struggle against crude German nationalism before 1848, during the 1848 revolution,[37] and later. But this is also more than just a momen-

---

33. Its real father is Hegel, who distinguished among *historical* and *unhistorical* nations, only the first objectifying the absolute spirit and playing an active role in history-making.

34. Engels, "Democratic Panslavism" (*Neue Rheinische Zeitung,* February 15, 1949), in Marx, *The Revolution of 1848* (London, 1973), 231.

35. Ibid., p. 234.

36. Engels, "The Magyar Struggle" (*Neue Rheinische Zeitung,* January 13, 1949), ibid., p. 218.

37. For example, they were resolutely opposed when the Frankfurt National Assembly claimed Polish territories in Prussia and Posnan for Germany.

tary expression of annoyance with the reactionary role played by "barbarious Asiatic" Russia and other Slavs. It is the consequence of a *global,* abstract, one-sidedly *centralistic, over-activistic* view, in which small things, including small nations, simply do not count, in which decisive events take place in the center of history and the impatient revolutionary wants to see them during his lifetime. Only from this point of view one can explain how it was possible for Marx and Engels to reject in 1848 "the principle of nationalities" by which each national group was considered entitled to self-determination. They found it idealistic, a principle of "abstract justice." Revolution was there, it had to win (in spite of the underdevelopment of precisely the four "revolutionary nations" in comparison with England or France). Europe had to be seen as *a system;* one had to disregard trifling, complicated elements at the periphery.

This kind of logic led the Georgian Josip Djugashvili to become the leading figure of Great Russian "socialist" nationalism, and the self-appointed judge over the destiny of dozens of "counter-revolutionary" or not-revolutionary-enough nations.

(6) Stalinism reduces all culture to the handmaiden of politics. The whole period between 1931, when Stalin personally attacked historians in his "Letter to the Editor of *Proletarskaia Revoliutsiia*" and Stalin's protégé Mitin rebuked philosophers for being "Menshevik idealists" or "mechanistic materialists," and the late forties, when Zhdanov led well-known campaigns against Aleksandrov's *History of Philosophy,* the formalism of Shostakovich's music, and the decadence of Akhmatova's and Zoshchenko's literature—that whole period was one persistent effort to compel intellectuals to follow every twist and turn of daily politics; to praise the ideas of the genius, the political boss; to imitate his style; to serve unconditionally.

Marx developed essentially different views on culture and its destiny in the process of communist revolution. It is true that Marxism shortened the distance between politics and culture, but not in the sense of allowing the hegemony of the former over the latter. Marx's point was rather that in the class society both politics and culture emerge on the objective historical ground of material production and class struggle. The emphasis was very strong and one-sided (as Engels later admitted), and that was the source of much later vulgarization. Stalin made a contribution of his own to the over-simplified base-superstructure scheme. Politics, which was treated by the Marxists of the Second International as just one sphere of the superstructure, became the very fundamental infrastructure: politicians had to decide about both economy and culture.

A number of Marx's most important and indeed illuminating ideas about the place and role of culture in the process of revolution were completely ignored or vehemently rejected by Stalinists.

Rather than serving a local political society, cultural and indeed all activity of the proletariat has to have a *universal historical* character: "It has to be directly connected with world history." [38] Science and the arts especially are a "universal human product."

---

38. Marx and Engels, *The German Ideology,* Part One, Introduction.

Rather than being a mere means to reach political goals, culture is one of the ends of human life. "In place of the *wealth* and *poverty* of political economy comes the *rich human being* and the *rich human need*. The *rich* human being is simultaneously the human being in *need* of a totality of human manifestations of life." The objects of culture are, on the one hand, creative objectifications of their authors; on the other hand, they awake potential senses of the persons who are exposed to them. "Only through the objectively unfolded richness of man's essential being is the richness of subjective *human* sensibility (a musical ear, an eye for beauty of form—in short, *senses* capable of human gratification, senses affirming themselves as essential powers of *man*) either cultivated or brought into being." [39]

Finally, if communist revolution is not the substitution of one form of domination for the other but the abolition of any domination by the reified social forces, such an emancipatory process is impossible without a critical consciousness mediated by the universal human culture. This critical consciousness will be *à la hauteur des principes* even when it deals with the most concrete phenomena. And the principles can be derived only from universal human experience condensed in the form of culture, and not from the sphere of ideology, which is a mystified expression of the particular interests of the ruling class. Thus a revolutionary movement must develop a *new* culture which will be a critique of every ideology and politics, including its own. Which presupposes freedom of cultural creation and expression, for which Marx and Engels always fought, from the early articles in the *Neue Rheinische Zeitung* against state censorship of the press to the letters of protest to the leadership of the German Social-democratic party because of party censorship almost four decades later.

In Conclusion

Marxism, at least in some of its interpretations, still remains the expression of epochal critical consciousness. To be sure, a creative interpretation involves an element of transcendence. There is a surface, descriptive layer in Marx's theory which refers to a no-longer-existing nineteenth-century world. There are contemporary problems which Marx anticipated but could not solve, and those which he was not yet aware of. There are simplifications, ambiguities, and contradictions between the principles and their application—which were amply used for all kinds of ideological purposes ever after. But there were in Marx's theory an extremely rich and sophisticated humanistic ground and a sufficiently general and profound critique of each alienated and reified society, which are still relevant and illuminating and constitute a necessary condition of all contemporary radical critical thought and praxis.

For a long time Stalinism has been preserving the appearance of its continuity with Marxism because of its genetic link with the Marxist-oriented Russian October Revolution, because its creators skillfully used various limitations of

---

39. Marx, *Economic and Philosophic Manuscripts of 1844,* ed. Dirk Struik (London, 1970), pp. 141–44.

classical Marxist texts, and because the conservative bourgeois ideologues had every interest in construing Stalinism as the legitimate heir and the necessary practical consequence of Marxism.

But the truth is that Stalinism—born as the product of an unfinished proletarian revolution amidst a backward peasant society encircled by a hostile capitalist environment—degenerated into a totally oppressive, dehumanizing ideology, expressing the interests of a gigantic international bureaucratic elite which nowadays constitutes a formidable obstacle to any genuinely revolutionary movement of the working class.

Some Questions on the Scholarly Agenda

Robert C. Tucker

Like any scholarly conference, the one on Stalinism at Bellagio was as useful (or more) for illuminating what still needs to be clarified and explained, and for the disagreements that developed, as it was for showing what some of us already more or less know and can agree on. The disagreements in this case were several and at times serious, although they did not result in a division of the conference group into warring camps or two distinct and definable schools of thought.

So, it seems fitting to bring this book to a close with a short report on some of the questions that arose in the discussions and some of the matters on which we disagreed. Perhaps in that way we can make the conference experience itself, and not just the papers here presented, contribute something to the advance of scholarship in Soviet and comparative Communist studies.

There arose, to begin with, a question of definition: Is it desirable and possible to define Stalinism in the effort to examine and interpret it as a phenomenon in the history of the Soviet and other Communist movements? "Definition" in this instance was taken to mean a listing of the particular attributes of a Communist system whose aggregate presence would stamp it as Stalinist. The reader familiar with the scholarly literature on totalitarianism will recognize this question as one that is implicit in that material too. In her classic study *The Origins of Totalitarianism* (1951, second edition 1966), Hannah Arendt gave a descriptive analysis of the phenomenon in historical terms, covering ideological, political, sociological, psychological, and structural aspects, but without any attempt at a formal definition in the sense just identified, whereas Carl Friedrich suggested subsequently that one could and should specify a "syndrome" of characteristics constitutive of totalitarianism.[1] The uses of a working definition of Stalinism were argued by some at the Bellagio conference, and Mihailo Marković has proposed in his paper a list of six characteristics which he believes to be "necessary and sufficient conditions" of Stalinism. Some participants were in agreement that it would be worthwhile to attempt a clarification of the term "Stalinism." Others, however, were of the view that, whatever the disadvantages of proceeding without

---

1. For the syndrome, see his introductory essay in *Totalitarianism*, ed. C. J. Friedrich (Cambridge, Mass., 1954). A further elaboration of the syndrome appears in C. J. Friedrich and Z. Brzezinski, *Totalitarian Dictatorship and Autocracy* (Cambridge, Mass., 1956).

a definitional structure, the difficulties of creating a workable such structure are so great that it is better not to try. As one participant put it, *words* can be defined, including "Stalinism," but when the word refers to such an extremely complex historico-socio-cultural-ideological-personal-political-and-economic phenomenon as Stalinism, this phenomenon is best simply studied, analyzed, described, thought about, interpreted, and explained. The question, needless to add, remained open; and the need for clarity is pressing. The reader will have to judge whether or not our volume would have gained in scholarly value if all the essays had proceeded from an agreed-upon group of characteristics taken as expressive of the nature of Stalinism.

Another contentious question, or set of questions, has to do with the ideological and politico-cultural determinants of the Stalinist phenomenon. The debate between Kolakowski and Marković, over the issue of whether Stalinism was the logical or inevitable end-product of the original Marxist *Weltanschauung,* which envisaged ultimate communism under the sign of a fully unified society, so straightforwardly and impressively speaks for itself in their essays that no extended commentary is needed here. Neither thinker doubts that Marx, if we can imagine him coming alive in Stalin's Russia (like Jesus Christ in the Spain of the Inquisition as depicted by Dostoyevsky in the famous chapter of *The Brothers Karamazov*) would have been horrified to see the reality that his thinking had spawned, to whatever extent that it had. Both parties agree that Stalinism was *in some sense* an offspring of classical Marxism; they differ over whether the offspring was natural and the one to be expected in view of the intrinsic texture of Marx's world-view and philosophy of history. For Kolakowski, Marxism was not essentially distorted in its Stalinist version; for Marković, it was. What the one views as a legitimate child, the other sees as a bastard.

Between the Marxism of Marx and the politico-cultural system forged under Stalin came the Leninist development of Marxist thought and revolutionary politics and the single-party dictatorship created under Lenin's leadership after 1917. That there were many differences between Lenin's NEP Soviet society of the early 1920's and Stalin's increasingly terrorized and dictatorially ruled one of the 1930's, and more broadly between Leninist and Stalinist Communism, no fact-minded student of Communist history can deny, although scholars will inevitably quarrel over the degree and significance of the differences. The question is: to what extent and in what ways was the Stalinist phenomenon in all its ideological, political, social, economic, and cultural expressions prefigured in Leninist Bolshevism as a movement, ideology and political culture, or to what extent was Stalinism an aberration that ran contrary to the traditions of Leninist Bolshevism and developed under the influence of such an historically accidental factor as the presence of the political personality of Stalin on the scene?

Nobody denies that Leninist Bolshevism as a movement, ideology, and system was—along with the Russian sociocultural and political environment—the historical crucible out of which Stalinism came. To quote a remark by Alexander Erlich, who kept lacing with humor our Bellagio discussions of even so lugubrious a subject as Stalinism, "It didn't develop out of Buddhism." But within the frame of our general agreement on that much, plenty of room remained for the serious differences which came out in the discussion. At least one participant, Leszek Kolakowski, forthrightly voiced agreement with the position that takes Stalinism as Marxism-Leninism in action: it was *not* to be seen as a monstrous aberration from Leninism. Against this view was ranged the argument, presented most forcefully perhaps by Stephen Cohen, that Stalinism was in sharp and basic discontinuity with Bolshevism, which itself was a movement with various political currents in the Lenin period and for some time after. Still another position represented in the papers contained in this volume (among them my own), and in the conference discussions, is that Stalinism, while an aberration from Leninism in some of its aspects, could properly claim to be in line with others—Leninism having itself been an internally diverse phenomenon which changed over time, as for example from the period of the Civil War and War Communism to that of the NEP.

The Bellagio discussion of Stalinism's relation to Leninism found a group of scholars from outside the USSR addressing themselves to a problem which has figured prominently in the dialogue which Soviet *samizdat* writings have brought into world-wide public view in recent years. In Aleksandr Solzhenitsyn's *The Gulag Archipelago,* it is argued that all the ugly phenomena which one might group under the heading of Stalinism, including the terroristic form of rule and the imprisonment of millions in Soviet "destructive-labor camps" (a truthful reformulation of their official designation, "corrective-labor camps"), not only are traceable to Leninism but began to sprout lustily in Lenin's post-1917 time of rule and under his personal auspices. In opposition to Solzhenitsyn's position is that of Roy Medvedev, who in *Let History Judge* and again in his essay for the present volume endorses, with qualifications, the "aberrational" school of thought. So the debate goes on. This volume makes no claim to resolving the issues involved. At most, it helps to clarify them, to show the range of possible positions, and the kinds of evidence that may be adduced for one or another among them.

The interpretation of Stalinism in culturalist terms as "revolution from above," which formed the subject of my conference essay, evoked, along with support, a number of pointed questions from various participants in the Bellagio discussion: Did it not go too far in using culture as an explanatory concept, considering that the latter tells more about how things are done than why they are done? Was it not misleading to treat Leninist thought as even *one* of the sources of Stalinist revolutionism from above, considering especially that Lenin's chief contribution to history was his leadership of the October Revolution of 1917, a clear case of revolution "from below"? In viewing the "Russian revolutionary process" as roughly a twenty-year one, with an interval of relative quiescence from 1921 to 1928, did the essay not dismiss the NEP as a sort of historical bivouac rather than the seminal period that it was? Did the essay not go too far in rejecting the adequacy of what it called the "circumstantial explanation" of Stalinist collectivization as found in the writings of Deutscher, Carr, and Gerschenkron? How strong was the evidence for the view presented in the essay that the Soviet

.revolution from above of the 1930's was a revival under Stalin's auspices of the historical Russian politico-cultural pattern of coercive, government-directed revolution from above, as seen, for example, in the reign of Peter the Great? Just how did this resurrection take place? Why did it happen in the 1930's and not in the 1920's? Why was this particular Russian historical pattern resurrected rather than some other that was also present in modern Russian history before 1917, such as the trend toward a Russian *Rechtsstaat?* And if a revival-of-the-Russian-past approach figures in the interpretation of Stalinism, with the corollary that we should see the forced economic development of the Stalinist 1930's as involving a strong element of "archaization" in the very method of its "modernization" of Russia, are we not in danger of overlooking the element of modernity that Stalinism produced by forging a nationally integrated society in Stalin's time? Finally, a question was raised which exposed, perhaps, our continuing lack of an adequate conceptualization of revolution, despite the huge literature now existing on this subject: Given that a real social revolution is, by its very nature, a liberating force, can a revolution from above which oppresses and enslaves people en masse properly be called a "revolution"? [2] Some of these questions seemed not overly difficult to answer; others pointed clearly to the need for more hard thinking and research.

Like some other fields, Soviet studies in the recent past has belatedly but increasingly been attracted to social history, which Alexander Dallin has described in a speech to another conference as "our next agenda." The significance of this is perhaps best indicated by citing Stephen Cohen's observation that Western Soviet studies have in the past been principally "regime studies," to the neglect of social history, which views the process from below. Our Bellagio discussions of Stalinism took up the theme of social history when we came to the question, which is dealt with in some of the essays in this volume,[3] of the extent to which the Stalinist revolution from above went on also from below, the extent to which some sections of the populace—such as the village poor during collectivization, not to mention elements of the Communist youth and party activists—took an active and willing part in the revolutionary changes which were occurring under Stalin. Here we have the problem of the interaction of state and society in Stalinism, of how social forces influenced and even supported—actively or passively—the Stalinist innovations from above.

This problem became entangled with the further one of periodizing the Stalinist

---

[2] Mihailo Marković, who raised this question, has set forth his view of "revolution as human emancipation" in *From Affluence to Praxis: Philosophy and Social Criticism* (Ann Arbor, Mich., 1974), esp. Chap. 6. The ancestry of this idea goes back to Condorcet, who wrote: "The word 'revolutionary' can be applied only to revolutions whose aim is freedom." Quoted by Hannah Arendt in *On Revolution* (New York, 1965), p. 21.

3. Moshe Lewin's essay in this volume is especially noteworthy in this connection. His essay likewise sees in Stalinism elements of a reversion to the tsarist pattern of revolution from above. See also Alexander Gerschenkron, *Economic Backwardness in Historical Perspective* (New York, 1965), esp. Chap. 6. Gerschenkron writes, *inter alia* (p. 147): ". . . the resemblance between Soviet and Petrine Russia was striking indeed."

revolution, which itself was taken by the participants to be a difficult task meriting much further study. It was generally agreed that one must allow for changes in both the degree and form of popular participation in the shift from the phase of the Stalinist revolution which took place in Russia between 1929 and 1933 (roughly the era of the First Five-Year Plan) and that which ensued after 1934, when the Stalinist Great Purge took place. Moreover, as H. Gordon Skilling observed, the problem of "from above" and "from below" takes on even greater complexity when we move from the Soviet revolution from above to the postwar export of Stalinist revolutionism from above to countries of Eastern Europe, such as Czechoslovakia; here one must distinguish those elements of the revolution from above which emanated from Stalin's Russia and those which were of local inspiration, even when the source of this local inspiration was the Communist party of the country concerned.

Needless to say, the discussion of the "from below" aspect of Stalinism led to no definite conclusions, other than the realization seemingly shared by us all that it is a question which needs much more research. Granted that the Soviet archives on the Stalin years remain for the most part closed to foreign scholars and are likely to remain so for the foreseeable future, enough material is already available to enable this work to proceed further without delay.

The range and richness of the Bellagio discussion on Stalinism defy full summary in this brief report. These, however, are some of the many issues that emerged in the course of it and found us either in disagreement over the solutions or in agreement that the solutions do not exist but ought to be sought. To paraphrase the old saying about art, scholarship is long and conferences are short.

The Contributors

WŁODZIMIERZ BRUS, professor of political economy at the University of Warsaw until his dismissal in 1968, is a senior research fellow of St. Antony's College, Oxford. His main publications in English are *The Market in a Socialist Economy* (London, 1972), *The Economics and Politics of Socialism* (London, 1973), and *Socialist Ownership and Political Systems* (London, 1975).

KATERINA CLARK is assistant professor of Russian in the Slavic Department of the University of Texas at Austin. She has in preparation a book on the Soviet socialist-realist novel, viewed in both a literary and a social context.

STEPHEN F. COHEN is associate professor of politics and director of the interdepartmental Russian Studies Program at Princeton University. He is the author of *Bukharin and the Bolshevik Revolution: A Political Biography, 1888–1938* (New York, 1973), and co-editor (with Robert C. Tucker) of *The Great Purge Trial* (New York, 1965).

ALEXANDER ERLICH is professor of economics and member of the Russian Institute at Columbia University. He is the author of *The Soviet Industrialization Debate, 1924–1928* (Cambridge, Mass., 1967).

LESZEK KOLAKOWSKI is a senior research fellow of All Souls College, Oxford. He was professor of the history of philosophy at the University of Warsaw until March 1968, when he was expelled for political reasons. His books in English include *Marxism and Beyond* (London, 1969), *Positivist Philosophy* (Harmondsworth, 1972), *The Devil and the Scripture* (London, 1973), *Husserl and the Search for Certitude* (New Haven, 1975), and *A Leszek Kolakowski Reader,* a special issue of *Tri-Quarterly* (Fall, 1971).

MOSHE LEWIN is reader in Soviet history and politics, Centre for Russian and East European Studies, University of Birmingham, England. He is the author of *Russian Peasants and Soviet Power: A Study of Collectivization* (Evanston, 1968), *Lenin's Last Struggle* (New York, 1968), and *Political Undercurrents in Soviet Economic Debates* (Princeton, 1974).

MIHAILO MARKOVIĆ has been professor of philosophy and director of the Institute of Philosophy at the University of Belgrade, and is a member of the Serbian

325

Academy of Sciences. During 1976 he was a fellow of the Woodrow Wilson International Center for scholars in Washington, D.C. His publications in English include *From Affluence to Praxis* (Ann Arbor, 1974) and *The Contemporary Marx* (Nottingham, 1974), and he is co-editor (with Branko Horvat) of *Self-Governing Socialism* (New York, 1975).

ROBERT H. MCNEAL is professor of history at the University of Massachusetts at Amherst. He is the author of *The Bolshevik Tradition: Lenin, Stalin, Khrushchev, Brezhnev* (Englewood Cliffs, 1975) and *Bride of the Revolution: Krupskaya and Lenin* (Ann Arbor, 1973), and has edited Stalin's *Works,* Vols. 14–16 (Stanford, 1967) and *Resolutions and Decisions of the Communist Party of the Soviet Union* (Toronto, 1974).

ROY A. MEDVEDEV, Moscow, is the author of *Let History Judge: The Origins and Consequences of Stalinism* (New York, 1971) and *On Socialist Democracy* (New York, 1975), and co-author (with Zhores A. Medvedev) of *A Question of Madness* (New York, 1971) and *Khrushchev: The Years in Power* (New York, 1976).

T. H. RIGBY is professorial fellow in political science, Research School of Social Sciences, Australian National University, Canberra. He is the author of *Communist Party Membership in the USSR, 1917–1967* (Princeton, 1968).

ROBERT SHARLET is professor of political science at Union College, Schenectady, New York. He is co-author (with Zigurds L. Zile and Jean C. Love) of *The Soviet Legal System and Arms Inspection* (New York, 1972). He is currently writing a book on *Pashukanis and Revolutionary Legal Theory in the USSR, 1917–1937.*

H. GORDON SKILLING is professor of political science at the University of Toronto. He is the author of *Communism National and International* (Toronto, 1964), *The Governments of Communist East Europe* (New York, 1966), and *Czechoslovakia's Interrupted Revolution* (Princeton, 1976), and co-editor (with Peter Brock) of *The Czech Renascence of the Nineteenth Century* (Toronto, 1970) and (with Franklyn Griffiths) of *Interest Groups in Soviet Politics* (Princeton, 1971).

ROBERT C. TUCKER is professor of politics at Princeton University. He is the author of *Philosophy and Myth in Karl Marx* (Cambridge, England, 1961; 2nd ed., 1972), *The Soviet Political Mind* (New York, 1963; rev. ed. 1971), *The Marxian Revolutionary Idea* (New York, 1969), and *Stalin as Revolutionary, 1879–1929: A Study in History and Personality* (New York, 1973); editor of *The Marx-Engels Reader* (New York, 1972) and *The Lenin Anthology* (New York, 1975); and co-editor (with Stephen F. Cohen) of *The Great Purge Trial* (New York, 1965). He is currently writing *Stalin and the Revolution from Above, 1929–1939: A Study in History and Personality.*

Index